INJURY AND INJUSTI

This book addresses some of the
over injury and law now taking
The essays tackle the inescapable
tions for social inequality in different cultural settings.
the tension between physical and reputational injuries, the construction of human injuries versus injuries to nonhuman life, virtual injuries, the normalization and infliction of injuries on vulnerable victims, the question of reparations for slavery, and the paradoxical degradation of victims through legal actions meant to compensate them for their disabilities. Authors include social theorists, social scientists, and legal scholars, and the subject matter extends to the Middle East and Asia, as well as North America.

ANNE BLOOM is Executive Director of the Civil Justice Research Initiative, a think tank affiliated with the University of California, Berkeley and University of California, Irvine Schools of Law.

DAVID M. ENGEL is SUNY Distinguished Service Professor of Law at the State University of New York at Buffalo.

MICHAEL MCCANN is Gordon Hirabayashi Professor for the Advancement of Citizenship at the University of Washington.

CAMBRIDGE STUDIES IN LAW AND SOCIETY

Cambridge Studies in Law and Society aims to publish the best scholarly work on legal discourse and practice in its social and institutional contexts, combining theoretical insights and empirical research.

The fields that it covers are the following: studies of law in action; the sociology of law; the anthropology of law; cultural studies of law, including the role of legal discourses in social formations; law and economics; law and politics; and studies of governance. The books consider all forms of legal discourse across societies, rather than being limited to lawyers' discourses alone.

The series editors come from a range of disciplines, including academic law, socio-legal studies, sociology, and anthropology. All have been actively involved in teaching and writing about law in context.

Series Editors

Chris Arup *Monash University, Victoria*

Sally Engle Merry *New York University*

Susan Silbey *Massachusetts Institute of Technology*

A list of books in the series can be found at the back of this book.

INJURY AND INJUSTICE
The Cultural Politics of Harm and Redress

Edited by

Anne Bloom
University of California, Berkeley

David M. Engel
State University of New York at Buffalo

Michael McCann
University of Washington

CAMBRIDGE
UNIVERSITY PRESS

University Printing House, Cambridge CB2 8BS, United Kingdom

One Liberty Plaza, 20th Floor, New York, NY 10006, USA

477 Williamstown Road, Port Melbourne, VIC 3207, Australia

314-321, 3rd Floor, Plot 3, Splendor Forum, Jasola District Centre, New Delhi - 110025, India

79 Anson Road, #06-04/06, Singapore 079906

Cambridge University Press is part of the University of Cambridge.

It furthers the University's mission by disseminating knowledge in the pursuit of education, learning and research at the highest international levels of excellence.

www.cambridge.org
Information on this title: www.cambridge.org/9781108413282
DOI: 10.1017/9781108332934

© Cambridge University Press 2018

This publication is in copyright. Subject to statutory exception and to the provisions of relevant collective licensing agreements, no reproduction of any part may take place without the written permission of Cambridge University Press.

First published 2018
First paperback edition 2019

A catalogue record for this publication is available from the British Library

ISBN 978-1-108-42024-2 Hardback
ISBN 978-1-108-41328-2 Paperback

Cambridge University Press has no responsibility for the persistence or accuracy of URLs for external or third-party internet websites referred to in this publication, and does not guarantee that any content on such websites is, or will remain, accurate or appropriate.

CONTENTS

List of Illustrations	*page vii*
List of Contributors	*ix*
Acknowledgments	*xv*
Introduction Michael McCann, David M. Engel, and Anne Bloom	1

PART I INJURY AND THE CONSTRUCTION OF LEGAL SUBJECTS

1 The Meaning of Injury: A Disability Perspective
   Sagit Mor — 27

2 Injury in the Unresponsive State: Writing the Vulnerable Subject into Neo-Liberal Legal Culture
   Martha Albertson Fineman — 50

3 "One Small Characteristic": Conceptualizing Harm to Animals and Legal Personhood
   Claire E. Rasmussen — 76

4 Righteous Injuries: Victim's Rights, Discretion, and Forbearance in Iranian Criminal Sanctioning
   Arzoo Osanloo — 96

PART II CONSTRUCTING INJURY AND IMAGINING REMEDIES

5 Chairs, Stairs, and Automobiles: The Cultural Construction of Injuries and the Failed Promise of Law
   David M. Engel — 117

CONTENTS

6 Incommensurability and Power in Constructing the
   Meaning of Injury at the Medical Malpractice Disputes
   Yoshitaka Wada   135

7 Injury Fields
   S. Løchlann Jain   154

8 Good Injuries
   Anne Bloom and Marc Galanter   185

9 Privacy and the Right to One's Image: A Cultural
   and Legal History
   Samantha Barbas   202

PART III INEQUALITY AND/AS INJURY

10 Injury Inequality
   Mary Anne Franks   231

11 The Unconscionable Impossibility of Reparations
   for Slavery; or, Why the Master's Mules Will
   Never Dismantle the Master's House
   Kaimipono David Wenger   248

12 Inflicting Legal Injuries: The Place of the
   "Two-Finger Test" in Indian Rape Law
   Pratiksha Baxi   267

13 The State as Victim: Ethical Politics of Injury Claims
   and Revenge in International Relations
   Li Chen   293

14 Law's Imperial Amnesia: Transnational Legal Redress in
   East Asia
   Yukiko Koga   317

   Conclusion
   Jonathan Goldberg-Hiller   351

Index   369

ILLUSTRATIONS

7.1 Hormone replacement therapy advertisement, circa 1960, suggesting that menopause will turn a woman into a nightie-clad lunatic who will strain the patience of her calm, professional husband. Proposing its own wet dream, the pharmaceutical company claims that "Premarin has the intrinsic ability to impart a sense of well-being" and should be used to "treat all women."   170

CONTRIBUTORS

Samantha Barbas is Professor of Law at the University at Buffalo School of Law. She holds a PhD in US History from the University of California, Berkeley, and a JD from Stanford Law School. Her research focuses on media law and history in the United States. She is the author of four books on American cultural history, film, journalism and the law, including *Laws of Image: Privacy and Publicity in America* (2015), and *Newsworthy: The Supreme Court Battle over Privacy and Press Freedom* (2017).

Pratiksha Baxi is Associate Professor at the Centre for the Study of Law and Governance, Jawaharlal Nehru University, New Delhi. Her research interests lie at the intersection of legal anthropology, feminist theory, and violence studies. She is the author of *Public Secrets of Law: Rape Trials in India* (2014), which was shortlisted for the Crossword Book Award (Nonfiction category). Baxi is the coeditor of the *Contributions to Indian Sociology*. Baxi anchors the *Law and Social Sciences Research Network* (LASSnet), which brings together scholars engaged in interdisciplinary research on law in the region.

Anne Bloom is Executive Director of the Civil Justice Research Institute, a think tank affiliated with the UC Berkeley and UC Irvine Schools of Law. Her background is in both academia and public interest law. Previously, she was Associate Dean for Research and Professor of Law at McGeorge Law School, Director of Public Programs at Equal Justice Works, and a staff attorney with the national public interest impact litigation firm, Public Justice. She holds both a JD and a PhD in political science and has authored many articles on injury-related topics.

Li Chen is Associate Professor of History and Chair of the Department of Historical and Cultural Studies at the University of Toronto. He is the founding president of the International Society for Chinese Law and History and a member of the Editorial Board of the *Law and History Review*. He holds a JD from the University of Illinois (Champaign) and PhD in history from Columbia University. Besides a number of articles on law, empire, and international politics, his recent publications include a monograph entitled *Chinese Law in Imperial Eyes: Sovereignty, Justice, and Transcultural Politics* (2016), which won honorable mention for the 2017 Peter Gonville Stein Book Award of the American Society for Legal History, and a coedited volume, *Chinese Law: Knowledge, Practice and Transformation, 1530s–1950s* (2015). His research focuses on the intersections of law, culture and politics in Chinese and global history since the sixteenth century.

David M. Engel is SUNY Distinguished Service Professor of Law at the State University of New York at Buffalo. He is former President of the Law & Society Association and the recipient of its 2017 Kalven Award for Outstanding Scholarship in Law and Society. Engel's research examines law, culture, and society in America and Thailand. His book, *The Myth of the Litigious Society: Why We Don't Sue* (2016) explains why American injury victims generally avoid claiming. His scholarship on Thailand, where he has lived, worked, and taught for many years, includes the book *Tort, Custom, and Karma: Globalization and Legal Consciousness in Thailand* (2010), which examines the effects of global transformations on Thailand's legal culture. Engel is a visiting professor at the Chiang Mai University Law School, where he received an honorary doctorate in 2011. He currently serves as an Editor-in-Chief of the *Asian Journal of Law and Society* and is a member of the inaugural Board of Trustees of the Asian Law and Society Association.

Martha Albertson Fineman is Robert W. Woodruff Professor of Law at Emory University School of Law. An internationally recognized law and society scholar, Fineman is a leading authority on family law and feminist jurisprudence. Before coming to Emory, Fineman taught at the University of Wisconsin and Columbia University, and was on the Cornell Law School faculty, where she held the Dorothea Clarke Professorship, the first endowed chair in the nation in feminist jurisprudence. Fineman is founder and director of the Feminism and Legal Theory Project, which was inaugurated in 1984 and also serves as director of Emory's Vulnerability and the Human Condition Initiative.

Mary Anne Franks is Professor of Law at the University of Miami and the Vice-President and Legislative & Tech Policy Director of the Cyber Civil Rights Initiative. Her publications include a forthcoming book on constitutional fundamentalism and dozens of articles in publications such as the *California Law Review*, *UCLA Law Review*, *The Atlantic*, and *TIME*. She is an internationally recognized expert on "revenge porn" and online harassment. She coproduced the documentary "Hot Girls Wanted" and is also a Krav Maga instructor. She holds a JD from Harvard Law School and received doctorate and master's degrees from Oxford University as a Rhodes Scholar.

Marc Galanter is Professor of Law Emeritus at the University of Wisconsin Law School. Previously he was the John and Rylla Bosshard Professor of Law and South Asian Studies at the University of Wisconsin–Madison and LSE Centennial Professor at the London School of Economics and Political Science. He has lectured at more than eighty universities in the United States and abroad. He has taught South Asian Law, Law and Social Science, Legal Profession, Religion and the Law, Contracts, Dispute Processing and Negotiations. He has authored numerous books and articles related to law, the legal profession and the provision of legal services in India.

Jonathan Goldberg-Hiller is Professor of Political Science at the University of Hawai'i at Mānoa where he teaches sociolegal theory. He is the author of *The Limits to Union: Same-sex Marriage and the Politics of Civil Rights* (2004), *Plastic Materialities: Politics, Legality, and Metamorphosis in the Work of Catherine Malabou* (2015; with Brenna Bhandar) and has published widely on issues of legal aesthetics, sexuality, and indigenous rights. He is coeditor of a book series, *Global and Insurgent Legalities* at Duke University Press, and former coeditor of *The Law & Society Review*. He is currently writing a book on the legal and political significance of night.

CONTRIBUTORS

Mary Beth Heffernan is Professor of Sculpture, Photography and Interdisciplinary Art and Chair of the Art and Art History Department at Occidental College. Her artwork explores representation and physicality, with a particular focus on the intersection of injury, illness, and images. Heffernan's Personal Protective Equipment (PPE) Portrait Project garnered international recognition for humanizing healthcare workers in the Liberian Ebola epidemic.

S. Løchlann Jain is on faculty at the Anthropology Department at Stanford University. Jain's publications include, among others, *Injury* (2006) and *Malignant: How Cancer Becomes Us* (2013). The latter won eight prizes, including the Victor Turner Prize, the Edelstein Prize, the Diana Forsythe Prize, the Fleck Prize, and the Staley Prize. Jain is currently writing a book on the history of vaccine development, and developing pedagogical and ethnographic methods based in theater and art practice. Jain also maintains an art practice (www.cardsthatart.com).

Yukiko Koga is Assistant Professor in the Department of Anthropology at Hunter College, City University of New York and Adjunct Associate Research Scholar at Weatherhead East Asian Institute, Columbia University. She is the author of *Inheritance of Loss: China, Japan, and the Political Economy of Redemption after Empire* (2016), which won two book awards from the American Anthropological Association: the Anthony Leeds Book Prize from the Society for Urban, National, and Transnational Anthropology and the Francis L. K. Hsu Book Prize from the Society for East Asian Anthropology.

Michael McCann is Gordon Hirabayashi Professor for the Advancement of Citizenship at the University of Washington. McCann is author of over sixty article-length publications, and author, coauthor, editor, or coeditor of eight books, including the multi-award-winning monographs *Rights at Work* (1994) and (with William Haltom) *Distorting the Law* (2004); each of these latter books won numerous professional prizes. McCann has been awarded many National Science Foundation (NSF) and other grants; was a Guggenheim Fellow and Fellow in Law and Public Affairs (Princeton); and won the Stanton Wheeler Mentorship Award (2017) from the Law and Society Association, of which he was the elected President (2011–13).

Sagit Mor is Senior Lecturer at the University of Haifa Faculty of Law, Israel. She holds an LLM and a JSD from NYU School of Law and was an Ed Roberts postdoctoral fellow in disability studies at UC Berkeley. She won the Association for the Study of Law Culture and the Humanities 2007 Dissertation Award. Mor is the cofounder of the Collaborative Research Network of Disability Legal Studies at the Law and Society Association. Her publications examine the sociolegal construction of disability in various fields including employment law, access to justice, bioethics, torts, and social welfare. She is coeditor of *Disability Studies: A Reader* (Hebrew). Her current research focuses on disability critique of torts.

Arzoo Osanloo is Associate Professor in the Department of Law, Societies, and Justice and Director of the Middle East Center at the University of Washington. She holds a JD and a PhD in cultural anthropology. As a legal anthropologist, her research and teaching lie at the intersections of law and culture. Her book, *The Politics of Women's Rights in Iran* (2009), analyzes the politicization of "rights talk" after that country's revolution. She is completing a manuscript that examines the Muslim mandate of mercy as it takes shape in Iran's criminal justice system. Prior to her academic work, she was an immigration and asylum attorney.

Claire E. Rasmussen is Associate Professor and Director of Graduate Studies in the Department of Political Science and International Relations at the University of Delaware. Her work in political theory is interdisciplinary and her work has appeared in journals in Political Science, Geography, Feminist Theory, and Law and Society. She is the author of *The Autonomous Animal: Self-Governance and the Modern Subject* (2011). She is currently completing a manuscript on the relationship between ideas about sexuality and self-governance at a personal and political scale.

Yoshitaka Wada is Professor of Law at Waseda Law School, Tokyo. A graduate of Kyoto University, he has been engaged in studies of the theory of law and society and dispute resolution, including analysis of the narratives of both injured victims and wrongdoers, and the power of legal discourse in medical or traffic accidents, based on social constructivism. He is one of the leading socio-legal scholars in Japan, a member of the Science Council and serves as Executive Officer for the Asian Law and Society Association. He has written many books, including *Process of Dispute Negotiation* and *Deconstruction of Sociology of Law: Beyond Postmodern Perspectives*, among others.

Kaimipono David Wenger is Associate Professor and Director of the Center for Law and Social Justice at Thomas Jefferson School of Law, California. His research and writing focus on a variety of civil rights topics in critical race theory, reparations and apology for slavery and Jim Crow, and law and religion. He has presented as an invited speaker for the Congressional Black Caucus in 2008, 2010, and 2014.

ACKNOWLEDGMENTS

We are grateful to the University of the Pacific McGeorge School of Law's Global Center for Business and Development and Loyola Law School's Civil Justice Program for their support of separate symposiums enabling initial development of this project. Thanks also to the Harry Bridges Center for Labor Studies at the University of Washington for financial support during the book's production phase. The extraordinary management skills of Adelina Tomova, at University of California, Irvine's School of Law, guided us through the production process. We are also grateful to Cambridge University Press, and especially to our editor John Berger, for their efficient and enthusiastic support. We deeply appreciate the intriguing intellectual contributions of our contributing authors, which have inspired us from beginning to end. Finally, we thank each other. Working together on this project has been a pleasure, and we are very glad to consider ourselves friends after the collaborative project has wrapped up.

INTRODUCTION
Michael McCann, David M. Engel, and Anne Bloom

Injury has been an inescapable part of human life since the dawn of civilization. Myths, epic poems, folk tales, and great works of world literature are all replete with stories of harms – accidental and intentional – and of the quest by victims to recover and set things right. Moreover, injury has always been entangled with law. Indeed, the very word "injury" derives from the Latin stem *jūs*, meaning "right" or "law," an indication of the presence of law at the core of the concept itself. We find it difficult to speak of injury in the Anglo-European tradition without referencing the legal interest it has impaired. Every legal system in the world concerns itself to some extent with the problem of injuries and the concerns of justice they raise.

As socio-legal research flourished in the second half of the twentieth century, scholars from many disciplines explored the mutually constitutive effects of law, culture, and society. A global interdisciplinary literature on "law and society" developed that portrayed law not as an autonomous body of knowledge or set of institutional procedures, but as forms of cultural practice and meaning making. Law, it was said, is too important to be left to the lawyers; understanding law in and as practice demanded the perspectives of anthropology, sociology, cultural studies, linguistics, and political science. From this multidisciplinary point of view, law appears as a dimension of culture, as a form of both official and informal "local knowledge," and as a particular discourse for expressing the "is" and the "ought" of social life.

To some extent, the problem of injury was addressed by this expansive and highly influential body of late twentieth-century socio-legal scholarship. Certainly the study of crime and criminal justice, which is one important legal response to the social problem of injury, has flourished among socio-legal scholars, generating thousands of studies, some of which illuminated the interaction between the justice system and criminally injurious incidents. Yet the noncriminal manifestations of injury practice, including what lawyers refer to as the law of torts, have remained oddly neglected by socio-legal scholars until relatively recently. Twenty-five years ago, in a landmark article on tort law and society, Michael Saks (1992) could still ask provocatively in his title, "Do We Really Know Anything About the Behavior of the Tort Litigation System – And Why Not?" In the years since Saks's article, the situation has improved somewhat, with the appearance of many new studies of civil trial juries, personal injury lawyers, the role of liability insurance, settlements and damage awards, the role of race and gender, and other relevant topics.

Yet, despite the profusion of these recent studies of tort law and society, there has been relatively little attention to the subject of our proposed book – namely, the cultural dimensions of injury and the law. Only a limited number of scholars, including the three co-editors of this book, have explored the mutually constitutive processes through which the legal and extra-legal domains of culture shape one another (like the two hands drawing one another in Saul Steinberg's famous cartoon), as they acknowledge and respond to the social problem of injury.

The primary concern of the contributors to this book, then, is not to identify and measure the effect of various independent social variables on the workings of injury law. Rather, this group of authors shares a more basic (and, we think, original) interest in the subtle, formative, interactive processes through which injuries are perceived, categorized, associated with particular cultural norms and practices, and – sometimes through the invocation of law – contested, resisted, or accepted by the injury victim and the broader public. Above all, the authors share a concern with the extent to which these cultural norms and practices related to injury tend to produce, reproduce, and even magnify inequality and injustice in society.

The chapters in the aggregate thus aim to advance comparative analytical mapping of the relationship between injury and injustice at two levels – first, how, in different times and places, injury is imagined, experienced, defined and responded to; and second, how legal institutions and cultural practices in different times and places facilitate or impede action to reduce and redress harm. This introductory chapter and the concluding chapter will generalize about these two analytical questions with an eye to guiding future inquiries and comparative theory building about injury and injustice.

CORE THEMES OF THE BOOK

The Social Construction of Injuries

The contributors to this book analyze different features in the broader landscape of injury. This landscape is found in every society, though its terrain varies from place to place. In general, however, the landscape of injury is distinctly uneven. Although injury and pain are universal experiences, they are not distributed equally. Injuries invariably affect the less privileged members of society disproportionately and thus create a hierarchy of risk and harm that mirrors social hierarchies of wealth, status, class, and power. The experience of injury, in short, flows down the social pyramid and pools among those who have the fewest resources to avoid it or mitigate its consequences. Hence the contributors' recurring attention to the interconnections among injury, inequality, and injustice.

Although the disparate frequency of injury among different social classes has been well documented, the analyses here go far beyond simple quantification. The authors resist a view of injuries as natural events, as things in the world that can be readily observed, counted, and tracked. Rather, the authors begin with the premise that injury is a social construct. What counts as an injury, indeed what counts as pain itself (see Jackson 2011), is the result of complex cultural and social processes, and it is their subtle and often invisible workings in particular social settings that produce outcomes that can be considered either just or unjust. Thus, all of the contributors to this book, in a variety of ways, attempt to make apparent and explicit those aspects of injury that are hidden or taken for granted. Using the tools of cultural interpretation, they attempt to reveal the origins of injustice and inequality that become connected through social practices to the problem of injury in society.

Our cultural analysis demonstrates in particular that experiences of injury are constructed out of the repertoire of cultural resources available to subjects. These cultural resources can include a multitude of religious, moral, technical, politico-ideological, and, of course, legal norms or discourses that structure social relationships in different cultural settings. People are exposed to these multiple modes of knowledge by their routine participation in various informal and formally institutionalized social settings. Popular understandings of injury, like most legal matters, are mediated by prior political beliefs, the social and religious networks in which individuals are situated, the frames of understanding crafted by political spokespersons, and media representations (Engel 2016, Ewick and Silbey 1998, Greenhouse 1986, Haltom and McCann 2004, Merry 1990). Many of the chapters that follow attempt to identify how structures of knowledge or discourse are deployed to construct the intersubjective worlds commonly inhabited by people who injure others or suffer injuries in particular times and places.

To some extent, the deployment of cultural knowledge in meaningful activity is a matter of relatively unreflective habit or practice, initially learned by instruction or example and galvanized into familiar routines and meaningful enactments through practical activity. At the same time, most constructivist scholars admonish against treating culture in deterministic terms; ideas do not "cause" specific meanings or choices (Pitkin 1972). Rather, experiences of injury become associated with different interpretations and practices through a complex process of meaning-making involving active subjects who operate within distinctive cultural contexts and draw on different legacies of life experience (Engel and Munger 2003). As Merry notes in her seminal study of legal consciousness, "the same event, person, action, and so forth can be named and interpreted in very different ways. The naming ... is therefore an act of power" (Merry 1990: 111). People are not rendered passive by the cultural milieu in which they live their lives, but culture plays an important part in delimiting and shaping the ways they identify, understand, and respond to their injuries.

The chapters in this book demonstrate that variations in social position – by class, race, ethnicity, gender, sexuality, religion, family, intelligence, physical capacity, and the like – produce enormous variation in practical access to cultural resources of meaning making and social action, including legal mobilization. And while social scientists have done a good job tracing patterns of variation along these lines of social difference, thus making sensible how differently situated people construct meaning in their lives, the ineffable qualities of human agency and individual histories render unreliable even the most expert predictions about experience based solely on social location. Most social constructivist analysts thus balance attention to patterned features of social context, social position, and cultural discourse with attention to the often surprising dynamics of individual actions.

Injuries are variably constructed along a variety of dimensions. For one thing, differently situated people may vary in whether they come to think of harmful events as injuries. We usually identify injury with harm to our basic interests or well-being, and especially with physical or emotional pain. But some kinds of harmful and even painful experiences are not viewed as injuries. For example, people sometimes inflict damage – such as tattoos, plastic surgery, or extreme exercise that cause pain and even leave scars – on their own bodies for enhancement, but most such subjects do not view these inflictions negatively as injuries (Bloom and Galanter, Chapter 8). One reason is that the subjects typically choose to undergo these inflictions for purposes of self-expression or otherwise. Other forms of culturally sanctioned disfigurement, however, are not chosen by the subjects themselves. Pain and disfigurement inflicted on children, such as foot binding and male circumcision, are often inflicted without the subjects' consent, yet are typically understood by parents and other adults as not abusive or injurious, but rather as an enhancement of their beauty, social status, or spiritual well-being.

Moreover, many harms experienced as injury are interpreted quite variably with regard to whether the subjects should demand remedies or compensation from others. David Engel's chapter probes the variety of interpretations of harm – as accidents, as results of fate or karma, as self-imposed – that discourage claims of injury against others or on society, leading injured persons to choose to "lump it" (Engel, Chapter 5). Again, whether pain is experienced as injury and whether it merits claims against others varies among different cultural traditions and among differently situated people within specific social contexts. Along similar lines, Sagit Mor (Chapter 1) writes from a disabilities rights perspective to show how injury can be understood in such different ways. Injury and disability alike can be viewed negatively as tragic misfortune, as a diminishment of a person, she argues, but they also can be viewed more positively in terms of different mixes of abilities. Mor's chapter underlines the ways that constructions of injury are contested, often by social groups, movements, and policy makers, as well as by ordinary individuals.

Likewise, many chapters in this book demonstrate that culturally sanctioned constructions of injury are constantly contested and in flux; what was an "accident" or matter of fate one day may become an actionable injury in another period, just as injuries familiar to one social or technological context may fade into irrelevance at another time. For example, Samantha Barbas (Chapter 9) shows how the rise of mass-mediated technologies gave rise to new categories of injury regarding images of the self, or representations of identity, that would have made little sense in different times. Løchlann Jain (Chapter 7) underlines that a plethora of historically new physical harms pervade our everyday lives in a technologically developed modern economy, so that we now find ourselves in a "time of injury." One implication is that we endure afflictions that are so common, so embedded in our lives, and so pervasive and enduring that we often do not even view them as injuries. Hence our project in this book of "mapping" the variety of changing ways that harms are or are not experienced as injuries and do or do not lead to claims for relief or reparation. While we look for patterns of interpretation and action among and within cultures, and among different spaces and times, our project again refrains from strong claims about social determinants. Authors in this collection return again and again to the active subjects who attempt to find meaning and determine a course of action that makes sense in the particular social position and cultural milieu in which they experience pain.

One theme that emerges from these chapters is how many members of society, in all societies, differ in their constructed "narratives of injury" from those of official legal actors, particularly judges and lawyers (see Yngvesson 1993). In many settings, official legal norms saturate social life and shape cultural understandings of denizens. But even these manifestations of law "in" social practice are highly variable. The often surprising finding is not just that disputes arise from different interpretations of official legal logics, but that social actors routinely construct their own terms of "legality" (Ewick and Silbey 1998) and often construct experiences of harm in ways that borrow little from, and even directly challenge, legal norms of injury. Yoshitaka Wada, in Chapter 6, is especially instructive in this regard. He shows how a medical malpractice dispute in Japan was understood through the very different standpoints of three key figures – the ordinary relational knowledge of a concerned mother, the medico-scientific knowledge of the doctor, and the legal knowledge of the lawyer. Law and injury, as we have said, are interrelated, but usually in complex, indirect, and shifting ways.

This fact of variability in constructions of injury and the appropriate or realistic responses to experienced injury underlines the important roles of non state cultural gatekeepers who interpret, mediate, or adjudicate among contending accounts, often adding authoritative weight to some versions over others. We can, after all, see normative weight in each of the accounts in Wada's analysis, but we know that they will not count equally, that some accounts are likely to draw on more cultural or institutional authority than others. In Chapter 7, Jain similarly shows how medical science generally reinforces the nearly obsessive focus on linear cause and effect in personal injury law, but other fields of injury disputing often take place absent scientific standards. Bloom and Galanter (Chapter 8) also show how body-refiguring practices of physical "enhancement," what they playfully designate as "good injuries," have ceded increasing gatekeeping roles to tattoo artists and plastic surgeons. The accounts by Rasmussen (Chapter 3), Engel (Chapter 5), Barbas (Chapter 9), Franks (Chapter 10), and others further call attention to how mass and social media shape attitudes, norms, and practices of injury construction and disputing (see also Haltom and McCann 2004).

We also highlight the different ways in which official legal systems categorize and compartmentalize institutional mechanisms for responding to, and deterring, various types of harm. Every advanced legal system provides multiple domains of law to address alleged harms, including especially criminal law, tort law, administrative law, and regulatory law. Public and private insurance mechanisms often figure prominently as well. Legal specialists tend to highlight in particular the differences between criminal and civil, especially tort, mechanisms. They emphasize the role of the state as prosecutorial representative of "the people" in criminal matters versus state mediation and adjudication of disputes between mostly private parties in torts. The different perspective of legal specialists also places great weight on the varying standards of liability (with criminal law emphasizing intent to a greater degree), different evidentiary rules and burdens of proof, and different remedial mechanisms (with criminal law relying heavily on punitive incarceration or payment to the state, while tort remedies focus on monetary compensation directly to victim claimants). But, viewed from the perspective of "the law in action," these purported differences seem greatly exaggerated and can be very misleading. Indeed, many harms experienced by citizens can be addressed through both criminal and civil actions; high-profile murder trials often are pursued through both state prosecution and wrongful death civil suits. Moreover, elements of multiple legal mechanisms are often combined in official legal proceedings and, especially, the broader politics of disputing in mass media and other institutional terrains of the state. For example, legal challenges to Big Tobacco transitioned from decades of civil tort litigation to hybrid "crim-tort" claims that mixed discursive elements and official roles from criminal and civil law (McCann, Haltom, and Fisher 2013).

The cultural accounts in this book recognize the porosity and malleability of official legal discourses and remedial mechanisms in practical interaction, within and beyond state institutional contexts. Arzoo Osanloo's intriguing study (Chapter 4) of how Iran's criminal code permits individual victims to demand or to forgo retribution, often based on a judge-led settlement, illustrates a creative melding of criminal and tort elements. Moreover, several later chapters in the collection (Chen, Chapter 13 and Koga, Chapter 14) disrupt and deconstruct traditional distinctions by focusing on how states sometimes position themselves as injured parties or are accused of being injurers. Even though states are representatives of their citizens in pressing these cases, the frameworks of disputing and claims for remediation tend to resemble civil law dynamics, often absent clearly established international or transnational rules, precedents, and institutional adjudicators.

That said, because criminal law frameworks and practices have been accorded by far the greatest attention by scholars, the studies in this book tend to focus more on injuries that are interpreted, disputed, negotiated, and adjudicated through civil tort conventions. We thus very self-consciously endeavor to rebalance scholarly engagement with these important if routine and sometimes less dramatic dimensions of injury practices in modern societies and states (see Engel and McCann 2009). And these are just some of the ways that the chapters that follow present both diversity in constructions of injury and variations in the institutional authority of norms and deciders for addressing competing claims by individuals, groups, organizations, corporate bodies, and states.

Causation and Responsibility

The chapters in this book reveal that narratives of injury, including those within and without official law, tend to vary along two separate but often related critical axes: interpretations of *causation*, and constructions of *responsibility*. "Causation" refers to analysis of the stimuli or actions that produce harmful results. A determination of factual causation connects the injury victim to another party – an individual, a group, society at large or the state – who might be held accountable, and even legally liable, for the damages. It is widely recognized, however, that not all attributions of factual causation will justify the legal attribution of responsibility for harm inflicted. Establishing causation in injury cases may help to identify a potentially responsible party, but causation in itself is not sufficient to determine liability. Even when it is clear that A has "caused" B's injury, the law still requires proof that A's actions were wrongful or fell below a legal standard of performance and were the "proximate" cause of the injury. In short, causation "in fact" is a necessary, but not sufficient, condition of legal responsibility. Furthermore, socio-legal researchers have demonstrated that people's thinking about causation can be biased by the attribution of moral blame. If A is viewed as a reprehensible person whose actions flagrantly violated social norms, then B (and other observers C) is far more likely to see a causal connection between A's actions and B's injury than under similar circumstances in which A is less morally blameworthy or suspect (Nadler and McConnell 2012). Once again, extra-legal moral judgments and legal protocols typically impinge on practices of injury determination, causation, and responsibility.

A good deal of scholarship has offered critical perspectives on the ways that the conventional legal preoccupation with causation narrows understandings of injury and liability. In particular, predominant discourses of causation tend to individualize responsibility for injury in ways that obscure and direct attention away from exposing broad, systemic patterns. For example, Løchlann Jain (2006) demonstrates how American law constrains constructions of injuries and of their causes, leading to the common perception that each injury is an isolated event with its own causal history, a view that obscures numerous easily foreseeable injuries that are systematically produced by the modern economic system. A broader understanding of the calculated decision-making that produces such injuries might lead to a very different conclusion about who should take responsibility for the victims of predictable "accidents" that are deemed acceptable in cost–benefit terms by product manufacturers. The principles of personal injury law, Jain writes, "narrow our modes of apprehension of what counts as injury, they divert attention away from other ways of understanding injury, and they miss the cultural implications of objects and the ways that objects are situated in networks of power" (Jain 2006: 151, see also Scales 2009).

The issue of temporality looms especially large in, and often challenges, most determinations of causality and, hence, responsibility. In general, the more remote in time the alleged source of a harm, the weaker is the claim of causality, not least because other intervening factors often complicate the chain of causality. To take a simple example, a claim that an automobile accident caused a neck injury is likely to be far stronger immediately after the incident than three years later. The very term "proximate" connotes imminence or immediacy in related causes and effects; as such, time is rarely on the side of injury claimants. This is especially true in matters of physical harm that allegedly result from exposure to toxic environmental causes – pesticide use by farmworkers, asbestos in construction materials and paint, coal dust for miners, and the like. While claims for redress for such injuries seem sensible to victimized workers, untangling specific causes that accrue over (often shortened) lifetimes complicates determinations of responsibility for wrongful action.

Kaimipono David Wenger's critical discussion about the impossibility of successfully demanding reparation for the harms of slavery imposed by dominant white populations on African slaves turns to a large extent on the extended passage of historical time (Chapter 11). He quotes the federal district court in the 2002 *Slave Defendants* lawsuit: "Plaintiffs cannot establish a personal injury sufficient to confer standing by merely alleging some genealogical relationship to African-Americans held in slavery over one-hundred, two-hundred, or three-hundred years ago." Simply put, "this causal chain is too long and has too many weak links for a court to be able to find that the defendants' conduct harmed the plaintiffs at all, let alone in an amount that could be estimated without the wildest speculation" (Wenger, Chapter 11).[1] And this was independent of the "fatal barrier" posed by the statute of limitations. Similar constraints on successful claims about the continuing injuries produced by historical wrongs of states are evident in the accounts of Li Chen (Chapter 13), regarding how European colonizers' allegations of barbaric practices rationalized imperial abuse, and Yukiko Koga (Chapter 14), regarding claims of Chinese victims against imperial Japan.

All of these chapters show how time figures prominently in shaping assessments about causation and which claims of responsibility for widespread injury count in different times and places. Two other important points are relevant here. First, as noted above, is the "tension between legal concepts of causation used by lawyers and judges and those found in the broader culture" (Engel 2009: 252–4). Official law

---

[1] In re African-American Slave Descendants Litigation, 304 F. Supp. 2d 1027, 1075 (2002).

neither determines nor exhausts the range of narratives about injury in society. Engel has illustrated this at length in his studies of injury narratives in Thailand as well as in the United States, specifically in "Sander County" (Engel 1984, 2009). Many studies of legal consciousness and legal practices in society have made the same point (Ewick and Silbey 1998). One of Jain's key points is that official tort law does not fully take account of how injuries are actually experienced in social life, and especially the context of unequal injury production that is often invisible to the most vulnerable persons in society (Chapter 7). Her account makes it clear that, in ordinary social life, blackletter legal principles and logics are often superseded or at least altered by engagement with competing normative, religious, or technical norms and proven experiential frameworks. This is one reason why she urges thinking of injury as a cultural "field" rather than a narrowly legal matter of linear cause and effect.

Second, such divergent ordinary, extra-legal normative discourses in turn often penetrate official legal practice, not only among jurors participating in official legal proceedings, but among lawyers and judges in trial situations as well. The lawyers and judges in "Hopewell," Georgia (Greenhouse 1986) and in western Massachusetts (Yngvesson 1993) constantly infused legal proceedings with their understanding of community norms and practices, even as they attempted to conduct those proceedings in a way that would reinforce what they considered core cultural values. Law in practice, whether within the courtroom or far from courts and judges in society, is almost always a jumble of legal and extra-legal discursive elements (Merry 1990).

These points again call attention to the role of extra-legal knowledge (as well as knowledge experts) in both determining causation and pressing beyond strict terms of causation in claiming or adjudicating responsibility. As noted previously, scientific and medico-scientific knowledge and norms can figure prominently. Pratiksha Baxi's chapter on the "two-finger test" in Indian rape cases (Chapter 12) underscores how medical knowledge and authority can significantly shape legal claiming and adjudication, and also how such authoritative knowledge itself is substantially shaped by colonial gender legacies and other biases. Yoshitaka Wada's (Chapter 6) constructivist study of a medical malpractice lawsuit likewise calls attention to the role of science and law as well as "ordinary" social experience in shaping the terms of claiming and adjudication of injuries. In sum, the chapters in this book cast doubt on the usual assumption that narratives of injury proceed necessarily from reasoning about causation to related reasoning about responsibility – from the "why" or "how" of an injury to judgments about "who" is liable.

Subject Construction

In addition to their reliance on concepts of causation and responsibility, injury narratives are also constructed around specific understandings of the legal subject, the person who experiences harm and may sometimes claim an entitlement to remedy. In many of the chapters that follow, the subjectivity of the injured victim is crucially important. The individual's position in the social order plays a role in this calculus, but so do self-perceptions and the viewpoints of third parties, including state and religious actors and institutions. We noted previously that assumptions about moral blame and the violation of cultural norms condition the causal stories that we tell. Judgments about liability – rendered by police, court clerks, lawyers, judges, juries, and by ordinary people throughout social life – routinely employ learned cultural scripts to determine who is and is not a disciplined, law-abiding, reasonable, "responsibilized," and thus justice-deserving person or collective. And this is another way that conventional morality and social norms often trump or complicate official legal norms in narrative development about injuries.

The chapters in this book vary widely in their attributions of agency and vulnerability, knowledge and naiveté, acceptance and resistance, power and powerlessness to legal subjects. Some emphasize the restricted social and institutional opportunities for effective action by more or less rational – and more or less well resourced – active agents, which liberal law posits. Others ask how the subjectivity of injury victims comes to be constructed in particular ways, and the answers often have deep histories, sometimes stretching back to colonial and postcolonial contexts.

Topics in this book related to subject construction include: how perceptions of injuries can help to create particular types of legal subjects; how subaltern perspectives on injury become mainstream and vice versa; the limitations of liberal legal theory for understanding how injuries are experienced from subaltern cultural perspectives; and the role of injuries in constructing (and challenging) social, sexual, and colonial inequalities. Several chapters address disputes over injury and liability among nation states, rather than among individuals, as with China's claims regarding the harms wrought by imperial Japan (Koga,

Chapter 14) as well as how American and other Western powers used claims of injury to justify imperial intervention (Chen, Chapter 13). The significance of new technologies of digital media also receives attention in a few of the chapters in the collection (Barbas, Chapter 9; Franks, Chapter 10). Additionally, several chapters consider how injuries are understood, and reconfigured, by actors and institutions in different geopolitical spaces and times (see, e.g., Engel, Chapter 5; Wada, Chapter 6; Barbas, Chapter 9). For example, several chapters address, explicitly or implicitly, themes of resistance and aspirational transformation, either individually through defiant norm violation (see, e.g., Bloom and Galanter, Chapter 8) or through the collective action of social movements and policy reforms (see, e.g., Koga, Chapter 14; Barbas, Chapter 9). They call attention to how injuries are at once personally, "privately" experienced and yet can be a basis of group identity and collective action. In the old lexicon of the Wobblies, "An injury to one is an injury to all."

Several chapters suggest new ways of thinking about injury that challenge conventional notions of the legal, rights-bearing individual subject. For example, one theme linking several chapters is a questioning of the liberal, self-sufficient, able bodied, autonomous legal subject, who usually is imagined to display great agency in mobilizing law and rights. Personal injury law presupposes the normalized healthy body and rational, fully developed human mind as the baseline to determine how injuries are compensated. Legally, tort remedies are intended to render damaged bodies and psyches whole again, whether literally or only figuratively. But the original whole is a fiction, and can be a destructive one at that. After all, most, people, and especially the poor and marginalized, are limited in agency and capacity even before they suffer a specific injury. That is, even before experiencing the trauma of an injury, an array of socially produced vulnerabilities and constraints define the "less than whole" person who must grapple with the additional burdens associated with serious accidents, toxic exposures, debilitating working conditions, and the like. Martha Fineman's influential and provocative argument for replacing the trope of the autonomous subject with a baseline "vulnerable subject," which is explained in her chapter, explicitly advances a critique of liberal legalism and agency (Chapter 2). Her prescription draws a mix of support and critique in turn from other scholars in the collection, especially Claire Rasmussen (Chapter 3) and Sagit Mor (Chapter 1). Mor questions whether highlighting people's vulnerabilities can escalate social stigmas of inferiority and undercut claims of entitlement. Rasmussen postulates that invoking similarities in vulnerability to establish rights entitlements of non-human animals as well as humans is likely to redraw rather than erase lines of hierarchy.

Mor and Rasmussen in some ways parallel the argument of theorist Wendy Brown, who goes further in emphasizing how civil law remedies actually tend to decrease the agency and increase the dependence of legal subjects. In her classic book, *States of Injury* (1995), Brown integrates Foucaultian analysis with Marxist sensibility to show how law participates in the disciplinary projects of liberal capitalist society. The liberal state, Brown argues, offers the legal processes as neutral arbiters of injury, thus removing them from complicity in the forces that systematically produce injury for many. Thus, the effort to define social injury as illegal powerfully legitimizes law and the state as appropriate protectors against injury and casts injured individuals as needing such protection by such protectors, and remedy by the mediators. "Whether one is dealing with the state, the Mafia, parents, pimps, police, or husbands, the heavy price of institutionalized protection is always a measure of dependence and agreement to abide by the protector's rules" (Brown 1995: 169). The preoccupation of rights-based "injury politics" is to promote reactive responses to harm that depoliticize citizens, both obscuring structural dimensions of injury and channeling people into reactive claims for restoration that sustain status quo inequalities rather than encourage collective efforts at egalitarian transformation of social relations. At its worst, a rights-based politics of injury fuels what Nietzsche called a "slave morality" of *ressentiment* rather than political citizenship. We might add that striving to realize the criteria that qualify people for claiming injuries in terms that deserve respect itself enforces normalizing discipline among citizens. While legal claims can sometimes reduce harm and empower in small ways, some chapters support Brown's view that more generally they sustain disciplined subjection to the hegemonic order.

Many chapters that follow, by contrast, portray an arguably more powerful subject that is continuously engaged in self-construction, in which injuries – and the reparation of injuries – play an important role (see, e.g., Bloom and Galanter, Chapter 8; Koga, Chapter 14). Some chapters also show how particular understandings of injury can play a central role in the construction of states as imperial protectors against injury as well as injurers (e.g., Chen, Chapter 13; Osanloo, Chapter 4). The sovereignty of most states, for example, seems to depend on claims of deterring or compensating injury to others, while the security of other states depends on their refusal to recognize injuries that seem so plainly to have occurred. As Robert Cover (1986) argued, law must exercise violence; law's violence is justified largely by the degree to which it, arguably, reduces the overall violence injuring its citizens, although many states – including the United States – arguably increase the net volume of harm and hurt in domestic society and the world beyond. However one calculates, though, these chapters caution that the agency of those claiming to be victims and to represent victims should not be discounted.

Cover reminds us that attention to the experience of injury also highlights the role of pain, both physical and emotional. The pain of injury, and its extra-rational or even irrational dimensions, propels much of the claiming and disputing over harms, and law often taps into heated emotions in ways that undercut its rationality. Mor (Chapter 1) emphasizes the pain of cultural stigma that compounds physical limitations for people with disabilities, and Barbas (Chapter 9) captures the emotional loss suffered by people who believe that their reputations have been undermined by others. In both criminal and personal injury law, the experience of pain often feeds the desire for vengeance, at once driving and arguably undercutting demands for legal retribution against injurers (see Sarat 2001). It is difficult to understand widespread support for mass incarceration and tolerance for extreme violence of police against black males in the United States without recognizing the public's fear of violence, however ill founded, and desire for vengeance. As Tom Baker has demonstrated, the emotion-driven demands for retributive "blood money" permeate tort disputing as well as prosecutor-driven criminal murder trials (Baker 2001). "Getting even" drives civil disputes as much as does "getting justice," as Sally Merry (1990) has demonstrated. Conversely, though, Arzoo Osanloo's chapter (Chapter 4) shows how the opposite emotions of forgiveness and forbearance can be mobilized among aggrieved families of murder victims in Iran, bolstering the promise of legal rationality, moderation, and community building.

Such complex relationships among subjectivity, injury, and the state call for new ways of thinking about personal injury law. While historically the focus on injury law has been on its claim to make individual injured subjects whole, this framework appears inadequate in light of our authors' demonstration that the individualized restoration after many injuries is no more than a convenient fiction, or that subjects may choose injury as part of a process of identity reconstruction, or that the state may spin injury narratives to justify imperial conquests and, at times, to ensure its own survival. After all, whole groups of people, especially lower income and marginalized minorities of the racialized laboring class, live in more or less permanent conditions of physical, emotional, and social injury. In this way, social norms stigmatizing particular subjects linked to undesirable traits of race, ethnicity, religion, and the like – as undeserving outsiders or Others – often prefigure and undermine the rationalistic pretenses of causal analysis and responsibility allocation in disputes over injury. Indeed, the standard response in most societies is for dominant or insider groups, and their official representatives, to simply "blame the victims" of systemic injury (Engel 1984, Haltom and McCann 2004).

What are the responsibilities of the state to remedy injury under these circumstances? Careful attention to the construction of subjectivity casts a new light on the conventional narrow aims of tort law. Does the collective nature of injury victimization, the vulnerability of the human (or nonhuman) subject, or the security of the state require new ways of thinking about injury, in which notions of corrective justice or making the subject whole play a less prominent role? How does the construction of subjects, as deserving humans or others, shape what we consider as "humane"? Indeed, what would it take to make the subject whole if the subject in question consists of thousands of similarly situated victims, or an entire community, or a colonized nation? What role does pain and suffering play in this alternative calculus? And how should compensation be conceptualized? These are some of the provocative new questions raised in this book.

Power and Injustice
This collection is committed to the position that injuries are produced amidst unequal, hierarchical power relationships (Franks, Chapter 10). Consequently, it is essential to recognize that neither injuries nor the mechanisms of personal injury law, or any domains of law for that matter, are neutral and removed from those relationships of power. Every rule institutionalizes affirmative action for some people over others; every causal judgment reflects and contributes to some version of redistributive justice (Scales 2009: 273). In the chapters that follow, multiple dimensions of unequal power – instrumental, institutional, and ideological (Lukes 2005) – are interrelated in multiple complex ways. The authors in this collection address at least four ways in which power disparities operate to produce injustice in injury cases.

First, many – perhaps most – injuries are not mere random accidents, but are produced systematically by larger forces and technologies of material production. This is the thrust of Jain's argument that American capitalism has created an "injury culture" that thrives and profits from refusals to make products and workplaces of production safe. Relegated to the status of economic "externalities," injuries are a central facet of capital accumulation. Invoking Ralph Nader, Jain argues that

> automobile deaths and disabilities pour billions of dollars into the economy, and … petrochemical pollution has remained virtually untouchable as a cause of death and decay. In fact, if nature was the "free" site from which capital could extract value, injury and illness has come to serve an analogical extractive role (Chapter 7: 3).

Indeed, predictable events causing massive numbers of preventable injuries and deaths are not merely justified as cost-efficient but also misleadingly characterized as unexpected "accidents." Those who manufacture pharmaceuticals, agricultural products, and consumer products, or who provide health services – indeed, those who participate in virtually all forms and sites of production and service – benefit from this logic. Personal injury law participates in protecting and legitimating this injury culture through its routine rejection of claims for diffuse harms and its demand that every accident victim prove an individual causal connection to a specific wrongful act. The presumptive freedoms and rights of propertied producers and privileged classes define the starting point for government obligations to reduce the harms of this arrangement. In this regard, law's neutrality is nested in pervasive legal protections for a hierarchical capitalist (and race-based) status quo that imposes injuries of widely varied types and degrees on large parts of the population.

Jain's analysis, underlining how legal interpretation of product liability law draws heavily on norms of individual consumption, parallels and builds on the work of critics such as Richard Abel. In a classic essay, Abel identified the linkage of torts to the rise of capitalism, and especially to the reproduction of a bourgeois ideology that enables producers to externalize costs, individualize exchange relations, commodify negotiations over harm, and justify unequal injury and access to remedies (Abel 1989–90). As a result, efforts to address injuries as collectively produced, or "structural" in form, and to frame entitlements to responsible actions by collectives, whether corporations or governments representing the people, are usually sidetracked and discouraged by legal mechanisms and even extra-legal normative traditions. "Class actions" in civil law and "disparate impact" in antidiscrimination law developed during the latter half of the twentieth century in US law in part to facilitate some claiming practices regarding structural harms, but those legal conventions have been dramatically narrowed in recent decades.

Second, we repeat that the harms of socially produced injury in virtually all societies fall disproportionately – and predictably – on the most vulnerable populations. Because of disparities in economic and political power, pain is distributed unevenly in society, and the prevalence of injury tracks the lines of inequality in society. People with low incomes are exposed to the riskiest and most unhealthy work conditions, food, clothing, appliances, residential environments, modes of travel, and overall lifestyles. To be poor is to lack the power to avoid disability, violence, and even terror at many levels. Inequalities of economic power intersect with racial, ethnic, gender, sexual, and other inequalities. The concept of "environmental racism" was developed to recognize the disproportionate distributions of pain and harm, but these inequities are ultimately a matter of disparate power among different social groups. And many of the most serious modes of injury – those that increase cancer rates, chronic diseases and disabilities, stress-related conditions, and much more – are largely invisible in everyday life and take their tolls on health and welfare slowly, incrementally, invisibly, masking the complex processes of causation that expose individuals and groups having the least control over their circumstances to the greatest risk of harm.

It is important to underline in this regard the disproportionate power exercised by dominant groups and organizations in determining the construction of injury, its causes, and the legitimacy of claims for redress. After all, it is the powerful who exercise the greatest control in making rules, adjudicating claims, and enforcing remediation or prevention. The narratives in this book are replete with accounts about how injury-claiming routinely expresses the will or benefits the interests of the haves over the have-nots. One classic example variously researched by all three of the co-editors, but not recounted in the following chapters, regards the politics of tort reform in the United States and other advanced legal systems. Tort law ostensibly provides workers and consumers victimized by reckless corporate power legal mechanisms for seeking damages. The insidious political gambit of the conservative tort reform movement, led by corporations in alliance with the mass media and political classes, reverses the constructed logic of victimization. Tort plaintiffs and their attorneys are often portrayed in politicized popular culture as irresponsible and greedy miscreants who victimize corporations and other large organizations with frivolous or vexatious lawsuits. The paradoxes of injury-claiming in capitalist society abound (Haltom and McCann 2004, McCann, Haltom, and Bloom 2001, Engel 2016). Parallel ironies and paradoxes of hierarchical power are evidenced in many of the chapters that follow (Mor, Chapter 1; Jain, Chapter 7; Franks, Chapter 10; Wenger, Chapter 11; Baxi, Chapter 12; Chen, Chapter 13; and Koga, Chapter 14).

Third, those with the least financial resources, organizational support, and social standing are least able to fashion viable responses and to compel relief for injuries imposed by the larger society. In the wealthy United States, large portions of the population do not have health insurance; in most of the Global South even fewer people are well insured. Likewise, the have-nots are least able to exert political influence – through elections, lobbying, protest, etc. – to compel safe processes of production and products, either though state regulation, worker control, or corporate commitment. Finally, and not least for this book, the have-nots are least well situated to compel remedies from personal injury law for serious injuries. Despite the unique availability in the United States of contingent-fee attorneys, inequalities of income and related racial, ethnic, religious, and gender status correlate with deficits in legal knowledge about possible courses of action. A great deal of research has demonstrated that disparities in social and economic power and status correlate with unequal understandings of rights and legal processes, access to lawyers, ability to devote time and financial costs to formal legal action, and independence from those who control productive and political processes. Researchers have also shown that most ordinary people are "one-shotter" amateurs in civil disputing, who face well-financed, experienced "repeat players" (Galanter 1974). Repeat players have the power and resources to play the long game and to dominate the creation of rules and procedures over time. Thus, the haves overwhelmingly tend to "come out ahead" in both informal and formalized legal disputing. It is true that injury victims have sometimes found it possible to aggregate their claims and expertise in certain ways, through class action lawsuits, the emergence of high volume "settlement mills," and the creation of alliances among personal injury lawyers to share data and develop common strategies (see, e.g., Engstrom 2011, Witt with Issacharoff 2004). But this kind of collaboration is confined to particular categories of claims and is of little use in the most common types of injuries. Moreover, even when claim aggregation is effective, the awards received by injury victims are extremely limited in comparison to the actual value of their claims. It seems that the disadvantages of relatively powerless injury victims are all but impossible to overcome.

Fourth, as we have already noted, civil disputing processes generally presume able bodied and self-sufficient subjects, and thus are systematically deaf and blind to the ongoing disabilities, disadvantages, and vulnerabilities that afflict most people's lives. Economic systems that produce injuries are routinely supported by law and insulated against challenges by those without power and resources who are most likely to be victimized by those production processes and consumption practices. Thus, it is not just the frequency of injury that is unequally distributed over the social hierarchy, but also the cultural interpretation and terms of legally actionable claims that constrain what counts as injury and the implications of remediation. For example, damage awards that take account of future earnings multiply the inequalities of wealth. It is thus much less costly to injure a poor person than a rich person (Scales 2009).

The unequal distribution of pain and injury is true for collectives and whole nations as well as for individuals. Injury is often experienced individually, but the motivations and terms of injury often are collective in nature. This is true for low-income and racially or ethnically marginalized people living in segregated urban neighborhoods, for immigrant and migrant workers in strange lands, for indigenous peoples in traditional lands or forced quarantine, and for peoples historically subjected to the violence of slavery (Wenger, Chapter 11), among others. It is also true for nation states such as China, which was victimized by both Japanese (Koga, Chapter 14) and Western (Chen, Chapter 13) imperialism. Injuries experienced by collectives in these various types of cases are complicated by the multiple and uncertain jurisdictions of official law that might address and redress large scale harms. The fact that such injuries take place over an extended time, often many decades of history, also often muddies the terms of claiming wrong and redress. And the perennial problem of legally protected "innocence" by dominant groups of states, like dominant groups in societies, commonly marks such experiences of injury and disputes over recognition and redress.

These common features of unequal power relations and inequalities of injury make issues of injustice central. Socio-legal researchers have consistently found that, in many situations, people who experience injury do not interpret their fate as one of injustice, or at least do not initiate claims to demand remedy for injustices that are perceived (Engel 2016). The reasons people without power and wealth typically do not pursue remedies are multiple: cultural norms opposing the assertion of their claim; their relative inability to discern causality and wrongdoing on the part of the injurer; lack of material resources necessary to pursue a claim; and the inadequate receptivity or accessibility of official legal forums for those without means. Lumping it is often a reasonable if tragic decision amidst limited opportunities, restricted capacities, and high costs. Indeed, narratives of experienced injury victims in the following chapters often highlight the inaccessibility or bias of legal institutions that should be sources of relief. But this book is also replete with stories of parties striving to articulate their claims of injury in terms that recognize power differentials and, at least potentially, frame demands for remedy in terms of justice.

CONCLUSION

Collectively, the chapters in this book demonstrate not only that injuries are socially constructed, but that disputes over injuries and remedies are inherently *political*. To properly address the problem of injuries in society, it is necessary to consider not only explicit contests over claims within settled normative terms, but also implicit contests among different normative frameworks and visions of the just community. Injuries, whether individually defined or collectively articulated, are always matters of contestation over "who gets what, when, how," as politics was famously defined by Harold Lasswell (1936).

We thus return to the centrality of themes about assignment of responsibility: to the victim, to a perpetrator, to collective injuries inflicted by organizations, institutions, and even an entire society and its representative, the state. From this vantage point, the question of rights takes on a rather different aspect than it does in conventional discussions of injuries and remedies. One takeaway from the book as a whole is that the endemic and systemic problem of injuries can never be addressed adequately by vesting individual victims with rights, since such rights could never be vindicated under current social arrangements; nor could they alter the broad-based foundations of injuries in society. This collection thus points to a practical, material failure of rights conventions broadly construed. At the same time, it is difficult to resist the normative thrust of the chapters in this book that all persons should be entitled to protection against seriously harmful injuries and – regardless of pervasive inequalities in wealth, status, and power – to expanded capacities to demand just remedies for injuries, both individually and collectively. In short, the book overall suggests how a deeper understanding of injuries can clearly expose ruptures in claims of legitimacy within societies, ruptures that occasionally find expression as legal demands but most often are "lumped," ignored, or suppressed. In this regard, we can do no better than to invoke the words of noted political theorist Judith Shklar (1986):

> It is not remembered that the history and present function of rights is the expression of personal outrage at injustice and cruelty. Rights are not a false front for impositions of power, as the Left so often claims. The call for rights is a response to very real dangers in an irrational world. Rectification is the chief task of the fair and the just or at least of those who are institutionally constrained to be so. It is the least one can do, and far less than most of humanity can hope for … [R]ights are asserted against power abused. To be heard and expressed at all, the voices calling for rights must address institutions of correction, however ineffective.

This book's focus on "injury and injustice" is, therefore, a singularly important way to achieve a deeper understanding, in Shklar's terms, of a dangerous and irrational world, riddled with a pervasive risk of harm and illness, distributed unequally across the human (and even the non-human) community. Although legal rights in their conventional form may fail to offer solutions or encompass the full extent of the injustice, rights in the broadest sense of the term provide a language to name the unfairness and cruelty associated with injuries in society and to begin to imagine solutions. Understanding the possibilities and limitations of seeking redress for injury is the challenge posed by this book. Whether or not individual authors find rights claiming useful in this regard, they agree on the need for greater commitment to reconciling the pervasive and unequal experiences of injury with the imperatives of social justice.

References

Abel, Richard L. (1989–90). "A Critique of Torts." *UCLA Law Review* 37:785–831.

Baker, Tom. (2001). "Blood Money, New Money and the Moral Economy of Tort Law in Action." *Law and Society Review* 35:275–319.

Brown, Wendy. (1995). *States of Injury: Power and Freedom in Late Modernity*. Princeton, NJ: Princeton University Press.
Cover, Robert M. (1986). "Violence and the Word." *Yale Law Journal* 95:1601–29.
Engel, David M. (1984). "The Oven-Bird's Song: Insiders, Outsiders, and Personal Injuries in an American Community." *Law and Society Review* 18:551–82.
   (2009). "Injury, Causation, and Responsibility: A Cross-Cultural Analysis of Tort Law and Society," in *Fault Lines: Tort Law and Cultural Practice*, edited by David M. Engel, and Michael McCann. Stanford, CA: Stanford University Press.
   (2016). *The Myth of the Litigious Society: Why We Don't Sue*. Chicago, IL: University of Chicago Press.
Engel, David M., and Michael McCann, eds. (2009). *Fault Lines: Tort Law as Cultural Practice*. Palo Alto, CA: Stanford University Press.
Engel, David M., and Frank W. Munger. (2003). *Rights of Inclusion: Law and Identity in the Life Stories of Americans with Disabilities*. Chicago, IL: University of Chicago Press.
Engstrom, Nora Freeman. (2011). "Sunlight and Settlement Mills." *New York University Law Review* 86:805–86.
Ewick, Patricia, and Susan S. Silbey. (1998). *The Common Place of Law: Stories from Everyday Life*. Chicago, IL: University of Chicago Press.
Galanter, Marc. (1974). "Why the 'Haves' Come out Ahead: Speculations on the Limits of Legal Change." *Law and Society Review* 9(1):95–160.
Greenhouse, Carol. (1986). *Praying for Justice: Faith, Order, and Community in an American Town*. Ithaca, NY: Cornell University Press.
Haltom, William, and Michael McCann. (2004). *Distorting the Law: Politics, Media, and the Litigation Crisis*. Chicago, IL: University of Chicago Press.
Jackson, Jean E. (2011). "Bodies and Pain." Pp. 370–87 in *A Companion to the Anthropology of the Body and Embodiment*, edited by Frances E. Mascia-Lees. Hoboken, NJ: Wiley-Blackwell.
Jain, Sarah S. Løchlann. (2006). *Injury: The Politics of Product Design and Safety Law in the United States*. Princeton, NJ: Princeton University Press.
Lasswell, Harold D. (1936). *Politics: Who Gets What, When, How*. New York: Whittlesey House.
Lukes, Steven. (2005). *Power: A Radical View*, 2nd edn. New York: Palgrave.
McCann, Michael, William Haltom, and Anne Bloom. (2001). "Java Jive: Genealogy of a Juridical Icon." *University of Miami Law Review* 56:113–78.
McCann, Michael, William Haltom, and Shauna Fisher. (2013). "Criminalizing Big Tobacco: Legal Mobilization and the Politics of Responsibility for Health Risks in the United States." *Law and Social Inquiry* 38(2):288–321.

Merry, Sally Engle. (1990). *Getting Justice, Getting Even: Legal Consciousness Among Working Class Americans*. Chicago, IL: University of Chicago Press.

Nadler, Janice, and Mary-Hunter McConnell. (2012). "Moral Character, Motive, and the Psychology of Blame." *Cornell Law Review* 97:255–304. http://scholarship.law.cornell.edu/cgi/viewcontent.cgi?article=3290andcontext=clr (accessed October 21, 2017).

Pitkin, Hanna Fenichel. (1972). *Wittgenstein and Justice*. Berkeley, CA: University of California Press.

Saks, Michael. (1992). "Do We Really Know Anything About the Behavior of the Tort Litigation System – And Why Not?" *University of Pennsylvania Law Review* 140:1147–291.

Sarat, Austin. (2001). *The Killing State: Capital Punishment in Law, Politics, and Culture*. New York: Oxford University Press.

Scales, Ann. (2009). "'Nobody Broke It, It Just Broke': Causation as an Instrument of Obfuscation and Oppression." Pp. 269–86 in *Fault Lines*, edited by David M. Engel and Michael McCann. Palo Alto, CA: Stanford University Press.

Shklar, Judith N. (1986). Injustice, Injury, and Inequality: An Introduction. Pp. 13–34 in *Justice and Equality Here and Now*, edited by Frank S. Lucash and Judith N. Shklar. Ithaca, NY: Cornell University Press.

Witt, John F., with Samuel Issacharoff. (2004). "The Inevitability of Aggregated Settlement: An Institutional Account of American Tort Law." *Vanderbilt Law Review* 57:1571–636.

Yngvesson, Barbara. (1993). *Virtuous Citizens, Disruptive Subjects: Order and Complaint in a New England Court*. New York: Routledge.

PART I

INJURY AND THE CONSTRUCTION OF LEGAL SUBJECTS

CHAPTER ONE

THE MEANING OF INJURY
A Disability Perspective

Sagit Mor

> The roots of tort law lie in human suffering, maimed bodies, shattered spirits, and extinguished lives.[1]

INTRODUCTION: DISABILITY AND INJURY

The meaning of injury is shaped by culture and depends on how a society or a community (however defined) understands the causes and the consequences of an injury. The meaning of injury shapes the experience of injury: the pain, the suffering, the tragedy, and the misfortune that are associated with bodily injury are not a-contextual bodily experiences, but rather culturally dependent occurrences that call for further interrogation and critique.

In this chapter, I would like to complicate the prevailing understanding of injury with the infusion of a disability perspective. I focus on injury as an experience of disablement (whether temporary or permanent) and suggest that the meaning of injury is shaped by one's understanding of disability. If disability is understood as pain, suffering, tragedy, and misfortune – injury, too, is understood this way. However, if this negative view of disability is challenged – and it has been challenged by disability advocates and critics – the taken-for-granted understanding of injury as a misfortune is also challenged. A critical view of disability and injury therefore brings a new perspective to the study of the legal regimes that address the consequences of injury, from the law of torts, the law of personal injury, to related legal arrangements, including no-fault schemes and social security-based mechanisms.

I suggest that the scholarly literature on disability studies and disability legal studies offers a new set of tools to investigate the relationships

This research was supported by the Israel Science Foundation (grant no. 719/16).

[1] Bell, Peter A. and Jeffrey O'Connell. (1997). *Accidental Justice: The Dilemmas of Tort Law*. Yale: Yale University Press.

between disability and injury, to interrogate the socio-legal construction of injury, and to examine the resulting implications for tort law and other related fields. A disability legal studies analysis seeks to examine the ways in which the law participates in the social construction of disability. The focus of inquiry is not merely on the promotion of disability rights and benefits, but rather on the ways in which biases and assumptions about disability permeate any field of law, shaping the design of legal norms and institutions, and being shaped by them (Mor 2006). In this view, tort law, like any other field of law, is not a mere reflection of social norms and values, but rather an active participant in the production of disability.

I further suggest that the disability perspective offers a particularly important prism for the study of the structure and logic of tort law, specifically, personal injury law, "the heart and soul of tort law," according to Lawrence Friedman (Friedman 2005: 349). So far, the study of disability and tort law has received little scholarly attention. Several studies have examined the place of disabled persons as injured or injurers, focusing mainly on the duty and standard of care toward and by disabled people (e.g., tenBroek 1966, Milani 1998). Others have attended to specific topics in tort law, such as wrongful life and wrongful birth lawsuits (Hensel 2005, Mor 2014),[2] and damages for pain and suffering (Bagenstos and Schlanger 2007), or on broader topics such as torts as a remedy and response to disability discrimination (Weber 2012). These pioneering studies demonstrate the intellectual contribution of disability critique to the study of tort law and the impact of disability rights on its development. Yet my goal is to go beyond the identity of the parties or a single issue and to explore the fundamental assumptions that underlie tort law as a field. This kind of analysis was first presented in Bloom and Miller's illuminating article on disability and stigma in tort litigation and its impact on litigants and public perception of disability (Bloom and Miller 2011).

This chapter interrogates the meaning of injury: How would a disability perspective complicate the meaning of injury and what would be its further implications for tort law? I look at the meaning of the injurious act and its societal, bodily, and economic consequences as an event

---

[2] Wrongful life and birth claims provide the site on which disability-based critiques and perspectives are most seriously and consistently considered. So far, these claims have largely been perceived as unusual tort claims. Yet I view them as indicative of the complexities of tort law from a disability perspective (Mor 2014).

that transforms one's status from a nondisabled to a disabled person. I argue that this understanding of the injurious act poses a fundamental challenge to tort law, as it provokes the following question: *Is it possible to reconstruct a concept of injury that is free of negative stigma and social bias against disabled people, but still acknowledges the pain and the moral wrong that an injury entails?* I suggest that the reconceptualization of injury requires a transformation in the social relations, social structures, and economic foundations that shape the meaning of disability. Such a fundamental change entails the implementation of disability rights, the expansion of social security and social welfare mechanisms, and the reframing of tort law's overt goals and underlying assumptions. As the following analysis shows, changing the social and material conditions that surround disability will have an impact on a broad range of social harms and injuries that currently lack adequate social response and are often treated in isolation.

THE DISABILITY CRITIQUE

The disability movement and the disability studies literature have transformed the meaning of disability – from an inherently inferior condition to a more complex social, political, and cultural phenomenon. They reject the prevailing individualistic medicalized view of disability and call for a more complex understanding of disability as a social construction and a human variation, an axis of identity and a platform for minority-based politics.

Early UK disability studies theory introduced the distinction between impairment, which is a "neutral" bodily variation, and disability, which is the meaning that is assigned to that variation, as shaped by power relations, cultural assumptions, and social practices (Oliver 1990, 1996). This powerful distinction was soon challenged, mainly because of its simplicity, its denial of the bodily experience of disability, and the resulting neglect of impairment as a category of social analysis (Shakespeare and Watson 2001). The importance of that distinction for now is the acknowledgement that disablement is not only physical (including cognitive or emotional), but also social – it is a bodily experience that is mediated through social attitudes, environmental design, the availability and quality of social services, and economic opportunities.

The disability–impairment distinction can enrich and complicate our understanding of injury as a concept that encompasses two dimensions: like impairment, injury has a seemingly value-free descriptive dimension as an event that causes a bodily change; like disability, injury has also a value-laden dimension when it is regarded as an event that transforms one's own self-perception, social position, political power, and even human worth and value. A substantial injurious event is often a disabling experience in which one is transformed from "capable," "whole," and "normal" to "incapable," "incapacitated," "damaged," and "abnormal." This is not solely because of the physical and emotional consequences of the injury, but also, and sometimes mainly, because of society's response to disability. The experience of injury is therefore informed both by the bodily change that one faces – whether physical or mental – and the disabling social conditions that he or she experiences.[3]

Tort law is a highly individualistic and medicalized societal response to disability and injury.[4] Under tort law, society ascribes responsibility to a person or an entity that was singled out of the many factors that contributed to that event and found liable for the injury; the wrongdoer is then obliged to compensate the injured person for the medical, financial, material, and emotional consequences of the injury; and the level of injury is measured primarily by medical and functional parameters. Accordingly, an undisputed function of tort law is to compensate persons who were wronged and to sanction those who caused these injuries. According to this basic type of corrective justice rationale, if there is no one to blame or to assign responsibility to – then the injury is perceived as merely a misfortune and there is no award of damages. Even under competing approaches that emphasize the regulatory role of law or its deterring function, there is a search for a specific individual or an entity that is responsible for the injury. This type of reasoning takes into account larger social goals that extend beyond the party's behavior and aim at preventing future injuries, but still employ a highly individualistic account of injury, according to which if an injury is cost-effective or unpreventable it is likewise a mere misfortune.

Yet these conventional views of tort law ignore the role of social structure in generating disablement (Bloom and Miller 2011). As I argued elsewhere, "The individual nature of tort law assumes that

---

[3] I leave aside for now people with pre-existing disabilities who face an injury.
[4] Other legal mechanisms may be insurance-based, administrative (such as social insurance), or informal (such as ADR). Nonlegal responses may be spiritual, religious, local, community-based, or social networks-based forms of support (see, e.g., Engel 2005, 2010).

damages should be awarded only to those whose disability results from an identifiable injury that was caused by someone's fault ... individual blame is perceived as a solution while the social structure is accepted as a given and remains unchallenged" (Mor 2014). The structural causes of social disablement are rooted in social relations and social structures, which tort law theory neglects to address and personal injury cases rarely acknowledge. These overlooked structural causes include several elements: first, the impact of prevalent stigmatic and unfounded views about disabled people and about life with a disability on the experience of disability; second, the ways in which the built environment excludes disabled people to separate spheres of living and renders them unfit to participate in social life; third, the impact of inadequate social services and support on the ability of disabled people to live an independent dignified life; and finally, the role of societal distribution of resources in rendering disabled people poorer than nondisabled people because of lack of employment opportunities and the extra costs of living with a disability (Officer and Posarac 2011).

The litigation of personal injury cases amplifies this individualistic understanding of disability and injury. Tort litigation functions as a spectacle of misery in which claimants are forced to participate in order to win their case and, if liability is established, to receive a higher amount of damages. Clearly, severe injury that leads to substantial disability involves increased expenses and may significantly decrease one's employment opportunities. It therefore deserves higher compensation. However, telling who is disabled, determining the level or percentage of one's disability, and deciding on the implications of one's disability are not clear-cut questions, particularly in an adversarial process. Cultural assumptions about disability produce implicit expectations about what disability "looks" like and what it entails, and may not allow for a more realistic and rounded depiction of the experience of disability. Moreover, what one may consider a mild injury can translate into substantial costs because of lack of access and services. The performance of misery is therefore not a deception, but rather a response to the complexity of disability and to assumptions of suffering and incapacity that underlie society's predominant understanding of disability.

The performance of misery has a role in establishing liability as well, though more subtly. Litigants may find it necessary as an underlying narrative in order to convince the court that the claim is justified and to interpret the rules in favor of the plaintiff (Bloom and Miller 2011, Hensel 2005). The severity of the injury may change the way that courts weigh both the arguments and the facts. The famous Learned Hand formula demonstrates this logic: when the expected loss is high, the law requires a higher level of precaution and is therefore more likely to award damages. The incentive for plaintiffs is therefore to emphasize their suffering and misery and to present high levels of dysfunction, inability to work, and low satisfaction from life in order to increase their chances of winning their claim and of receiving proper damages. This individualistic and medicalized view of disability turns tort law into a site that produces, maintains, and reinforces negative views about disability.

The above concerns are most evident in two issues that have already received much scholarly attention: pain and suffering damages, and wrongful life/birth liability. Compensation for pain and suffering is a branch of nonpecuniary damages that is heavily influenced by judges', lawyers', and juries' negative assumptions about life with disability and what it involves (Bagenstos and Schlanger 2007). These nondisabled actors attribute much higher levels of pain and suffering to disability than those experienced by disabled people, even those who became disabled following an injury (ibid.). Studies have found, for instance, that juries base their assessment on their own fear of disability and not on the lived experience of disability (ibid.). Wrongful life and wrongful birth cases provide an even more extreme example than pain and suffering. These claims are grounded in ableistic social conventions: wrongful life claims assume that disabled people would have been better off, from their own perspective, had they not been born; wrongful birth claims assume that parents' expectations to prevent the birth of a disabled child are protected interests, since having such a child is a harm to the family (Hensel 2005, Mor 2014). While most jurisdictions reject wrongful life claims as immoral and impossible, wrongful birth claims are widely accepted based on tort law's classic doctrines (ibid.).

Despite these highly problematic features of tort law, it serves several other functions that a disability perspective should take seriously: first, it expresses a social and sometimes moral disapproval of the injurious action; second, it serves to deter and prevent future injuries; and third, it provides a remedy for the economic consequences of disability. I will address these three aspects later on, in this order, as I further develop my argument. The mutual challenge to tort law and disability is therefore to reconstruct a personal injury law that accomplishes its various functions without employing a highly individualistic medical view of disability. The following sections attempt to respond to these challenges.

AWARENESS OF DISABLING IMAGES AND ENVIRONMENTAL BARRIERS AND THEIR CONSEQUENCES

A disability approach to tort law first necessitates an increased awareness of disabling images and environmental barriers. This means transforming how all legal actors, particularly lawyers and judges, understand disability and talk and write about disability. It means viewing disability not in a medicalized–individualized fashion, but rather through a socio-cultural-political lens that acknowledges and even emphasizes the material dimension of the social construction of disability and the many roles that society plays in generating disablement. Including, as discussed earlier, the impact of stigma and stereotypes on social participation, the bearing of social structures and institutions on disabled people's ability to participate in public life, and the ways in which misallocation of societal resources has led to poverty and lack of opportunities for disabled people (Bagenstos and Schlanger 2007, Bloom and Miller 2011).

One immediate implication for tort law would be to avoid presenting disability as a source of agony and misery, and instead acknowledge and stress the social difficulties that disabled people encounter, the role of the environment in shaping the experience of disability, and the material consequences that an injurious event may entail. This also means developing a way to understand impairment and talk about it in a nonnegative way. Adrienne Asch, for example, maintained that "having a capacity can be good, but the absence of capacity is simply an absence" (Asch 2003: 326). She further explained that "[t]he absence of capacity it is 'not necessarily' 'bad'; the opposite of having a capacity is not having it; having it and not having it can be equally legitimate ways of living a life" (ibid.).

A further step would be not only abandoning the view of disability as inferiority and avoiding the tragic view of disability, or advancing a view of disability as mere absence, but rather espousing an "affirmative view" of disability that fosters disability pride and celebrates disability culture. In the words of Swain and French: "It is essentially a non-tragic view of disability and impairment which encompasses positive social identities, both individual and collective, for disabled people grounded in the benefits of life style and life experience of being impaired and disabled" (Swain and French 2000: 569). The persistent implementation of disability rights is of great importance here, because disability rights offer an alternative vision in which such understanding of disability is a viable option.

However, this positive alternative view of disability poses several, sometimes conflicting, difficulties. First, it goes against tort law's basic doctrines, including harm, fault, and causation, which are required for establishing liability. The understanding of disability as a source of pride may impact its framing as a harm; the understanding of disability as a product of social barriers may undermine causation; and the destabilization of harm and causation may impede the attribution of fault to an individual wrongdoer. If the fault is society's, with strong structural aspects, then the harm is social harm, which the individual involved cannot be responsible for. In the absence of liability, no damages will be awarded.

A second set of concerns relates to the level of compensation that such awareness would yield, even if liability is established. One direction may suggest that turning tort litigation from a spectacle of misery to an exhibit of disability pride would *decrease* the ascribed damages, since "happy" or "content" litigants do not seem to be injured or disabled enough and might therefore have lower chances, compared with "miserable" ones, for sufficient compensation that covers their losses and expenses. Another direction may suggest that the level of compensation would actually *increase*, since a social understanding of disability would expose the wide-ranging implications of social disablement (Bloom and Miller 2011). In any event, the greatest challenge that remains is imposing the extra costs of these social implications on a random wrongdoer. According to this logic, if it is society that can and should remove social barriers, then individual liability only diverts public attention away from society's responsibility (Mor 2014).

Third, these debates carry the risk of associating the struggle for disability pride and recognition with tort reform efforts. While tort reform represents reactionary efforts to reduce damages based on anti-plaintiff and pro-business interests (Finley 2004), the disability critique seeks to provide more plaintiffs with better chances for economically secure and emotionally and physically fulfilling lives. This uneasy alliance between progressive disability forces and conservative causes is not unique to the context of torts. It appears in beginning and end of life discussions, as well as when pro-disability arguments are confused with pro-life arguments. The disability-based critiques of prenatal testing, for instance, maintain that prenatal selection of embryos or fetuses based on their expected impairment is morally problematic, as it assumes that life with a disability is a life not worth living, and are therefore often mistaken for a sanctity of life line of argument. However, for disability scholars of bioethics, there is a clear line between these two types of reasoning: the disability critique is not pro-life, but rather pro-disability (Asch 2003). Similarly, there should be a clear line between disability pride arguments, on the one hand, which are pro-disability and aim to provide more options and support to disabled people, and tort reform efforts, on the other hand, which do not attend to the corporal, material, and social consequences of injury, but rather focus on the interests of the wrongdoer. While the former is concerned with plaintiffs' well-being and social inclusion, the latter favors defendant's financial interests and works to delegitimize otherwise justified claims.

Finally, the argument against a tragic view of disability may contradict some progressive campaigns in support of emergent or particularized injuries, such as hate crime and domestic violence or disaster relief, whether caused by the natural environment (e.g., earthquake, hurricane) or by human intervention (e.g., terror attacks).[5] Such campaigns recognize the complex nature of these injuries, the diverse social factors that shape the circumstances of these injuries, and the importance of formalized redress mechanisms that ameliorate the emotional, physical, and economic consequences of an injury. However, in advocating for redress (whether administrative or court-based) they often employ, express, and reinforce a negative view of disability.

Interestingly, the campaigns to acknowledge these injuries face similar dynamics and dilemmas that tort litigation does. They carry a negative message about disability for two related reasons: one is a deeply embedded tragic view of disability; another is strategic – to mobilize public support by relying on narratives and images of misery and tragedy that bring awareness to the problem and to the need to provide relief. Second, they already grapple with a somewhat similar tension: how to raise awareness of the cause of injury without victimizing the injured or reinforcing their social marginality (see, e.g., Gondolf and Fisher 1988, Minow 1992).[6] Often, the anti-victimization efforts may be compromised by the short-term practical goal of providing economic relief and social services to mitigate the costs and consequences of injury – care, cure, rehabilitation, and continuing support.

---

[5] A similar claim may be raised with regard to disaster relief, whether caused by nature (e.g., earthquake, hurricane) or by human intervention (e.g., 9/11, school shooting) and with regard to privacy-based claims, particularly in the age of Internet and cellular-based modes of communication.

[6] Especially when related to identity based concerns, such as gender, race, or LGBT.

However, I argue that if society were more supportive of disability, in terms of social acceptance, disability rights, and social services, then many of the needs of persons in extreme situations would have been met by the existing net of support, and efforts could have been dedicated to the larger social issue that requires attention. Furthermore, the lack of such universal services leads to fragmentation, since each group fights for its own interests and must demonstrate a higher level of misery and suffering.

To conclude this point, emphasizing social disablement takes the discussion away from medical–individual understanding of injury, but carries its own risks and dilemmas. Some are inherent to the logic of tort law, some are closely related, and some are associated with the broader social issues of injury. In other words, increased awareness of disabling images and environmental barriers is not a "sectarian" concern of disabled people. It is rather a new perspective through which to understand a broad range of injury-related social and legal problems.

THE EMBODIED EXPERIENCE OF DISABILITY AND INJURY AS MORALLY WRONG

In this section, I argue that the fundamental problem with the emphasis on disabling images and environmental barriers is that it tends to stress the social context and to neglect the embodied experience of injury that may entail pain and limited ability. Earlier I presented the usefulness of the disability–impairment distinction for a richer understanding of injury. In this section, I would like to complicate this distinction and to argue that a more complex understanding of the relationships between disability and impairment could be beneficial to the reconstruction of injury as morally wrong, and therefore deserving of legal remedy.

The classic division between impairment and disability maintains that impairment is a bodily characteristic, while disability is the social meaning that attaches to that trait. However, several disability studies scholars have criticized that distinction for its neglect of the body – the physical experience of pain and more broadly the lived experience of the disabled body. These scholars argue that impairment is not a neutral bodily trait that is free of context and power relations and that disability is not a purely social phenomenon, unrelated to bodily experiences. "The sharp distinction between impairment and disability," so the critique goes, "creates a series of binary opposites which constitute theoretical territories with clearly marked boundaries" (Hughes and Paterson 1997: 330):

The biological	The social
impairment	disability
the body	society
medicine	politics
therapy	emancipation
pain	oppression
the medical model	the social model

The body in these discussions represents the limitations that disabled people experience due to their physical, mental, or cognitive condition rather than those that stem from the social structure. Jenny Morris was one of the first to note that the social model of disability denies or erases the embodied experiences of disability. She argued that "to deny the personal experience of disability is, in the end, to collude in our oppression" (Morris 1991: 120). Morris's argument is grounded in a feminist perspective on disability, which:

> must focus, not just on the socioeconomic and ideological dimensions of our oppression, but also on what it feels like to be unable to walk, to be in pain, to be incontinent, to have fits, to be unable to converse, to be blind or deaf, to have an intellectual ability which is much below the average. There are positive and strong elements to these experiences but there are also negative and painful elements. The tendency of the disability movement to deny the difficult physical, emotional and intellectual experiences that are sometimes part of the experience of disability is a denial of "weakness," of illness, of old age and death (Morris 1991: 48–9).

The challenge, as Hughes and Paterson put it, is "to rescue the concept of 'suffering' from its reactionary and tragic association ... [And] to think of suffering as a concept which reflects the mutual engagement of pain and oppression" (Hughes and Paterson 1997: 336). Pain is not only a product of our anatomy and physiology, but rather located at the intersection between biology and culture (ibid.: 329, Best 2007: 165). In his work on *The Culture of Pain*, Morris (1991) attempted to deconstruct the prevailing understanding of pain as shaped by the dominant scientific and medical discourse and to offer a more discursive account of pain, which is, as Best articulated it, "always a cultural artefact ... always an experience in need of interpretation" (Best 2007: 168). Following Morris and Hughes and Paterson, Best argued that we lack "cultural resources to fully describe and explain the nature of painful experiences" (ibid.: 170). He forcefully stresses, "Pain is a material barrier that exists beyond the politicoaesthetic level" (ibid.: 169) and that we need to include a concept of pain that acknowledges its potential to disrupt and shape one's identity and sense of self (ibid.: 170). Aware of the difficulties that this stance may stir among disability critics, Best argues that "[t]o recognize the existence of biologically based realities is not to accept biological dysfunction as the sole cause of disability or any other form of reactionary politics of disability" (ibid.: 170).

It is therefore important to stress that even in a fully accessible and inclusive society, the very experience of becoming injured is painful and the loss of some physical or intellectual capacity does not become meaningless. This is true for disabled persons too: being disabled does not mean being indifferent to changes in one's bodily condition, whether they are associated with aggravating one's impairment or with acquiring a new type of impairment. Acknowledging these experiential aspects of disablement and the difficulties they entail should be reconceptualized as a source and sign of strength, not weakness.

The sociology of impairment and the social construction of pain may offer an alternative meaning of injury that accounts for both pain and oppression. It allows more space for discussing the painful aspects of injury and, therefore, the wrongs of injuring. Injury is wrong because it does cause suffering and pain. Yet, if suffering and pain are mediated through the social and the cultural, then they can also be mitigated by them: first, by changing the social and built environment, and second, by developing linguistic possibilities to talk about pain in a nonreactionary way. The first step would be to acknowledge that while it is impossible to deny pain, its meaning is not necessarily a tragic one. The second step would be to recognize that people can endure pain and at the same time experience happiness and live fulfilling lives.[7]

Martha Fineman's conceptualization of the vulnerable subject may provide a bridge between the disability critique and its legal implications (Fineman 2008). Fineman argues that the vulnerable subject is a "far more representative of actual lived experience and the human condition" than the liberal ideal of the autonomous self (ibid.: 2). This vulnerability arises "from our embodiment, which carries with it the ever-present possibility of harm, injury, and misfortune from mildly

---

[7] Research shows that persons who were injured do restore a sense of meaning and happiness in their lives (see, e.g., Albrecht and Devlieger 1999, Oswald and Powdthavee 2008). Other research shows that children with disabilities can have a positive impact on the family (Stainton and Besser 1998).

adverse to catastrophically devastating events, whether accidental, intentional, or otherwise" (ibid.: 9). While this view of vulnerability is not entirely a tragedy-free approach, it does allow more space for a non-tragic view of injury and disability. On an individual level, it embraces dependency and assumes "a wide range of differing and interdependent abilities over the span of a lifetime" (ibid.: 12). On a state level, it demands an active and responsive state that provides individuals "a true opportunity to develop the range of assets they need to give them resilience in the face of their vulnerabilities" (ibid.: 21).

Following Fineman, I suggest that tort law is a law of vulnerable subjects in time of crisis. As personal injury law, it deals with "[b]odily needs and the messy dependency they carry" (Fineman 2008: 12). The harm that an injury entails is the epitome of universal human vulnerability, yet this harm is context-dependent. In Fineman's terms, the state's response to harm shapes the experience of injury, as its institutions "play an important role in lessening, ameliorating, and compensating for vulnerability" (ibid.: 13). The structure of these institutions may increase or decrease resilience. The embodied experience of injury underscores its material implications – bodily, financially and otherwise. It calls attention to the actual reality of the human condition, which includes pain and vulnerability, and requires a modified legal language and modified legal institutions. There is a need therefore to reimagine a new role for tort law that takes seriously its role as a major mechanism of state response to injury and disablement. From a disability perspective, tort law's language, doctrine, and practice should incorporate both a commitment to disability rights and an understanding that injuring someone, causing pain, is morally and socially wrong. The disability and vulnerability challenge to tort law is therefore to promote human resilience and to minimize inequality and disadvantage.

TORT LAW AS PREVENTION, NOT ELIMINATION

So far, I have focused on tort law as an instrument that addresses the consequences of injury. Yet tort law also has a role in preventing injuries. Current discussions in tort law theory with regard to prevention revolve around the notion of deterrence. However, I prefer prevention, because it is more suitable to my project, although carries its own challenges.

Both prevention and deterrence acknowledge and sometimes even celebrate the regulatory role of tort law in setting standards to corporations and big industries that tend to maximize profit and self-interest. Yet I argue that each one offers a different frame of meaning to the regulatory function of tort law. *Deterrence* has become a primary goal of tort law since the introduction of the economic analysis of law, which found tort law a particularly fruitful field to demonstrate and develop its arguments (Calabresi 2008). The main problem with this type of analysis, however, is that its core value is efficiency and its primary goal is the reduction of accident costs, with no specific interest in the individual who was injured or the morality of harm. While other economic principles and apparatuses, such as spread loss and insurance, may be in line with an injury-centered analysis, deterrence remains very individualistic in its nature and focuses on the wrongdoer's conduct and not on the injured perspective. The term *prevention* is more appropriate for my purposes because, as I suggest, its core value is safety, not efficiency. Prevention focuses on proper guidance for human and enterprise conduct to avoid injuries and harm. Moreover, it puts more trust in the state and its regulatory capacities (Sugarman 1985), thereby allowing the state to become responsive, to intervene in market forces, and to create the conditions for human resilience. Furthermore, by emphasizing safety, prevention sets forth a more human-centered vision that seeks to protect potential injured persons. Nevertheless, prevention also carries its own complexities from a disability perspective.

Despite the above advantages, the preventive function of tort law poses the following challenge from a disability perspective: what message is embedded in the attempt to prevent injuries? The understanding that disability should be prevented when possible is not exclusive to tort law, but exploring its anti-disability sentiment is crucial for a disability analysis of tort law. The attempt to reconstruct a concept of injury that acknowledges the complexities of disability, but avoids the denigration of disabled people, requires a disability-sensitive understanding of prevention. The following suggests that a more nuanced conception of prevention may rely on the distinction between prevention and elimination of disability.

The distinction between prevention and elimination, or the attempt to draw such a distinction, is evident in discussions concerning medical and safety-related issues. While the elimination of disabled people is an absolute wrong, following the lessons of the Eugenic movement, the prevention of disability is a goal shared by all. It is shared by disability scholars and disabled people, too, who disapprove of the violation of autonomy and the infringement of bodily integrity that an injury entails and are aware of the social consequences of an injury (Asch 2003, Wasserman 2013). Interestingly, there is not much literature on this tension, maybe because of its puzzling nature. One solid voice is that of Davis Wasserman, a disability bioethicist, who has argued: "We must acknowledge that it is sometimes appropriate to prevent functional limitations, and thereby reduce, often dramatically, the number of people with various disabilities" (Wasserman 2013: 270).

This tension is perhaps most apparent in the attempt to draw a line between *prenatal diagnosis*, which is highly controversial within the disability community, and *prenatal care*, which is instead legitimate and is widely regarded as responsible pregnancy. If disability-based termination of pregnancy is morally problematic, what should be the disability position regarding the precautionary measures that pregnant women are expected to follow, such as taking folic acid, eating properly, and avoiding alcohol? For Adrienne Asch, there is a clear difference between "selecting out fetuses and protecting them" (Asch 2003: 326). She argued: "We protect the possibility for capacity when we promote fetal health, but we refuse to acknowledge or permit the growth of people who will not have such capacity when we select against fetuses as potential people with disabling traits" (ibid.: 326). Asch's distinction between selection and protection echoes the distinction between prevention and elimination and offers disability-based support to prevention as protection, which correlates with the core value of safety that I offered earlier.

For Wasserman the tension between selection and protection is more acute and harder to resolve. In his view, disability entails an "undeniable tension" between equality and health protection (Wasserman 2013: 276). He argues that this undeniable tension makes disability discrimination different from gender and race discrimination, where the close relations between prevention and elimination make prevention an illegitimate cause. Wasserman's conclusion urges a call to "prevent disabilities in ways that do not exaggerate the difficulties of life with a disability" or "encourage pity" or condensation (ibid.). Aware of the limited nature of this solution, Wasserman stresses that such an approach should be viewed as "a matter of respect, not of political correctness" (ibid.); that is, as a matter of human dignity and human diversity and not an empty rhetoric. Similarly, disability advocates find the overemphasis on cure and rehabilitation contradictory to the disability movement's goals, but would not oppose medical care and technological innovation altogether – to allow the person to maximize her potential (Shakespeare 2006).

Another analogy, closer to tort law, is the enactment and enforcement of safety rules and laws. The goal of these rules is to prevent injury and disablement. Should we not care about safety because we find positive, affirmative, and even joyful aspects to life with a disability? Emens (2012) offered "framing rules" to guide prevention and safety campaigns so that they present more realistic, balanced information about disability. She calls to incorporate "more of an inside perspective [of disabled people] on disability into driver's education – which is generally more positive, as well as more informed, than the outside perspective" (ibid.: 1419). She also suggests that "cigarette warning labels should be examined through what we might call the disabled-listener heuristic" (ibid.: 1426), which means to imagine a disabled listener.

Wasserman and Emens offer solutions based on language and information. This direction is important, but insufficient for tort law. First, as I argued earlier, awareness of disabling images and environmental barriers carries its own limitations. Second, unlike safety rules and policies, tort law responds to an already existing injury by imposing a sanction on a specific wrongdoer, and compensating an actual injured person. They should therefore be supplemented by a more structured response that attends to the moral aspects of personal injury law and to the economic consequences of injury and disability.

I started with the challenge to tort law, which is to condemn the injurious act and avoid the devaluation of the injured person. However, as the analysis progresses, parallels with other domains emerge. Thinking about prevention broadly, through all fields of inquiry – torts, prenatal care, work and road safety, public health, and so forth – reveals how interconnected disability and injury are and how many other fields of regulation, human behavior, and well-being may be impacted from this type of analysis. All these domains share the task of preventing injuries and attend to their consequences, and face the challenge of doing so without viewing those persons who were injured as less than fully human.

REMEDYING THE ECONOMIC CONSEQUENCES OF DISABILITY

An additional important function of tort law is its role in remedying the economic consequences of injury. That is a primary concern that either underlies or overshadows the discussion on injury from a disability perspective. The concern here is rooted in the pragmatic realization that tort law is a source of financial relief to disabled people. This financial relief is needed because of the economic consequences of disability, which are partly a result of the bodily injury and partly a result of inaccessible society and inadequate social welfare policy. Once a person wins a tort law suit, he or she is compensated based on the estimated costs of living with a disability, which may rise to several millions of US dollars. Clearly, tort law is not the only form of state response to injury. Other mechanisms, such as health insurance, social security, and safety regulations provide support and seek to prevent future injuries. While tort law may not be the most suitable mechanism to find the root causes of social problems or the best platform for fixing them, it provides a remedy to the individual litigant and by that expresses social disapproval of the injurious act. The analysis so far has supported this assertion. Yet in this section, I would like to complicate this view and offer some alternative directions.

In her work on vulnerability, Fineman calls for reimagining the state as a responsive state. She stresses that "we must think beyond current ideological constraints and consider the possibility of an active state in non-authoritarian terms" (Fineman 2008: 19). Fineman's search for an alternative to the liberal antidiscrimination paradigm leads her back to the state and the support that its institutions can provide if designed properly: "Certainly state mechanisms that ensure a more equitable distribution of assets and privilege across society would contribute to a more robust democracy and greater public participation. The choice, then, is not one of an active versus inactive state per se, but rather whether the state is constructed around a well-defined responsibility to implement a comprehensive and just equality regime" (ibid.). It is not surprising, therefore, that responsive mechanisms may impact the level of tort litigation. Thus, where robust national health insurance exists, levels of tort claiming and litigation tend to be low (Kerr, Ma, and Schmit 2009). Conversely, in the United States where there is meager health insurance and inadequate regulation, tort remedies are more important and exercised more often (ibid.).

The problem with a tort-based approach to remedying the consequences of injury is that it benefits only the few: only those who file a lawsuit and who succeed in settling or litigating that suit receive compensation. Other persons do not usually win that amount of money and do not have all their needs met (Abel 1989–90, Sugarman 1985). As classic socio-legal theory has taught us, the transformation from unperceived injury to perceived injury and from naming an injustice to claiming a remedy is not an easy task, and it requires psychological, social, and economic resources that not all people have (Felstiner, Abel, and Sarat 1980). Even after filing a claim, other social forces may interfere with the process due to power differences between the parties (Galanter 1974). Eventually, difficulties in proving one's case may lead to a loss that is legally justified, but result in no relief to the claimant.

If we care about disabled people's economic opportunities, we should actually take a different direction and rethink the relationships between tort law and other forms of response to injury, such as social security. A true and deep commitment to the economic and personal well-being of all disabled people should lead us to examine more carefully the structure of the welfare system, social insurance, and social security more broadly. Adequate health services, adequate social services, and adequate disability-related allowances would allow more injured persons to remain fully integrated in society and to feel valued and worthy following an injury.

Currently, torts and social security are viewed as two distinct spheres of state response to injury. Yet this distinction reinforces and legitimizes the problematic division between the injured persons who deserve full compensation because they were wrongly harmed, and those who deserve a minimal safety net because their injury was a mere misfortune. The disability critique helps to undermine this division because its view of disablement is not individualistic, but rather social: disability and injury often occur because of the existing environmental and social conditions, including pollution, crime, war, sanitary infrastructure, nutritious food, or work safety (Officer and Posarac 2011). The state has the power and the means to prevent and ameliorate these conditions through its regulatory agencies and social welfare policies. Furthermore, the state can promote access and equality by removing the social and environmental barriers that contribute to the costs of living with a disability and limit the opportunities that disabled people have following an injury. The disability critique turns what was previously conceptualized as misfortune into injustice (Shklar 1990) and demands an appropriate state response that acknowledges its role in disablement processes; it demands a responsive state.

A social view of disablement adds an additional dimension to the socio-legal and egalitarian critique and thus blurs the lines between the deserving and nondeserving and between misfortune and injustice. It calls for an egalitarian alternative that may lead to the dismantling of personal injury law as we know it. So far, I have focused on reforming tort law from within. At this point it seems that a total reconstruction is needed. The argument follows its predecessors, as developed by Sugarman (1985) and Abel (1989–90), but it adds a disability perspective that has not been discussed so far. The disability justification for "doing away with tort law" is not disability-specific in the sense that it aims to benefit disabled people only; rather, it is universal in the sense that it benefits any person who faces an injury of any kind or any source.

The egalitarian alternatives rest on two related dimensions of equality: political and material. Political equality rests on the logic of recognition, while material equality rests on distribution (Fraser 1999). While political equality is promoted through disability rights, material equality depends on the structures of social welfare policies. Yet the two are interdependent, as each realm of equality supports and enhances the other. The structural egalitarian response to the consequences of injury would be based on a broad-based no-fault system, one that follows the New Zealand model, or on a progressive social security system that provides disabled people with economic security. While the former is more egalitarian than the current system, the latter covers more people and conditions and stays away from any division that is based on the circumstances of injury. At the same time, disability rights promote economic opportunities and reduce the costs of disability.

The disability challenge to tort law further exposes the interconnections between the two levels of equality: the more social and medical services, including healthcare, rehabilitation, education, housing, and personal assistance, are provided by the state, the more the level of pecuniary damages awarded in courts can be expected to decrease. Furthermore, the more accessible, accommodating, inclusive, and egalitarian society becomes, the more injured people's needs for compensation for wage loss, and for pain and suffering, can be expected to decrease as well. Again, this argument should not be aligned with tort reform efforts to reduce tort-based compensation. It rather seeks to reimagine alternative or complementary mechanisms to torts that would better benefit a larger population of injured persons, no matter what the reasons or circumstances of their injury. The role of torts would need to be reconceptualized through the lens of social justice and human dignity.

CONCLUSION: A NEW ROLE FOR TORT LAW

As this chapter comes to an end it becomes clear that the disability critique poses a fundamental challenge to personal injury law. It requires a new framing for personal injury law that accounts for its political, expressivist, moral, and distributive dimensions. This new direction must face the question: what is left of tort law? In this chapter I offered two possible directions: reforming tort law or revolutionizing tort law. Both require a new framing and a new role for tort law.

In a 1997 piece entitled *Tort Law's Role as a Tool for Social Justice Struggle*, Lesley Bender argued that tort law was always about social justice and human dignity achieved through compensation. But somehow, with time, "the means ... came to be understood as the end" (Bender 1997). According to Bender: "Injured people suffer two distinct assaults to their dignity: ... the economic and emotional consequences of the physical injury itself, which if uncompensated can encroach upon one's dignity, and the dignitary injuries imposed by a social order that seems to permit people to conduct themselves in ways that injure others for their own benefit or in promoting their own interests" (ibid.: 251).

Bloom and Miller have followed this line too, arguing that a rights-based narrative may substitute for the tragedy-based narrative in tort litigation and instead "emphasize the right to be free from unwanted bodily interference. Such an approach recognizes that, while people may adapt to changes in their physical condition, they resent changes imposed on them without their consent" (Bloom and Miller 2011: 743).

Bender's understanding of the future of tort law moves torts away from the far end of private law toward the realm of public law and allows for questions of social justice to take a central place. Both unwanted bodily interference and the devaluation of life following an injury fit into Bender's argument because they are both issues of social justice, social cohesion, and human dignity.

Is it possible then to reconstruct a concept of injury that is free of negative stigma and social bias against disabled people, but still acknowledges the pain and the moral wrong that an injury entails? The simple answer is yes. The more complicated answer is that it requires more than a conceptual, linguistic, or awareness-based change. It requires a new social structure and a transformation in social conditions and social relations.

References

Abel, Richard L. (1989–90). "A Critique of Torts." *UCLA Law Review* 37:785–831.

Albrecht, Gary L., and Patrick J. Devlieger. (1999). "The Disability Paradox: High Quality of Life Against All Odds." *Social Science & Medicine* 48(8):977–88.

Asch, Adrienne. (2003). "Disability Equality and Prenatal Testing: Contradictory or Compatible?" *Florida State University Law Review* 30:315–42.

Bagenstos, Samuel R., and Margo Schlanger. (2007). "Hedonic Damages, Hedonic Adaptations, and Disability." *Vanderbilt Law Review* 60:697–745.

Bender, Leslie. (1997). "Tort Law's Role as a Tool for Social Justice Struggle." *Washburn Law Journal* 37:249–60.

Best, Shaun. (2007). "The Social Construction of Pain: An Evaluation." *Disability & Society* 22(2):161–71.

Bloom, Anne, with Paul Steven Miller. (2011). "Blindsight: How We See Disabilities in Tort Litigation." *Washington Law Review* 86:709–53.

tenBroek, Jacobus. (1966). "The Right to Live in the World: The Disabled in the World of Torts." *California Law Review* 54(2):841–919.

Calabresi, Guido. (2008). *The Cost of Accidents: A Legal and Economic Analysis*. New Haven, CT: Yale University Press.

Emens, Elizabeth F. (2012). "Framing Disability." *University of Illinois Law Review* 2012:1383–441.

Engel, David M. (2005). "Globalization and the Decline of Legal Consciousness: Torts, Ghosts, and Karma in Thailand." *Law & Social Inquiry* 30(3):469–514.

⸺ (2010). "Lumping as Default in Tort Cases: The Cultural Interpretation of Injury and Causation." *Loyola LA Law Review* 44:33–68.

Felstiner, William L. F., Richard L. Abel, and Austin Sarat. (1980). "The Emergence and Transformation of Disputes: Naming, Blaming, Claiming." *Law & Society Review* 15(3–4):631–54.

Fineman, Martha Albertson. (2008). "The Vulnerable Subject: Anchoring Equality in the Human Condition." *Yale Journal of Law & Feminism* 20:1–23.

Finley, Lucinda M. (2004). "The Hidden Victims of Tort Reform: Women, Children, and the Elderly." *Emory Law Journal* 53:1263–314.

Fraser, Nancy. (1999). "Social Justice in the Age of Identity Politics: Redistribution, Recognition, and Participation." Pp. 25–52 in *Culture and Economy after the Cultural Turn*, edited by Larry Ray and Andrew Sayer. London, UK: Sage Publications.

Friedman, Lawrence M. (2005). *A History of American Law*. New York: Simon and Schuster.

Galanter, Marc. (1974). "Why the 'Haves' Come Out Ahead: Speculations on the Limits of Legal Change." *Law & Society Review* 9(1):95–160.

Gondolf, Edward W., and Ellen R. Fisher. (1988). *Battered Women as Survivors: An Alternative to Treating Learned Helplessness*. Lexington Books/DC Heath and Com.

Hensel, Wendy F. (2005). "The Disabling Impact of Wrongful Birth and Wrongful Life Actions." *Harvard Civil Rights–Civil Liberties Law Review* 40:141.

Hughes, Bill, and Kevin Paterson. (1997). "The Social Model of Disability and the Disappearing Body: Towards a Sociology of Impairment." *Disability & Society* 12(3):325–40.

Kerr, Dana A., Yu-Luen Ma, and Joan T. Schmit. (2009). "A Cross-National Study of Government Social Insurance as an Alternative to Tort Liability Compensation." *Journal of Risk and Insurance* 76(2):367–84.

Milani, Adam A. (1998). "Living the World: A New Look at the Disabled in the Law of Torts." *Catholic University Law Review* 48:323–417.

Minow, Martha. (1992). "Surviving Victim Talk." *UCLA Law Review* 40:1411–45.

Mor, Sagit. (2006). "Between Charity Welfare and Warfare: Privilege and Neglect in Israeli Disability Policy." *Yale Journal of Law and the Humanities* 18:63–137.

(2014). "The Dialectics of Wrongful Life/Birth Claims in Israeli Law: A Disability Critique." *Studies in Law, Politics and Society* 63:113–46.

Morris, Davis. B. (1991). *The Culture of Pain*. Berkeley, CA: University of California Press.

Morris, Jenny. (1991). *Pride against Prejudice: Transforming Attitudes to Disability*. London: The Women's Press.

Officer, Alana, and A. Posarac. (2011). "World Report on Disability." World Health Organization.

Oliver, Michael. (1990). *The Politics of Disablement*. London, UK: Macmillan Education.

Oliver, Michael. (1996). *Understanding Disability: From Theory to Practice*. Palgrave, London: Macmillan Press.

Oswald, Andrew J., and Nattavudh Powdthavee. (2008). "Does Happiness Adapt? A Longitudinal Study of Disability with Implications for Economists and Judges." *Journal of Public Economics* 92(5):1061–77.

Shakespeare, Tom. (2006). *Disability Rights and Wrongs*. London, UK: Routledge.

Shakespeare, Torn, and Nicholas Watson. (2001). "The Social Model of Disability – An Outdated Ideology?" Pp. 9–28 in *Exploring Theories and Expanding Methodologies: Where We Are and Where We Need to Go*, edited by Sharon N. Barnartt and Barbara M. Altmann. Bingley, UK: Emerald Group Publishing Limited.

Shklar, Judith N. (1990). *The Faces of Injustice*. New Haven and London: Yale University Press.

Stainton, Tim, and Hilde Besser. (1998). "The Positive Impact of Children With an Intellectual Disability on the Family." *Journal of Intellectual and Developmental Disability* 23(1):57–70.

Sugarman, Stephen D. (1985). "Doing Away with Tort Law." *California Law Review* 73(3):555–664.

Swain, John, and Sally French. (2000). "Towards an Affirmation Model of Disability." *Disability & Society* 15(4):569–82.

Wasserman, David. (2013). "Is Disability Discrimination Different?" In *Philosophical Foundations of Discrimination Law*, edited by Deborah Hellman and Sophia Moreau. Oxford: Oxford University Press.

Weber, Mark C. (2012). "A Common Law of Disability Discrimination." *Utah Law Review* 1:429–72.

CHAPTER TWO

INJURY IN THE UNRESPONSIVE STATE
Writing the Vulnerable Subject into Neo-Liberal Legal Culture

Martha Albertson Fineman

INTRODUCTION

This chapter considers the limited ways in which "injury" or harm is understood in American political and legal culture. In particular, I am concerned with the inability of contemporary constitutional or political theory to interpret the failure of collective or state action as constituting harm worthy of recognition and compelling remedial action.[1] Here, I am not focused on laws redressing harm to private individuals and entities caused by other private individuals and entities. These legal harms are defined in areas of private law, such as tort and contract. Nor am I focused on those legal harms addressed by areas of regulatory law, such as criminal or administrative law. Rather, I am interested in the norms and values that inform the principles governing the exercise of action and restraint on the part of the state when it acts as sovereign and in relationship to individuals as political or legal subjects. As reflected in these foundational documents and constitutional

---

[1] See, e.g., *Town of Castle Rock v. Gonzales*, 545 U.S. 748, 768–9 (2005): "Although the framers ... did not create a system by which police departments are generally held financially accountable for crimes that better policing might have prevented, the people ... are free to craft such a system under state law." See also *DeShaney v. Winnebago Department of Social Services*, 489 U.S. 189, 195 (1989): "But nothing in the language of the Due Process Clause itself requires the State to protect the life, liberty, and property of its citizens against invasion by private actors. The Clause is phrased as a limitation on the State's power to act, not as a guarantee of certain minimal levels of safety and security."

jurisprudence of the United States, these principles express a theory or philosophy of what constitutes legitimate state authority.

The idea that constitutional injury or harm can be caused by state *inaction* is not well developed in American political and legal culture. The norms and values informing our ideas of appropriate actions on the part of the state, as well as defining the corresponding entitlements of political or legal subjects, are firmly anchored in the principle of nonintervention or *inaction*. The specter of state or public interference with individual privacy or liberty interests haunts our constitutional order and shapes what we perceive as constituting injury by the state. Restraints on state action are viewed as arising from the terms of the social contract and are often referred to as "negative rights." By contrast, the term "positive rights" is used to refer to affirmative obligations placed on the state (and/or others) to provide rights-holders with needed goods or services.[2]

American constitutional jurisprudence, as it has developed within the framework of negative rights, elevates the ideal of individual liberty over any robust sense of the necessity for collective or substantive equality. The liberty limitations placed on governmental action resonate in the very documents comprising the terms of the American social contract.[3] By contrast, positive rights or entitlements are

---

[2] A negative right is a right *not to be* subjected to an action of another person or group – a government, for example – usually in the form of abuse or coercion. A positive right is a right *to be* the recipient of an action by another person or group. In theory, a negative right forbids others from acting against the right holder, while a positive right obligates others to act with respect to the right holder. The holder of a negative right is entitled to noninterference, while the holder of a positive right is entitled to provision of some good or service. A distinction between negative and positive rights is popular among some normative theorists, especially those with a bent toward libertarianism. The idea of positive versus negative rights (or duties) also shapes theories in regard to individuals: negative rights are prohibitions; positive rights connote obligations or duties. However, this essay is concerned with the state, not individual manifestation of rights.

[3] A social contract is defined as "[a]n implicit agreement among the members of a society to cooperate for social benefits, for example by sacrificing some individual freedom for state protection" (*Oxford Dictionaries*, s.v. "social contract," accessed February 16, 2016, www.oxforddictionaries.com/definition/american_english/social-contract?q=social+contract). The documents comprising the American social contract – the Declaration of Independence, the Bill of Rights, and the Constitution with its federalist structure and enumerated powers – uphold individual liberty at the expense of a more substantive equality. The Bill of Rights enumerates some specific prohibitions or limitations on state action. The Constitution also imposes duties of equal protection and due process, and there are legal remedies for individuals

generally considered legitimately based only on current and specific consensual arrangements, such as those found in public legislation or private contract.

The denial of positive rights means that the state has no constitutional responsibility to guarantee access to basic goods and services. As a result, the Constitution, as it is interpreted, thus tolerates (and even condones) state disregard for or abandonment and neglect of basic human needs. Profound inequalities in circumstances, status, and well-being are accepted – even justified – by reference to individual responsibility (see, e.g., Brooks 2015).[4] Proposed remedial and altruistic responses are deflected with warnings about the addictive dependency asserted to be inherent even in the highly stigmatized system of welfare currently in place (see Eberstadt 2015).[5]

State neglect of the needs of those individuals living in poverty or suffering under social, economic, and material disadvantage is not seen as requiring legal or political remedy. Quite the contrary: state inaction is typically viewed as the appropriate manifestation of state restraint in the face of individual liberty or autonomy rights that condemn any move toward the "redistribution" of private wealth or property. "Private" structures, such as the family, market, charity, or the workplace, are designated as the prime mediating institutions to provide for the needs of individuals.[6] Arguably, the state may be seen as having

---

excluded from preexisting benefits or protections offered under law. Some exclusionary categories or classifications made in laws or practice receive greater scrutiny than others, with race classifications being the most suspect in case law.

[4] Brooks (2015) discusses Putnam's (2015) research on inequality and the divide between children growing up in college-educated and high school-educated homes: "The first response to these stats ... should be intense sympathy ... But it's increasingly clear that sympathy is not enough ... There are no basic codes and rules woven into daily life, which people can absorb unconsciously and follow automatically. Reintroducing norms will require, first, a moral vocabulary ... Next it will require holding people responsible" (Brooks 2015).

[5] Eberstadt (2015) asserts that the trajectory of the current "entitlement state appears to be degrading standards of citizenship" by not only "undermin[ing] ... the legitimacy of utilizing stigma and opprobrium to condition the behavior of beneficiaries" and the mental state of the middle class as "hard-working and self-sufficient," but by encouraging the "mass gaming of the welfare system [as] a fact of modern American life."

[6] Absent extraordinary failures, such as abuse or neglect, the caretaking of individual needs has been considered beyond the scope of state concern (Fineman 2010). This privatization masks dependency and other implications of human vulnerability, allowing us to indulge in fantasies of independence, self-sufficiency, and autonomy (Fineman 2012b).

some responsibility in regard to the conduct and operation of those institutions, but at best the state is seen as an incremental and contested residual actor when they fail. This understanding of state inaction as not constituting injury or harm is both validated and compelled by the ways in which, over the course of American political history, the political subject and social contract have been understood as anchored in liberty and autonomy.

This chapter considers how this hierarchy of liberty over equality developed and questions whether it should continue to prevail. It asks when state inaction in the face of some forms and magnitudes of inequality should be considered an injury in and of itself. When should the disregard of impoverishment, disenfranchisement, alienation, and exploitation of substantial numbers of individuals within and through the systems of law and politics rise to the level of "gross negligence" on the part of the state? And when should such neglect be understood as the "social-contractual injury" of the state effectively institutionalizing subordination and inequality? To begin to answer these questions, the next section considers the origins of political and legal subjectivity and offers the "vulnerable subject" as an alternative to the liberal legal subject that has impaired our political and legal imagination for over two centuries.

THE POLITICAL (AND LEGAL) SUBJECT

In western political traditions, the idea of political (and legal) subjectivity[7] places the individual in relationship to the state and its institutions.[8] The terms of the social contract, as they are articulated and

---

[7] I use "political subject" to encompass both legal and political subjectivity. Law is fashioned in the shadow of the political subject and as a broad and universally applicable manifestation of the relationship between the state and the individual. Law relies on categories that are necessarily broad in nature and take legal subjects outside of personal history (Fineman 2015). Legal theory, like political theory, must to some extent assimilate concrete and material differences into the dominant meta-narratives and can have only a limited ability to theorize around particulars (ibid.). Significantly, law is less flexible and more resistant to reformulation or radicalization than political theory. Law is rule- and precedent-bound and operates as a dominant structural paradigm co-opting the experiences of nondominant groups (ibid.). Co-optation is achieved through classification and tinkering reforms, while the disqualification and silencing of individuals is accomplished in legal constructs, such as the adversarial process, rules of evidence, and the structured elements of causes of action and claims for relief, making it impossible to tell stories outside of legal narratives (ibid.).
[8] That relationship also influences the way the law understands and defines the nature of the relationship among individuals, and between individuals and societal institutions.

understood, define the quality and nature of that relationship. Specific conceptualizations of the political subject and terms of the social contract will affect the status of everyone in society, although not everyone may be considered a fully realized and legally capable subject.[9] For example, at the formation of American democracy (and within its foundational documents), fully realized political subjectivity was limited to white, male, property-owning or tax-paying individuals of a certain age and religion, who were also "free."[10] Over the course of the nineteenth and twentieth centuries, some of these qualifiers were removed and full political subjectivity was recognized for members of previously excluded groups.[11] However, the expansion of the population did not automatically transform the perceived nature or assumed capabilities of the political subject. Indeed, the inclusion of previously excluded actors was based on the assertion that there were no relevant differences between these parties and the original political subject. The mode of inclusion was assimilation, underscored by the application of a principle of formal equality.[12]

The implications of this exclusion and eventual assimilation of women and significant numbers of nonconforming men were significant. While the contemporary race- and gender-neutral political subject may look different than the original, many aspects of the constitutional relationship between the political subject and the state remain close to

[9] When everyone in society is judged against an unattainable ideal, it is inevitable that many will be found wanting and deemed deviant (Fineman 2012b: 88).

[10] Women, children, and slaves, among others, had a lesser, diminished, form of political subjectivity and were entitled to fewer rights, as well as having different obligations.

[11] Certain aspects of political citizenship, such as eligibility to vote, hold office, or serve on juries, remain limited to citizens of a certain age. In addition, minors and others are not granted full protection of some constitutional protections: First Amendment, etc. (See also Witte and Nichols (2016); documenting how political rights and privileges flowing from religious affiliation were gradually removed, providing additional opportunities for excluded groups of people.)

[12] Formal equality eschews "special" treatment and affirmative action. It has problems with substantive equality because of the nature of the political subject as traditionally imagined – these ideas cannot be accommodated consistent with that subjectivity. Over time, the role of the state has changed to be more or less supportive or charitable (contrast current welfare policy with the New Deal or Great Society), but the battles are always defined by and anchored in the Lockean vision of the liberal political subject. Even in the New Deal era, nonconforming individuals had to cast themselves as victims or blameless and unjustly injured or discriminated against (see Dauber 2012).

those developed hundreds of years ago.[13] Our long-standing universal legal subject is envisioned as an autonomous, independent being along the lines of Lockean lore.[14] This liberal legal subject is a competent social actor capable of playing multiple and concurrent adult (formerly all-male) roles: the social, and legally defined, roles of the employee, the employer, the spouse, the parent, the consumer, the manufacturer, the citizen, the taxpayer, and so on (Fineman 2008).

This liberal subject informs our economic, legal, and political principles (see Deneen 2012: 25).[15] He is indispensable to the prevailing ideologies of autonomy, self-sufficiency, and personal responsibility (see ibid.: 28). He hides the ways in which social roles also reflect allocations of social power and prestige and define institutional relationships of inequality, such as employer/employee, teacher/student, or parent/child (see Fineman 2014).[16] His society is one in which competent, self-interested individuals possess the capacity to manipulate and manage their independently acquired and overlapping resources and may exercise a range of options in pursuit of their individually defined good lives (see Offer 2012).[17] Rather than being seen as dependent on others and in need of state provision or assistance, the liberal subject demands only the autonomy that will enable him to provide for himself and his family as he sees fit (see Eichner 2005).[18] The liberal subject's demand for liberty may be distilled into the freedom to make choices, as exemplified in the right to contract (see Titlestad 2010).[19] It is through contract that his relationship to both the state and its institutions are to

---

[13] The American Constitution is ancient by international standards, with an amendment process that is difficult and results in few amendments (see Fineman 2012a). While there may be adaptations in light of technology or catastrophe, our overall understanding is shaped by the Constitution and the political subject it imagined. See generally Chemerinsky (2000), critiquing Justice Scalia's jurisprudence of originalism; see also Senior (2013), briefly discussing originalism and textualism.

[14] For centuries, John Locke's philosophy of liberal individualism has inspired Western concepts of equality and the liberal subject (see Locke [1689]1988).

[15] Deneen (2012: 25) discusses the influence of liberalism.

[16] See also generally Deschamps (2010), explaining that social identity is a concept believed to be fluid and dependent upon an individual's position in society.

[17] Offer (2012) discusses the doctrines of self-interest and market efficiency and its relation to society.

[18] Eichner (2005) reviews Fineman (2004), which discusses how the United States has failed at meeting dependency needs.

[19] Titlestad (2010) discusses multiple philosophical views of liberalism and liberalism in the judiciary.

be ordered. Significantly, this perception of the essence of the liberal subject also defines the terms of the social contract and has effectively operated as a significant restraint on the state, which above all must not interfere with individual liberty (ibid.).[20]

When considering the continued viability and justice of this version of the social contract, it is relevant that the founding fathers were not merely white, male, and propertied, but shared a remarkably privileged phenomenological perspective as compared with the situations of those not possessing their specific characteristics and attributes. As a result, the founding fathers fashioned a political subject deemed to naturally possess idealized qualities and characteristics as derived from the aspirations, experiences, and perceived capabilities of the members of their limited and unrepresentative group. They failed to comprehend that the legitimacy of the social contract might be undermined because the experiences and perceptions of those previously excluded were in some significant ways different from that political subject, and perhaps incompatible with the norms and values underlying the original organization of state and individual responsibilities.[21]

To a large extent, the experiences of those excluded were not considered public or appropriate for "political" consideration. Those experiences were rooted in what were deemed to be "private" arrangements: politically invisible and publicly assumed institutions, particularly the family with its defined hierarchical relationships of husband or wife, parent/child, and master/servant. "Natural" entitlements, such as rights in private property (even in other human beings), allowed the illusion of independence even as they offered a range of options and access to

---

[20] Titlestad (2010) discusses John Locke, his view on liberty's effect on societal restraint, and the battle between free-market economics and socialism during the nineteenth century.

[21] In so far as those qualities and characteristics were seen as intrinsic to the individual and not the products of institutional and social relationships that compensated, complemented, and enhanced that individual, they were at best misleadingly simplistic. In particular, the emphasis on the political subject's entitlement to individual autonomy or liberty as a protection against state intervention assumed an inherent self-sufficiency that masked any actual individual's reliance on family, community, social, and political structures, and law in producing the ability to act or be independent. In fact, the political subject's position within these societal structures was not seen as undermining or compromising the ideas of autonomy and independence, but as manifestations of those characteristics as he assumed responsibility for family members, servants, residents, and others who occupied statuses with lower political subjectivity.

political and economic power that was denied to many others. Like all human beings, the founding fathers were inevitably entwined with and dependent upon social, political, familial, and economic structures and relationships for care, nurture, and support over the course of their lives. In fact, the very social arrangements they neglected to recognize as implicating the political placed them in a privileged position by subordinating others. Even if they recognized the inequality of these social arrangements, they could afford to ignore them within their constructed realms of public versus private spheres. Thus insulated, the privileged few did not need to consider the implications of inevitable human vulnerability and dependence as they crafted their social contract. Their perspective on what its terms should be was shaped by revolution, and they sought primarily to codify the results of a struggle with an exploitative monarch, shedding the status of "subject" and becoming "citizens."

Based as it was on a limited set of both experiences and objectives, it is not surprising that the political subject reflected in the original American constitutional order incorporated only some of the host of possible variations in human characteristics, experiences, and capabilities. The political subject projected in the constitutional era was a fully functioning, independent, and self-sufficient adult, fully capable of taking care of his own needs and the needs of those subordinated and dependent upon him. However, from the perspective of the twenty-first century's supposed beneficiaries of the social contract, this political construct is theoretically inadequate. We inhabit a world of dynamic complexity, uncertainty, and technology, unimagined by the founding fathers. Their social contract is incapable of fully (or fairly) informing the development of political and legal norms to address many, if not most, of the situations and circumstances that occur over the life-course of most actual individuals living today (Boyd 2017).[22] The inaction

---

[22] Notably, peer nations have much more modern constitutions defining state responsibility. Other nations replace their constitutions wholesale approximately every nineteen years, the same length of time Thomas Jefferson suggested, in a 1789 letter to James Madison, as marking a constitution's natural expiration, because "the earth belongs always to the living generation" (Liptak 2012, quoting a letter from Thomas Jefferson to James Madison on September 6, 1789). The United States Constitution and its first ten amendments, known as the Bill of Rights, are well over 200 years old (ibid.). The Constitution is notoriously difficult to change, currently having only twenty-seven amendments (ibid.). There is a declining tendency of foreign judges to cite decisions of the United States Supreme Court because of its "parochialism" (ibid.). Aharon Barak, former president of the Supreme Court of Israel, wrote in the

compelled by their vision of a restrained state should be understood as constituting gross neglect in modern society, and the social contract should be amended so that the contemporary political subject is more inclusive of and responsive to the universal human condition.

VULNERABILITY THEORY

Often narrowly understood as merely openness to physical or emotional harm,[23] vulnerability should be recognized as *the* primal human condition (Fineman 2014: 310). As *embodied* beings, we are universally and individually constantly susceptible to harm, whether caused by infancy and lack of capacity, by disease and physical decline, or by natural or manufactured disasters (ibid.). This constancy recognizes that there is no position of invulnerability. In this sense, vulnerability is a precursor for dependency, and dependency should be understood as one manifestation or realization of embodied vulnerability.[24]

Embodied Vulnerability

A vulnerability analysis asks us (and our economists, philosophers, and politicians) to embrace a more complicated and comprehensive understanding of vulnerability and dependency than is reflected in either common usage or the image of the reductive liberal subject. Vulnerability theory insists that human vulnerability and dependency

---

Harvard Law Review that the Supreme Court was "losing the central role it once had among courts in modern democracies" and identified Canadian law as serving as a "source of inspiration for many countries around the world" (ibid., quoting Barak 2002). Justice Michael Kirby of the High Court of Australia reportedly stated in a 2001 interview that, "America is in danger, I think, of becoming a legal backwater" (Liptak 2012, quoting Kirby 2001).

[23] *Oxford Dictionaries* defines vulnerable as, "susceptible to physical or emotional attack or harm" (*Oxford Dictionaries*, s.v. "vulnerable," accessed June 18, 2015, www.oxforddictionaries.com/us/definition/american_english/vulnerable); *Merriam-Webster Online Dictionary* defines vulnerable as "capable of being physically or emotionally wounded" and "open to attack or damage" (*Merriam-Webster Online Dictionary*, s.v. "vulnerable," accessed February 16, 2017, www.merriam-webster.com/dictionary/vulnerable).

[24] Dependency on others and on resources for our care is often inevitable at certain stages of life and can also arise as a result of our vulnerable embodiment. This form of dependency is not constant, but episodic over any individual life-course. But dependency must also be understood as a universal aspect of the human condition – the inevitable manifestation of human embodied vulnerability (see Fineman 2015: 620). For the development of the dependency theory, see generally Fineman (2004).

are indispensable to, and should therefore be brought into the center of, any theory of what it means to be human. The theoretical inquiry asks what this understanding of the human condition means for the construction of the political subject, the social contract, and an appropriately responsive state.[25]

The Life-Course and Embodiment
Unlike the abstract liberal subject, the embodied vulnerable subject is dynamic and reflects the fact that humans have a "life-course" (Fineman 2012a: 1753). While the liberal subject is static, the vulnerable subject is inclusive of all stages of human development, reflecting a comprehensive understanding of the human condition, with implications for defining the nature of the relationship between the state and the individual legal subject (see Fineman 2008: 10–12).

Over the course of a normal lifespan, we experience a range of developmental and social stages (Fineman 2012a: 1753). We are born helpless and totally dependent on others for care and the provision of basic needs. While only some return to that form of total dependency as we age, or become ill or disabled, most humans experience intermittent and varying degrees of dependency throughout their lives. Our dependencies are mostly addressed through institutions, be they deemed "private," such as the family, or "public," such as the social safety net or "welfare" (ibid.: 1756).

The trope of the liberal subject at best captures only one stage – the freely functioning, unencumbered adult stage of human existence – which is also the stage least likely to reflect the constant vulnerability and potential dependency inherent in the human condition (Fineman 2012a: 1753). By contrast, the vulnerable subject anticipates that every individual will encounter a myriad of opportunities, frustrations, challenges, successes, and defeats, necessitating a wide range of expertise and capabilities during his or her life in which there will be varying degrees of dependence and shifting levels of reliance on others (ibid.). These encounters can be catastrophic, such as disease pandemics, environmental catastrophes, or terrorism; mundane, such as street crime, crumbling infrastructure, recession, corruption, or other indications of failing societal institutions; or merely developmental, such as illness or physical

---

[25] And if our bodily fragility, material needs, and the possibility of messy dependency that they signify cannot be ignored in life, how can they be absent in our theories of equality, society, politics, and law? (Fineman 2010: 263).

decline in aging (see ibid.: 1753–4). Importantly, this myriad array of life events also includes many positive possibilities, such as encounters that evoke strong pleasurable feelings as we encounter nature, art, or a person who generates within us feelings of love, friendship, and compassion (ibid.: 1754). Human vulnerability and need is thus manifested in creative and productively generative ways, as well as having more negative aspects. The significant point is that we are situated beings who live with the ever-present possibility of changing circumstances – negative and positive – that may alter our needs and desires both individually and in our collective lives (ibid.). As we will have little or no control over many of these circumstances, the liberal subject's reliance on concepts such as liberty, autonomy, and individual agency are at best only appropriate for some situations and at some stages of human development.

Differences and Embodiment
Vulnerability cannot be eradicated – there is no invulnerability, only the prospect that we will have sufficient resources and capabilities to respond successfully in specific times of crisis or opportunity.[26] A consideration of resources and capabilities highlights one of the paradoxes of a vulnerability approach: while initially it is theoretically important to understand vulnerability as universal, constant, and arising from embodiment, vulnerability must simultaneously be understood as particular, varied, and unique on the individual level (Fineman 2014: 317). It is in the consideration of such differences that the real promise of the theory is evident; it brings to the fore the social and institutional dimensions of human vulnerability. Two forms of individual difference are relevant, reflecting both the embodied and the embedded nature of vulnerability (see Fineman 2013: 619, 637).

There are individual variations in physical, mental, intellectual, and other components of human embodiment (Fineman 2013: 619, 637). These differences are not necessarily socially neutral, and historically, specific variations in embodiment have led to the exclusion of certain people and the perpetuation of hierarchy, discrimination, and violence (Fineman 2012a: 1754; see Shilling 1993: 55–9, 111–12). Some individuals have been subordinated because others thought their differences indicated that they were dangerous or interpreted those differences as

---

[26] As there is no invulnerability, the counterpoint to vulnerability is the resilience that comes from having the means to confront and address misfortune (Fineman 2010: 269).

inadequacy, inferiority, or weakness.[27] These differences or variations are also the basis for the segregation of some individuals from general society and clustering them into a stigmatized "vulnerable *population*" category (see Fineman 2008: 4).[28] This fragmentation of humanity into discrete populations tends to locate differences within individuals, obscuring universal, and inherent vulnerability and the ways in which the meanings and consequences of variations are shaped within social structures.

Some physical, mental, intellectual, sexual, and other variations are developmental or age-related in nature (Fineman 2014: 318). Developmental differences can bring physical or emotional dependence on others (ibid.). This is particularly evident in infancy and childhood, but is also often provoked by severe illness, disability, and advanced age (ibid.). Significantly, developmental differences show the inevitability of human dependence on others and on society and its institutions: this is inevitable when we are young and not unusual as we become ill, disabled, or elderly (ibid.).

Understanding embodied vulnerability allows us to appreciate the many ways in which human beings are, from the moment of birth until we die, in relationship with and dependent upon society and its institutions and on each other (Fineman 2014: 318). We are inevitably, although differently, situated within webs of economic, social, cultural, and institutional relationships that profoundly affect our individual destinies and fortunes (see Fineman 2012a: 1755). Those relationships structure our options, creating or impeding our opportunities, but they often operate outside our individual or even collective control (Fineman 2014: 319).

---

[27] See, e.g., Integrating Gender into the Third World Conference against Racism, Racial Discrimination, Xenophobia, and Related Intolerance (South Africa, August 31–September 7, 2001), 21 *J. Muslim Minority Aff.* 373, 377 (2001) ("[M]icroenterprise development must recognize the fact that race and gender discrimination may limit access to resources, such as credit, for women from disadvantaged racial, ethnic and immigrant communities."); Amy L. Knickmeier, "Blind Leading the 'Colorblind:' The Evisceration of Affirmative Action and a Dream Still Deferred" (1997) 17 *N. Ill. U. L. Rev.* 305, 351 ("Societal racism against African Americans continues to present obstinate socio-economic and psychological barriers to achieving access to higher education.").

[28] The appropriate legal response to such instances is an improved and strengthened antidiscrimination system, complemented by affirmative action and social welfare to make up for past discrimination and reduce the probabilities of future discrimination (Fineman 2013: 637–8).

Embedded Vulnerability – Societal Institutions and the Social Contract

A vulnerability approach focuses primarily on exploring the theoretical significance of the fact that, as embodied beings, we are inevitably and inextricably embedded within society and its institutions throughout the life-course (Fineman 2013: 622). This reality should have significant implications for the ways in which we reimagine the social contract and how it might define the legal, cultural, and societal role of institutions within the state in the twenty-first century.[29] Indeed, one way to think about the formation of society is to posit that it is human vulnerability that brings individuals into families, families into communities, and communities into societies, nation states, and international organizations (Fineman 2012a: 1756). Further, the terms of any social contract should anticipate that individuals are inevitably dependent not only on their relationships with each other, but also on the interactions they have with the institutions and political structures constructed within society (ibid.).[30]

Recognizing the importance of institutional arrangements and the individual situational differences generated or produced within them argues for moving critical inquiry beyond embodied differences and the individual identities derived from them. This expansion of inquiry does not mean ignoring bias and exclusion or abandoning equal protection measures, but recognizing that discrimination is a limited concept and fails to adequately capture current and pervasive social injustices (see Fineman 2008: 3). Many of these injustices are found within the practices and procedures of institutions, manufactured through structure and operation and by the misallocation of power in the creation of social or institutional roles. These injustices are pervasive, elusive, and entrenched, and they affect everyone positioned inside (as well as standing outside) specific institutions, and they demand a responsive state.

In considering the structuring power of institutional arrangements, a vulnerability approach assumes an integrated vision of society, not

---

[29] While the current liberal social contract privileges liberty and formal equality, the vulnerable social contract would seek a more substantive sense of equality, privileging inclusion, opportunity, and resilience.

[30] This formation of social foundations touches on John Locke's characterization of the development of familial and social bonds. Locke posited that an urge toward self-preservation through association with others led to the creation of society (see Locke [1689] 1988: 318–19).

one of autonomous individuals and separate spheres.[31] There is no public/private divide and the identity categories of critical interest are the social identities prescribed by law, practice, and culture: employer/employee; creditor/debtor; adult/minor; stockholder/stakeholder; parent/child; teacher/student, and so on. A vulnerability analysis contextualizes the vulnerable subject within the social contract, recognizing that it is only through societally produced institutions and identities that the individual can gain the resources necessary to ameliorate, address, or compensate for human vulnerability (see Fineman 2010: 269). That reality must be taken into account.

Resilience

The concept of resilience is centrally important in a vulnerability analysis, signifying the role of essential resources in counterbalancing vulnerability.[32] The degree of resilience that individuals possess is largely dependent on the quality and quantity of resources or assets they have at their disposal or command.[33] While there is no position of invulnerability, resilience is the measure of the ability that an individual has to recover from harm or setbacks (Fineman 2010: 269). Resilient individuals can take advantage of opportunities or take risks in life, confident that if they fail the challenge or meet unexpected obstacles they are likely to have the means and ability to recover (Fineman 2014: 320).

Resilience greatly affects an individual's ability to evaluate and act in making choices or decisions. It should be apparent that a certain measure of resilience is essential before there can be any semblance of agency or autonomy.[34] Significantly, human beings are not born resilient

---

[31] State restraint is often expressed in terms of separate spheres ideology, contrasting the public and private domains (see Fineman 2008: 5).

[32] *Oxford Dictionaries* defines resilience as, "the capacity to recover quickly from difficulties" (*Oxford Dictionaries*, s.v. "resilience," accessed February 2, 2017, www.oxforddictionaries.com/us/definition/american_english/resilience); *Merriam-Webster Online Dictionary* defines resilience as, "the ability to become strong, healthy, or successful again after something bad happens" (*Merriam-Webster Online Dictionary*, s.v. "resilience," accessed February 2, 2017, merriam-webster.com/dictionary/resilience).

[33] See generally Kirby (2006), discussing how institutions, together and independently, provide assets – advantages, coping mechanism, or resources – that cushion us when we are facing misfortune, disaster, and violence.

[34] We must realize that, regardless of how desirable autonomy may be as an aspiration, it is meaningless and unattainable without an underlying provision of substantial support from society and its institutions (Fineman 2010: 260). Without that support network, individuals do not have the resources they need to create options and make choices (ibid.).

(Fineman 2012b: 110). Rather, resilience is produced over time and within social structures and under societal conditions over which individuals may have little control (ibid.). The concept of resilience as an accumulation of resources resonates with vulnerability theory's insistence that the state's relationship with the political subject be conceived as over the life-course, not statically, as it is with the liberal subject.

It is also evident that resilience is not distributed equally – some have more than others.[35] While sometimes a lack of resilience can be deemed an individual failing, sometimes inequality in resilience is a function of unequal access to certain societal structures. Sometimes it is a result of unequal allocations of power and privilege within social relations. These structural factors are surely as significant as individual character or values in achieving success in life. Those who fail are not differently or particularly vulnerable; rather, unlike more well-positioned individuals, they lack sufficient resources and resilience to address their vulnerability. Their status or position should not be automatically dismissed as individual failure; while they may not have the levels of resilience necessary to respond successfully to life's travails, perhaps this deficit reflects an institutional or societal failing as much or more than it does an individual one.[36]

Resources

Resources can come in material forms, such as the goods and services we can acquire with wealth produced through participation in business, economic, and financial systems, or nonmaterial forms that contribute to the development of resilience (Fineman 2010: 270, citing Kirby 2006).[37] These nonmaterial resources can be in the form of social goods, human capital, existential resources, and environmental resources (ibid.). Social goods, such as well-developed and supportive relationships and emotional and psychological stability, are produced within families or social networks.[38] Similarly, "human capital" comes from education or training

---

[35] Individuals are positioned differently within society; some are more privileged and others are relatively disadvantaged (Fineman 2008: 15).

[36] The failure of such institutions to function in an inclusive, equitable, and just manner should be just as important to law and policy as deliberate discrimination (Fineman 2015: 624–5).

[37] This list of resource types was developed as an expansion of the four types of assets identified in Kirby's *Vulnerability and Violence* (2006): physical, human, social, and environmental.

[38] Social networks might include unions, community or political interest associations, or groups formed around such identity categories as sexuality, gender, or race. Social

across the life-course, as well as subsequent work experience and professional development (Fineman 2010: 270). Existential resources can be built through religious affiliation or may emerge from the acquisition of philosophical or ascetic sensibilities that provide a sense of meaning and belonging in life.[39] Environmental resources are also critical, as the condition of both the built and natural environments profoundly affects individual and communal health and well-being.[40]

Our experiences with resource-producing societal institutions and the systems comprising them are often concurrent and interactive, but can also be sequential (Fineman 2012a: 1757). For example, the relationships between the educational system and the employment and social security systems are sequential (ibid.). Collectively, they provide for the accumulation of resources, creating assets for use in the present and preserving possibilities and opportunities for the future (Fineman 2010: 269–70). Significantly, the failure of one system in a sequence, such as a failure to receive an adequate education, affects future prospects (Fineman 2012a: 1757). It is often impossible to compensate fully for this failure, given that the systems further down the line are constructed in reliance on successfully fulfilling the earlier steps (Fineman 2010: 270).[41] Someone who misses out on education typically will have fewer options and opportunities in the workplace, making for more a precarious retirement and lower savings (see Ross and Van Willigen 1997).[42]

On the other hand, and also worth noting, is the fact that sometimes privileges conferred in one concurrent system can compensate for, or

---

support and networks have been linked with rates of cardiovascular disease and with recovery from heart attacks (Wilkinson and Pickett 2010: 76). One experiment showed that people with friends were less likely to catch cold (ibid).

[39] "Existential" may be defined as: "involved in or vital to the shaping of an individual's self-chosen mode of existence and moral stance with respect to the rest of the world" (Rooney et al. 2001).

[40] See, e.g., Katzand (2012), discussing a 2012 Yale University study finding that "tiny particles of air pollution contain more hazardous ingredients in non-white and low-income communities than in affluent white ones," meaning that "communities of color and those with low education and high poverty and unemployment face greater health risks."

[41] "Initially, human abilities and experience are primarily developed through systems that provide education, training, knowledge, and experience. Accumulation of a degree of human capital is essential in gaining access to employment systems, which themselves can provide further resources" (Fineman 2010: 270).

[42] Ross and Van Willigen (1997), documents how one's lack of education leads not only to low employment status, but also affects marital status, a sense of control over one's life, social and emotional support, and economic resources.

even cancel out, disadvantages encountered in others (Fineman 2012a: 1758). For example, a good early start in regard to education, such as that provided by universal pre-kindergarten classes, may triumph over poverty as a predictor of success later in school, particularly when that education is coupled with a strong and supportive social or relational system, such as a supportive family or community network (Fineman 2008: 15–16).[43]

In other words, society's institutions interact in ways that actually produce (or fail to produce) social, political, and economic equality. They can and do operate to privilege or disadvantage each individual during the life-course, and an initial privilege or disadvantage may determine whether an individual is able to benefit fully from other systems.[44] Because accomplishment in one arena is often contingent on success in another, the impact of the allocation of privileges and disadvantages is cumulative (Fineman 2012a: 1758).

VULNERABILITY AND THE RESPONSIVE STATE

The most important aspect of reimagining undertaken in a vulnerability analysis involves understanding how the social contract should envision state responsibility with regard to both the vulnerable subject and resource-conferring institutions. The first step in a vulnerability analysis is to develop an understanding of the nature of the political subject as vulnerable across the life-course; the second step places that complex and comprehensive subject within the social and institutional contexts that shape its prospects and possibilities. The third step locates the contextualized vulnerable subject and its institutional arrangements within the framework of state power and responsibility. How should our understandings of human vulnerability, the nature of institutions, and the role of institutions in providing resilience inform our politics and law?

---

[43] There is substantial evidence that investments made in childhood are differently effective than those made in adults. A study by James Heckman, a Nobel Prize-winning economist at the University of Chicago, tracks the notion that dollars invested in early childhood yield even greater returns as children grow, illustrating the role of resilience in improving well-being across the life-course and the interactive and sequential implications of an early accumulation of the assets that give us resilience (see Cohn 2014: 7–8).

[44] See Ross and Van Willigen (1997: 276–9), explaining that education opens doors to better employment and economic resources which increase the overall subjective quality of life.

We begin with the observation that the state is always at least a residual actor when it comes to societal institutions. The state brings societal institutions into being through law and regulation, as well as defining the nature and consequences of the social relations and roles within them.[45] It also works to protect or privilege certain entities and allocates power between and among constituents, stakeholders, and members of institutions.

Powerful, resource-giving institutions like the family, corporations, schools, and financial institutions are constructs of the state (see Fineman 2008: 6). It is the legitimating authority of law and the regulatory machinery of the state that create marriage, define the family, and mandate the corporate form, for example. The state brings these entities into existence as legitimate institutions.[46] The law both assigns and enforces content and consequences, and by doing this the state asserts that it has a monopoly over legitimate means of coercion. This exercise of power is one way in which the state constitutes not only its institutions, but also itself.[47] State mechanisms also enforce "private" agreements (contracts) and provide security for and structure private property.

These examples of state action in regard to institutional formation and operation make it clear that the choice is not one between an active state on one hand and an inactive state on the other – action is what defines the state (see Fineman 2010: 273).[48] Because societal institutions are so vitally important, both to individuals and to society, their flaws, barriers, gaps, and potential pitfalls must be monitored, and these institutions must be adjusted when they are functioning in ways harmful to individuals and society.[49]

---

[45] A few examples of how the state creates and influences even "private" institutions are legal documents such as charters, documents of incorporation, licenses, and permits.

[46] Robert Dahl, Yale professor, observed that, "without the protection of a dense network of laws enforced by public governments, the largest American corporation could not exist for a day" (Alperovitz and Daly 2008, quoting Dahl 1982). Dahl also noted that the view of economic institutions as "private" is an "ill fit" for their "social and public" nature (ibid.: 139).

[47] The state must be understood as a political construct as well as a functioning entity, expressing certain preferences and values that should be explored for their accuracy and desirability (Fineman 2012a: 1760).

[48] Instead, the choice is whether the state will act to fulfill its responsibility to ensure access and opportunity for all consistent with a realistic conception of the human subject (Fineman 2010: 273–4).

[49] The state must be responsive to individual, social, and institutional vulnerabilities in a way that is anchored in the realities of the human condition, rather than some

The Already (and Unequally) Responsive State

One way of understanding how the state is active is to look at the ways in which it currently responds to individual vulnerability through its creation and maintenance of institutions. Significantly, those institutions that serve as artificial entities should also be understood as vulnerable, although differently so than are individuals. Institutions may not be injured or die as human beings do, but they can suffer decline or decay, be captured or controlled by destructive forces, or be susceptible to environmental, political, or economic changes (Fineman 2008: 12). Interestingly, the state as it has been imagined in contemporary political theory is much more inclined to be directly responsive to institutional, rather than individual, vulnerability. Paradoxically, the relative robustness of state response to institutional vulnerability is justified by reference to the role that institutions have in providing resources to both individuals and the larger community. For example, the vulnerability of corporate or business institutions as job creators and/or economic stimulators to startup or ongoing production or operating costs is routinely evoked to justify subsidies.[50] These subsidies can be quite generous, whether they take the form of tax policies, direct transfers, or investment, or are delivered through facilitating access to the mechanisms of state authority, such as law or utilization infrastructures.[51]

Of course, it is not the state response to market or institutional vulnerability that fuels the calls for restraint by small government adherents. Rather, the demands for a restrained state are in response to the monitoring and regulation of the marketplace, which is viewed as increasing market vulnerability. Critics argue that for economic prosperity and job creation the state must assume a position of benign neglect (Leef 2013).[52] Considering the complexity and nature of

---

abstract and unachievable ideal (Fineman 2012a: 1752). It must have a rigorous duty to ensure that everyone not only has equal protection of the law, but an equal opportunity to enjoy the benefits of society and its institutions (ibid.).

[50] But see, e.g., Story (2012), discussing the increasing prevalence of corporate subsidies and incentives over the past thirty years, despite little evidence of their effectiveness in creating jobs or benefitting local communities.

[51] Some state institutional responses to individual vulnerability can also provide benefits to institutions; a publicly educated workforce can save an employer from investing time and money in training.

[52] Leef (2013) argues that "[f]ree markets and smaller government means greater opportunities for everyone."

institutional vulnerability, however, this argument is both unreasonable and disingenuous.[53]

Institutions are not only vulnerable to market and economic uncertainties. They are also vulnerable to manipulation, misbehavior, and corruption. This can result from things like the structure of corporate law demanding that corporations produce hefty profits for shareholders and allowing massive salaries for CEOs, while frustrating access to power on the part of employees and other stakeholders.[54] The vulnerability of the corporation is created by the fact that it is primarily a profit-driven entity, providing a compelling argument for a much more attentive and responsive state: one that exposes, contemplates, and balances the competing vulnerabilities of all the interested parties, including society, that are inherent in institutional arrangements.

This is not an argument that the state should not respond to institutional vulnerability, but a demand that it does so in a balanced and measured fashion that is as attentive to human as it is to institutional vulnerability. Consider how the lack of such a state response contributed to the practices that led to the Great Recession. The state responded to the increasingly vulnerable position of certain big businesses caused by the failing market during the recession, and the heightened risk of loss was met with loans to the auto industry and bailouts for the financial industry (see Kiel 2012). At the same time, the exposed vulnerability of and heightened risks for individual mortgage holders created in the wake of the same crisis was largely ignored. Their plight was assigned to the realm of individual responsibility, and pleas for governmental aid were deflected with cries of "moral hazard."[55]

---

[53] In addition, this critique of government is at odds with evidence presented in recent studies: social welfare and a responsive government can inspire more economic prosperity and job creation by providing resilience in the form of economic security and empowering citizens to take more risks (see Frick 2015).

[54] See, e.g., Yang (2013), discussing how corporate America's focus on maximizing shareholder value led to "an economy in which companies are increasingly disconnected from the state of the nation, laying off workers in waves, keeping average wages low[,] and threatening to move operations abroad in the face of regulations and taxes").

[55] "'Moral hazard' refers to situations in which economic actors, because they do not bear the full consequences of their actions, maximize their utility at the expense of others. A common example is an individual with theft insurance not protecting an easily-replaceable item" (Kordana 1997, citing Kotowitz 1987). During the Great Recession, "the preoccupation with moral hazard was targeted at homeowners instead of banks, creating overlapping income and asset double-checks to weed out the unworthy" (Dayen 2015).

In other words, the state played favorites, choosing to respond to vulnerable institutions over vulnerable individuals. This ill-considered and unreflective choice failed to take into account the ways in which corporations, acting in ways consistent with the profit motivation, can exacerbate their own vulnerability, create hazards for society, and dissipate the resilience of others. A truly responsive state would consider all interested parties and their competing vulnerabilities.[56]

Of course, it is important to recognize that the state does make erroneous and biased responses to economic, as well as other, crises. The state is capable of being abusive, over-reaching, and authoritative.[57] Like all human institutions, the state is vulnerable to capture, corruption, and misdirection. State misdirection can come from external forces, as happens when powerful entrenched interests hijack even the most egalitarian impulses for their own purposes (Fineman 2012a: 1762). It can also be the product of flaws or weaknesses in the design or operation of state structures and practices. Massive misdirection has attended the current corrupted legislative culture produced by ineffective campaign financing and other reform that provides incentives for repressive tactics, distortions of the truth, and democracy-frustrating partisanship.[58]

To many progressive commentators, the failures of the state are reason enough to move beyond politics, even beyond law. This reaction, while perhaps understandable, is naïve and ultimately reactionary.

[56] Our current system of responding to institutional vulnerability over individual vulnerability is far from balanced. See, e.g., Johnston (2014), stating that the burden of corporate welfare, i.e., subsidizing corporations, is "especially hard on the poor. The bottom fifth of households in all but one state pay a larger share of their income in state and local taxes than the top 1 percent of earners. This means that corporate welfare effectively redistributes from the poor to those rich enough to own corporate stock." See also Daily Take (2017), which states that: "[T]he American taxpayer isn't paying much for social safety net programs like food stamps and Medicare. But we are paying a lot for the billions of dollars the U.S. government gives to corporate America each year."

[57] Avoiding this overreaching requires vigilance, but advocating for vigilance is not the same as urging abandonment or retreat on the part of the state (Fineman 2012a: 1760).

[58] See Levi (2011), exploring the potential long-term impacts of *Citizens United* in light of data from the 2010 electoral cycle showing increases in private donations, overall advertising expenditures, the number of involved "super PACs," and the use of negative campaigning). See also Pildes (2011), finding that polarization leads to a lack of effective internal checks and balances during times of unified government and deadlock during times of divided government.

We need the state; we cannot do without it. Society, like all collective human relations, needs rules, which operate as constraints on individuals for the good of the collective, be that collective in the form of a family, a corporation, an economy, a community, or a state or governmental entity.

Further, it is important to remember that although we may talk about "the state," it is not a monolith. The state is actually a cluster of relationships, entities, and agencies reflecting and shaping public norms and values through law and policy. Those relationships include the relationship between citizen and state, as well as between state and institutions. And as a democratic institution, the state is also susceptible to political pressure and collective calls for reform.

To realize a responsive state, individuals must appreciate that we too are part of the state and are inevitably affected by its policies and law. We do not – we cannot – stand outside the state, and we therefore have a responsibility to participate in the formation of its policy and practices. We must be vigilant in ensuring that the state is working effectively and in an egalitarian manner, with values and norms of equality and justice being paramount in defining state actions. State vulnerabilities are present whether the state is constituted as restrained or as responsive (Fineman 2012a: 1762). Orienting the state to be responsive to the vulnerable subject would require dedication to a different set of values – more egalitarian and collective in nature – than those that informed the state built on an image of the liberal subject.

Vulnerability's values prefer connection and interdependence rather than autonomy and independence in both political and personal visions. This would require the state to respond to the damage done by privileging liberty over equality, necessitating a look at the existing structures of inequality. Institutions serving to allocate society's resources unequally to the benefit of the few must be monitored and reformed. Politicians will tell us that this is an impossible task, but what they really mean is that it will place them in an uncomfortable position, particularly with those who are currently privileged.[59] Perhaps it is no more than a utopian fantasy, but I believe that

---

[59] For example, the livestock lobby spent $2,906,571 on lobbying expenses in 2013 alone (Center for Responsive Politics 2013b). That same year, the agribusiness sector spent $153,732,176 on lobbying (Center for Responsive Politics 2013a). On February 4, 2014, the Senate passed a bipartisan farm bill estimated to cost nearly $1 trillion over the next ten years while cutting $8 billion in food stamps over that same period (Nixon 2014).

organizing around our shared vulnerability provides the foundation for building an inclusive and democratic political coalition – one that can both expose and displace unwarranted privilege and demand that the terms of the social contract require the state to ensure a more level playing field, genuine access and opportunity, and institutions that build resilience.

References

Alperovitz, Gal and Lew Daly. (2008). *Unjust Deserts: How the Rich Are Taking Our Common Inheritance*. New York: The New Press.

Barak, Aharon. (2002). "Foreword: A Judge on Judging: The Role of the Supreme Court in a Democracy." *Harvard Law Review* 116:19–162.

Boyd, Julian P, editor. (2017). "Letter from Thomas Jefferson to James Madison." Pp. 392–4 in *The Papers of Thomas Jefferson*, Volume 15: March 1789 to November 1789.

Brooks, David. (2015). "Op-Ed., The Cost of Relativism." *New York Times*, March 10. www.nytimes.com/2015/03/10/opinion/david-brooks-the-cost-of-relativism.html?_r=1 (accessed November 3, 2017).

Chemerinsky, Erwin. (2000). "The Jurisprudence of Justice Scalia: A Critical Appraisal." *University of Hawai'i Law Review* 22(2):385–402.

Center for Responsive Politics. (2013a). "Lobbying: Agribusiness Sector Profile 2013." *OpenSecrets.org*. www.opensecrets.org/lobby/indus.php?id=A&year=2013 (accessed November 3, 2017).

   (2013b). "Lobbying: Livestock Industry Profile, Summary 2013." *OpenSecrets.org*. www.opensecrets.org/lobby/indusclient.php?id=a06&year=2013 (accessed November 3, 2017).

Cohn, Jonathan. (2014). "Leave No Parent Behind." *New Republic* 245(12):7–9.

Dahl, Robert. (1982). *Dilemmas of Pluralist Democracy: Autonomy vs. Control*. New Haven, CT: Yale University Press.

"Food Stamps are Affordable; Corporate Welfare is Not." (2017). *Daily Take*. Truth-out.org. www.truth-out.org/opinion/item/19844-food-stamps-are-affordable-corporate-welfare-is-not (accessed November 3, 2017) [cited as *Daily Take* 2017].

Dauber, Michele Landis. (2012). *The Sympathetic State: Disaster Relief and the Origins of the American Welfare State*. Chicago, IL: University of Chicago Press.

Dayen, David. (2015). "A Needless Default." *The American Prospect Longform*, February 8. www.prospect.org/article/needless-default (accessed November 3, 2017).

Deneen, Patrick J. (2012). "Unsustainable Liberalism." *First Things* (August/September 2012):25–31.

Deschamps, Jean-Claude. (2010). "Social Identity and Relations of Power between Groups," In *Social Identity and Intergroup Relations*, ed. Henri Tajfel. Cambridge: Cambridge University Press.

Eberstadt, Nicholas. (2015). "American Exceptionalism and the Entitlement State." *National Affairs* 22(Winter):25–38. www.nationalaffairs.com/publications/detail/american-exceptionalism-and-the-entitlement-state (accessed November 3, 2017).

Eichner, Maxine. (2005). "Dependency and the Liberal Polity: On Martha Fineman's 'The Autonomy Myth.'" *California Law Review* 93(4):1285–86.

Fineman, Martha Albertson. (2004). *The Autonomy Myth: A Theory of Dependency*. New York, NY: The New Press.

(2008). "The Vulnerable Subject: Anchoring Equality in the Human Condition." *Yale Journal of Law and Feminism* 20(1):1–23.

(2010). "The Vulnerable Subject and the Responsive State." *The Emory Law Journal* 60:251–75.

(2012a). "Beyond Identities: The Limits of an Antidiscrimination Approach to Equality." *Boston University Law Review* 92:1713–70.

(2012b). "'Elderly' as Vulnerable: Rethinking the Nature of Individual and Societal Responsibility." *The Elder Law Journal* 20(1):101–41.

(2013). "Feminism, Masculinities, and Multiple Identities." *Nevada Law Journal* 13(2):619–39.

(2014). "Vulnerability, Resilience, and LGBT Youth." *Temple Political and Civil Rights Law Review* 23:307–29.

(2015). "Equality and Difference – The Restrained State." *Alabama Law Review* 66(3):609–23.

Frick, Walter. (2015). "Welfare Makes America More Entrepreneurial." *The Atlantic*, March 26. www.theatlantic.com/politics/archive/2015/03/welfare-makes-america-more-entrepreneurial/388598/ (accessed November 3, 2017).

Johnston, David Kay. (2014). "The Shocking Numbers Behind Corporate Welfare." *Al Jazeera America*, February 25. america.aljazeera.com/opinions/2014/2/corporate-welfaresubsidiesboeingalcoa.html.

Katzand, Cheryl. (2012). "People in Poor Neighborhoods Breathe More Hazardous Particles." *Scientific American*, November 1. www.scientificamerican.com/article/people-poor-neighborhoods-breate-more-hazardous-particles/ (accessed November 3, 2017).

Kiel, Paul. (2012). "The Bailout: By the Actual Numbers." *ProPublica*, September 6. www.propublica.org/article/the-bailout-by-the-actual-numbers (accessed November 3, 2017).

Kirby, Michael. (2001). "Think Globally." *The Green Bag 2d* (Spring):287–95. www.greenbag.org/v4n3/v4n3_dialogue_kirby.pdf (accessed November 3, 2017).

Kirby, Peadar. (2006). *Vulnerability and Violence: The Impact of Globalization*. Ann Arbor, MI: Pluto Press.

Kordana, Kevin A. (1997). "Tax Increases in Municipal Bankruptcies." *Virginia Law Review* 83:1035–108.

Kotowitz, Y. (1987). "Moral Hazard." Pp. 549–51, In *The New Palgrave: A Dictionary of Economics*, Volume 3, ed. John Eatwell, Murray Milgate and Peter Newman. London: Macmillan.

Leef, George. (2013). "Op-Ed., Trickle-Down Economics – The Most Destructive Phrase of All Time?" *Forbes*, December 6. www.forbes.com/sites/georgeleef/2013/12/06/trickle-down-economics-the-most-destructive-phrase-of-all-time/ (accessed November 3, 2017).

Levi, Lili. (2011). "Plan B for Campaign-Finance Reform: Can the FCC Help Save American Politics After Citizens United?" *Catholic University Law Review* 61:97–104.

Liptak, Adam. (2012). "We the People' Loses Appeal with People around the World." *New York Times*, February 6. www.nytimes.com/2012/02/07/us/we-the-people-loses-appeal-with-people-around-the-world.html.

Locke, John. ([1689] 1988). *Two Treatises of Government*, ed. Peter Laslett. Cambridge, England: Cambridge University Press.

Nixon, Ron. (2014). "Senate Passes Long-Stalled Farm Bill, With Clear Winners and Losers." *New York Times*, February 4. www.nytimes.com/2014/02/05/us/politics/senate-passes-long-stalled-farm-bill.html (accessed November 3, 2017).

Offer, Avner. (2012). "Self-Interest, Sympathy and the Invisible Hand: From Adam Smith to Market Liberalism." www.nuff.ox.ac.uk/economics/history/Paper101/offer101.pdf (accessed November 3, 2017).

Pildes, Richard H. (2011). "Why the Center Does Not Hold: The Causes of Hyperpolarized Democracy in America." *California Law Review* 99:10–47.

Putnam, Robert D. (2015). *Our Kids: The American Dream in Crisis*. New York, NY: Simon & Schuster.

Rooney, Kathy et al. eds. (2001). *Microsoft Encarta College Dictionary* 501.

Ross, Catherine E. and Marieke Van Willigen. (1997). "Education and the Subjective Quality of Life." *Journal of Health and Social Behavior* 38(3):275–97.

Senior, Jennifer. (2013). "In Conversation: Antonin Scalia." *New York Magazine*, October 6. http://nymag.com/news/features/antonin-scalia-2013-10/ (accessed November 3, 2017).

Shilling, Chris. (1993). *The Body and Social Theory*. London: SAGE Publications.

Story, Louise. (2012). "As Companies Seek Tax Deals, Government Pays High Price." *New York Times*, December 1. www.nytimes.com/2012/12/02/us/how-local-taxpayers-bankroll-corporations.html?_r=1& (accessed November 3, 2017).

Titlestad, Peter James Hilary (2010). "Liberalism." *English Academy Review* 27(2):94–100.

Wilkinson, Richard and Kate Pickett. (2010). *The Spirit Level: Why Greater Equality Makes Societies Stronger*. New York, NY: Bloomsbury Press.

Witte, John, Jr. and Joel A. Nichols. (2016). *Religion and the American Constitutional Experiment*, 4th ed. New York, NY: Oxford University Press.

Yang, Jia Lynn. (2013). "Maximizing Shareholder Value: The Goal That Changed Corporate America." *The Washington Post*, August 26. www.washingtonpost.com/business/economy/maximizing-shareholder-value-the-goal-that-changed-corporate-america/2013/08/26/26e9ca8e-ed74-11e2-9008-61e94a7ea20d_story.html?utm_term=.78e4f69c3c4f (accessed October 19, 2018).

CHAPTER THREE

"ONE SMALL CHARACTERISTIC"
Conceptualizing Harm to Animals and Legal Personhood

Claire E. Rasmussen

> [Have you considered] what your desire [to free Tommy] does to our legal system and the standing of mankind and our primacy in our vision of the universe is just detritus and wreckage on the way to your mad goal to release one chimp.[1]
>
> Fiat justitia, ruat coelom. (Let justice be done, though heavens may fall.)
>
> Lord Mansfield, Somersett v. Stewart, a 1772 ruling finding chattel slavery to be unsupported by the law.[2]

In December 2013, an activist organization filed a habeas brief on behalf of Tommy. A young male, Tommy was living in a trailer park in upstate New York. Borrowing language from *Romer v. Evans*, the brief argued that Tommy was being denied his legal rights – including a legal right to challenge his captivity – on the basis of "one small characteristic."[3] The relevant "characteristic" was that Tommy is a chimpanzee. Tommy's case was one of several pursued by the Nonhuman Rights Project (NhRP) on behalf of animals. In a series of cases, they have argued that legal personhood does not require the individual be human. While not yet successful on behalf of Tommy or other nonhuman plaintiffs, the NhRP has attracted a great deal of attention by challenging the assumption that all legal subjects are by nature human.

The legal strategy pursued by the NhRP suggests that the interests of nonhuman animals may be best achieved in the courts not only by regulating specific acts of harm – as animal cruelty laws tend to do – but also by directing attention to the moral and political

---

[1] Stephen Colbert to Steven Wise. *The Colbert Report*. July 17, 2014.
[2] *Somerset v. Stewart*, 98 Eng. Rep. 499 (K.B.) (1772).
[3] *Romer v. Evans*, 517 U.S. 620 (1996).

conditions that have enabled injuries to be inflicted upon animals more generally. In other words, these suits suggest that the initial injury to animals happens not at the moment of abuse, confinement, or slaughter, but in the overall conceptual framework that defines nonhuman animals as property within the legal system. To deny animals recognition as legal subjects prevents any ability to make claims on society to prevent or compensate for injuries. To change the idea of legal personhood would thus be a transformative act on behalf of animals, providing a new ground for legal action. Legal personhood for animals would also be transformative in how we conceptualize the relationship between legal subjectivity (who counts within the legal system) and injuries.

In this chapter, I explore two specific cases involving innovative legal strategies attempting to redress injuries done to nonhuman animals. In addition to the case of Tommy, I explore the case of the fighting dogs seized from Bad Newz Kennels, the dogfighting operation infamously run by National Football League (NFL) quarterback Michael Vick. Both cases explicitly or implicitly suggest a heightened legal responsibility toward animals that is not dependent upon proving that animals are equal to humans in capacity or even rights. Instead, they focus on the actual harm inflicted on the animals and appeal to a shared desire to create new conditions that mitigate these harms. These arguments reflect a shift in thinking about nonhuman animals as legal subjects from a model that required demonstration of their capacity as rights-bearing subjects toward an emphasis on corporeal vulnerability, or a capacity to experience pain. This shift mirrors arguments from political and legal theory, addressed below, that suggest this model of vulnerability may present a new legal framework for marginalized subjects, including animals, to make legal claims against injustice. Rather than basing these claims on legal status or recognition as rights-bearing subjects, these claims of injustice shift the focus to the injury itself and its causes. Scholars like Martha Fineman suggest that this model of thinking about legal subjectivity can expand our moral and legal universe in ways that create new avenues for those subjects rendered most vulnerable to injury by unjust societal conditions.

These cases demonstrate the value of legal innovation in challenging conceptions about how, in Colin Dayan's (2011) terms, the law can make and unmake persons, particularly in those moments when the law is called upon to clarify the boundaries around personhood. However, the emphasis on corporeal vulnerability, while intended to dismantle hierarchies, may reinforce existing power relationships in ways that are problematic not only for animals, but also for other subjects understood as vulnerable. My argument proceeds in three stages, first exploring the arguments about a subjectivity grounded in a shared sense of vulnerability. Second, I explore the arguments and consequences of the two cases in which the boundaries of personhood are challenged by legal advocacy on behalf of animals. Finally, I explore how, in practice, these arguments can in fact reinforce the primacy of the autonomous subject in problematic ways. I conclude that while the project of vulnerability presents an alternative to conventional rights-based models that emphasize either the rights derived from the biological fact of being human or rights derived from a demonstration of capacities, it may be less successful in undermining the kinds of hierarchy that enable the exclusion of vulnerable subjects.

VULNERABILITY AS SUBJECTIVITY

The ideal of the autonomous, rights-bearing subject has long been scrutinized as descriptively and normatively problematic (Denbow 2015, Gill 2001, Rasmussen 2011). Feminist scholars in particular have called into question the ideal of the independent, rational, and self-interested subject at the heart of liberal political and legal theory (Keller 1997, Mackenzie and Stoljar 2000). The idea of the *vulnerable* subject has gained some traction among critics of the liberal subject as diverse as Judith Butler, Cary Wolfe, Martha Nussbaum, and Martha Fineman, all discussed in this chapter, as an alternative that highlights the relational nature of subjectivity and supports a political project challenging hegemonic power relationships.

This emphasis on subjectivity rooted in vulnerability derived from corporeality has significant overlap with arguments emerging from animal rights scholarship and advocacy (Deckha 2007). Accounts in favor of moral or legal consideration of animals have sought to reject rationalist accounts of subjectivity that require a subject's demonstration of rational self-mastery or capacity for the rational pursuit of self-interest. Similarly, animal rights advocacy rejects an anthropocentric account of subjectivity that conflates species being (human being) with being a subject (of rights, of law, or of politics) (Gunnarsson 2008). The proposed alternative is often derived from Jeremy Bentham's famous question "The question is not, can they reason, nor can they talk but can they suffer?" (Bentham 1879). As with theories of vulnerability, Bentham bases his question on the corporeal capacity for pain and a presumed empathetic response to that corporeal suffering that can bring together a moral and political community not on the basis of shared interests or universal capacities, but according to a shared experience of vulnerability to suffering. While shifting away from an explicit focus on pain as vulnerability, recent literature on vulnerability has similarly sought to expand our moral and political universe by rethinking the nature of those included. As described by Deckha, this strategy aims to shift away from "metrics of ethical worth such as whether or not they possess a sufficient capacity to reason, suffer, emote, use language, make tools or exhibit some other trait presumed to define what it means to be human" (Deckha 2015: 49).

One of the most prominent accounts of the vulnerable subject in political theory comes out of the work of Judith Butler (2003, 2004), who seeks to decenter notions of individual agency while retaining a capacity for political agency. Butler discusses the idea of vulnerability relative to subjectivity in two different contexts in her work. In earlier works, Butler uses the language of vulnerability to describe the nature of subjectivity formed through language (Butler 1997a, b). Our social existence is enabled through access to a common language, meaning that our self is constituted via a system of language external to ourselves through which we relate to others. Since signification is external, we are neither fully in control of the meaning of our own utterances and how they will be received and interpreted, nor can we be certain that the system of signification itself is stable, since its meaning relies upon shared usage. Butler here is drawing upon a structuralist account of language and a post-structuralist/Foucaultian account of power, suggesting that our selves are formed within rather than existing prior relationships of power; we are effects and causes of systems of meanings. We are thus vulnerable in the sense of being subjects to existing systems of power. As Catherine Mills describes, "the subject emerges through a primary submission to the categories, terms and names established by the concatenations of power relations that precede and extend beyond the subject they hail into meaning. Thus, the subject is condemned to seek recognition of its own existence in a discourse which is both 'dominant and indifferent.' Hence, the social categories through which the subject comes to exist come to signify subordination and existence simultaneously, such that 'within subjection, the price of existence is subordination'" (Mills 2000: 270). Vulnerability in this context is generated by a lack of identity external to power relations and the absence of an ability to control the effects of one's own (speech) acts. We must use language to become subjects (legible to others), but in doing so we become subject to that language.

Butler later more explicitly uses the language of vulnerability to unpack a specific political vision not unrelated to her earlier work. Following 9/11, and in the wake of political violence, Butler argues that the experience of corporeal vulnerability should not be seen as a political problem to be solved through an assertion of strength and a reassertion of identity. Instead, she argues that witnessing violence opens a political conversation about "who counts as human? Whose lives count as lives? And, finally, what makes for a grievable life?" (Butler 2003: 10). These questions are meant, on the one hand, to gesture toward thinking about what constitutes subjectivity and, on the other, to explore the ways that political community is constituted and how that community might be constituted in less violent or exclusionary ways.[4]

As with the account of the self-interpolated by language, Butler highlights a relational sense of self, made vulnerable by its dependence upon others for its meaning. This account, however, is more explicitly corporeal, formed "in part by virtue of the social vulnerability of our bodies – as a site of desire and physical vulnerability, as a site of a publicity at once assertive and exposed … socially constituted bodies, attached to others, at risk of losing those attachments, exposed to others, at risk of violence by virtue of that exposure" (Butler 2003: 10). Butler goes on to argue explicitly that this notion of the vulnerable self can remake our sense of rights, shifting from a self-presentation as a bounded, rational being capable of making demands, to experiencing ourselves as a corporeal member of a material community on which we rely. Opening up the question of who counts and why, the shock of vulnerability can help us to recognize or see the other as constituted through a shared vulnerability. In this way, while here emphasizing the corporeal over the linguistic, Butler is utilizing vulnerability to generate political community with the Other while undermining the stability of the self. In recognizing

---

[4] Derrida makes similar arguments about violence as disruptive to the self, making us more open to the Other. He, however, utilizes a more mundane form of violence – the regular slaughter of animals as a part of the regular human diet – to expose us to the shock of embodied vulnerability. See Calarco (2004: 175–201) for a discussion of this argument.

our own vulnerability, we may reach out to others upon whom our self depends. As Oliver describes Butler's political community based on a shared experience of suffering, it can be a "strange kinship ... based not on blood or generation but on a shared embodiment and the gestures of love and friendship among living creatures made possible by bodies co-existing in a world on which we all depend" (Oliver 2009: 228).

In a similar vein, the idea of vulnerability has gained traction in legal literature in large part through the work of Martha Fineman. Building on her existing critique of the ideal of the autonomous subject, Fineman seeks to argue that vulnerability is a descriptively accurate understanding of the human condition and is a politically useful concept in positing a political and legal project of managing "common vulnerabilities" (Fineman 2008, 2010).

As with Butler's later arguments, Fineman rests her idea of vulnerability in human embodiment, recognizing the ways that our bodies' vulnerability to harm prevents us from ever being fully independent, implying that a lack of full autonomy is not a characteristic of marginal subjects – those who are unable to fully self-govern – but a basic part of being a subject, and thus cannot be grounds for political exclusion. The chief role of the state becomes not responding to the interests of autonomous subjects but managing our collective experience of vulnerability. Further, societal relations position us differently relative to our vulnerabilities, and thus the state has a role in managing inequities of vulnerability. Vulnerability can thus be the grounds of a political project that challenges the social context in which vulnerabilities emerge, demanding the state and society be "responsible to, and responsible for, vulnerability" (Fineman 2008: 13).

For Fineman, the advantage of the vulnerable subject is in shifting the focus from the individual to social relations. Rather than demanding that a subject meet a set of criteria for being recognized as an autonomous, rights-bearing subject, the vulnerable subject turns our attention to the social relations that constitute our lives. As with Butler, she emphasizes the ways that we are all subject to relationships that prevent us from ever being fully in control of our own lives. Rather than seeing this as a detriment, she sees political opportunity in addressing the ways that vulnerabilities are created, distributed, and addressed.[5]

---

[5] This argument has obvious similarities to Fineman's earlier work on independence and the myth of autonomy, though she argues that the idea of vulnerability, while including the model of dependence, is a broader concept.

Animal rights arguments have often drawn from a similar critique of the centrality of autonomy-based approaches to rights that require subjects to be able to make demands upon the law, suggesting that membership is predicated on an ability to make claims in the language of the law. Instead of requiring that political recognition require a similarity with already demonstrated legal subjectivity, a vulnerability approach draws our attention to "both the responsibility and vulnerability of living together with other species" (Shukin 2009: 223). Accounts based on vulnerability shift the burden from those who speak to those who hear, connecting legal and political theory by rethinking the political subject more generally to the project of animal rights (Wolfe 2010: 136). Significantly, the appeal to corporeal vulnerability is an attempt to move away from a requirement to establish an essential sameness between the excluded subject and those already recognized, whether that be an essential nature, the capacity for autonomy, or recognition under the law. Instead, appeals to vulnerability begin from the "material needs of embodied and corporeal existence" that compel us to recognize the injuries experienced by others, even those who may be different (Deckha 2015: 60). Therefore, the political project of animal rights may be a site for examining the consequences of the utilization of vulnerability as an alternative model for thinking about rights, because nonhuman animals are an exemplar of subjects rendered vulnerable to injury by societal practices, but who lack, at present, legal recognition as subjects capable of challenging this injury (Wolfe 2010).

VULNERABLE OTHERS: THE CASES OF TOMMY AND JOHNNY JUSTICE

Turning away from a demand that a subject must affirmatively demonstrate a right to rights and toward a responsibility to otherness, theories of vulnerability seek to circumvent the exclusive and often status quo-affirming nature of the ideal of autonomy. In this section I consider two recent cases in which novel arguments are made on behalf of animals based in an argument for responsibility toward vulnerable subjects. The first case is that of Tommy the Chimpanzee. The NhRB filed a writ of habeas corpus on his behalf and received a hearing in court. While ultimately unsuccessful in challenging his confinement or changing his status as property under the law, the attention brought to the case has refocused interest and energy on animal rights issues. The second case is that of Johnny Justice and the Vick-tory dogs, forty-nine dogs seized from a dogfighting operation. In addition to animal cruelty prosecutions, the court appointed a guardian and established a trust on their behalf as a means of rectifying the harm done to them. In both cases, the injury done to the animals and the responsibility for rectifying that injury are foregrounded, suggesting a novel interpretation of our legal responsibility for animals.

Tommy is a twenty-six-year-old male chimpanzee owned by a private citizen in upstate New York. He has lived most of his life in a structure in a trailer park where he lives in a cage and has a small, enclosed area outside. Tommy was legally purchased and displayed as a part of a chimpanzee show in a circus. After his original owner died, ownership of the chimpanzee passed to the owner of the trailer park, Patrick Lavery. The NhRP selected Tommy as a part of a broader legal strategy seeking to challenge the status of animals as "property." Writs were also filed on behalf of three other chimpanzees – Kiko, Hercules, and Leo – though only Tommy's motion received a hearing. The group has established a trust on behalf of Tommy and received permission from a primate sanctuary to eventually relocate him to their facility.[6]

The NhRP, led by Steven Wise, selected the three chimpanzees living in New York State because of the precedent of *Somerset v. Stewart* (1772), a case in which a judge issued a writ on behalf of a slave (James Somerset) who could not himself file a writ because he was not a legal person. Wise argued that legal personhood does not necessarily require the ability to represent oneself in court nor does it require being a human being.[7] Neither the fact that Tommy was not a human being nor that he could not make a claim on his own behalf should bar a legal claim being made on his behalf. Legal personhood, the writ argued, is not a biological category, but one constructed in and by the law itself and thus subject to reconsideration and revision. Being human does not automatically confer legal personhood nor, in a legal environment

---

[6] While Tommy's case has received the most media attention, his was not the first application for writ on behalf of an animal. PETA (People for the Ethical Treatment of Animals) filed a writ on behalf of an orca whale being held in a Sea World aquarium, alleging illegal enslavement. The NhRP is currently suing the SUNY system for the continued use of three chimpanzees in research facilities (see Kerr et al. 2013, Trouwborst et al. 2013).

[7] For a fuller accounting of the case, see the Nonhuman Rights Project webpage, where they have compiled the legal documents associated with the case (see also Siebert 2014).

in which corporations are legal persons, does legal personhood require being human (Kennedy 2013).[8]

The goal of filing the writ is two-fold. The first is to liberate the individual Tommy from his confinement in the private facility and allow him to live among his fellow primates in a dedicated facility. The second is a more long-term goal to expand the legal opportunities available to animals by suggesting that animals may be plaintiffs via legal proxies.[9] The NhRP states its goals as "Our mission is to change the common law status of at least some nonhuman animals from mere 'things,' which lack the capacity to possess any legal right, to 'persons,' who possess such fundamental rights as bodily integrity and bodily liberty, and those other legal rights to which evolving standards of morality, scientific discovery, and human experience entitle them."[10]

While Tommy remained at his previous home, the NhRP has been successful in getting an injunction against his current owners, preventing them from moving Tommy outside of the state of New York, suggesting some sympathy to the argument that Tommy was more than just property.[11] Their second goal – challenging our certainty in the biological basis (membership in the human species) of our ethical and political community – may be the more successful front. Tommy's case has received a great deal of public attention. Wise appeared on *The Colbert Report*, where the host asked his staff to take down a picture of Tommy in his cage because it was "sad making."[12] The *New York Times Magazine* also featured a cover story about Tommy's case in April of 2014. The online version included a short documentary about Wise entitled "Animals Are People Too." These public appeals foregrounded the experience of confinement and pain suffered by Tommy,

---

[8] For more on debates around legal personhood and recent "personhood bills" that have sought to bestow legal personhood on fetuses, see Hunt (2011).

[9] Those familiar with animal rights advocacy may recognize some similarities to arguments made by Cass Sunstein: that the problem with existing protections for animals is not the law itself, but the ability to enforce them. Sunstein has argued that cases like Tommy's, in which the animal – via proxies – is able to sue its "owner" can provide an alternative means of enforcing the law (see Sunstein and Nussbaum 2004). For further discussion of the benefits and costs of the property framework see Bryant (2007).

[10] Nonhuman Rights Project. www.nonhumanrightsproject.org/.

[11] After losing his last court hearing, Tommy was relocated out of the state by his owner and the NhRP has been unable to locate him.

[12] *The Colbert Report*. July 17, 2014.

highlighting the consequences of his legal status as property rather than as person.

The case of Johnny Justice and the dogs of Bad Newz Kennels also represents a novel legal argument on behalf of animals that reconfigures the relationship between animals, injury, and the law by making the dogs property owners, albeit via a guardian. Johnny was among forty-nine dogs seized in 2007 from a kennel owned by NFL quarterback Michael Vick. Vick and three other men were convicted on charges of illegal gambling in addition to animal cruelty and conspiracy charges. Affidavits from the case reported that in addition to having physical injuries related to fighting, dogs used in the facilities had been killed by drowning and electrocution, while others had endured physical abuse.

In many legal cases involving dogfighting, the animals are held by public shelters as evidence. Quite often the dogs are eventually euthanized because of their physical condition and a belief that the dogs cannot be rehomed due to emotional problems and the potential for violence. In the Vick case, the combination of public attention and a wealthy defendant led to a very different outcome. In settling his case with the U.S. Attorney's office, Vick was ordered to place $928,073 in a trust for the future care of the dogs. The surviving forty-eight dogs were assigned a legal guardian, Rebecca Huss of Valparaiso University, selected by the U.S. Attorney's office.[13] Huss was given the authority to determine the best outcome for the dogs and to oversee the distribution of the monies. Against the wishes of some of the highest profile animal welfare organizations, the dogs were placed in rescue groups with experience with bully breeds and fighting dogs: Best Friends Animal Sanctuary and Bad Rap, a San Francisco-based bully breed rescue. Most of the dogs were eventually re-homed with some remaining in sanctuary settings. Johnny Justice is the most famous of the dogs, appearing in *Parade* magazine and having a GUND beanie baby doll modeled on him. The dogs have achieved minor celebrity, having an active online presence and appearing in national media.

Both legal cases demonstrate the shifting role of the law in determining the status of animals relative to human beings. For the animals, the litigants deliberately or inadvertently shift the focus from establishing standing or on the capacity of the litigants to rectifying the suffering experienced by the animals. Rather than beginning from a claim of fundamental equality between humans and animals, the stories of

---

[13] For a first-hand account of this process see Huss (2008).

these animals focused on a common experience of pain and an appeal to a responsibility to end the pain and rectify its source. Foregrounding the corporeal experience of imprisonment, physical harm, and emotional abuse, Tommy and Johnny become visible to the law as vulnerable rather than as autonomous subjects and their legal cases implied a responsibility for their well-being beyond their utility to humans.

This focus, as Fineman suggests, then highlights a sense of responsibility to these legal persons. The establishment of trusts on behalf of animals as a fiduciary responsibility to harmed subjects transforms the animals from property to property owners, an argument that challenges the clear distinction between persons and property in the law. In an Austrian case the court refused to recognize a trust established by an animal rights organization on behalf of the chimpanzee Haisl precisely because, the court argued, to own property would make Haisl a legal person (Belivaqua 2013: 75–7).[14] The use of trusts and the desire to remedy past wrongs implies a sense of legal responsibility for injury inflicted upon the recipients of the trust. The legal move is thus a dual one that, on the one hand, achieves a pragmatic goal of demanding and receiving compensation for a past wrong. In doing so, however, these claims also challenge the very grounds that enabled the harm to be inflicted in the first place, the idea that animal bodies and their experience of pain is not legible or important to the law. Tommy and Johnny, in becoming named litigants represented in the law, transcend the category of "mere animal," an undifferentiated mass distinguished primarily by the fact of being not human, to become subjects of the law. Their vulnerability, and the call to address it, demonstrates the vulnerability of the category of "human" and its supposed primacy within the law.

THE LIMITS OF THE VULNERABLE SUBJECT

The idea of the vulnerable subject is intended to not only be a means of reconsidering the moral, political, and legal worth of animals, but as a transformative discourse more generally that can move the law away from the limitations of the ideal of the autonomous, rights-bearing, liberal subject. In challenging the "juridical technology of the 'person'" on which many of our jurisprudential principles are built, can

---

[14] For more on the relationship between personhood and property and the ways in which the denial of property rights has been a way of denying legal personhood or making a person experience "civil death" see Dayan (2011).

the vulnerable animal subject be revolutionary? (Mussawir and Otomo 2013). This section considers some of the limitations of the vulnerable subject in light of the specific challenges to the law represented in these cases. From this analysis, there is reason to question whether the vulnerable subject in fact challenges or reinforces existing technologies of power. I examine both of the central claims about the vulnerable subject. First, the claim that an emphasis on vulnerability (especially through the figure of the animal) can challenge the hegemony of the autonomous, rights-bearing subject and the ways in which this ideal is used to stigmatize other subjects. Second, I explore the claim that the vulnerable subject presents a dramatically new way of thinking about responsibility and especially, for Fineman, the relationship between the state and its subjects.

The vulnerable subject is intended to be a more expansive and potentially more egalitarian way of conceptualizing subjectivity. Rather than relying upon a qualifying characteristic (humanity) or capacity (autonomy) possessed by the subject who makes claims, vulnerability requires only a recognition of the other's pain that provokes a sense of shared corporeal vulnerability. What is common is the recognition of the other through *similarity*: in one case of another reasonable being, in the other, of another suffering being. This moment of recognition, however, becomes problematic in practice in the two most common ways in which this relationship of similarity is understood.

While often defended as a pragmatic rather than philosophical position, one of the most common ways in which the relationship of similarity is drawn is through denying any significant difference between humans and animals, either through a biological claim of similarity (humans are, in fact, animals and are genetically nearly identical to chimpanzees) or an attempt to demonstrate that animals are like humans in morally relevant ways. This desire for similarity may explain why the legal cases that are the most successful and gain the most media traction are those in which the animals are either most human-like in appearance (like apes) or are domesticated animals (like dogs) and, especially have been given human names like Johnny and Tommy.[15] In depicting the plight of Tommy, the *New York Times Magazine* showed

---

[15] The tendency to generate a hierarchy among animals according to criteria of similarity, usefulness, and familiarity, and the ways in which this often reflects cultural bias, is discussed at length in the animal studies literature. See Nagy and Johnson (2013) and Herzog (2010).

a photograph of Tommy alongside an artist's rendering of Tommy as a chimpanzee in a suit sitting upright and testifying in a courtroom, humanizing his appearance.

This need for similarity also manifests itself in the ways in which the corporeal suffering of others becomes legible in the law. The law distinguishes between necessary and unnecessary suffering, that is, forms of pain that are acceptable as a part of the course of life and those that are unnecessary and thus justice demands compensation.[16] Of course, recognizing the pain of others is itself an interpretive process, as much as the recognition of the status of others involves political interpretation. While some forms of pain – the wounds from a dog fight or a beating – may seem self-evident, accounting for the suffering and vulnerability of others often requires an analogy with the self. This is clear in the evidence presented in support of Tommy's writ, in which the authors make a clear case that Tommy's imprisonment is problematic because he is an autonomous being like other human beings. They argue that he "is possessed of autonomy, self-determination, self-awareness, and the ability to choose how to live his life, as well as complex cognitive abilities" (Nonhuman Rights Project (NhRP) 2013: 77). While seeking to avoid a catalog of capacities that firmly fixes the grounds for subjects that matter, clearly the articulation of a need for freedom for Tommy leads to a specification of a catalog of necessary characteristics that defines an autonomous subject worthy of consideration. The affidavits highlight several features including language usage, self-awareness, manipulation of objects, and other tests that redraw the boundaries of subjectivity to include Tommy, but without undermining the exclusive nature of this version of subjectivity in which a set of characteristics are defined by those already considered autonomous and against which suspect subjects may be measured. Thus, while the language of vulnerability is meant to avoid the requirement of sameness between subjects, making injury visible to others, especially in a way that can be recognized by the

---

[16] This distinction is highlighted by animal rights supporters as particularly problematic, in that it permits a wide range of actions against animals on the grounds that some forms of pain endured by animals are acceptable in the name of, for example, scientific advancement or food production, and so long as pain is minimized in ways that don't threaten the desired end then that pain is morally and legally justified. Of course, a similar distinction is also drawn with humans all the time in terms of what kinds of suffering are normal or even desirable (such as the pain from surgery, a hard workout, or mourning a loss) and which are unacceptable (such as pain from an assault, an act of negligence, or an untimely death).

law, requires some appeal to an essential sameness. Making vulnerability visible relies upon either a presumed self-evident harm of corporeal suffering or a deeper sense of injustice caused by certain forms of suffering that are presumably universal such as confinement or deprivation. Similarity still stands as a prerequisite for acknowledging vulnerability.

While the standard of self-sufficient autonomy is deployed on behalf of Tommy in ways that can reaffirm the norm of the autonomous subject, the claim of being like a human can become problematic in ways in which these comparisons can also highlight the ways in which vulnerable subjects lack autonomy. In particular, the common strategy of portraying animals as like other "marginal" subjects on the "frontiers" of justice as Nussbaum defines it. Most often, animals are depicted as deficient humans, either similar to cognitively disabled persons, unborn fetuses, or "locked in perpetual childhood ... cases of arrested development" (Belivaqua 2013: 81). From an historical standpoint, these comparisons have rarely had a positive outcome for either the nonhuman or human animals being compared. Quite often, marginal subjects, including women, racial minorities, disabled persons, or others, have been compared with animals on the basis of a similar corporeality. As a political matter, the status of "vulnerable subject" often has a stigmatizing effect, portraying some subjects (such as "at-risk youth") as both insufficiently autonomous and potential threats to society as a whole (Brown 2011).

Theoretically, the emphasis on vulnerability is meant to challenge the privileging of rationality above corporeality by emphasizing the inherent corporeal vulnerability that characterizes all subjects. In practice, however, the hierarchy among subjects may be retained by highlighting the relative vulnerability of some subjects to their own corporeality in contrast to other, more suitable, subjects. This tension is present even in Fineman's work, in which, while she highlights the universality of vulnerability, she also sees that vulnerability as the basis for political change, suggesting that vulnerability is an undesirable if unavoidable part of the human condition. Some subjects remain defined chiefly by their relative vulnerability, and this perceived lack can make individuals or groups the target of intervention in ways that do not necessarily address inequality or injustice, but merely enhance state power over them (Brown 2012). The analogy that is made between vulnerable subjects demonstrates the ways that highlighting the vulnerability of specific groups can draw attention to their inequality and lack of stature, further stigmatizing them rather than challenging societal practices. This problem was highlighted by the case of several

Austrian chimps, in which a judge rejected a petition to assign a legal guardian to a chimp because the instances in which guardians could be appointed – severe cognitive impairment or being an endangered child – simply did not describe the status of the chimp. In defining a chimp as like an impaired or immature human, the specific qualities of those humans and of the chimp are lost. Belivaqua (2013: 80) argues,

> In the framework of a legal-political imagination which depicts the individual as a self-contained and holistic unit, endowed with an autonomous will, much of the debate about human rights has focused on the legal status of so-called marginal cases (fetuses and newborns, disabled). What the court proceedings involving chimpanzees bring to light, however, is precisely the difference between the human marginal cases and those that could similarly be designated "non-human marginal cases" since they concern individuals whose living conditions are far removed from those of the majority of their conspecifics.

The ways in which this unequal distribution of corporeality (and corporeal vulnerability) manifests in the law can be seen in the role of legal representation and guardians in these legal cases. In order to make their claims legible, the animals in these cases are dependent upon human legal representation in order to interpret and represent their suffering. Not only does the possession of a guardian imply a deficiency on the part of the subject in need of representation, but it also generates a hierarchy amongst those deemed fit to represent animals. In the case of animals this often results in a struggle over the legitimacy of different forms of knowledge and a hierarchy of proper relationships to animals that has often marginalized different human groups.

As with the differences of opinion even among animal welfare groups in the case of the Vick dogs, the interpretation of suffering – both what constitutes suffering and how it can be remedied – remains an open and irreducibly political question. Quite often the struggle over who is permitted to interpret the needs of animals is itself a site of political contestation. Multiple works have discussed the ways that proper treatment of animals was and is used as a means of judging the relative civilization or humanity of different groups.[17] The improper treatment of

---

[17] Dayan (2011) discusses, for example, how slave laws did not permit slaves to engage in animal husbandry because it was improper to give property dominion over property. See also Feder (2007), Elder et al. (1998), and Deckha (2007, 2008, 2012). For a further discussion of the ways in which animals were used to define proper citizenship in a democratic context see Rasmussen (2015).

animals has often been used to show the moral deficiency of particular cultures, including condemning the methods of slaughtering animals, criminalizing the use of animals in religious ceremonies, or banning animal sports engaged in by the lower classes or cultural minorities. While certain forms of violence are normalized and therefore tolerated (such as industrial food production), others are stigmatized (such as halal slaughter), thereby creating a hierarchy among those deemed "humane" in their treatment of animals. The right to be a custodian of animals is thus often seen as evidence of being a rational or civilized human being. This mediating role thus establishes a hierarchy not only between those who must be represented and those who may represent themselves, but further between those who may do the representing. Rather than disrupting hierarchy, the vulnerable subject merely displaces it to another location, establishing a hierarchy not only between those who are more and less vulnerable, but potentially between those who are seen as moral guardians of the vulnerable and those who are stigmatized for inflicting pain.

The complicated roles that recognition and representation continue to play bring me to a final question about whether the vulnerable subject displaces or reaffirms the power relationships it is meant to dismantle. Fineman argues that the vulnerable subject can create a space for increasing claims to be made about our responsibility for vulnerability, in her case particularly in making claims on the state.[18] In the cases of Tommy and Johnny, the state is called upon to disrupt private property relationships in order to rectify relationships that create the subject's vulnerability.

Nonetheless, we may be skeptical about whether the utilization of the law in this manner is a transformation of the liberal state or merely an affirmation of its existing parameters. The story of the possibility of animal rights often describes the expansion of rights to nonhuman animals as a general story about the expansion of rights to various groups excluded on the basis of, for example, class, race, sex, or sexuality. Other accounts trace the changing perception of animals. The extension of legal and state-based concern for animals, however, must also be placed in the context of a changing view of the role of the state within, in particular, the horizon of liberalism. As Smith argues

---

[18] I would specifically highlight that this is Fineman's argument and not necessarily Butler's; although she does imply that the political community may be more responsive, she does not necessarily indicate that the state is the instrument for doing so.

"indeed, the concept of animal rights would hardly make sense before we had a concept of the state as a guarantor of individual rights, just as the concept of animal welfare depends on the concept of the state as a guarantor of individual welfare. Thus the development of the liberal welfare state changes the context of our ethical relations with animals ... it asks: What responsibility does the state have for their welfare?" (Smith 2012: 16).

This understanding of the rise of animal rights within a context of a changing perception of the state (and the law) overlaps with the framework of biopolitics, which suggests that power is aimed at the management of life itself (Foucault 1997: 252). Animals are inserted into new networks of power that include not only the rise of a range of biopolitical practices of medical science, public health regimes, capital extraction, and environmental management. While it may challenge the certainty of the biological basis of a regime of human rights that has excluded consideration of animals except as moral patients, it does not preclude simply enfolding animals into a regulative regime of the biopolitical management of life that justifies violence through other means. Thus, thinking of nonhuman animals as vital subjects is not, strictly thinking, to remove them from the exercise of power over them, but to insert them into different networks of power made possible by the liberal state. The management of animal life by the liberal state does not eradicate injury or injustice, but shapes the means by which injury and injustice are understood and can be addressed. The shift to the language of vulnerability implies the ethical pull of a shared experience of corporeal pain and injury that might create a wider circle of consideration. This ethical and legal claim does shift attention away from the need to catalog characteristics that define when a legal subject "counts" and instead focuses on the injury itself, creating a presumed sense of ethical responsibility for harm and the conditions that generate these injuries. This account, however, fails to adequately address the political conditions in which vulnerability, like injury and injustice themselves, is constructed within relationships of power, hierarchy and violence. The constitutive nature of power means that vulnerability, as much as autonomy or legal subjectivity, is always constructed within particular contingent relationships that require us to be attentive to the multiple effects of these claims, which may alleviate some injuries while generating others.

The idea of the vulnerable subject can be valuable in providing a critique of the autonomous rights-bearing subject and in presenting opportunities to rethink the boundaries of political community. In the context of nonhuman animals, it presents a challenge to explain *why* animals ought to be excluded from moral and legal consideration. While opening up the category of "legal personhood" and revealing it to be a political rather than natural construct, focusing on vulnerability may reiterate the political hierarchies that have made the achievement of legal personhood so important.

References

Belivaqua, C. B. (2013). "Chimpanzees in Court: What Difference Does it Make?" Pp. 71–87 in *Law and the Question of the Animal: A Critical Jurisprudence*, edited by Y. Otomo and E. Mussawir. New York: Routledge.

Bentham, J. (1879). *An Introduction to the Principles of Morals and Legislation*. Oxford: Clarendon Press.

Brown, K. (2011). "'Vulnerability': Handle with Care." *Ethics and Social Welfare* 5(3):313–21.

(2012). "Re-moralising 'Vulnerability.'" *People, Place and Policy* 6(1):41–53.

Bryant, T. L. (2007). "Sacrificing the Sacrifice of Animals: Legal Personhood for Animals, the Status of Animals as Property, and the Presumed Primacy of Humans." *Rutgers Law Journal* 39:247–330.

Butler, J. (1997a). *Excitable Speech: A Politics of the Performative*. New York: Routledge.

(1997b). *The Psychic Life of Power: Theories in Subjection*. Palo Alto, CA: Stanford University Press.

(2003). "Violence, Mourning, Politics." *Studies in Gender and Sexuality* 4(1):9–37.

(2004). *Undoing Gender*. New York: Routledge.

Calarco, M. (2004). "Deconstruction is Not Vegetarianism: Humanism, Subjectivity, and Animal Ethics." *Continental Philosophy Review* 37(2):175–201.

Dayan, C. (2011). *The Law is a White Dog: How Legal Rituals Make and Unmake Persons*. Princeton, NJ: Princeton University Press.

Deckha, M. (2007). "Animal Justice, Cultural Justice: A Posthumanist Response to Cultural Rights in Animals." *Journal of Animal Law and Ethics* 2:189–230.

(2008). "Disturbing Images: PETA and the Feminist Ethics of Animal Advocacy." *Ethics and the Environment* 13(2):35–76.

(2012). "Toward a Postcolonial, Posthumanist Feminist Theory: Centralizing Race and Culture in Feminist Work on Nonhuman Animals." *Hypatia* 27(3):527–45.

(2015). "Vulnerability, Equality, and Animals." *Canadian Journal of Women and the Law* 27(1):47–70.

Denbow, J. M. (2015). *Governed Through Choice: Autonomy, Technology, and the Politics of Reproduction*. New York: New York University Press.

Elder, G., J. Wolch, and J. Emel. (1998). "Race, Place, and the Bounds of Humanity." *Society and Animals* 6:183–202.

Feder, E. K. (2007). "The Dangerous Individual('s) Mother: Biopower, Family, and the Production of Race." *Hypatia* 22(2):60–78.

Fineman, M. A. (2008). "The Vulnerable Subject: Anchoring Equality in the Human Condition." *Yale Journal of Law and Feminism* 20(1):8–40.

——— (2010). "The Vulnerable Subject and the Responsive State." *Emory Law Journal* 60(2):251–76.

Foucault, M. (1997). *The History of Sexuality*, vol. 1. New York: Vintage.

Gill, E. (2001). *Becoming Free: Autonomy and Diversity in the Liberal Polity*. Lawrence: University of Kansas Press.

Gunnarsson, L. (2008). "The Great Apes and the Severely Disabled: Moral Status and Thick Evaluative Concepts." *Ethical Theory and Moral Practice* 11(3):305–26.

Herzog, H. (2010). *Some We Love, Some We Hate, Some We Eat*. New York: Harper.

Hunt, A. (2011). "Rightlessness: The Perplexities of Human Rights." *CR: The New Centennial Review* 11(2):115–42.

Huss, R. J. (2008). "Lessons Learned: Acting as a Guardian/special Master in the Bad Newz Kennels Case." *Animal Law* 15:69–85.

Keller, J. (1997). "Autonomy, Relationality, and Feminist Ethics." *Hypatia* 12(2):152–64.

Kennedy, M. (2013). "Judge Rejects Habeas Petition for Tommy the Captive Chimpanzee." *Courthouse News Service*, January 23. www.courthousenews.com/2013/12/23/63980.htm.

Kerr, J. S., M. Bernstein, A. Schwoerke, M. D. Strugar, and J. S. Goodman. (2013). "A Slave by Any Other Name is Still a Slave: The Tilikum Case and Application of the Thirteenth Amendment to Nonhuman Animals." *Animal Law* 19:221–497.

Mackenzie, C. and N. Stoljar. (2000). *Relational Autonomy: Feminist Perspectives on Autonomy, Agency, and the Social Self*. Oxford: Oxford University Press.

Mills, C. (2000). "Efficacy and Vulnerability: Judith Butler on Reiteration and Resistance." *Australian Feminist Studies* 15(32):265–79.

Mussawir, E. and Y. Otomo. (2013). "Law's Animal" in *Law and the Question of the Animal: A Critical Jurisprudence*, edited by Y. Otomo and E. Mussawir. New York: Routledge.

Nagy, K. and P. D. Johnson. (2013). *Trash Animals: How We Live with Nature's Filthy, Feral, Invasive, and Unwanted Species*. Minneapolis, MN: University of Minnesota Press.

Nonhuman Rights Project (NhRP). (2013). "Memorandum of Law in Tommy Case." www.nonhumanrightsproject.org/wp-content/uploads/2013/12/Memorandum-of-Law-Tommy-Case.pdf.

Oliver, K. (2009). *Animal Lessons: How They Teach Us to Be Human*. New York: Columbia University Press.

Rasmussen, C. (2011). *The Autonomous Animal: Self-Governance and the Modern Subject*. Minneapolis: University of Minnesota Press.

—— (2015). "Domesticating Bodies: Race, Species, Sex, and Citizenship," in *Political Theory and the Animal/Human Relationship*, edited by J. Grant and V. Jungkunz. Albany, NY: SUNY Press.

Shukin, N. (2009). *Animal Capital: Rendering Life in Biopolitical Times*. Minneapolis: University of Minnesota Press.

Siebert, C. (2014). "Should a Chimp Be Able to Sue Its Owner?" *New York Times Magazine*, 23 April.

Smith, K. K. (2012). *Governing Animals: Animal Welfare and the Liberal State*. Oxford: Oxford University Press.

Sunstein, C. R. and M. C. Nussbaum, eds. (2004). *Animal Rights: Current Debates and New Directions*. Oxford: Oxford University Press.

Trouwborst, A., R. Caddell, and E. Couzens. (2013). "To Free or Not to Free? State Obligations and the Rescue and Release of Marine Mammals: A Case Study of 'Morgan the Orca.'" *Transnational Environmental Law* 2(1):117–44.

Wolfe, C. (2010). *What is Posthumanism*. Minneapolis, MN: University of Minnesota Press.

CHAPTER FOUR

RIGHTEOUS INJURIES
Victim's Rights, Discretion, and Forbearance in Iranian Criminal Sanctioning

Arzoo Osanloo

INTRODUCTION

On a breezy summer day in August 2013, twenty-six-year-old Sogand was to be hanged for killing her husband, Hamid, six years earlier. As required by law, the victim's family, represented only by the mother of the deceased, was in attendance. Instead of carrying out the execution, however, the prison magistrate in charge of implementing the punishment called a reconciliation meeting between the accused and the family of the victim. Her aim was to bring about an agreement between the victim's family and the perpetrator. After several hours of discussion, finally, Hamid Heydari's mother, who was meeting her former daughter-in-law for only the second time since the tragic death of her son, consented to forgo her right of retribution, thus sparing Sogand's life. When I interviewed the mother of the deceased in September 2013, Mrs Heydari told me, "I forgive Sogand with all my heart."

Iranian criminal sanctioning is notoriously tough. According to Amnesty International, Iran executes more people per capita than any other country in the world.[1] One aspect of Iran's death penalty that is often overlooked and under-studied is the victim-centered approach to crime. In certain crimes deemed to be private harms, the Iranian judicial system affords the right of retributive sanctioning to the injured

---

I would like to acknowledge Michael McCann for providing key insights and vital suggestions that helped improve this chapter.

[1] Amnesty International Global Report: Deaths and Executions 2016, April 11, 2017. www.amnesty.org/en/documents/act50/5740/2017/en/ (accessed October 20, 2017).

parties. Injured parties can also forgo this right. These crimes, including homicide, are effectively treated as torts. Thus, in homicide cases, injured parties possess wide latitude in determining whether offenders live or die. The penal code also specifies that government officials and their agents must work toward reconciliation to achieve forbearance of retribution to the extent possible. That is, the law compels all interested parties, including judicial officials, to work to persuade the injured parties to forgo their right of retribution. How parties arrive at forbearance, however, is by and large beyond the formal sanctioning process. Neither the consideration, nor the stipulations used to bring about forbearance, enter into the legal process, and there are few formal regulations that guide reconciliation. This moral and legal compulsion to procure forbearance, on the one hand, and its informal and unregulated nature, on the other, have, in the intervening years, opened new avenues for negotiation, bargaining, and indeed reconciliation between victims and perpetrators. These avenues, moreover, are populated by numerous groups, including state officials, NGOs, social workers, village leaders, and of course, families of defendants and injured parties, who work toward forbearance and reconciliation, in a sort of state-sanctioned anti-death penalty cottage industry – all in the face of severe restrictions against overt resistance to the death penalty.

In Mrs Heydari's case, the decision to forgo sanctioning Sogand with the ultimate penalty came after six years of private contemplation, conditioned by intense and sustained social interactions with different interested parties, including the mother of the offender, her own family members, prison officials, and social workers. In response to my simple question, "Why did you forgo retribution?" Mrs Heydari offered a similarly unaffected answer, "Because of my faith."

Aiming to tease out the depth of meaning in Mrs Heydari's response, in this chapter, I navigate the legal framework that affords individuals this right and explore its religious roots. In order to contextualize the moral and legal obligation to bring about forbearance, I consider Iran's post-revolutionary criminal justice system and the foundational logic of this hybridized "crimtort" system (Koenig and Rustad 1998). As I do, I argue that the legal and moral requirement of mercy, alongside the absence of any meaningful regulation, conditions an affective space through which various social agents press their cause, and injured parties, like Mrs Heydari, are left to contemplate, often over a period of years, what it means to choose to execute a guilty party – or not. This space, moreover, generates performances of righteous suffering by both injured parties and offenders that correspond with tropes of grace, grief, and magnanimity, specific to an Iranian national expression of *Shi'i* Islam. I pay close attention to how the possibility of forbearance plays upon the religious compulsion to be merciful and forgiving in ways that are particular to Iranians' ethico-religious values.

THE POST-REVOLUTIONARY CRIMINAL JUSTICE SYSTEM

In 2013, both the Iranian parliament and its oversight body, the Council of Guardians, passed and approved the revised penal code. The following year, they ratified a new code of criminal procedures as well. These events were notable because when the penal codes were altered soon after the 1979 revolution, ostensibly to conform to the *shari'a*, they were considered temporary until the new government could introduce a comprehensive Islamic penal code. Thus, with the passage of the amended version of the codes, some three and a half decades after the revolution, the judiciary finalized Iran's *Law of Islamic Punishment*.

The codification of Islamic principles into law is an important component of legal modernization in many Muslim-majority societies, and the debates around the Islamicized codes expose the difficulties of integrating scriptural texts into a centralized legal system. A study of the historical foundations and present-day effects of codified *shari'a* allows for a more nuanced understanding of how civil (tortious) and criminal proceedings are blended and how this form serves certain logics surrounding punishment.

After the constitutional revolution of 1906–11, the new Iranian parliament drafted the country's first constitution. To construct a centralized body of law, the government imported civil and penal codes primarily from France and Belgium, while also asserting the law's conformity with *Shi'i* Islamic principles (Banani 1961). Between the constitutional period and the 1979 revolution, Iranian criminal codes went through a series of secularizing reforms that systematized offenses and punishments while establishing a hierarchy of courts to adjudicate allegedly criminal behavior and to arbitrate over disputes. By 1939, the Iranian civil and criminal codes no longer contained references to *shari'a* (Mohammadi 2014: 230).

In 1979, when the popular revolution removed the monarchy, a coalition of leaders, including religious and secular nationalists, established a new system of governance: an Islamic Republic. A referendum vested the *'ulama* (religious scholars) with great political authority through the power of the *Velayat-e Faqih* (Guardianship of the Jurist). In this newly envisioned branch of government, the religious leadership consolidated state power by supervising all judicial, military, and other matters deemed important to the political organization of the state. When Ayatollah Khomeini was elected as the country's highest authority, as the *Vali-ye Faqih* (Ruling Jurist), he moved quickly to dissolve the bases for the existing judicial apparatus and renewed his call to integrate *shari'a* into state law. In an apparent revitalization of *shari'a*, Khomeini and the supporting *'ulama* called for conformity of state laws to Islamic principles. The appeal to conform to the *shari'a* represented a manifest change from the previous era in which laws were simply to avoid conflict with it (Gholami 1999: 214). The new state dismantled much of the systematization of the pre-revolutionary period. For instance, municipal courts that handled a wide range of disputes were initially replaced by revolutionary *shariat* (Islamic) courts that gave judges broad jurisdiction over the kinds of cases they heard, with marked attention to crimes against the state and the aims of the revolution.

Many of the post-revolutionary revisions to the law arose from the leadership's goal of grounding the institutions of government in *Shi'i* Islamic traditions. Between 1982 and 1983, the Council of Guardians introduced new penal codes. Crimes are categorized according to prescribed punishments, and thus organize the criminal legal system. Criminal laws are divided into four categories, according to punishment: *hudud* (crimes against God), *qisas* (retributive crimes), *diyat* (compensatory crimes), and *ta'zir* (discretionary crimes). The first three sets of laws are those deemed to be grounded in scriptural texts and are thus less amenable to reform, while the last category of laws, the *ta'zir*, are nonsacred, discretionary punishments that serve a deterrent purpose in criminal sanctioning. *Ta'zir* consist of public offenses considered immoral or threats to security and order.

The first category, *hudud*, consists of crimes against God, which are deemed by the religious leaders in power to have punishments prescribed in the scriptural texts. As such, the punishment, often severe, is very difficult to alter. The categories of *qisas* (retribution) and *diya* (compensatory crimes) consist of offenses that have private plaintiffs, and are deemed to be private matters, independent of the state. These crimes, including homicide, are first and foremost treated as tortious injury. In such crimes, the state delegates the determination of sanction to the victims or, if deceased, their next-of-kin. *Ta'zir* are crimes against the public interest and are prosecuted by the state's attorney, ostensibly on behalf of the people.

By 1991, an amendment to the penal code created a category of public injury for murder, which was, until then, regarded as solely private. This provision made homicide both a private injury, with the next-of-kin as the plaintiff, and a public harm, prosecuted by the state. Thus, in murder cases, private injury and criminal liability are assessed by the same court and there are two complainants, the next-of-kin and the public. First, under a theory of tort, the family of the victim, as a private plaintiff, files a complaint for *qisas*. Only the private plaintiff has a case for retributive punishment, and only the private plaintiff may forgo it. Once a judicial panel, consisting of a majority of three judges, rules the death a homicide, it has no discretion in the punishment awarded to the plaintiff. The punishment is fixed by the scriptural principles upon which the law is based. Essentially, the court awards a property right, of in-kind extraction of life or limb, to the family of the victim. The logic of the state's case for punishment is based on public harm, protection from further injury, and deterrence under the discretionary *ta'zir* provision. The state's sanction applies only if the family of the victim forgoes retributive sanctioning. In such cases, the judicial panel possesses broad discretion to sentence the perpetrator to a minimum of three years up to a maximum of ten years imprisonment.[2] New provisions to the revised penal codes added a variety of complementary and alternative sanctions.[3]

In this victim-centered approach to sanctioning, the state affords injured parties wide latitude in determining whether the offender should live or die. Many social and legal actors, including judicial officials, work toward reconciliation and forbearance. Offenders are scrutinized – by victims, judges, lawyers, and other interested parties – on a broad array of factors to assess the appropriate sanction and whether they are worthy of forbearance.

Iran's crimtort system, then, is seemingly the reverse of that described by Koenig and Rustad (1998). At the outset, it seems that Iran's judiciary,

---

[2] The time the offender serves in prison before being spared counts as time served toward the final *ta'zir* sentence.

[3] The complementary and alternative sanctions include probation, house arrest, banishment from a town or province, suspended sentencing, deferred sentencing, and a requirement of a course of study or work or prohibition thereof.

in keeping with the original inspiration for states to criminalize what are essentially private harms, reworked its tort system to provide criminal sanction for a private harm. However, the important point of distinction is that in the crimtort paradigm, the state changed the primary function of torts, which is to settle individual disputes, and amplified tort remedies to fill a void in the criminal law (Koenig 2008: 736). Such actions in the American tort context permitted civil lawsuits to expose and punish powerful corporations for violations against groups, both with increased monetary damages and sometimes imprisonment. In large-scale civil actions, crimtort litigation also possesses a significant potential for "a symbolic politics of agenda transformation" (McCann, Haltom, and Fisher 2013: 295). Being able to characterize corporations' actions as criminally fraudulent allows for increased and sustained public interest that inspires support for social and legal mobilization against large-scale violators.

In Iran, lawmakers did just the opposite. While they determined a need for a state sanction of a private injury, they did not augment the remedy. And while the new penal code provides a whole host of new remedies under the public sanctioning action, they can only be assessed in the event that the family of the victim forgoes the ultimate punishment of death. The Iranian government has preserved the privilege of victims' rights in murder cases, granting them vast discretionary authority. In the next section, I will explore the underlying logic of this discretion through an exploration of its relationship with mercy in the Iranian Islamic context.

Merciful Discretions

Retributive punishment alongside the possibility of forbearance is hardly unique to Iran, and exists with broad variation in diverse criminal justice systems around the world. What has been less studied, however, is what happens when the state affords vast discretionary power to private individuals, as part of the broader fabric of tort law. In his study of crime, capital punishment, and class in eighteenth-century English law, Douglas Hay noted the availability of the pardon power as a discretionary tool of state legitimacy and control (Hay 1975). Applying a Marxist class analysis, Hay argued that criminal laws that punished property violations with death were a means for the ruling classes to control the lower classes and to protect elite victims of crime. However, despite the frequent issuance of death sentences, execution rates did not rise. Instead, Hay contended, state officials routinely made use of the pardon power, which, although "erratic and capricious," served as a "useful palliative" against such an extreme sanction (Hay 1975: 44). This show of magnanimity, Hay suggested, was an exercise of elite power that served to legitimize its control over the masses. Responding to Hay's claims, John Langbein (1983) conducted an empirical study of the criminal records of that time to argue that the discretionary pardon served as a mechanism to curb the severity of the law.[4] According to Langbein, the use of the pardon was not the unique exercise of elite forbearance toward the masses, and the laws served to protect the victims of crime, who, he found, were "overwhelmingly" nonelites (ibid.: 97).

Thus, codification limited discretion, but it also tailored redress to the customs of the times. In England, new Anglo-Saxon codes did not codify tribal practices, but the codes were "directed at readers who could be presumed to know the customs already, and offered fixed rules to govern situations which must previously have rested on discretion" (Baker 2002: 3).[5] As with eighteenth-century England, the Iranian criminal justice system codified fixed rules, yet it also affords broad discretion. In cases of retribution, that discretion remains with the victims of crime, rather than being redirected to the state. Iran's system, moreover, is governed by the intermingling of three modalities of social control: the modern criminal law, through which the state exercises its sovereign power, the moral principles of the *shari'a*, which take up and reconfigure pre-Islamic social rituals, and tribal and cultural practices. This hybrid and multivalent criminal justice system accounts for group injuries (families of victims), but not by augmenting criminal penalties, rather, by preserving and fortifying private sanctioning.

Nevertheless, the codification of tort laws, not just in Iran, but even in western societies, remains bound up with pre-legal customs that sought to extract damages incurred from the staining of tribal

---

[4] Langbein (1983: 109) refers to the pardon as an "adjunct" to the system of sentencing because, in the mid-eighteenth century, trial judges did not have the direct authority to issue pardons and had very little discretion in sentencing. Their recommendations to the monarch, however, were often met with deference. In a similar fashion, trial judges in Iran are restricted in sentencing, as punishments for private injuries, such as murder, are fixed (and the definition of intentional murder is broad). Given their social standing, however, judges can be influential in convincing families of victims to forgo retributive punishment.

[5] Compare with Bassiouni (2014: 121), who says that the "Islamic criminal justice system somewhat superimposed itself on indigenous systems, but regional differences were significant."

honor, albeit now limited in most societies to monetary damages.[6] In his classic essay on "primitive law," Robert Redfield described how simple societies moved from employing retaliatory sanctions to developing proto-legal institutions. He suggested that the formalization of law emerged through "the development of systems of compensation or of forms of socially approved retaliation in the development of what might be called a rudimentary law of torts" (Redfield 1964: 13). This rudimentary tort law included a formal process and a specific sanction. Legal process resulted, in effect, when "retaliative force is stylized by custom into a sort of ritualistic revenge" (ibid.: 12). The overall goal of primitive law, Redfield suggested, was to rein in "unlimited revenge" between families or tribes (ibid.).

As this proto-tort law developed into a modern justice system, however, the harm that the law punished was that which was committed against society as a whole, not just the victims and their next-of-kin, and it became "something that we are likely to think of as criminal law" (Redfield 1964: 13). Referencing Maine's assertion "from status to contract," Redfield recognized the shift from primitive to modern law as being one in which the legal institutions recognized their roles as adjudicating harm done to the greater society (criminal law) and to the individual victim (tort law) as opposed to simply mediating disputes between families or tribes. Legal codes secularized and individuated earlier practices, and ultimately privileged the harms done to society over those of the family. For Redfield, this was best evidenced in the development of a body of criminal law. Thus, modern laws emerged not only because of codification, but also by distinguishing criminal law from tort, giving crimes against the state and society the higher privilege and harsher punishment: whether a perpetrator lived or died was the prerogative of the state. However, as the laws changed in this way, they also moved away from the restorative aims that sanctions in private contexts possessed (Braithwaite 2002: 7).

In Iran, while the state maintains broad control over legitimate violence, it preserves the essential attributes of ritual, the excesses of which, vengeance and collective punishment, are curbed by the limits brought to bear by *shari'a*, not by virtue of its codification alone. The central feature of this resulting legal order is that the family of the victim possesses the right of punishment, albeit to a limit. This resulting system permits the state to maintain order, while at the same time

---

[6] This may explain why Iran's new criminal codes have increased monetary damages.

it fuels concerns with family or tribal codes of honor, but also reconciliation. So, as with Hay's model, the system allows for legitimation of state authority, while the delegation of the right of retribution and the exercise of forbearance as a right of victims corresponds more with Langbein's finding that the system is set up to protect victims of crime, who, are often nonelites. The problem with mercy, however, is that the discretion with which it is dispensed erodes the classic indicators of a modern justice system: consistency and uniformity of punishment.

Iran's project of Islamicizing the laws, especially the penal codes, involved reducing broad "ethico-religious principles" into positive law (Izutsu 2002). For instance, religious ethics demand that Muslims be merciful and compassionate in their dealings with others. Numerous verses of the Qur'an, the *hadith* (narrations of the Prophet's words, deeds, and omissions), and other scriptural sources acknowledge this commitment to humanity. Verses of the Qur'an specify limits with respect to revenge, and entreat believers to be merciful and to forgo retribution. With respect to retribution and forbearance in criminal sanctioning, Chapter 5 (*The Cow*), verse 45 is the source that gives expression to Iran's *Law of Islamic Punishment*.[7] Four propositions underlie this verse and define the penal code's murder provisions: (1) equal justice (2) is a right (3) that belongs to victims, and (4) forgiveness is better.

Iranian foundations of forbearance, which in one way take on a modern formulation in the penal code provision, derive not only from sacred texts, but also from the example of the first *Shi'i* Imam 'Ali, noted for his magnanimity (Corbin 1973), as well as the Persian Sufi traditions (Lewisohn 2006). Other sources of forgiveness can be attributed to pre-Islamic folkloric or ritual practices, such as the *qahr va ashti* (conflict and reconciliation) dialectic (Behzadi 1994).

The Iranian case can be distinguished from other Muslim-majority societies, as well as the English, by virtue of the fact that the leaders of the Iranian revolution arrogated to themselves not only a monopoly on legitimate violence, but also the final authority to interpret the sacred scriptures, something that for many Muslims is a deeply personal spiritual exegesis. The state took open, context-driven, and (what are

---

[7] The verse states, "We ordained therein for them: 'Life for life, eye for eye, nose for nose, ear for ear, tooth for tooth, and wounds equal for equal.' But if any one remits the retaliation by way of charity, it is an act of atonement for himself. And if any fail to judge by (the light of) what Allah hath revealed, they are (no better than) wrong-doers" (Ali 1983: Q5:45).

for some) mystical values, and concretized them, while conferring on themselves an exclusive authority to interpret them. As a result, broad moral principles became ossified and separated from their threshold values, underlying intentions, and relationship to the higher aims of the *shari'a* (*maqasid al-shari'a*) (Mir-Hosseini 1993, Zubaida 2005).

Quite apart from Weber's characterization of '*qadi*-justice' as the model of irrational and arbitrary decision-making, discretion in the Islamic juristic context was derived from a place of learned analytical expertise. The discretion afforded, or at least was intended to afford, jurists qualified to evince the righteous aims of the *shari'a* the liberty with which to issue rulings tailored to the specificities and nuances of the cases before them.[8] In the ideal system of Islamic justice, the judge would possess the jurist's ability to bring the breadth of principled moral reasoning to bear on each case. The fact that three judges hear murder cases is perhaps an acknowledgment of, if not corrective to, the difficulties inherent in such principled discretion in a modern bureaucratic system, whose very purpose in fixing punishments is to remove discretion.

Thus, alongside the fixed, rigid, and decidedly retributive nature of Iran's criminal laws, said by its leaders to be in conformity with the *shari'a*, lies also a space where discretion enters into the decision-making process. In murder cases, in particular, this doubly legitimized legal system, with its scriptural-turned-statutory provisions, engenders an affective space of adjudication.

AFFECTIVE SPACES

An important element of my argument is that alongside the fixed laws of retributive punishment for murder, the Iranian penal code compels

---

[8] Scholars of Islamic law have criticized Weber's '*qadi*-justice,' a demeaning description of jurisprudence and law in Muslim-majority societies, which attributed to judges a monolithic irrationality and arbitrariness, altogether lacking in the normative qualities of justice – consistency, transparency, and predictability (Weber 1978). Such scholars responded with clarifications on many levels. Some highlighted the rationality, order, and logic in Islamic law and practice (Messick 1993, Rosen 1989, Tucker 2000). Others distinguished judicial reasoning by Muslim jurists qualified to give legal opinions from legal rulings issued by civil law judges to whom Weber implicitly compared the *qadi*: the jurist's law versus judge's law distinction (Arjomand 1988, Schacht 1964). The post-colonial framework of governance in many of these contexts, however, demands still deeper analysis into the complexity of legal reasoning, as it is fashioned by the intermingling of at least two modalities of juridical thought in these societies, and indeed in their courtrooms, where laws of evidence are also in play.

all parties involved to try to arrive at a reconciliation that will lead the family of the victim to consent to forbearance. I argue that one of the effects of this moral and legal obligation, absent any meaningful regulation, is that it engenders the affective space in which negotiations take place. By affective space, I do not suggest a space of emotions alone. In this context, affect is much broader than emotion; it is characterized by pre-linguistic registers of experience, which include the interiorized cognitive or spiritual fields that precede intersubjective relationships. Scholars of the "affective turn" draw on the work of Spinoza in attempting to bring concordance to mind and body behaviors (Clough 2007). Implicit in this argument is a strong critique of Cartesian dualism.

Building on this work, anthropologist Yael Navaro-Yashin (2012) extends affect to the material environment, suggesting that it is found not only in pre-personal psychic states, but also in the hazy and atmospheric spaces of the exterior world. Material environments contain "affective energies" that are themselves transmitted to and between human subjects (ibid.: 18). Affect in this context is a nondiscursive sensation that a space generates and consists of "charges emanating from the natural and built environment" existing between, through and around human and nonhuman worlds (ibid.: 21).

Physical environments, whether they be built or natural, discharge affect; they are populated with both meaning-laden material objects and psychically informed subjectivities. Thus, the environment and the physical objects arranged in them are spaces of meaning that act on the interiority of the subject (subjectivity). Navaro-Yashin (2012: 24) suggests that we study the exterior spaces, that is, the active physical life of affect, alongside subjectivity's interior affective space. Among the meaning-laden material environments that evoke affect are legal spaces of bureaucratic administration. While bureaucracies serve as rationalizing and disciplining apparatuses of governance, they are also producers of an "emotive domain" (ibid.: 82).

Drawing from the co-implication of the interior and exterior realms of affect, I attempt to make sense of Mrs Heydari's ability to consign herself to forbearance when the law permits her to exact equal justice. To understand Mrs Heydari's decision to forgo retribution and forgive Sogand, I explore the affective bureaucracy of the law. As I do, I underscore the emotive domain that emerges through her active interior life, brought about by prayer, contemplation, and meditation, but also her exterior surroundings where reconciliation meetings call upon passionate performances of remorse, pain, suffering, honor, and even pride.

Such performative exercises, however, operate through the multiple registers of *Shi'i* sentiment as well as other cultural practices. In the absence of legal guidelines, forbearance work comes to be regulated through long-held ritual practices that take place between victims' families and numerous interlocutors, who prevail upon the families' faith and their feelings of loss and injury, and appeal to them to cultivate grace and magnanimity. Through the course of negotiations, victims' families frequently engage in such rituals, and often come to expect them as a condition of forgiveness itself.

Such processes draw upon and incorporate wider cultural practices, such as *qahr va ashti*. Parents or other social actors, teach *qahr va ashti*, a socially recognized "emotional-cognitive-behavioral cultural script," to children, who then internalize it in their own social interactions into adulthood (Behzadi 1994: 322). *Qahr* begins with a social rupture, then comes a silence that signals feelings of hurt by the victims. It also evokes the compassion and love of others, including family members, friends, and neighbors, and motivates them to get involved in resolving the conflict and to arrive at reconciliation. In one case where I interviewed family members who agreed to relinquish their right of retribution, they did so only after meetings with the family of the perpetrator, especially the family matriarch. Originally steadfast in their decision to seek retribution, the victim's family members told the many social workers and faith leaders who came by that they were surprised and offended by the failure of the perpetrator's family to come to see them. Upon hearing this complaint, social workers arranged a meeting between the two families. The perpetrator's relatives, who had originally kept their distance out of a desire not to upset the grieving family, met them, paid their respects to the family's deceased son, and listened to the angry complaints about their own son, the perpetrator.

Thus, I suggest that Iran's criminal justice system, after sanctioning, produces a particular kind of affective space – evoking *Shi'i* sentimentality for suffering, grace, and magnanimity and culturally entrenched ethical practices, like the *qahr va ashti* – in an attempt to yield forth a feeling of forgiveness in the victim's family. This is not to suggest that affect is synonymous with sentiment or emotion, which are attitudes, thoughts, or judgments prompted by feeling; they are entirely exterior (Navaro-Yashin 2012). What I am suggesting is that the affective space draws from both interior and exterior dimensions and conditions and shapes the *kinds* of exterior feelings, emotions, or sentiments that emerge from this forgiveness work. The affective space shapes the sentiments or emotions cultivated by the actors involved. And thus, sentiment and emotion in this context are not part of pre-existing legal regulations on how to forbear, as there are none, but rather become part of the intersubjective work between the many parties that ultimately make up or entail the work of getting parties to reconcile.

In the four decades of Islamic governance in Iran, thus a cottage industry, of sorts, has emerged to fill the regulatory void of the forbearance provisions in the penal code. This industry is populated by secular and religious persons, government officials, and anti-death penalty activists working in numerous social, legal, and political arenas to attempt to moderate the effect of death sentences in homicide cases in Iran. They involve social workers, judges, and the families of victims, but also celebrities, politicians, and well-respected members of the community, including the *'ulama*, Sufi mystics, and village elders. State-run television and radio dramatically recount true stories of forgiveness, as do newspapers and magazines.

Negotiations set off by this cottage industry emerge through the very logics of the system of criminal sanctioning that privilege victims' rights, even arguably, over those of the state, and create the conditions of possibility of forbearance, and to an extent, forgiveness.[9] They are enmeshed and intermingled with everyday life in particular ways, and as such they draw upon particular dimensions of Islam, especially as they are attuned to the ritualized aspects of (Iranian) *Shi'i* practices, which include grace in suffering (*mazlumiyyat*), compassion (*rahmat*), reason (*aql*), and the inspiration wrought by God's divine wisdom (*hekmat*), all of which are expressions of "true" faith (Momen 1985).

Calls for compassion and forbearance pervade daily life in numerous contexts, including in the state-owned television and radio, as well as newspapers and magazines. They highlight stories of forgiveness among

---

[9] While I distinguish forbearance and forgiveness, my interlocutors did not always do so. The word Iranians employ to denote forbearance in the legal context is *gozasht*, while forgiveness is expressed by the term *bakhshesh*. In legal settings, the term my interlocutors employed is *gozasht*, signifying forgoing a right that they possessed, that of retribution. *Baskhshesh*, however, is the term my interlocutors use more colloquially, in interviews, for instance. So it was clear that my interlocutors distinguished the former as a legal term with instrumental, not emotional, meaning. However, in interviews, I posed clarifying questions to attempt to ascertain if and how my interlocutors distinguished the terms outside of the legal context and what it meant to them to forgive someone. It was not always the case that someone who agreed to forgo retribution also personally or emotionally forgave the perpetrator.

the Prophet and his family or they recount true stories of forbearance in local cases of homicide. Television shows query jurisprudential scholars and psychology professors about the effects of forgiving and not doing so. The various media outlets reveal a pedagogical aim to influence everyday social interactions by displaying the language and embodiment of compassion, mercy, and forbearance, in a sense, to show viewers how it works.

In this unregulated almost liminal space between law and social practice lies the neither ossified (as legal codes are) nor fluid (as social practice can be) space of forbearance decisions. These decision processes can go on, quite literally, for years, usually while the defendants are in prison.[10] Throughout this period, victims' families, not to mention defendants' families, are in a protracted agony. For injured parties, there is the double agony of loss and decision-making. From there, the emotional path to healing may begin with heated anguish reflected in indecision, anger, despair, and helplessness, all of which appeal for revenge or at least retribution. For some, however, the distress may dissipate to allow for tranquility accompanied by resignation, and ultimately perhaps, forbearance, if not forgiveness, altogether.

CULTIVATING FORGIVENESS

For Mrs Heydari, whose bride, Sogand, killed her son, Hamid, peace came slowly, at first only during prayer. "It was the only time when I could quiet my mind and stifle my anger towards Sogand," she said. Mrs Heydari explained that it was the constant repetitions in her prayers that focused her attention away from her son's death, and what she would do about Sogand. She prayed to ask God what to do. Her family, including a husband and four sons, had given her their power of attorney. "Because you are the mother," her husband had said to her. Since her husband did not want *qisas*, he said that Mrs Heydari should decide. He wanted her to be satisfied with any decision she would make. For six years, Mrs Heydari lived with the agony of deciding what to do. She could not sleep through the night. She thought about only this – what to do about Sogand – most every day. She frequently visited her son's tomb. In interviews I had with her during the summer of 2013,

---

[10] A provision in the new penal code (Article 427) permits a prisoner to petition for release if the family of the victim has still not made its decision after ten years. Ten years, of course, is the maximum sentence the state can give for homicide.

Mrs Heydari told me about her torment. She said, "I would lie on Hamid's grave and cry and ask him what I should do." I asked her if she discussed it with her husband or family members or others. She said everyone tried to talk to her; social worker set up meetings, religious people came over to pray. No one told her what to do, but still they gave her suggestions. Her husband, suggesting she would be troubled with the moral burden of having a person's death on her hands, said, "Don't soil your hands with her [Sogand's] blood."

Many people had dreams about it and related them to her. Her cousin told her that Sogand came to her in a dream asking for her forgiveness. However, Mrs Heydari thought, if Sogand wanted her forgiveness, then why did she not ask to see her (Mrs Heydari). Her brother, who was her best friend, was the only person to whom she posed the question of what to do directly. He said, "I can't tell you what to do. You have this right, but forbearance is better."[11] Finally, one night, after six years, Mrs Heydari was able to make her decision. "Hamid [her son] came to me in a dream and told me 'Mother, forgive her.'" It was not so much that Mrs Heydari wanted retributive sanctioning to be carried out, but that she could not bring herself to forgo it either. As she saw it, she would be disposing of the right of retribution on her son's behalf. She did not feel that she could exercise it or forgo it without knowing what Hamid would do. And so she did not, until he came to her and told her.

Mrs Heydari ended her indecision, her search for a solution, after seeing her son in a dream. Her final words as I left her home after our last interview were, "I don't want her death; my son didn't want her death." A number of the family members whom I interviewed, who consented to forbearance, came to their ultimate decision through a dream. Social workers confirmed to me that this was a common route to the families of victims deciding against retribution. One social worked explained why she thought this happened.

> Seeing her son in a dream was just the relief she needed to let go of the pain and grief, not of his loss, but of executing his right. It is very difficult to make a decision like this. To be burdened with carrying out justice on behalf of your child, your mother, father or closest and most beloved relative. The dream is usually a turning point.

[11] This statement, which in many ways has become idiomatic, draws from the key Qur'anic verse (5:45) on retribution to which I earlier referred.

Prior to the dream, Mrs Heydari had to carry the burden of trying to determine what he would have wanted. She could not be sure until the dream told her that she would not be committing an injustice against her beloved by forgoing retributive sanctioning on his behalf.

For Mrs Heydari and other pious Muslims, dreams are interiorized spaces of "divine inspiration" (Edgar 2011: 7). Mrs Heydari's dreamworld became a "landscape of imagination," where she could work out her ethical questions and be moved to take "concrete action" (Mittermaier 2011: 50). Ultimately, her decision did not involve money or any other conditions; it was her son's appearance to her in a dream. Dreaming of Hamid, she explained, was God's divine wisdom and "God's wisdom is never without reason." I asked her whether she was satisfied with her decision. She said that she had found repose, release, tranquility, but she still hurt all the time.

If her attitude exhibited grace in suffering (*mazlumiyyat*), she also sought it in her adversary, the defendant, as well. Sogand had been locked up for the past six years. At first, Mrs Heydari did not want to see, let alone talk to, Sogand, her daughter-in-law. As time passed, however, the one and only thing she wanted was to see Sogand, one last time, to witness the pain and regret in her face. She wanted to see Sogand as *mazlum* also. As with other families of victims, for Mrs Heydari, the defendant's remorse was a crucial factor for forgiveness. In a number of interviews I had with victims' families, remorse was a key element in their decision to forgive. The families were looking for that essential, relational quality that humanized the defendant to them, thus providing a sign of the humanity the victims shared with the perpetrator. Facing the perpetrator and looking into his or her eyes could bring about a Levinasian recognition of the perpetrator's humanity through which, then, forgiveness would be warranted (Levinas 1969: 198). After Mrs. Heydari saw Sogand, her remorse and humility suitably befitting, she agreed to forgo her right to retribution.

Over time, through the cases and an emergent expertise cultivated by the social workers, prison and judicial officials, and others, a fluid but discernible processes for arriving at forbearance begins to take shape. Not only do they involve emotional meetings, but also some financial settlement. In Mrs Heydari's case, the matter of financial settlement was a problem because she did not want anything. As she told the prison officials, "You can fill a house full of gold and give it to me, but it won't change anything for me." But negotiators, social workers on her behalf, had come up with a sum, and told the judge that Mrs Heydari needed to have it.[12] The payment of this sum became a contingency for the defendant's release, even though Mrs Heydari had not asked for it.

When I asked Mrs Heydari whether she forgave Sogand or only consented to having her not executed, she said, "I did it from my heart; I forgave her. But my heart still hurts." Then, after a moment's reflection, she added, "I entrust her to God. I don't want her death; my son didn't want her death."

CONCLUSION

Much has been written about the role of victims in sanctioning processes in western legal scholarship; to understand the Iranian context, it is important to consider that role as well. As I have already noted, few regulations guide the operation of forbearance. I do not suggest, however, that this void of regulation constitutes an oversight or a failure on the part of the state to rationalize law. Rather, I suggest that in the very ambiguity of forbearance practices lies an intentionality which arises first from the state's recognition that the victim is the primary victim, and who, as a result of the loss or injury, acquires a property right. The state's lack of guidelines, then, lies in its role in preserving the rights of property owners to dispose of their possessions as they see fit, albeit within the broad parameters that the state determines. In the context of the right of retribution, the state aims to prevent parties from taking the law into their own hands. The lack of guidance on forbearance is accompanied by a compulsion, both moral and legal, to seek reconciliation. This codified compulsion also suggests that positive law is inadequate to facilitate so deeply emotional a process as reconciliation between perpetrators and victims. In a sense, the state's acknowledgement allows interested parties to sidestep the rationalizing features of law and cultivate a space for victims to process and perform their emotional journeys during the months and years of deciding what to do. Such a journey allows for faith as well as other ritual practices to enter into the forbearance work. Prior to codification, Muslim forbearance existed already as a hybridized form of justice. *Shariʿa* prescribed limits aimed to curbed revenge practices among tribal groups. So now, these practices, mediated and bureaucratized by this novel state form,

---

[12] The social workers explained that the paying of a fine would serve as a further sanction, since six years for murder was so little. In addition, they suggested, it would serve a deterrent purpose to prevent Sogand from committing further violence.

an Islamic republic, both reproduce older practices and afford new possibilities for ethical practice. The forgiveness work being forged in this affective space is an important avenue and dimension of legal reform, one that may bridge the challenges in achieving quasi-liberal Western-style reforms, such as the wholesale abolition of the death penalty. In this way, the involvement of so many actors and open, public discussion may share some of the same effects of the large-scale crimtort suits that McCann, Haltom, and Fisher (2013) described, potentially permitting wider social transformations to arise, and possibly shifting attitudes about the death penalty in Iran.

References

Ali, Y. (1983). *The Holy Qur'an: Text, Translation, and Commentary*. Lahore: Amana Corp.

Arjomand, S. (1988). *The Turban for the Crown: The Islamic Revolution in Iran*. New York, NY: Oxford University Press.

Baker, J. H. (2002). *An Introduction to English Legal History*, 4th ed. London: Oxford University Press.

Banani, A. (1961). *The Modernization of Iran, 1921–1941*. Stanford, CA: Stanford University Press.

Bassiouni, C. M. (2014). *The Shari'a and Islamic Criminal Justice in Time of War and Peace*. New York, NY: Cambridge University Press.

Behzadi, K. (1994). "Interpersonal Conflict and Emotions in an Iranian Cultural Practice: *Qahr* and *Ashti*." *Culture, Medicine, and Psychiatry* 18(3):321–59.

Braithwaite, J. (2002). *Restorative Justice and Responsive Regulation*. New York, NY: Oxford University Press.

Clough, P. T. (2007). "Introduction." Pp. 1–33 in *The Affective Turn: Theorizing the Social*. Edited by P. T. Clough with J. Halley. Durham, NC: Duke University Press.

Corbin, H. (1973). *Traites Des Compagnons – Chevaliers: Recueil de sept 'Fotowwat-Nameh.'* Téhéran: Institut Français de Recherche en Iran.

Edgar, I. (2011). *The Dream in Islam: From Qur'anic Tradition to Jihadist Inspiration*. New York: Berghahn Books.

Gholami, H. (1999). "The Islamisation of Criminal Justice and Its Developments in Iran." *Tilburg Foreign Law Review* 7(3):213–20.

Hay, D. (1975). "Property, Authority and the Criminal Law." Pp. 17–63 in *Albion's Fatal Tree: Crime and Society in Eighteenth-Century England*, edited by D. Hay, P. Linebaugh, J. G. Rule, E. P. Thompson, and C. Winslow. London: Allen Lane.

Izutsu, T. (2002). *Ethico-Religious Conceptions in the Qur'an*. Montreal, QC: McGill-Queen's University Press.

Koenig, T. (2008). "Crimtorts: A Cure for the Hardening of the Categories." *Widener Law Review* 17:733–81.

Koenig, T. and M. Rustad. (1998). "'Crimtorts' as Corporate Just Deserts." *University of Michigan Journal of Law Reform* 31:289–352.

Langbein, J. H. (1983). "Albion's Fatal Flaws, Past and Present." Yale Faculty Scholarship Series Paper 545:96–120. digitalcommons.law.yale.edu/fss_papers/545.

Levinas, E. (1969). *Totality and Infinity: An Essay on Exteriority*. Translated by Alphonso Lingis. Pittsburgh, PA: Duquesne University Press.

Lewisohn, L. (2006). "Ali ibn Abi Talib's Ethics of Mercy in the Mirror of the Persian Sufi Tradition." Pp. 109–46 in *The Sacred Foundations of Justice in Islam*, edited by M. A. Lakhani. Bloomington, IN: World Wisdom Inc.

McCann, M., W. Haltom, and S. Fisher. (2013). "Criminalizing Big Tobacco: Legal Mobilization and the Politics of Responsibility for Health Risks in the United States." *Law & Social Inquiry* 38:288–321.

Messick, B. (1993). *In the Calligraphic State: Textual Domination and History in a Muslim State*. Berkeley, CA: University of California Press.

Mir-Hosseini, Z. (1993). *Marriage on Trial: A Study of Islamic Family Law*. London: I.B. Tauris.

Mittermaier, A. (2011). *Dreams that Matter: Egyptian Landscapes of the Imagination*. Berkeley, CA: University of California Press.

Mohammadi, M. (2014). *Judicial Reform and Reorganization in 20th Century Iran: State-Building, Modernization and Islamicization*. New York: Routledge.

Momen, M. (1985). *An Introduction to Shi'i Islam*. New Haven: Yale University Press.

Navaro-Yashin, Y. (2012). *The Make-Believe State: Affective Geography in a Postwar Polity*. Durham, NC: Duke University Press.

Redfield, R. (1964). "Primitive Law." *University of Cincinnati Law Review* 33:1–22.

Rosen, L. (1989). *The Anthropology of Justice: Law as Culture in Islamic Society*. Princeton, NJ: Princeton University Press.

Schacht, J. (1964). *An Introduction to Islamic Law*. Oxford: Clarendon Press.

Tucker, J. (2000). *In the House of Law*. Berkeley, CA: University of California Press.

Weber, M. (1978). *Max Weber: Selections in Translation*. Edited by W. G. Runciman. Translated by E. Matthews. New York: Cambridge University Press.

Zubaida, S. (2005). *Law and Power in the Islamic World*. New York: I.B. Tauris.

PART II

CONSTRUCTING INJURY AND IMAGINING REMEDIES

CHAPTER FIVE

CHAIRS, STAIRS, AND AUTOMOBILES
The Cultural Construction of Injuries
and the Failed Promise of Law

David M. Engel

INTRODUCTION

Tens of millions of Americans experience physical injuries each year. Approximately one in eight Americans requires medical treatment after being seriously injured, and nearly 130,000 suffer injury-related fatalities (National Safety Council 2014: 2). These figures, although alarming, are almost certainly underestimates. As we shall see, injuries are difficult to define and a great many of them go uncounted. It cannot be doubted, however, that the risks and costs associated with injuries pose a serious social problem. In fact, it would be more accurate to say that the problem of injuries in society is actually a cluster of interconnected problems, among them the following: How should injuries be prevented and the risk of injury in society reduced? How should injurers be deterred from exposing society to unnecessary risk of harm? How should injurers be held accountable or even punished when they inflict harm on others? How should injury victims be compensated? How should they be rehabilitated and reintegrated into society after they recover from the harm they have suffered? How should the public be made aware of injury risks in order to guard against them?

Every society in the world faces these questions and provides its own set of answers, which usually include some combination of government regulation, private or public insurance, informal social or market-based sanctions, tort law, and criminal law. Because of differences in culture, history, and legal traditions, different societies bundle these approaches in different ways. Some place greater emphasis on government regulation and social welfare, while others rely more on market solutions and private insurance. America is distinctive in its frequently stated preference for market-based approaches and – paradoxically – its robust tort law jurisprudence. In fact, American tort scholars sometimes convey the impression that tort law in itself has the capacity to address our injury problem by providing the necessary deterrence, compensation, moral accountability, punishment, and loss distribution. It is ironic that this grandiose vision of tort law coexists with a uniquely American suspicion of intervention by "big government" in so-called private disputes and transactions.

But does American tort law actually function as a one-stop solution for the multiple problems of injury? Does it really resolve society's need for safety, for control and punishment of misconduct, and for the need to compensate and rehabilitate injury victims? Setting aside the speculations of tort law theorists about what the law should do, if we want to learn what it actually does it is instructive to consider a rapidly growing research literature about the behavior of individuals who suffer injury. Surprisingly, the answer is that they very seldom invoke tort law or benefit from its indirect or "shadow" effects. Although conventional wisdom would have us believe that Americans are extraordinarily litigious and that most injury victims rush – or hobble – to a lawyer's office in order to file a lawsuit as quickly as possible, it turns out that injured Americans rarely do so. After suffering an injury, even a serious one, the vast majority of Americans don't sue, don't consult a lawyer, and don't make any claim against another party. Sociolegal researchers use the term "lumping" to describe this kind of inaction; and by lumping they mean that the injured party contends with the costs and consequences of the injury without any significant attempt to hold the injurer responsible.

Researchers have found that roughly nine out of ten injury victims in America engage in lumping, not claiming.[1] Only 3–4 percent hire a lawyer; and only 2–3 percent end up suing, even when their injuries are likely to have been caused by negligence (Hensler et al. 1991, Saks 1992, Baker 2005, Engel 2016). Although cross-cultural comparisons are notoriously problematic, the best evidence suggests that injured Americans are no more litigious than their counterparts in

---

[1] In this chapter, I define "claiming" as an effort to obtain compensation from the injurer or her insurance company and not from a third party, such as a victim's compensation fund, government benefits, the workers' compensation system, or one's own health and medical insurance.

other countries, despite our unusually robust tort law "on the books."[2] In short, there is little evidence to support the widely shared view that Americans are notable for their litigiousness. The absence of legal claims is indeed the most distinctive aspect of American legal culture.

There is something mysterious about this massive tendency to lump our injuries. The overwhelming preference for lumping has never been fully explained or theorized. Why do so few injury victims assert claims, and where do all the other injury cases go? In this chapter, I suggest that the explanation for the predominance of lumping in American injury cases lies in the social construction of injury itself and in the cultural norms and concepts that shape the identities and actions of injurers, injury victims, and their social and physical surroundings. I will describe six ways in which the cultural construction of injury operates to suppress claiming and encourage lumping:

1. *Pain perception.* The experience of pain – and whether it is thought to exist at all – varies across social and cultural settings.
2. *Beneficial pain.* Painful experiences can be interpreted as eufunctional, not harmful. When that is the case, such experiences, even if unbearably agonizing or traumatic, are not considered injuries, and lumping naturally follows.
3. *Natural injuries.* Even if a painful experience is deemed an injury, it may be viewed as the inevitable result of interacting with features of the physical or social environment that are natural, and not the product of human choice or wrongdoing.

---

[2] Research on injury victims in England and Wales has revealed a claiming rate of 10.5 percent, which is roughly equivalent to the rate cited by studies in the United States (Genn 1999). Surprisingly, Japanese people tend to have much higher claiming rates than Americans in injury cases, yet their lawyer consultation rates are a little less than ours and their litigation rates are substantially lower (Murayama 2007). All of these differences are difficult to interpret because of definitional variations among researchers. Other cross-national studies proceed from a different baseline – the existence of a grievance rather than the experience of an injury – so the calculation of claiming and litigation rates is skewed. Nonetheless, such studies tend to portray Americans' responses as not strikingly more adversarial than those of citizens elsewhere. For example, Americans' claiming rate and litigation rate per tort grievance are roughly the same as those of Australians (FitzGerald 1983). Our claiming rate per injury grievance is higher than that of Canadians, but our lawyer consultation rate is lower than theirs, and our litigation rate for civil cases in general appears to be approximately the same (Kritzer et al. 1991).

4. *Invisible choices.* Although it is sometimes apparent that an injury was caused by conscious choice – the deliberate weighing of risks and benefits by injurers – the decision-making process may be hidden from view and the victims may not understand how and why they have been exposed to harm. The resulting injuries in such cases take on a false appearance of unavoidability – and they are most likely to be lumped.
5. *Self-blame.* Those who suffer illness or injury very often blame themselves, a widespread tendency that is reinforced by society's propensity to blame the victim. Self-blame and blaming the victim tend to reduce the likelihood of claiming.
6. *The cultural environment.* Cultural norms generally extol personal responsibility and condemn the pursuit of compensation. Such norms tend to shape the interpretations and choices of those who suffer harm. They also influence the views of family members, friends, and colleagues, who reinforce the decision to avoid claiming.

PAINFULNESS IS NOT A GIVEN

Although one might think that pain is one of the few universal constants, and only its interpretation varies across cultures, that is not entirely true. Wounds or fractures that are extremely painful to an office worker or a classroom teacher may seem less intense to a professional athlete, for whom they are a normal and expected hazard of everyday activities (Howe 2001). Hockey or football players often deny that they are in pain – to themselves as well as to others. Farmers who suffer injuries that a white collar worker would consider excruciating may simply consider them part of their daily life and not necessarily debilitating (Engel 1984). A study of servicemen during the Second World War found that they required lower levels of pain medication when they were wounded if they associated their pain with an honorable discharge (Jackson 2011: 52, citing research by Beecher 1946). There is good reason to view pain as a cultural construct that may vary from one social context or historical era to another (Gergen 2009: 126).

To the extent that an individual does not experience an event as painful – even though others might – the likelihood of an injury claim is greatly reduced. This simple fact helps to explain lumping in at least some cases of what would generally be considered injuries.

PAIN MAY BE BENEFICIAL NOT HARMFUL

Not all painful events are injuries. Pain can be interpreted in different ways, and sometimes it actually appears to confer a benefit – even when the results leave lasting marks on the body. A classic example is foot binding in China, a pre-revolutionary practice that was excruciatingly painful and made it difficult to walk without the assistance of servants (Levy 1966, Blake 1994). Chang (2003: 4) describes her grandmother's painful experience during a period when foot binding was a common practice among upper class Chinese women:

> Her mother [i.e., Chang's great-grandmother], who herself had bound feet, first wound a piece of white cloth about twenty feet long round her feet, bending all the toes except the big toe inward and under the sole. Then she placed a large stone on top to crush the arch. My grandmother screamed in agony and begged her to stop. Her mother had to stick a cloth into her mouth to gag her. My grandmother passed out repeatedly from the pain.

Without question, Chang's grandmother suffered pain. Yet it is unlikely that any of the participants would have characterized foot binding as the infliction of an injury. Rather, it was an enhancement of the girl's beauty and a symbolic token of nobility. When pain is accepted as beneficial, it does not become the basis for an injury claim.

A modern example is male circumcision. The American medical establishment endorsed male circumcision for more than a century, starting in the late 1800s, based on the view that it prevented disease and deformity (Waldeck 2003). And, of course, the Jewish and Islamic traditions have for centuries portrayed circumcision as conferring an important religious benefit. But today some critics consider male circumcision a form of child abuse and even a human rights violation. The procedure is so painful for adults that it requires general anesthesia, yet it is typically performed on infants without this precaution, despite the fact that, according to scientists, infants are fully capable of sensing pain (ibid.: 477).

It cannot be doubted that circumcision causes male babies to feel pain, but, as was the case with foot binding in China, defenders of the practice argue that the pain actually confers a benefit. In the words of one model:

> There is a misconception that pain is a bad thing to be avoided at all cost. Pain is part of life as a human being. We could not survive without

pain ... We could not grow and learn as individuals without pain. You cannot give your child a life without pain. The consequence of doing that would be disastrous (Davis 2001: 527, quoting Berlin 1989).

In the year 2005, more than 1.2 million circumcisions were performed on 56 percent of newborn male babies in the United States (the number fluctuates with changes in the position of the American Academy of Pediatrics). For the most part, these children are not seen as injury victims, but as the recipients of a religious or medical benefit. This perspective may change, as did the view of foot binding in China. More people may come around to the critics' view that this particular experience is not only painful but also injurious. If that should occur, then what was once viewed as a health precaution or a religious rite would come to be viewed instead as an injury.

So long as beneficial pain is not perceived as injurious, lumping is such an obvious response that few would even consider the individual to have foregone the opportunity to lodge a claim. Claiming in response to beneficial pain appears absurd, unthinkable. It is only when societal perceptions change and the beneficial character of the painful practice is questioned that it can become evident – to some, at least – that an injury has occurred. Only at that juncture does the possibility of a claim arise, though the likelihood may remain very small. Before that moment, however, when the pain is not seen as harmful, lumping is the only imaginable response.

NATURAL INJURIES

Even when individuals feel they have been injured, their suffering may seem natural and not the basis for lodging a claim. The naturalization of injuries occurs in at least two different ways. First, damage to the body may be explained as a normal consequence of the life cycle rather than a harm that could be avoided by taking precautions. Chairs are a case in point. Consider the case of an imaginary middle-aged office worker who suffers from back pain or spinal deformity. This individual cannot recall any traumatic incident that caused these symptoms, just the development of physical discomfort and disability over a period of years. Her condition seems a normal part of the aging process to her and to her coworkers, who may experience similar symptoms. They do not consider it an injury and surely not a reason to seek a remedy from anyone else. Lumping would nearly always be the expected response.

It may be surprising, then, to learn that these very ailments can be caused by a familiar feature of our physical environment – the chair. The presence of chairs in our lives does not appear to be the result of human choices among competing options or a preference for risky technologies over safer ones. They are simply what most of us do with our bodies when we are not moving around or lying down. They seem almost like natural objects, the equivalent of rocks and trees in our homes, work places, and public areas.

Yet a growing body of research now suggests that chairs not only cause back pain and spinal deformity but also diabetes and cardiovascular disease (Cranz 1998, Buckley et al. 2013). Those who study "sedentary science" contend that there is nothing natural about chairs or the harms they cause. In some cultures, people do not use chairs at all; they simply squat, stand, or sit on the ground or floor – and in those cultures, people have healthier spines. If more office workers used stand-up desks rather than conventional desks and chairs, or even if they took frequent breaks from their sitting positions, they would enjoy better health, live longer, and suffer fewer musculoskeletal problems (Buckley et al. 2013).

Might chair-related injuries be the basis for claims against others? It is certainly possible to interpret the absence of claims as a form of lumping. Even though it is difficult to imagine America as a totally chairless society, variations in chair design can cause more or fewer physical symptoms. If the most advanced ergonomic practices were adopted, we could significantly reduce the number of injuries and illnesses associated with chairs (Cranz 1998: 101–2). The ideal chair would have lower seats, front rails that curve downward, seat depths and widths of only seventeen inches, less padding, and a space between the seat and the back of the chair. Adopting these changes in the design of most chairs, Cranz argues, would yield "an enormous benefit for public health" (ibid.: 105).

From this perspective, then, the ailments of our hypothetical office worker are actually injuries caused by manufacturers and designers who failed to take proper precautions. The problem, however, is that people who suffer the consequences of improper chair design seldom conceptualize their physical problems as avoidable injuries that have been inflicted on them by others. Indeed, the vast majority do not perceive that they have been injured at all. Lumping occurs as a matter of course, not as a conscious decision by the victim. Litigation in such circumstances is unthinkable. The perception of chair-related illnesses and injuries as "natural" is likely to persist as long as chair sitting for extended periods of time remains culturally normative. Scientists like James Levine (2014) are currently campaigning for a change in our perceptions about sitting, standing, working, and exercising, and in the United Kingdom a movement called "Get Britain Standing" has been launched (www.getbritainstanding.org). If such efforts succeed, a cognitive shift may occur and an enormous number of health problems in our society may come to be viewed as injuries that could result in legal claims. Until that shift takes place, however, lumping will remain the only conceivable response.

A second reason for the naturalization of injuries is that they result from risks that are viewed as a normal part of life, such as the risk of falling down the stairs. Stair injuries are different from chair injuries, where, as we have seen, the victim does not even associate her physical condition with exposure to a risky object. People who fall while ascending or descending the stairs know they have been injured, and they certainly associate their accident with the stairs they were using. What they may not know, however, is that falling on stairs need not be viewed as normal. Unnecessarily dangerous design rather than their own clumsiness or inattention may very well have caused their mishap.

Between one and two million Americans are injured on stairs each year, and thousands are killed, many of them older people (Pauls 1991: 128, Cohen 2000). The cost to the public is more than $10 billion dollars annually (Cohen 2000). But stairs are a ubiquitous part of our physical environment, and the risks associated with them are usually seen as unavoidable. To the extent that anyone is blamed for injuries on stairs, the problem is typically attributed to the inattentiveness or physical shortcomings of the victim.

In fact, however, ergonomics engineers have demonstrated that such injuries can be significantly reduced by better stair design: broader treads, shorter risers, and the elimination of variability in stair dimensions within a given staircase. That is, some researchers now maintain that stair injuries are not a "natural" or inevitable result of humans' interaction with their physical environment, but are caused by faulty design (Cohen et al. 2009). Viewed from this emerging perspective, many of these injuries could be considered actionable harms. They could give rise to claims rather than simply being lumped by the victim.

But people who fall on stairs seldom view their mishaps as potential claims. They interpret their injuries according to a normalized view of their physical surroundings. Stairs are simply there, and it is normal for some people to fall when they use them. Stairs do not hurt people; people on stairs hurt themselves. As long as few of us know about the unnecessary risks posed by certain stair designs, lodging a claim is unlikely to cross the minds of most injury victims, and we would expect lumping to occur in nearly every case.

In sum, the naturalization of injury results in the lumping of enormous numbers of potential claims each year. Naturalization occurs either because certain harms are considered a part of the body's inevitable decline and degeneration or because they are viewed as the result of normal interactions with our physical environment. In both circumstances, a shift in perception could result in a radical change in public understanding. What are currently viewed as natural injuries could come to be viewed as avoidable harms caused by blameworthy decisions to expose us to unnecessary risks. Until such a shift occurs, however, we may assume that nearly all "naturalized" injuries will result in lumping rather than claiming.

INVISIBLE CHOICES

Even when harms are created by conscious decisions – the deliberate weighing of risks and benefits by injurers – these deeply embedded and often profit-motivated choices may not be fully understood or even apparent to the victims or to society in general. This is an additional reason that injuries caused by unnecessarily risky design choices come to be naturalized and result in lumping. Unreasonable or self-serving processes of risk allocation may simply be invisible to those who are harmed as a result. Injury victims end up lumping because they view their injuries as inherent in the product or activity and not as the consequence of faulty risk–benefit analysis or other undesirable design choices.

Sarah Lochlann Jain has provided an excellent account of these invisible choices in the field of product liability. In her book, she describes the social distribution of injury that is encoded in product design: "Design decisions ineluctably code danger and injury at the outset of the production process ... [and] raise the question of how human wounding counts, who 'owns' health, and how it is to count as a social good" (Jain 2006: 56).

Automobiles provide many illustrations of the "ineluctable" coding of danger and injury. One classic example is air bags, which automobile manufacturers resisted providing long after it was known that they would prevent many injuries and fatalities. Over time, the manufacturers' cost–benefit justification for withholding this safety feature became more and more visible, until the point was reached when a societal consensus characterized cars without air bags as "defective." The shift in perception from nondefective to defective occurred not because of a major technological advancement, but because the public came to understand that it was no longer "natural" for drivers and passengers to be thrown against the steering wheel, dashboard, or windshield in an accident. Manufacturers' decisions to introduce automobile safety features often lag behind what is technologically possible and reveal a more fundamental set of assumptions about how much injury it is appropriate (or efficient) for them to impose on society.

A more recent example of a shift in the coding of danger and injury involves rear view cameras on automobiles. According to recent estimates by federal regulators, 267 deaths and approximately 15,000 injuries are caused each year by vehicles backing up. The victims are mostly young children, in contrast to stair injuries, where the victims are mostly elderly (Office of Regulatory Analysis and Evaluation, National Center for Statistics and Analysis, National Highway Traffic Safety Administration 2014). One study found that 80 percent of individuals struck in driveways by cars backing up were younger than five years old and the victims' average age was only two years (Hurwitz et al. 2010).

Surely all would agree that these tragic incidents should be counted as injuries, but are they "actionable" injuries that could plausibly become claims? Not if it is assumed that cars are a ubiquitous part of our physical environment and they "naturally" come with a blind spot, making risk to small children unavoidable. According to this line of thinking, injuries from backing up, though regrettable, are a normal concomitant of the automobile combined with inattentive caretakers. Responsible parents keep their kids away from driveways where they might be injured in this way; and good kids listen to their parents. The absence of claims does not seem to be the product of lumping. It is just common sense.

It does not appear that a major technological breakthrough was required to install rear view cameras in cars. Their absence simply reflected a set of assumptions about who should be responsible for such risks, and whose costs and whose benefits should be given the most weight. These choices about risk were, however, invisible to most of us until the issue began to receive publicity and eventually the attention of Congress. A consensus now appears to be growing that a vehicle without a rear view camera is defective – that this type of injury should *not* be encoded in the vehicle design, to use Jain's terminology, and there should be a change in the allocation of risk and responsibility among auto manufacturers, drivers, and children. Not surprisingly, a new regulation has now been promulgated making rear view cameras mandatory in all new cars and light trucks starting in May 2018.

When shifts of this kind take place over time, injuries are increasingly perceived as "actionable" that were previously seen as unfortunate yet natural features of our automotive age. Unless and until such a perceptual shift occurs, however, these injuries and others like them are almost certain to be lumped. Claiming seems both absurd and inappropriate, an attempt to cash in on a child's misfortune and to shirk one's personal responsibility. As Jain points out, virtually every product might, if closely examined, reveal the silent encoding of risk that it contains. When injuries result from these invisible choices, lumping rather than claiming is all but assured, except in extremely rare circumstances.

SELF-BLAME

Astonishingly, a great many injury victims blame themselves for their suffering, even when it seems obvious that their accident resulted from another person's wrongdoing. And, to some extent, society supports this perverse tendency to blame the victim. In theory, self-blame should not foreclose the possibility of claiming, but in practice it is a powerful factor leading countless injury victims to lump their harm.

Contemporary tort law allows injury victims to recover compensation if their harm results *both* from the wrongful act of another *and* from their own contributory negligence. Under modern "comparative fault" regimes, when both the injurer and the victim breach a duty of care, the injured person can receive a damage award reduced by the proportion of the harm attributable to her own carelessness. She is not precluded from recovery altogether. When it comes to injuries in real life, however, neither injury victims nor the general public seem to accept the legal principle of comparative fault. Many victims and third-party observers simply assume that, when the victim has done something wrong, she has completely absolved the injurer of any responsibility.

Even in our supposedly litigious society, self-blame is a common reaction to injury. Jean Jackson notes that one of the most deep-seated associations with pain and suffering is the idea that the injured person must have somehow deserved his or her fate: "The Latin root for 'pain,' after all, means punishment. In a just and orderly world, our reasoning goes, innocent people would not be suffering like this, so something must be *wrong*" (Jackson 2011: 378). The association of pain with punishment tends to be shared by the victim as well as the society that witnesses her suffering.

Although it may seem irrational and counter-productive for victims to view their injury as a form of punishment, this tendency has been widely documented. Considerable evidence points to the prevalence of victim-blaming – the assumption that victims should have taken greater care, that they somehow deserve the harm that befell them, and that the injury itself was fated to happen or may even have been a form of cosmic retribution. The religious roots of such assumptions are unmistakable (Wright 1983: 64, Schulz and Decker 1985: 1166, Bendelow and Williams 1995: 92, Cook 2004: 462).

The psychology of self-blame is far more powerful than the rule of law, which would allow some compensation for the injury victim who did indeed do something wrong. The perception that injury victims are responsible for their own suffering expands beyond reason to preclude any possibility that the injurer should be called to account. Self-blame explains a great deal of the lumping that occurs in our society.

LIVING IN A CULTURE THAT DISAPPROVES CLAIMING

Cultural norms are more likely to be influenced by "haves" than "have-nots" (Galanter 1974). This simple fact helps to explain why injury victims formulate their responses in a cultural environment hostile to the very idea of asserting rights against injurers. Personal injury claims, unlike most legal actions, are usually brought by have-nots against haves. Less wealthy and legally inexperienced individuals are the ones most likely to suffer injuries and, if they do choose to sue, they are most likely to litigate against "deep pocket" defendants. It shouldn't be surprising that persons and corporations with greater wealth and social status would adopt anti-claiming perspectives, since they are the most likely targets of tort claims. Nor is it surprising, given their greater social clout, that their anti-claiming perspectives have become highly influential. What they consider an appropriate response to injury pervades much of American society and stigmatizes injury claims and claimants.

In their study of tort law and the media, Haltom and McCann (2004) reveal one way in which this process of cultural production works. The mass media, even when reporting basic facts, draw selectively on contrasting versions of "common sense" about injuries and litigation in American society. Haltom and McCann found that newspapers have a strong tendency to report about injuries in terms of the ideology of "personal responsibility" rather than the equally legitimate ideology of risk reduction and corporate responsibility. "Personal responsibility" has, of course, become a catchphrase of those who oppose claiming and litigation by injury victims. In this context, it means that lumping is the most culturally legitimate course of action.

Haltom and McCann persuasively demonstrate that the dominant media perspective grew directly from a strategy coordinated by such organizations as the Manhattan Institute, the American Tort Reform Association (ATRA), the Association of Public-Safety Communications Officials (APCO), and locally based Citizens against Lawsuit Abuse (CALA) groups. Funding for these organizations came from insurance companies, large corporations, and "wealthy individual patrons and foundations that traditionally have supported conservative, pro-business causes, including the John Olin Foundation, the Sarah Scaife Foundation, and the Starr Foundation" (Haltom and McCann 2004: 46). A massive advertising campaign in the 1980s and 1990s disseminated the anti-claiming viewpoint in clear and simple terms. This campaign was so successful that a majority of Americans still believe its erroneous assertions about hyper-litigious Americans to be based in fact.

The so-called "tort reform" movement became highly politicized. Its positions were adopted, primarily but not exclusively, by political conservatives and figured prominently in political campaigns. At the same time, voices on the other side of the policy debate were weak or ineffectual in their impact on popular culture. Referring to the pro-plaintiff American Trial Lawyers Association, Haltom and McCann entitle one of their chapters, "ATLA Shrugged." The mass media playing field came to be dominated by ideas and images associated with a highly critical view of personal injury claimants, and the contrary view began to seem indefensible.

The politics of tort reform have had a powerful impact on the new common sense about claiming and lumping in our society. Tort reformers have been far more savvy and effective in their media strategies than those who speak for injury victims. Their success goes a long way to explain why our social and cultural environment is so supportive of lumping and so skeptical about claiming.

Once cultural frameworks of this kind become well entrenched, they affect Americans' thoughts and choices even at the nonconscious level. Although the dominant perspective on injuries reflects the interests of those against whom claims might be asserted, it paradoxically influences the cognition of those who are injured as well. Even when it might be in the victims' interest to bring a claim, they often adopt the tort reformers' "personal responsibility" ideology, and they support the belief that our society suffers from too many claims. In short, injury victims tend to share the position that upstanding citizens, those who are not greedy or selfish, should simply lump their losses or settle for minimal compensation (Greenhouse et al. 1994). And they respond to their mishaps by joining the vast majority who refrain from lodging a claim against their injurers.

Furthermore, because the anti-claiming ideology of "personal responsibility" has become so pervasive in American culture, it is likely that influential third parties will reinforce the victims' inclination to lump. Most people consult with friends and family before making major life decisions, and even those who decide alone are swayed by the anticipated approval or disapproval of those with whom they interact. It is highly probable that these third parties will, in any given injury case, reflect the majority view – that claiming in personal injury cases is socially unacceptable. Moreover, those who are close to the victim may want to shield him or her from the social opprobrium a claim might evoke, as well as the stress, anxiety, and uncertainty associated with the legal process.

Thus, the individual who lives in a culture that generally disapproves of personal injury claims is much less likely to claim than to lump. In countless ways, cultural images that discourage claiming can influence the thoughts and actions of injury victims. These cultural factors provide powerful explanations for the predominance of lumping in American society.

CONCLUSION

I began by asking why lumping and not claiming is the predominant response to injury in American society. Why is it, in other words, that the vast majority of injury victims respond to the harm they have suffered by absorbing the costs and consequences without making any sort of claim against the injurer? As we have seen, lumping is even more widespread than we thought. That is because so many injuries go uncounted, and in such cases no claim is typically made or even imagined. The concept of injury itself is a moving target, socially constructed in ways that make lumping all but inevitable.

Commentators have tended to assume that the decision to claim, as opposed to lumping, is made consciously by individuals who weigh the costs and benefits of seeking a remedy from their injurer. The prevalence of lumping, in other words, is usually thought to result from deliberate choices made by fully aware individuals. But this understanding of perception and decision-making by injury victims now seems inadequate. Furthermore, conventional models have failed to problematize the concept of injury itself and have seldom considered how it is that so many painful and debilitating life experiences come to be viewed as no one's fault, as natural, and even as beneficial.

Injury is a social and cultural construct, not a fact of nature, and a closer examination of the ways in which we construct injuries helps to explain the prevalence of lumping rather than claiming. I began by discussing "beneficial pain," incidents that some might in theory view as injuries but, because of historical, religious, medical, and other framings, Americans instead tend to view as eufunctional and not harmful. Despite the criticism of recent activists, few people, even today, would consider the millions of infants who undergo male circumcision to have suffered injuries. Although this sort of painful experience may someday be viewed as an injury — perhaps even an actionable injury — as of today most people tend to perceive the practice as no more than a normal medical procedure or religious ritual. If we don't see the injury, we don't even notice that lumping has occurred.

Other painful experiences are indeed considered injuries, but are nevertheless lumped because they appear to the victim — and to nearly everyone else — as natural occurrences. These injuries are explained as the normal and inevitable result of human interaction with the physical environment — with the chairs, stairs, and automobiles that are a daily part of our lives. But, as we have seen, many of these seemingly "natural" injuries could indeed have been made less serious or averted altogether. From a different and more critical perspective, therefore, it becomes clear that the risk of harm in many instances is not really inherent in our physical surroundings. Often designers and manufacturers actually recognize and weigh the risks.

Their intentional decisions to embed those risks in their products or services, however, remain invisible. The resulting injuries appear to be natural or unavoidable, when in fact the means to prevent them may be close at hand. And finally, even when injury victims do conclude that they have been wronged by another person or corporation, they are deterred from taking action by the psychology of self-blame and by a widely-shared hostility to claiming in their social and cultural surroundings.

It follows, then, that lumping is the default response by most injured Americans, and tort law is therefore playing an even more marginal role than we might have thought. This chapter has suggested six reasons why lumping predominates in injury cases. If valid, this analysis casts serious doubt on tort law's capacity to provide compensation, deterrence, loss distribution, and moral justice to injury victims – either directly or through its shadow effects. If, among the millions of Americans who suffer injuries each year, few claims are ever asserted against the injurers, tort law's promise has failed – not only through the efforts of conservative tort reformers, but through broader processes of social construction. The belief that American tort law can reduce injuries and provide justice may be nothing more than a comforting myth.

References

Baker, Tom. (2005). *The Medical Malpractice Myth*. Chicago: University of Chicago Press.

Beecher, Henry K. (1946). "Pain in Men Wounded in Battle." *Annals of Surgery* 123:96–105.

Bendelow, Gillian and Simon Williams. (1995). "Pain and the Mind–Body Dualism: A Sociological Approach." *Body and Society* 1:83–103.

Berlin, Stuart M. (1989). "From the Jewish Journal: Don't Fear 'Brit Milah.'" *Berit Milah Newsletter* October 6.

Blake, C. Fred. (1994). "Foot-Binding in Neo-Confucian China and the Appropriation of Female Labor." *Signs* 19:676–712.

Buckley, John P., Duane D. Mellor, Michael Morris, and Franklin Joseph. (2013). "Standing-Based Office Work Shows Encouraging Signs of Attenuating Post-Prandial Glycaemic Excursion." *Occupational and Environmental Medicine* 71:109–11.

Chang, Jung. (2003). *Wild Swans: Three Daughters of China*. New York: Simon and Schuster.

Cohen, H. Harvey. (2000). "A Field Study of Stair Descent." *Ergonomics in Design: The Quarterly of Human Factors Applications* 8:11–15.

Cohen, Joseph, Cindy A. LaRue, and H. Harvey Cohen. (2009). "Stairway Falls: An Ergonomics Analysis of 80 Cases." *Professional Safety* January:27–32.

Cook, Douglas H. (2004). "A Faith-Based Perspective on Tort Causation." *St. Thomas Law Review* 16:455–67.

Cranz, Galen. (1998). *The Chair: Rethinking Culture, Body, and Design*. New York: W.W. Norton.

Davis, Dena S. (2001). "Male and Female Genital Alteration: A Collision Course with the Law?" *Health Matrix: Journal of Law–Medicine* 11:487–570.

Engel, David M. (1984). "The Oven Bird's Song: Insiders, Outsiders, and Personal Injuries in an American Community." *Law and Society Review* 18:551–82.

——— (2016). *Why We Don't Sue: Injuries and the Non-Litigious American*. Chicago: University of Chicago Press.

FitzGerald, Jeffrey. (1983). "Grievances, Disputes and Outcomes: A Comparison of Australia and the United States." *Law in Context* 1:15–45.

Galanter, Marc. (1974). "Why the 'Haves' Come Out Ahead: Speculations on the Limits of Legal Change." *Law and Society Review* 9(1):95–160.

Genn, Hazel. (1999). *Paths to Justice: What People Do and Think About Going to Law*. Portland, OR: Hart Publishing.

Gergen, Kenneth J. (2009). *Relational Being: Beyond Self and Community*. New York: Oxford University Press.

Greenhouse, Carol J., Barbara Yngvesson, and David M. Engel. (1994). *Law and Community in Three American Towns*. Ithaca, NY: Cornell University Press.

Haltom, William and Michael McCann. (2004). *Distorting the Law: Politics, Media, and the Litigation Crisis*. Chicago: University of Chicago Press.

Hensler, Deborah R., M. Susan Marquis, Allan F. Abrahamse, et al. (1991). *Compensation for Accidental Injuries in the United States*. Santa Monica, CA: RAND.

Howe, P. David. (2001). "An Ethnography of Pain and Injury in Professional Rugby Union." *International Review for the Sociology of Sport* 36:289–303.

Hurwitz, David, Anuj Pradhan, Donald L. Fisher, et al. (2010). "Backing Collisions: A Study of Drivers' Eye and Backing Behaviour Using Combined Rear-View Camera and Sensor Systems." *Injury Prevention* 16:79–84.

Jackson, Jean E. (2011). "Pain and Bodies." In *A Companion to the Anthropology of the Body and Embodiment*, edited by Frances E. Mascia-Lees. Chichester, UK: Wiley-Blackwell.

Jain, Sarah S. Lochlann. (2006). *Injury: The Politics of Product Design and Safety Law in the United States*. Princeton, NJ: Princeton University Press.

Kritzer, Herbert M., W. A. Bogart, and Neil Vidmar. (1991). "The Aftermath of Injury: Cultural Factors in Compensation Seeking in Canada and the United States." *Law and Society Review* 25:499–543.

Levine, James. (2014). "Killer Chairs." *Scientific American* 311:34–5.

Levy, Howard S. (1966). *Chinese Footbinding: The History of a Curious Erotic Custom*. New York: Walton Rawls.

National Safety Council. (2014). *Injury Facts*. Itasca, IL: National Safety Council.

Office of Regulatory Analysis and Evaluation, National Center for Statistics and Analysis, National Highway Traffic Safety Administration. (2014). "Backover Crash Avoidance Technologies." FMVSS No. 111, *Final Regulatory Impact Analysis*, U.S. Department of Transportation.

Pauls, J. L. (1991). "Safety Standards, Requirements, and Litigation in Relation to Building Use and Safety, Especially Safety from Falls Involving Stairs." *Safety Science* 14:125–54.

Saks, Michael J. (1992). "Do We Really Know Anything About the Behavior of the Tort Litigation System – And Why Not?" *University of Pennsylvania Law Review* 140:1147–292.

Schulz, Richard and Susan Decker. (1985). "Long-Term Adjustment to Physical Disability: The Role of Social Support, Perceived Control and Self-Blame." *Journal of Personality and Social Psychology* 48:1162–72.

Waldeck, Sarah E. (2003). "Using Male Circumcision to Understand Social Norms as Multipliers." *University of Cincinnati Law Review* 71:455–526.

Wright, Beatrice A. (1983). *Physical Disability – A Psychosocial Approach*, 2nd ed. New York: Harper and Row.

CHAPTER SIX

INCOMMENSURABILITY AND POWER IN CONSTRUCTING THE MEANING OF INJURY AT THE MEDICAL MALPRACTICE DISPUTES

Yoshitaka Wada

INTRODUCTION

In every culture, the meaning of injury is socially constructed and extends beyond personal physical pain. First, injury always contains emotional or psychological dimensions, involving sorrow, grief and anger. Second, it is not excusive to the person actually injured, and extends to socially connected people, including family, friends and so on. When a loved one is injured or killed, the pain, grief and anger are naturally shared with them. Third, injury involves people who contribute to its emergence. In this sense, injury is constructed as a social event and people defined as wrongdoers also face another kind of injury. In all of these dimensions, social constructions of injury result from a complicated struggle among a variety of discursive powers and narratives. In this chapter, we examine the construction of injury in a medical malpractice death case, including how the injury was constructed in each actor's everyday world and how the political struggles over the injury's meaning took place in courtroom interactions.

Several different narratives come together in a conflicting manner during the process of dispute resolution after a medical accident. In particular, when the accident requires complicated evaluations from an expert point of view, we often face a deep chasm between the lay victim's construction of the meaning of injury and that of physicians and other healthcare professionals involved in the case. A lay victim's construction of the meaning of injury takes place in relation to their family history and everyday life. For example, the death of a family member means the eternal loss of an irreplaceable person, whereas the same death can often be a statistical fact from the physician's point of view. Here we find a kind of incommensurability (Kuhn 1962) that tends to heighten the conflict between them.[1]

Law and the legal system can be understood as a project to bridge the chasm by providing acceptable fair resolutions to both parties from neutral positions based on legal norms. However, law itself is nothing but an external discourse for both the lay person whose injury is embedded in his or her everyday life and for the specialist, whose perspective is based on expert medical knowledge. As a result, we find another layer of incommensurability of discourses in relationships between law and both parties' perceptions. Incommensurability in the construction of meaning, thus, can be observed in two dimensions: First, the chasm of the meaning of the accident between a lay victim and a healthcare professional and, second, the chasm between the legal discourse and both parties.

In the complicated intersections of the different narratives, we can find not only a conflict of perspectives, but also the formation of political power and dominance embedded in the disputing process. As long as the incommensurability cannot be overcome, power will take center stage, although tacitly, in the process of resolving conflicts that stem from different perspectives and narratives. In a courtroom, legal discourse dominates other discourses in the process of constructing the meaning of injury. Even in alternative dispute resolution (ADR) or private negotiation, legal discourse has an indirect but strong influence on parties' construction of reality and, of course, the third party's view.[2] However, it is also true that the direct, simple narratives of victims or scientific narratives of expert physicians implicitly infiltrate into legal discourse. Here, we observe a more complicated and often ambivalent process at work in mobilizing power in courtrooms, as legal discourse can work, on the one hand, as a tool to enhance parties' positions, but, on the other hand, as a dominating power to suppress their original narrative.

---

[1] In the philosophy of science Thomas Kuhn and Paul Feyerabend introduced the concept of "incommensurability" in the 1960s, which was originally invented in Greek mathematics. Generally, it means there is no common measure to evaluate or compare conceptions among different theoretical paradigms.

[2] In Japan, even in ADR and the process of mediation, mediators suggest and persuade their settlement proposal referring to legal norms. Although parties can reject it, the process is much more like arbitration than facilitative mediation.

This chapter examines how the incommensurability of perceptions produces and enhances conflicts after an accident happens, the ambivalent role that law takes in this process, the power struggles that take place in dispute resolution processes, and what strategies can work in this context by looking closely at a particular medical malpractice case.

THE STRUCTURE OF NARRATIVE AND THE POWER OF ALLEGORY: THEORETICAL FRAMEWORK

The Positioned Self and the New Concept of Universality

When we try to understand the meanings of discourse or narratives, we should keep in mind that understandings always take place as an interpretation by "the positioned subject." The interpretation of some discourse or narrative is without exception colored by a particular inclination of the positioned or situated subject (Sandel 1982)[3] that has been constructed through her or his concrete experiences in the everyday world. This implies two things. On the one hand, interpretation by the positioned subject continuously produces differences depending on the particular situation and time. On the other hand, in spite of this fluctuation, we can find that some universality stemming from human experience is embedded in the self, though it is considered to be made up of numerous concentric layers of community where her or his experiences take place. We should know that we may overlook the power of feelings and emotion contained in narratives if we insist on the Western conception of "transcendental universality" and the position of "objective observer" without a concrete situation. It is when we listen to the local voice of people as a positioned self – constructed from concrete experiences – that we can catch the exact universality embedded in human experiences and its narratives.

These arguments lead us to new conceptions of "universality." It is the power of emotions stemming from the unexpected death of a loved one that makes us understand the other person's narrative on injury. This "power" embedded in human experiences and its narratives seems to reach human emotion or feeling directly. We may find an alternative source for new concepts of universality in the "power" rooted in particular local human experiences. Rejecting neither transcendental

---

[3] Sandel describes a concept of the "radically situated self" as constituted by community attachments and principles, unlike the "unencumbered self," who is detached from any community and has no attachments.

universality nor skeptical relativism, we can still look for universality among positioned subjects who live in a different local-life world by introducing the dimension of "power" of emotional feeling embedded in human experiences and its narratives.

If we take the above arguments seriously, a researcher should listen to voices, interpret narratives and read discourses about experiences of unexpected death not by pretending to be an objective observer, but as a particular individual who is also a positioned subject in some culture.

In the field of law, again, lay people's narratives are interpreted through a transcendental legal point of view and their voices seem to be eliminated in formal legal discourse in courts. However, as I have already pointed out, disputants' voices often successfully resist and intrude implicitly into the meanings of legal discourse. How is it possible that everyday narratives intrude into and construct in part the meaning of "universal" legal language?

To answer this question, we refer to arguments on the concept of allegory in the field of ethnography.

An Allegory and the Structure of Narratives

James Clifford, an anthropologist, examines the concept of allegory in ethnography, referring to critical discussions in literature (Clifford 1986). According to him, allegory denotes a practice in which a narrative fiction continuously refers to another pattern of ideas or events. He wrote that any story has a propensity to generate another story in the mind of its reader (or hearer), to repeat and displace some prior story. In other words, when reading or listening to a story, readers and listeners always interpret it and construct their own version of a story referring to their life experiences. If we feel sympathy with an injured person's grief and anger, we are, at the same time, recalling and displacing our own experiences. This is nothing but a function of allegory embedded in particular narratives.

Here we can again find a way to universality evoked by allegory in narratives. It may be said that the power of emotional feeling, as a source for human universal understandings, is transmitted through the work of allegory and is contained in local voices and narratives.

Let me note some additional points of allegory, in order to examine the relationship between legal language and everyday narratives. In the first place, the work of allegory occurs not only in the content of text, but also in the form of it. When we examine narratives appearing in a court, which is regarded as an unusual place organized by unfamiliar authoritative local rules, it is important to take account of the allegorical function of the form of narratives as well as their content.

Moreover, these allegorical functions are always related to the dimension of discursive or nondiscursive power. An ethnography cannot escape from the moral and political problems that lie in the power relationships. When we examine the narratives and their allegories in a court, this political dimension, including the dominance of legal language, should be given proper attention.

Thus, through the examination of the allegorical function of narratives, we can understand the mechanism by which we can reach and feel sympathy with human universality by carefully reading and listening to the voice of a positioned subject in the local narrative.

Relationships between legal discourse and everyday narratives should be regarded not as a simple confrontation, but as a complicated reflective one in which, through the work of allegory, each discourse may intrude into and implicitly construct each other.

THE MEANING AND POLITICS OF INJURY IN MEDICAL MALPRACTICE

Medical Malpractice Litigation in Japan

Medical malpractice is a typical area in which multiple voices rooted in parties' everyday discourses encounter and reconstruct each other in a conflicting manner. Although medical malpractice litigation in Japan has recently increased rapidly, it is still at a very low level compared with the United States: around 800 cases per year.[4] Generally speaking, because of the extremely small number of lawyers (about 30,000) and their high fees, Japanese people refrain from using courts.

Moreover, the likelihood of patients winning their case was between 20 and 40 percent in the last decade, although it was between 80 and 90 percent in other categories of civil action. In this situation, a lot of medical malpractice accidents must be concealed and, even if the patient's side suspects its possibility, most of them have no option other than to give up.

---

[4] The highest number of cases of medical malpractice litigation in Japan is 1,110 in 2004. Although the number is small compared to that in the United States, physicians are members of an exceptional profession who think about the possibility of being involved in lawsuits among a general Japanese populace who never consider the possibility.

However, even with this difficulty, some patients and their families do bring their case to court. What makes them sue? It is certain that those litigants construct their own ideas on the accident from their everyday point of view, which may quite often be inconsistent with the legal definition of the case. After bringing the case to court, they usually have to begin another struggle with another kind of professional knowledge and practice. Here is a case in which a young boy unexpectedly died from a medical malpractice accident and his parents had to fight with both doctors and legal professionals.

The Patient and Family's Construction of the Meaning of Medical Injury

When facing medically adverse events like death or serious injury, patients and their family members are thrown into deep sorrow and the stable realities of their everyday lives sometimes suddenly collapse. Although each case has its own particular aspects and history, the shared story of the loss of a loved one, which is repeatedly shown in literature, movies or other popular media, follows a framework to construct the reality they are faced with and gives shape to their amorphous emotion. On the basis of this story of the loss of a loved one, they construct a more complicated reality concerning adverse medical events and injury that makes the meaning of injury change from a personal event of pain and grief to an event that must be socially addressed.

In Japan, where mobilizing lawsuits still leaves a negative impression, families tend to construct a reality which excessively emphasizes grief and blame on physicians without referring to compensation. Here, there can be incommensurability within their own narratives.

Healthcare Professionals' Construction of the Meaning of Medical Injury

Healthcare professionals are also faced with emotional confusion immediately after an adverse event, such as a patient's death. Here we find a variety of stories that influence their construction of reality that again embraces contradiction and conflicts. First of all, as professionals, they understand the event from the perspective of medical expertise, in which death is not a particular event but a statistical reality. From this viewpoint, the relationship between the medical treatment taken and the result could be recognized as the effect of complications, which may be perceived as nothing but a result of negligence from the family's lay perspective.

In addition, healthcare professionals' everyday narrative consists of a particular professional cognitive framework. Their perspective contains the limits and risks of medical care, and death can be a part of their everyday life. The death of an irreplaceable loved one for a family is just the death of one patient among many, even though the event may also cause the physicians' pain.

The personal feelings of a physician may often contradict organizational guidelines that prescribe the action to be taken after a serious adverse event. Here we can find different voices and incommensurability in healthcare professionals' construction of reality.

Legal Discourse: The Effort to Overcome Incommensurability or the Power Game

Incommensurability can, of course, be found between a patient's reality and a physician's. Based on and influenced by different cognitive frameworks of dominant discourses, it is extremely difficult for both sides to jointly construct a common or coordinated recognition of the reality of events that took place and the meaning of the injury that resulted.

Here legal discourse can be viewed as a mediating tool to overcome the incommensurability. However, here again we find incommensurability between the legal discourse and a patient's or a physician's perspective. Among this complicated interaction of different discourses, we also find a power relationship – domination and subordination – in the process of meaning making. In many aspects, legal discourse not only dominates physicians' viewpoints, but also suppresses patients' everyday voices. Actually, legal discourse has already penetrated implicitly into a patient's or physician's recognitions of injury and events in different ways.

However, under this incommensurability, weak voices sometimes intrude into the content of stronger narratives. These struggles among voices can be heard in a room at a hospital just after an adverse event or in a conversation in a courtroom.

LEGAL DISCOURSE AND EVERYDAY NARRATIVE IN A MEDICAL MALPRACTICE CASE

The Case

On the evening of January 19, 1994, returning home by motorcycle, Masaki, a seventeen-year-old high-school student, crashed into an illegally parked freight truck and was struck hard in his face and abdomen. He was immediately taken to hospital by ambulance. When checking the X-ray and CT scans that were taken the next day, two doctors could not find the shadow of gas, which later turned out to be decisive evidence of the rupture of the duodenum, and thought it was just a bruise. They told the parents that there was nothing to worry about. On the same day, when Masato vomited blood and his mother asked if an internal organ was damaged, doctors said that it was a nosebleed. After that, without considering the possibility of the rupture of an internal organ, doctors gave him just pain relief, and three days later allowed him to eat. A couple of days later, Masato's white blood cell count increased rapidly and his temperature climbed. On January 25, doctors took another X-ray, but again they overlooked a shadow of gas, or at least did not take it seriously.

It was not until January 27 that one of the doctors began to suspect the possibility of rupture of the enteric canal, and he performed an X-ray examination with an imaging agent. Finding that the imaging agent was coming out of the duodenum, the doctor was first to notice that the duodenum was ruptured. Immediately, an abdominal operation was carried out, but it was too late. Masato suffered excruciating pain that became worse and worse. Although the doctors tried to persuade his parents to have another operation on January 31, the parents had already lost their trust and moved him to another hospital. Masato passed away on February 3.

Although his parents tried to obtain a persuasive explanation for their son's unexpected death from those doctors and the hospital, their answer and attitude was far from satisfactory and only made them angry. For the parents, the most important thing was to know why their young son had to die in order to give some positive meaning to his untimely death. To overcome the anger of grief, the parents needed to do something. Suspecting the possibility of medical malpractice, they finally brought the case to a lawyer, who was well known in medical malpractice litigation.

The lawyer immediately obtained all the related documents, including X-ray photographs, following pre-litigation legal procedure and found that a shadow of gas in one of the X-rays could be strong evidence for their side to prove the doctors' medical malpractice. She sued the doctors and the hospital.

The lawyer's legal definition of the case and her strategy were appropriate and efficient. The litigation process seemed to proceed as usual

INCOMMENSURABILITY AND POWER

as per legal professions in the court. This could be another rare medical malpractice case in which the patient's side would unquestionably win. However, for the parents, the lawyer's documents, filled with objective descriptions of the accident and legal terms, never reflected the "reality" and "truth" of their unfortunate experience. They requested the lawyer submit some documents that had been written by them and used everyday narratives about the unexpected death of their young son. Although the lawyer accepted their request, a couple of times, she finally rejected submitting it to the court. It is said that judges do not like to receive too many documents written by disputants themselves, because they usually contain too many things that have no bearing within a legal framework and are quite often a waste of time to read.

When the lawyer began to recommend conciliation, the parents made the decision to dismiss her. They wanted to fight using their own version of the case in court, and acceptance of conciliation would make them lose that opportunity. The parents dismissed the lawyer and paid 2,000,000 yen ($16,000). After that, they did everything themselves, including cross-examination without lawyers. They submitted a lot of documents filled with the parent's voices and narratives on the experience of the unexpected death of a loved one. Finally, on January 31, 1997, they won the case.

In this case, we can find a severe conflict between the lawyer's perspective, constructed from a legal and strategic point of view, and the parents' interpretation of the case, defined from the position as "parents who lost their young beloved son." In the rest of this chapter, I will examine this conflict in interpretation of the case, the interrelationship between everyday narratives and legal discourse after dismissal of the lawyer, and the defendant's lawyer's strategy and discourse, pointing out the function of allegory. I will refer to documents of the case, my own interview with the parents, and the lawyer's and mother's narratives, which appeared in a TV program (a documentary made because this case was unique in that the parents were able to win without lawyers in a difficult medical malpractice case).

Dominance of Legal Discourse

For a while, after the case was brought to court, litigation proceeded smoothly as usual, through exchange of legal documents that were adequately constituted from a legal point of view. Although we can find a few passages and words that contain evaluation based on everyday values, such as "promising young boy," most parts of the plaintiff lawyer's documents consisted of "objective" and efficient descriptions of the case. The defense lawyer's documents also focused efficiently on the legal issue of doctors' negligence, mobilizing medical jargon. Masato's death was almost perfectly positioned in the professional, scientific, objective languages of law and medicine. Masato's voice, as well as his parent's voices, was almost erased in the professional discourse.

The plaintiff lawyer's strategy was to reach a conciliation agreement as soon as possible and obtain advantageous compensation, because she truly believed it was the most desirable outcome for victims of medical malpractice cases. One reason why she preferred conciliation was that, even if they won the case finally, the defendants would appeal and the litigation would last for many years. In an interview for the TV program she said: "I think it meets the objective interest of litigants to settle the case as soon as possible. In a civil action, what the litigants can get is limited to monetary compensation. So, it meets the clients' interest to obtain the biggest monetary compensation as quick as possible without a burden on them."

Even if this plaintiff lawyer's strategy, sincerely thinking about the client's interest, is adequate and "objectively advantageous" from the legal profession's point of view, it could not persuade the parents, who were fighting another dispute caused by their young son's unexpected death. Because of this gap of perspective, the parents wanted to submit their own documents, filled with everyday narratives.

Now let me briefly examine the allegory in legal language. As long as this grammar of legal language itself has been developed from and constructed of numerous previous concrete cases of accidental death, it may to some extent contain an allegorical function about grief and anger. However, it is too abstract and technological to admit the work of allegory.

First, in order to accept it as allegory, we usually need some more concrete and rich discourse or narratives. Just as we cannot sympathetically feel the anger of grief of an Ilongot man when we read an explanation of headhunting customs from exchange theory, we cannot feel the allegorical function only from a technological legal discourse detached from everyday life.

Second, the legal language was united with another kind of allegorical effect – that is to say, the forms and content of legal language that make it necessary for lay people to be helped and led by legal professionals, who impress us with the story of "sincere remedy for the weak by the legal profession." Of course, this sincere story is, at the same time, very oppressive. Moreover, legal language itself implies the story of "social ordering with law." Accepting this power of allegorical function, most lay people in the courts usually never object to it and their own voices are oppressed and eliminated.

Voices and Narratives of Victims

When the parents' intention to carry out the litigation contradicted the lawyer's strategy to settle the case by conciliation, they dismissed the lawyer. This point in the litigation process was filled with everyday narratives, though taking account of and loosely shaped by legal language. Here, let me pick up some topics on which their narratives developed and examine the relationship between those topics and the allegory of "unexpected death of a loved one." Those three topics are (a) the purpose of litigation, (b) the doctors' behavior and responsibility and (c) the dismissal of their lawyer.

The Purpose of Litigation

According to the grammar of legal language, the purpose of medical malpractice litigation is to claim monetary compensation. For the parents this legal definition is, of course, too narrow. There is a deep gap between a lawyer's idea of the "objective best interest for a client – that is, quick recovery of monetary compensation" and the parents' version of the "best solution." We can find their narratives on the purpose of litigation in documents submitted by them and in cross-examination.

> Please understand that we thought seriously before we made the decision to sue. We will not compromise easily and will fight it out until we can clarify the malpractice. We think it will contribute to prevent another medical malpractice accident. This litigation is not only for us, but for our people and society. (Plaintiff document no. 4)
>
> I trusted doctors. I believed they would save my son's life. But my son lost his life because of medical malpractice and I feel Masato's deep sorrow caused this unreasonable fate. I decided to sue, in order to know what happened to my son, why he had to die. (Cross-examination)
>
> We do not mind how long it takes, how much money it costs, we will fight until our opinion will be admitted to be right. This is the crusade for my son. (Plaintiff document no. 6)

These narratives are found more or less commonly among the victims of some accidents. We can derive a variety of interpretations from these narratives, listening to sometimes too fierce a voice of anger, because they can be united with some different allegories. For example, we can hear the voice of grieving parents who have unexpectedly lost their beloved son, based on the allegory implying a story of a parent–child relationship. On reading fierce words like "crusade for my son," some may hear the voice of parents who have lost reason and have become occupied by hate and hostility. Or others may feel that words like "in order to know what happened" or "this litigation is not only for us, but for our people and society" seem just to be excuses, and their true purpose of litigation must solely be monetary compensation.

In fact, the defense lawyer seemed to construct this image of a greedy plaintiff. He wrote: "Quite often plaintiffs in medical malpractice cases lack the intention and attitude to pursue the objective truth and are guided by the greedy principle of behavior to maximize the compensation" (Defendant document no. 6).

However, "the greedy principle of behavior to maximize the compensation" is more appropriately applied to a lawyer's "strategy in tort litigation" and their idea of "objective best interest" than lay litigants' consciousness. Even if lay litigants appear greedy to maximize the compensation, the grammar of legal language in court, which limited the content of solutions to monetary compensation, imposes it forcefully on lay people, for whom monetary compensation is not the main purpose.

Moreover, as for the image of "the litigants who lost reason and are occupied by hate and hostility," we can say that the structure of an adversarial system and the grammar of legal language, in which process moves by exchange of attack and defense, forces litigants to be excessively hostile. If the parents' narratives indicate that they had lost reason, the above-mentioned defense lawyer's words also imply that he had lost his temper to the same extent. These fierce words may be tactical.

Anyway, here we have found that there can be multiple interpretations of the plaintiff's purpose in suing. Can we regard the parents' words as sincere and serious in their purpose? Should we interpret them as greedy, as the defendant's lawyer pointed out? Do the parents lose their reason because of the fierce feeling of hostility? We cannot decide which interpretation is appropriate here. I think the judges in this case were faced with the same problem we were faced with when they read and listened to the parents' narratives. In order to solve this problem, we need to examine narratives on other topics.

Physicians' Behavior

As the possibility of negligence in finding the rupture of the duodenum was a critical point in the grammar of law, narratives on the doctors' behavior had important effects on the result of the case. The critical issue was whether the doctors should have found the rupture of the duodenum from the X-ray with the shadow of gas and Masato's appearance. The defense lawyer submitted plenty of medical documents and described Masato's appearance as follows:

> The patient had never severely complained about abdominal pain. The patient's abdominal pain was not strong enough to require an operation. (Defendant document no. 2)
>
> The patient's abdominal pain had been consistently limited to a controllable level. After January 20, it gradually changed to just a feeling of abdominal distension (Defendant document no. 6)

Next, let us listen to the mother's voice on their son's situation.

> Throughout the night Masato suffered terribly, bending his body like a prawn. I made a call to the nurse's station three times around four o'clock. But only a doctor of cerebral surgery came to us. (Cross-examination)
>
> As Masato vomited blood, I asked a doctor many times as to the possibility of rupture of an internal organ. But he answered I had no need to worry about it, and that it was just an abdominal bruise. According to the defendant's document, my son had never complained about pain. It is not true. It was recorded every day in his medical chart and the nurse's record that my son had suffered from abdominal pain. I heard Masato always complained about the pain. (Plaintiff document no. 1)

The mother's voice, speaking based on her own experience, seemed to shift the focus of the court from the exchange of attack and defense. That is to say, discourse on the possibility of negligence in the court had transformed from medical scientific language to the everyday narrative of Masato's bedside scenes. Litigation that proceeded through the quiet exchange of legal and medical knowledge and language by lawyers, who were both familiar with medical malpractice cases, was now intruded on by the particular local voice of parents based on their everyday knowledge and experiences once their plaintiff's lawyer was dismissed. The defendant's scientific medical explanation, which was filled with medical jargon, did not seem as impressive as the mother's narratives of experience, which described her son, who suffered terribly after having his body bent like a prawn. Judgment as to medical issues is difficult because, in many cases, scientific medical knowledge does not give a clear answer, especially in the process of litigation when both sides try to emphasize the advantageous interpretation of medical opinions. Thus, even if the medical discourse is not necessarily reliable, the allegory of the parent–child story based on the experience of the unexpected death of their son may have some impact, even in court.

Dismissal of the Lawyer
The parents wrote about why they dismissed their lawyer.

> We thought again and again and reached the conclusion that it will be riskier to continue to be represented by the lawyer. There are many reasons. The lawyer who should be just a representative of us did not accept our demand adequately. Sometimes we felt that she was full of pride and too dogmatic as a legal expert. We suspected she had some hidden relationship with the defense lawyer and judges. As a result of all of this, we can not trust her any more. (Plaintiff document no. 6)
>
> My lawyer said that as we rejected the conciliation, she had to prove every legal issue including doctors' negligence and we returned to the starting point. (Plaintiff document no. 20)

The plaintiff's lawyer must have thought that conciliation would have given the parents the "objective best interest," and rejected their own documents filled with legally irrelevant narratives, which judges do not welcome. As long as the monetary compensation principle is taken for granted, obeying the grammar of legal language, the plaintiff's lawyer's judgment and behavior was adequate. However, the plaintiff's lawyer's behavior, which seems to be "adequate" for the legal profession, was "inadequate" for lay litigants.

This suggests that the problem lies not in the plaintiff's lawyer's behavior in the case, but in the grammar of legal language and its oppressive function. This point was made clear in the defense lawyer's words just after the dismissal of the plaintiff lawyer.

> After we dismissed the lawyer, who understands legal issues, the significance of the conciliation agreement and the defendant's sincere intention, the court process was confused by the plaintiffs. Although they submitted numerous documents, most of them were irrelevant to legal issues and they do not understand the difference between maintaining the facts and proving them. (Defendant document no. 6)

In his discourse, the grammar of legal language was taken for granted and he completely denied the significance of the narratives of the plaintiffs, who did not have legal knowledge. It was these points, which were denied or said to be irrelevant by the defense lawyer, that had critical importance for the lay plaintiffs. But both the plaintiffs' lawyer and the defense lawyer, accepting the common sense of the legal profession that litigation should be performed with legal expertise, tried to oppress the everyday definition of the problem. It is symbolic that, in the above-mentioned words by the defense lawyer, when the dismissed plaintiffs' lawyer was referred to, the polite form of expression was used in original Japanese. Here, we can find an allegory that implies the story of "hidden domination over lay people by expertise." Moreover, the defense lawyer seems to try to provoke the allegory of "greedy tort litigation plaintiff."

On the contrary, there is a possibility that this dismissal of the lawyer may indicate the lay litigants' sincerity, because it means they had something to do in court, even taking the risk of dismissing a famous expert lawyer in the medical malpractice field.

Here again we cannot tell what interpretation is appropriate as to the plaintiffs' decision to dismiss the lawyer. How are we to read or listen to their narratives for the purpose of litigation? The doctors' behavior and the dismissal of their lawyer seems to depend on another level of allegory embedded in their voice and narratives. Before we examine this, let's take a look at the defense lawyer's strategy as well.

The Defense Lawyer's Strategy
At the first stage of litigation, the defendant's discourse was almost exclusively occupied with a plain description of the facts and scientific medical language related to the legal issues. But after the dismissal of the plaintiff's lawyer and the emergence of the lay plaintiffs' voices in the court, the defense lawyer began to respond critically to them. As I have already mentioned, he oppressively criticized the lay litigants' confusing narratives, mobilizing an ideal image of litigation as a forum for legal experts. In addition to this general criticism of the lay litigants' behavior, he tried more positively to construct a bad image of the plaintiff, provoking the allegory of the "greedy tort litigation plaintiff."

In fact, this image of "greed for money" always casts a shadow on plaintiffs in tort cases. Suing for compensation is often viewed and criticized as a behavior of getting money in exchange for the death or suffering of a loved one. In this sense, every plaintiff in a tort case is united with the allegory of "greed for money." The defense lawyer's strategy in our case also provokes it effectively.

Besides the direct expression, "guided by the greedy principle of behavior to maximize the compensation," said in order to construct the image of the "greedy plaintiff," the defense lawyer mobilized some supplementary information.

First, he pointed to the existence of the mother's brother, an ex-policeman, who helped to give advice to the plaintiffs in preparation for litigation. The defense lawyer seemed to imply that the man was the parents' backstage mastermind.

Second, the defense lawyer pointed out that the patient (Masato) rode a motorcycle, in spite of the fact that he was still a high school student – in Japan there are gangs of young, rough riders who neglect traffic rules. But in the case of Masato, he was officially permitted to ride a motorcycle by his school. The defense lawyer tried to imply that Masato's rough driving may have caused this unfortunate event.

Third, criticism of the dismissal of the lawyer, who recommended an amicable conciliation agreement, also contributed to the construction of the image of the "unreasonable and greedy plaintiff."

Although these narratives of the defense lawyer were not directly relevant to the legal issue, they were continually provoking an allegory to imply the story of the "objective neutral language of law," "fair litigation performance by legal experts" and the "unreasonable greedy tort plaintiff" by pointing out that the case was confused by unreasonable parents who wanted too much from the legal system.

Here again, whether this defense lawyer's strategy would be successful or not depended on the power of allegory that the lay plaintiffs' side unconsciously continued to provoke.

"Grief in the Unexpected Death of Loved One": The Allegory of the Parent–Child Tie

I pointed out that the plaintiffs' narratives as to "purpose of suing," "doctors' behavior" and "dismissal of lawyer" were open to different possibilities of interpretation. If the defense lawyer's strategy is successful, we may find unreasonably greedy parents and their excuse-ridden, tactical narratives. If the defense lawyer's strategy is ignored and we accept the parents' voices more positively, that is because we found the strong power of allegory embedded in their narratives coming from their particular experience.

In this case of medical malpractice, it is the allegory that provokes the story of "grief in the unexpected death of a loved one" and "parent–child tie."

> Masato often told me 'Mom, I do not like this hospital. Transfer me to another big hospital, please'. My son was so pitiful, his consciousness

INCOMMENSURABILITY AND POWER

had been clear until the moment of death. When we transferred to Saiseikai Hospital, it was too late. We had nothing to do for him. Just before dying, Masato made a sign with his fingers. Yes, he notified me that he was dying. (Plaintiff document no. 1)

Masato had been conscious until the last moment. He asked me to put water into his throat to clean up. He vomited it, following your (doctor's) instruction. A couple of hours after this, my son died, making a sign with his fingers. He was conscious even at the last moment. Can you imagine his suffering? (Cross-examination)

Even if you escape by lying, or even if the truth is revealed, my son will never come back. I have no word to express my grief as a parent who lost my beloved son. The only thing that will comfort us is if you tell us everything that happened in truth. (Cross-examination)

Although these narratives are based on the particular experience of Masato's mother, they give us "universal" understanding and sympathetic feelings through the strong power of allegory. In legal documents, we can see plain descriptions, such as "the patient died in Saiseikai Hospital" followed by lines of accounting compensation. Far beyond the effects of this legal language, readers or listeners will read or hear in local narratives both the voices of the particular parent's grief and some "universal," as well as their own, feelings.

This allegory of "grief in the unexpected death of a loved one" and the "parent–child tie" is the keystone for all the plaintiffs' narratives. By sharing this powerful allegory, readers find consistency and persuasiveness in their narratives on the "purpose of suing," "doctors' behavior" and the "dismissal of their lawyer" and also find not unreasonable, greedy plaintiffs, but rather sincere parents.

One more important point is that the cross-examination was performed by Masato's mother. This added the power of the allegory of the "mother–child tie" to their narratives. The power of allegory came not only from the content of their narratives, but also from the forms in which the narratives were presented. Although this allegory may be gender-biased, it is true that it can have power in Japanese society.

Thus, the keystone allegory of "grief in the unexpected death of a loved one" and the "parent–child tie" gives live meanings to all the plaintiffs' narratives. It should be noted that, on the contrary, the persuasiveness of the keystone allegory in turn depends on and is reinforced by each part of the narratives on "purpose of suing," "doctors' behavior" and "dismissal of lawyer." Allegory in narratives should be understood to have a reflexive character.

BRIDGING THE LEGAL DISCOURSE TO THE EVERYDAY NARRATIVE

In this chapter, I have pointed out that power of allegory embedded in the everyday narratives of positioned subjects has some effects on the court process, which is theoretically dominated by legal language. It is beyond my aim here to answer whether the power of allegory drove the judgment in this case or not. I add that the plaintiff finally won the case, in spite of the fact that only 20 to 40 percent of plaintiffs' medical malpractice cases are won in Japan.

This case suggests that the possibilities of interpreting the case may change if courts accept everyday narratives more flexibly. As long as the dominant position of legal language is taken for granted, the legal system will oppress the everyday understanding of life and not be responsive to lay people's needs.

For example, the image of "unreasonable, greedy litigants in medical malpractice cases" that the defense lawyer tried to invoke, is, in fact, constructed and imposed on litigants by the legal system itself, and limits the solution to monetary compensation. For the litigants, there is no other way than to claim for monetary compensation in order to bring the case to court, even if their purpose is different. If they try to pick up another nonlegal issue, the legal system rejects it as "irrelevant." If they adhere to the grammar of legal language and focus on the legal definition of monetary compensation, they may be regarded as an "unreasonable, greedy plaintiff." This is the dilemma. This criticism against tort litigants indicates the arrogance, oppressive power and contradiction of legal expertise. At the same time, it implies that even the "objective," "neutral," "fair" legal language of lawyers in fact always invokes some allegory, such as "greedy litigants." This is why lay litigants have to resist the oppressive power of legal language by introducing everyday narratives and voices into the courtroom, even though their effort is mostly blocked by their lawyers. The plaintiff in our case wrote:

> My son would have been saved if it was another hospital. Nobody can understand our feeling. Only a parent who has experience of losing a beloved child. Can you imagine how painful it is to count the damage in exchange for his life? Masato was only 17 years old. I cannot imagine how chagrined he felt. It is impossible to convert his life to monetary damage. (Cross-examination)

The grammar of the legal system including "the principle of monetary compensation" and "aggressive adversarial system" exercises discursive oppressive power against lay people. What we should do is to open the way and provide an opportunity to listen carefully to lay people's voices in the courtroom. It will make the litigation process richer, more responsive and more persuasive. Our plaintiff's words may be suggestive.

> We need the opportunity to explain my case. We would like to know what happened to my son and want their sincere apology. We do not want to finish our case with superficial monetary compensation. (Plaintiff document no. 4)

References

Clifford, James. (1986). "On Ethnographic Allegory." Pp. 98–121 in *Writing Culture: The Poetics and Politics of Ethnography*, edited by James Clifford and George E. Marcus. Berkeley, CA: University of California Press.

Kuhn, Thomas. (1962). *The Structure of Scientific Revolutions*. Chicago, IL: University of Chicago Press.

Sandel, Michael. (1982). *Liberalism and the Limits of Justice*. London: Cambridge University Press.

CHAPTER SEVEN

INJURY FIELDS

S. Løchlann Jain

My career has been dedicated to understanding how the distribution of the physical wounding inevitable to mass production has been rationalized and justified in the United States (Jain 2004, 2006, 2013). As one of the few places one can make a compensatory claim for an allegedly avoidable injury, the law has taken a central role in this investigation. I have used the very narrowness of the legal endeavor – the kinds of claims that can be brought, the arguments that are legible to the courts, the method of *stare decisis*, and even the particular ways in which legal opinions sometimes defy reason – as a knife edge with which to cut into the broader problem of wounding in American practices of production and consumption.

While injuries have always been distributed unevenly, as a legal term, injury requires one key comparison. A claim of injury relies on a prior, uninjured body. Personal injury law operates through a mechanism by which the uninjured – whole, well – body serves as the collateral for a system based on the right not to have been injured by negligence, oversight, or carelessness. For this reason, tort law has always struggled with understanding and regulating toxic chemicals, since incremental injuries over long periods of time are difficult to fit into the models of proximate cause that courts rely on. Perhaps in part as a result of the law's unwillingness and inability to take on toxic chemicals, even the organisms in the deepest part of the sea are now contaminated with PCBs. Lead and DDT, substances that were, like PCBs, banned decades ago, still course through soil, water, and blood. Perhaps thousands more chemicals, known and unknown, have made their way into our bodies and life worlds. Living now means living with and within known and unknown kinds of injury. There is no untouched, uninjured body that we might imagine can be recouped through the promise of a compensatory legal award.

While American law, policy, medicine, and experimental science still valorize cause and effect as a necessary condition of regulation, how might "injury" maintain conceptual or political meaning in a post nuclear-testing, post-Monsanto, post-pension world? In other words, how might we consider injury as always already in process, rather than as an event constituted by a clear cause and effect? Injury is a field, a range, an ongoing process. And yet I want to suggest that it still has value, for everyone does not romp equally in these grounds.

There are plenty of examples in which courts have taken a lead in changing how and what injury means, particularly in toxic torts, but also in redefinitions of what consumers should be able to expect from an everyday object. But these exceptional cases belie their rarity, for the structure of tort law requires that individuals or groups bring claims against other individuals and corporations and prove their cases in situations that are usually dramatically unequal. While the courts have, given the regulatory vacuum of the United States, taken on a governing role, there are limits to what even an "activist" court can do. They simply are not institutions funded to do independent research and adjudicate safety measures for products, chemicals, and the environments through which people negotiate everyday life. Legal regulation of products through tort law is piecemeal and random.

Still, it is the very potential of courts to make injuries visible and compensable that has spurred a tort reform movement. The "movement," largely funded by corporations and their insurers, has done a spectacular job of misinforming citizens about the mechanisms of the law and all but dismantling this last bastion of consumer protection. It is not until, say, a Californian finds themselves desperately ill or hurt after medical malpractice that they realize that their potential compensation is capped at $250,000, and that this sum wouldn't buy the research to prove even an obvious case.

At best, then, courts are not well situated to understand the current forms of always-already injured subjects and to grasp injuries as occurring on multiple planes. At worst, courts enable the ruse that everyone can have a day in court, that injury is in general something we don't want, and that we do have tools to protect the average Joe. The law, in its form and method, offers the false promise that injury could conceivably not exist with enough care in design and use of products. At double worse, personal injury law obscures the reality that injury is one of the primary products of capitalism, that it is a source of enormous profit, and that while its distribution is unequal and unfair, no one escapes – not even the 6'1" white male CEO, not even the crustaceans at the bottom of the Mariana Trench.

Ralph Nader was not wrong when, over fifty years ago, he wrote that the profits of automobility lay in accident cleanup, emergency medicine, and the sale of fast cars. There was no profit in safety and thus no safety even at low speeds (Nader 1965). While it is undeniably true that Nader's book and personal injury litigation led to increased auto safety after sixty years of slaughter (Jain 2004) and that profits were, finally, to be found in that arena, it is also true that the crash remains a huge boon to the economy, that automobile deaths and disabilities pour billions of dollars into the economy, and that petrochemical pollution has remained virtually untouchable as a cause of death and decay. In fact, if nature was the "free" site from which capital could extract value, injury and illness have come to serve an analogical extractive role.

Pharmaceutical companies rush in to fill the gaps that underfunded, ignored, preventative medicine could not hope to fill (Jain, Masco, and Murphy, Suicidal Circuits, forthcoming) and spend their R&D on "drugs for life" (Dumit 2012). In *Malignant*, I parsed this argument in detail through the example of cancer, demonstrating how the disease is embedded within a sophisticated rhetoric that situates it outside of our medical and industrial cultures as something to be battled and cured. At the same time, both treating and producing it are billion dollar industries (Jain 2013). Disavowing, causing, and treating injury creates value – as does the PR claiming that "it didn't happen, and if it did it was an accident, and if it was we take full responsibility, and if we do, we don't need any oversight." My colleague Michelle Murphy calls it what it is: gaslighting (Murphy 2017).

So, if we take this claim seriously, that injury serves as a key site for capital accumulation, offers a gleam of hope for those suffering, and is unevenly but indisputably ubiquitous, then injury is no longer, if it ever was, a thing that can be determined by, defined through, or compensated with existing equations and mechanisms. We need to develop vocabularies with which to understand, compensate, and come to terms with the new course of human and nonhuman wounding.

In this chapter, I offer an analysis of *in vitro* fertilization (IVF, or assisted reproductive technology – ART) as a way to better understand the ways in which multiple layers of injury operate simultaneously to enable clinics to harvest profit from this procedure. IVF, part medical and part capitalist (to the extent that there is a difference anymore), offers a particularly fascinating place to think about these issues for several reasons that are so ingrained as to be nearly invisible (and thus as easily harnessed by the industry), starting with the belief that reproduction is a natural and healthy social and medical right and that nuclear families with children are to be rhetorically, if not in reality, encouraged.

Further, we *want* to think that that the doctors who perform the procedure work primarily in the interests of health rather than out of intellectual curiosity or for financial gain, and most people make the assumption that they do. Indeed, such a conjecture enables clinics to mislead egg donors into accepting treatments that lack substantive data of their safety, even within a decades-long history of proof that exogenous hormones deliver a great deal of danger. These donors are further led to believe that their product, the raw material of IVF, should be given up freely or cheaply, virtually without consideration of the physical or psychological consequences, but certainly with no recourse when things go wrong. One does not want to call them naïve, but, by definition, young healthy people will not have experience with health advocacy. Beyond these considerations lies an even trickier black hole, into which seems to tumble the too-hot-to handle issue of whether an embryo, as a potential person, should have a right to the conditions that give it the highest possible chance for a healthy life, or that the parent(s) of those children have a similar right to the conditions that give the highest possible chances of having a healthy child. Even the simplest calculus for this, the practice of implanting multiple embryos, and therefore exponentially increasing the chance of multiple births, has produced tens of thousands of children who have suffered the risks and consequences of prematurity and other issues related to the conditions of their births. For some unfathomable reason, this obvious, purposeful, and profitable harm visited by IVF physicians has been barely noted and completely excused. The fact of multiple births has even been used to argue that problems associated with IVF are not due to the procedure, but to the fact of multiple birth. This point willfully ignores on the one hand that without multiple births the industry would founder, and on the other, that IVF is the prime cause of multiple births and will be for the forseeable future.

It may come as a matter of astonishment to many to learn that neither clinics nor governments in the United States track the continued health of the main players in IVF – the genetic parents, the birth parents, or even the babies. Though couched in terms of the well-being of families, IVF is in actuality, a barely regulated multi-billion-dollar market. Unlike any comparable commodities-based system (the stock market, futures, meat production), this one exists without the usual legal or regulatory protections against injury or expected guarantees of the product's or contract's quality. Very few plaintiffs sue for egregious errors involving IVF; people find it galling to sue for a poorly designed product when that product is their baby.

For these reasons, it serves as one perfect case study for understanding the complexity of injury fields and the ways in which contemporary science and technology can utterly evade any framework the law once had for adjudicating injury, harm, and responsibility.

THE PROCEDURE

IVF refers to a process of removing eggs from a woman's ovaries, combining them with sperm, and then implanting the resulting embryo into a woman's body. In 1983, a live birth resulted by extracting an egg cell from one woman and implanting it into another, and the first donation program started in 1987 (Lutjen et al. 1984, Kennard et al. 1989). For the donor, although the extraction of one egg doesn't require it, drugs are almost always administered to stimulate the production of extra egg cells (also referred to as ova or gametes). Hormones also stimulate the uterine tissue of the birth mother to encourage an implanted embryo to develop into a fetus. Donated eggs account for over a quarter of IVF live births, even though only about 12 percent of IVF procedures use them (Family Issue Fact Sheet 2010). In other words, the practice of using donated eggs – like the practice of creating the conditions for multiple births – underpins the very viability of a multi-billion-dollar industry, whose success rates would be too low without them. The use of IVF (or ART) has doubled in the last ten years.

The IVF industry portrays the procedure as generally successful and extremely safe. IVF advertisements peddling parenthood portray sweetly swaddled babies, and the IVF clinic welcomes would-be patients with pastel pink-and-blue walls replete with large framed pictures of chubby little hands and feet (quite different from the screaming-bloody-murder babies used to advertise condoms). Neither of these representations is based on anything but spin. For most people the decision to have children is no decision at all, it is an accident, a religious calling, or just what one does.

Despite the fertility industry's ubiquitous ruddy-baby advertising, it is neither easy nor inexpensive to produce an IVF baby. Roughly 30 percent of IVF procedures result in a live birth (CDC 2014), a statistic just large enough to prompt would-be parents to spend between $12,000 and $30,000 or more per cycle, often multiple times. This gamble has even opened a niche market for lenders (Silver-Greenbert 2012). Contingent on age, success rates that hover at 40 percent for women under thirty-five plunge to about 10 percent for women over forty-two. However, if older women use an oocyte from a markedly younger woman, the chances of a live birth leap to just over 50 percent (Pacific Fertility, cit. 18).

According to the most recent CDC statistics at the time of writing, which is for year 2014, IVF resulted in "57,323 live births (deliveries of one or more living infants) and 70,354 live born infants" (CDC 2014). It's difficult to tell from these numbers the absolute numbers of single vs. multiple births, but the *minimum* number of children born in multiples, if there were only twins and no triplets, would be 26,062 – well over a third of all babies produced. There is *no* medical controversy about the vastly increased health and disability risks of multiple births. Despite these potentially severe risks, and the low success rates, the CDC web page also sports photos of handsome, proud, smiling, *young* couples and their calm healthy babies. The information, while statistical, is emphatically not given neutrally and not, I will suggest, accurately.

Egg recruiters, sometimes as discrete agencies and sometimes as part of IVF clinics, represent the egg extraction process in various ways in their attempts to encourage young fertile women to undergo the procedure. One broker, for example, invites women to consider selling oocytes because Egg Donation, Inc., is "Where Dreams Come True, since 1989" (www.eggdonor.com 2017). Another program plays the gamete market as if it were recruiting models, calling itself "the Agency for Super Donors, known for representing the brightest, most beautiful and accomplished donors in the country" (www.eggdonation.com 2017). This agency encourages young women to think of the process as giving a gift, telling women that "egg donation is possible through ... the beauty of the human heart. Without angels like you, loving couples who are struggling to have a child would have little hope."

One previous Donor Angel testifies to the pleasures of giving the "gift of life to a deserving couple." These recruiting themes reflect dual psychological tactics: on the one hand – as in the promotional material of a company known as the Donor Source – young women are invited to help further the great march of humanitarian scientific progress, while on the other, websites uphold a conservative model of procreation reiterating that the donations are for couples. These sites use language that represents egg retrieval as itself a "medical procedure," drugs as "medications," and the doctor as "your physician." The Donor Source emphasizes, too, the importance of the potential donor's kindly nature, noting that "the journey of donation involves … most of all, willingness to help a couple struggling with infertility to realize their dream of a child" (Donor Source 2017). The tone of recruitment blends scientific euphemism with moral superiority to conjure an irresistible call to participate.

Anthropologist Gaylene Becker interviewed one man who was going through photographs of women in inviting poses in order to select eggs for transplant. He said, "With the pictures, you start looking at them as people, and that made it more difficult. I found myself thinking, 'This is a really nice looking woman.' Then I felt like, 'What do I care? I'm not calling her up on a date!' But it was distracting from the birth data, from the genetic factors" (Becker 2000: 154). His dilemma is understandable: After all, the people selecting eggs and sperm are partaking in a highly intimate process, one that in the case of 98.3 percent of births results from a sexual encounter. The precedent and cultural expectations for flirting, dating, and mate selection simply do not exist for gamete selection. As this man experienced, the selection of a donor inhabits an odd space ghosted with values and codes from a different set of practices. Gamete consumers half cruise, half mail-order their way through quasi-understood reproductive science (Berger 1999). Another ambiguity pervades the process of gamete selection: although the buyers purchase sperm more or less as a commodity on the free market, no regulations insist that clinics test the donors or the collected sperm for genetic flaws. In this *hors la loi* frontier, it's buyer beware all the way. But of what?

The recruitment sites actively palliate another unspoken anxiety about donation: the third parent. After the announcement that Dolly the sheep was cloned from three sheep ova in 1996, President Clinton withdrew federal funds for human cloning and called on private companies to do the same. The creation of a cloned sheep created much uproar, yet the similar processes involved in egg donation have barely been discussed. One reason may be that the cloning of Dolly required three egg cells, represented by sheep scientists and the press as "three mothers." Using sheep terms, a child produced with a donor egg cell has, in a way, three parents (two genetic donors and a birth mother). If we used to disparage a child with only one obvious parent by calling her a bastard, how might we legitimate a child with three? The translation from sheep to human reproduction seems to require wrapping the third "parent" in a ribbon of discretion and topping him or her with a gift card labeled "donation."

The Pacific Fertility Center's ads target the serious crowd: gorgeous young women in graduation caps or thoughtfully posed with pencil in hand. The Center's booklet offers nourishing imagery, while its website magically turns a frightening and intrusive event (making one's way to an office, sitting in a waiting room, dealing with strangers, being poked and prodded, giving self-injections, having numerous blood tests) into one that "many of our egg donors say ... has been one of their most rewarding experiences" (Pacific Fertility Center 2017). It is almost impossible to believe that the carefully choreographed ads use actual testimonials, so perfectly do they address every possible hesitation a young woman might have. While one plucky testimonial claims, "It's such a neat feeling to know I have helped to give new hope to a childless couple," another implies that she gets to give something away at no cost to her, since "all those eggs would be wasted anyway." If a potential donor were concerned about the drugs, worry no more: "It was exciting to see my body respond to the treatments as I daily got closer to giving my recipient the opportunity to bring a new life into the world" (Pacific Fertility Center 2017).

In sharp contrast to the media representations of "welfare moms," who presumably should not have children at all, let alone support for those children through entitlement programs, egg-donation ads portray infertile couples as loving, deserving, struggling, and dreaming, a rhetoric that juxtaposes these victims of tragic infertility with hazy-edged photos of laughing babies and children. The noble and innocent goal of wanting a child tints the whole IVF infrastructure as similarly unimpeachable. Through alchemy, say these ads, we all can participate in the miracle of life.

Loosely extrapolating from the time involved for sperm donation, the American Society for Reproductive Medicine, in a report titled "Financial Compensation of Oocyte Donors," suggests that eggs should be priced at around $5,000. The price should not be so high that "women will discount the physical and emotional risks of oocyte donation out of eagerness to address their financial situations or their infertility problems" (Ethics Committee 2007: 306). The organization's concern implies that the physical and emotional risks are known and can be measured (and hence discounted), while this very group has consistently opposed tracking women after they've donated (Levine 2010).

Soft-focus nostalgia blurs a not so warm-and-fuzzy fact: the word *donor* actively misrepresents the exchanges at play in the gamete market. Of all the ethical and practical considerations attending egg extraction, the most vibrant ones fizz around the issues of reimbursement and payment, as we fret over the commodification of human life. Donor payment structure reflects real-world salary distribution: Harvard donors make more than women from the University of Kentucky; straight-A students make more than C-average students. A recent report found that the price scale advertised for eggs correlated nearly exactly with SAT scores. To the young people who are the most coveted donors, even a small amount of cash can be a large motivator.

The label *donor* could more accurately be substituted by "person undergoing extraction," "seller," or "genetic parent." In addition to evading the financial issue, the euphemism *donor* bolsters the normative, heterosexual, nuclear economic unit of reproduction – ironically, given that the actual practice of IVF expands single people's and same sex couples' ability to have children. The money doesn't discriminate; a cheap egg supply works for nearly everyone.

The following statement by an ethicist illustrates the typical divide between intent and commodification: "When people want to [provide an egg] for altruistic reasons, it's a wonderful gift ... When donation becomes commercialized, it raises all sorts of deep, philosophical questions about using humans as a means to an end" (Ernlé Young, director of the Center for Biomedical Ethics at Stanford, quoted in Hamilton 2000). The assertion suggests that altruistic intent in itself defers the "deep, philosophical issues," which surely range from coercion to eugenics, that a purely commercial venture might raise. This false distinction between gifting and commerce, common also in organ exchange debates, confuses a critical point. Even when the gamete is freely given, doctors, nurses, moneylenders, accountants, pharmaceutical companies, lawyers, and many others profit from commercialized, for-profit IVF. Donation is anything *but* a "wonderful gift," regardless of a donor's intent and even if the donor herself never sees a penny, because it takes place within an already commercialized ethos.

Anonymity has also been used to assuage anxiety about both the Three Parent problem and the baby-exchange market. Many potential egg recipients insist on anonymity. Some others – recruiters, physicians, recipients, even donors themselves – also prefer donor anonymity. When the United Kingdom banned anonymous donation, donation rates in that country decreased by 25 percent. Anonymity is the primary reason the industry gives for not wanting long-term follow-up on donors, despite the fact that critical genetic information about the donor will not be accessible to the children. To properly track people over time, you have to know who they are.

The private, often anonymous nature of donorship can be both socially and medically isolating. Anonymity also leaves people exceptionally vulnerable in medical emergencies. One college student suffered a severe stroke in reaction to Lupron. Since her parents hadn't known that she was undergoing the extraction procedure, they were called in only after she was in the emergency room. Medical settings often require full disclosure to ensure proper diagnosis or treatments, especially in emergencies, and secrecy or unease around medical history heightens risk. To add insult to the injury, despite over $100,000 in medical bills that she was responsible for, she received only a "dropped cycle" fee of $650 (Hamilton 2000). Stories like this one make it clear that, just as different parties need their own lawyers, different parties should have their own doctors (Lahl 2009). Francine Coeytaux recommended that each woman should have her own doctor whose "only job is to look out for the well-being of the woman" (Coeytaux 2005).

Quite simply, no one tracks donors to try to understand the physical or psychological consequences of donation, and in the twenty-year history of artificial egg extraction, no one ever has (Schneider 2007, Kramer et al. 2009). No protocol or requirement mandates that clinics contact women after egg extraction, and no agency collects data on subsequent health issues that a woman may want to report.

This is somewhat counter-intuitive for two reasons. First, some of these drugs are being used off-label; that is, they have been tested for other illnesses (in one case, prostate cancer, a disease of old men) and not for use in young women. Second, the hormones used in IVF have been shown in not dissimilar circumstances, such as hormone replacement therapy (HRT), to cause cancer. The high stakes for young women and for the practice of medicine mar the issue even further.

Until the last couple of years, virtually no research has focused on young adult cancers. Yet one in forty-nine women under the age of thirty-nine is diagnosed with an invasive cancer. Unlike for children and for older adults, survival rates for young adults have not improved. Given the inability of the medical system to access young adults (due to the often limited insurance coverage), diagnose this group (due to the belief that cancer is a disease of older folks), and treat them (given poor understanding of their cancers), even a small possibility of a medical procedure causing cancer in this demographic seems like a good moment to pause (Bleyer 2011, National Cancer Institute 2013). The dicey medical experiment of giving fertility hormones to the young, fertile women who are recruited to donate provides a good example of the money to made in putting people at risk of cancer in addition to that made from treating it.

The relationship between the hormones used in IVF and cancer would seem to be an obvious area of research. Hormones have been used in medicine and agriculture in the United States since the 1930s for everything from fattening livestock to stunting the growth of girls at risk of becoming offputtingly tall, from attempting (without success) to prevent miscarriages to trying to reduce the effects of aging in women. The history of synthetic hormones includes the purposeful withholding of the correlations between hormone use and cancer by physicians when giving drugs to women in the 1960s so they would not worry (Langston 2010). Still, estrogen and progesterone, considered to be the core, natural "messengers of femininity and masculinity," have been the most widely used drugs in the history of medicine (Oudshoorn 1994, Jordan-Young 2010).

The lack of research puts everyone in a bind; without data, anecdotes and assumptions drive the conversation, and any position one can take on the issue becomes a personal one. Any of the players here might be dismissed as having too much at stake in the issue: perhaps one has an ax to grind with doctors, with medicine, with progress, or with children. Perhaps doctors or would-be parents do not want to consider that they may be agents within a cancer-causing industry. In any case, it is an unpopular move to seem to impugn the child and a person's desire for one.

Each live birth requires, on average, four IVF attempts. Each attempt (or cycle) requires several weeks of hormone use for either one woman or, in the case of donor eggs, two women. In the United States, clinics administer about 120,000 IVF cycles annually (no central agency collects data, so numbers are estimates). Despite the immense difficulty and expense of creating embryos, each year approximately 40,000 are discarded in the United States because people either do not want to keep them, do not want to pay for freezing them, or decline to donate them to other potential parents (Roberts 2011).

Several commentators point out that the lack of long-term health data means that IVF remains experimental and thus precludes the possibility of informed consent (Coeytaux 2005, Magnus and Cho 2006, Uroz and Guerra 2009). Clinics and spokespeople uniformly communicate the lack of health data on egg donation and hormone use as evidence that no risk exists. For example, a 2012 study found that the risk of breast cancer for those who take hormonal drugs for IVF at a young age (precisely the demographic targeted by egg recruiters) actually *increased* by 59 percent after sixteen years – when most were still under forty (Pearson 2006, Stewart et al. 2012). A Reuters report on this study cited the American Society for Reproductive Medicine (or ASRM, a self-proclaimed interdisciplinary group of fertility experts that represents IVF clinics) as claiming that this should reassure women, since IVF *overall* is "not associated with an increased risk for development of ... cancer" (Dr Linda Giudice, president of the American Society of Reproductive Medicine, quoted in Seaman 2012). As a result of this informational quagmire and the ongoing misrepresentation of data, many prospective clients and donors, as well as potential regulators, falsely assume that the hormonal drugs used in IVF procedures have been assessed by the Food and Drug Administration (FDA) for their safety in egg extraction.

Because of this lack of data, at first, the IVF story seems to follow the simple plotline of a profitable business in need of an extractive resource (in this case, eggs). To be sure, this oversimplification is not entirely wrong. Studies have shown that many clinics do not follow even the few unenforceable guidelines laid out by the ASRM (Levine 2010). In one of the very few instances in which the FDA has been involved with IVF, it recommended against (but did not disallow) the use of the Vero cell line, created from African green monkey kidney epithelial cells, that had been used to culture human embryos. The FDA warned that this xenotransplantation could result in cross-species infection of the sort that is believed to have caused HIV/AIDS, and recommends that when co-cultures are used that doctors should maintain contact with "patients for their lifetimes and counsel them to be alert to any unusual symptoms" (FDA 2017). After all the research I've done on

IVF and cell cultures over the years, this web page, buried away, is the only trace I've found of this issue – never have I come across the lifetime tracking of patients or even a frank discussion of what co-cultures are used in individual cases.

I needn't argue here that the data *should* be collected. That's obvious: they should. And the very lack of collected data on hormones and egg extraction seems to suggest that the data are still out there to be collected and that if a registry were set up, in thirty or forty years we would know any dangers. Then again, to set up such a study now would be to virtually admit to women that they are being guinea pigs. Such a consent form would virtually guarantee a loss for clinics.

Because good health is required of donors, those considering selling or donating eggs have typically not had to deal with or understand the health system before, nor have they developed the skills to successfully negotiate the multiple demands of being a patient. At the time I embarked on the project, I thought of giving over an egg or two (or seven) as the equivalent of handing over some sperm – with injections in the place of magazines. In that trust – or naïveté – I was the perfect candidate.

The system discourages young women with little or no medical experience from thinking too much about fair and legitimate payment, encourages them toward secrecy even at their own physical peril, and requires them to take untested drugs without any warnings of the decades-long history linking hormones to cancer. Often clinics underplay even the acknowledged health risks, such as ovarian hyperstimulation syndrome, by as much as 400 percent (Sauer et al. 1996, Maxwell et al. 2008, Lahl 2009). The industry represents all this as part of an innocent process in the higher service of the Family (or more accurately, specific Families).

HORMONES

In 1978, British physicians announced the birth of the first test-tube baby. Robert Edwards, one of the scientists who developed the procedure, first with mice and then with Ms Brown, was awarded the 2010 Nobel Prize in Medicine for his work on IVF. Louise Brown's mother did not take fertility drugs, nor was she aware at the time of the procedure that IVF had not yet yielded a live birth. In this instance, the doctors removed the single egg produced in an ovulation cycle, fertilized it in a lab, and implanted it back into her uterus. In the 1980s, doctors began injecting hormones to artificially increase the number of eggs produced in one cycle, enabling them to implant more than one egg at a time and thus increase the chance of pregnancy (as well as the chance of twins and triplets). Multiple egg harvesting also enabled the freezing of embryos, making possible several pregnancies from one round of superovulation. The number of women over thirty-five having children has increased twelve-fold since 1970.

Central to the functioning of the endocrine system, hormones control growth, mood, and the messaging required for reproductive cycles. In the first phase of egg extraction, called hyperstimulation, doctors serially administer three potent hormonal drugs to encourage the development of extra eggs. The brain processes these synthetic hormones as if they had been produced by one's own body to magnify aspects of the reproductive cycle.

First, a gonadotropin-releasing hormone agonist (GnRHa, a.k.a. luteinizing hormone-releasing hormone, or LHRH) is self-administered daily for one to two weeks (yes, you give yourself a needle!). This blocks pituitary function and creates a temporary menopause that enables the physician to sync the donor's ovulation with that of the woman who will receive the embryo. They affect not only gonadal hormones, but are also "powerful modulators of autonomic neural function" (Mathias and Clench 1995). Lupron, a drug initially approved for the palliative care of prostate cancer, is currently the most popular GnRHa, despite an ongoing criminal investigation into its fraudulent marketing, the falsification of data, numerous settlements for price fixing, and findings of significant and damaging irreversible effects (Norsigian 2005).

Lupron is on the lists of the NIH and OSHA as a hazardous drug and a teratogen (an agent that increases the risk of abnormal fetal development) (Shepard 1992: 233). Lupron was originally researched and indicated for the palliative care of prostate cancer (a disease that affects older men); when tested in rat studies, all rats at all doses developed pituitary adenomas (tumors) (Millican 2003).

Second, gonadotropin is injected with Gonal-f, Perganol, or Clomid. Normally used to promote fertility in women who have a deficiency of the hormone, the overdose of gonadotropin in fertile women triggers the ovary via the pituitary to develop several egg-containing follicles. A third injection, this time of human chorionic gonadotropin, forces an extreme ovulation with the goal of producing several eggs at one time. By now you've swollen up and are doing your best not to get body-checked on the ice hockey rink.

Beyond these basic functions, the precise mechanisms of these drugs remain largely unknown. One of the main stumbling blocks for both studying and regulating hormone use is the fact that these notably finicky drugs can have opposing effects at low and high doses: low doses of Lupron, for example, "result in the ovaries producing estrogen or the testes producing testosterone; only after reaching a high dose is the drug's desired effect, inhibition of estrogen or testosterone production, achieved" (Myers and vom Saal 2008: 30–1). As a result, hypothesizing the effects based on assumptions about larger or smaller doses working in a linear, rather than opposing, way have missed the mark. Scientists' use of experimental animals that have greater or lesser susceptibility to hormones than humans also skews results.

The Scottish surgeon George Beatson researched hormones and reproductive cancers in the 1890s (Beatson 1896). His discovery that cancers contain hormone receptors that feed on the hormones either produced by the body or taken in by the body exogenously lay behind a whole series of twentieth-century treatments meant to "starve" reproductive cancers, including hysterectomy, removal of the pituitary gland, and ovarian ablation.

Despite the temptation to think of these hormones as safe because bodies already produce them, the contemporary use of synthetic hormones in no way augments a natural ovulation process. As is true with most supplements, including vitamins, just because a body produces a substance does not make it safe. A more "natural" state for women of reproductive age may well be that of constant pregnancy. In fact, the very idea of monthly menstruation is only about fifteen decades old, so in a way the cycles that synthetic hormones adjust and modify are remnants of the industrial revolution itself. Not giving birth is a known risk for breast and ovarian cancer, since the hormones released during ovulation overload the hormone receptors in those tissues. Pregnancy gives a break of nine months per child from these overloads, and over the course of two to four decades, the breaks add up. In other words, without the hormone vacations that pregnancy brings, the overloaded hormone receptors can create malignancies (Russo et al. 2005, Bandera 2005). Most pregnant women don't think of their pregnancy as a holiday from anything except possibly tampons and taking out the garbage, but the link is clear.

The tie between hormones and hormone receptors also supports the recent finding that estrogen and progesterone hormone replacement therapy (HRT) significantly increases the risk of cancer and heart disease (Collaborative Group on Hormone Factors 1996, Chlebowski et al. 2010). Many experts attribute the recent small decline in breast cancer mortality (from 178 per 100,000 in 1998 to 160 per 100,000 in 2008) to the decline in the use of HRT by postmenopausal women (Watkins 2007, Sprague et al. 2011).

Drug companies promoted HRT for decades for reducing hot flushes, weight gain, and heart disease and as a cure-all for the decreases in skin tone, muscle mass, bone density, and memory that come with aging, without any evidence that HRT could in fact fulfill such promises (Figure 7.1). The ad is, of course, horrifically misogynist, as would have been obvious to any woman at the time. So the point is not just that the company could advertise a product, targeting *all* women in their own wet dream, by so offensively denigrating the very people it was targeting. The point is not just that the company was promoting the idea that all women should take an entirely untested drug. The point is that the company could portray the frustration over a lifetime of having been expected to make coffee for men, having to treat men as if you thought they were smarter when you knew they weren't, and of having men constantly looking over their glasses at you as if you were a crazy idiot, as if it were a simple matter of biology. This was part of the vast infrastructure, from the market in dolls to the withholding of birth control, that kept women as baby-making machines. Within this historical context, only a generation or two in the past, how are we to consider the "choice" of having children?

In 2010, fifty years after the introduction of HRT treatments, enough convincing evidence was found against Pfizer that juries awarded millions of dollars in punitive damages to plaintiffs, indicating reckless disregard for women's health in selling the drug without warnings or adequate study. Since then, more than 9,000 other women with cancer have sued Pfizer (Prempro Settlement 2010). Some plaintiffs who alleged their cancers were caused by HRT showed that Wyeth knew the dangers of hormone replacement therapy well before the Women's Health Initiative found that it caused increased rates of cancer, stroke, and other health problems; in other cases, however, Pfizer has successfully argued that cancer has many causes and therefore couldn't be traced specifically to its products. HRT is one strand in a complex story of the way synthetic hormones have been falsely marketed as natural substances. It also illustrates how easily we assume that data are being collected and regulation is taking place as drugs become increasingly common. In fact, the opposite is often true. The creeping normalcy of

he is suffering from estrogen deficiency

Figure 7.1 Hormone replacement therapy advertisement, circa 1960, suggesting that menopause will turn a woman into a nightie-clad lunatic who will strain the patience of her calm, professional husband. Proposing its own wet dream, the pharmaceutical company claims that "Premarin has the intrinsic ability to impart a sense of well-being" and should be used to "treat all women." Source: DES Action USA, www.desaction.org

certain procedures and drugs in the medical field still renders invisible whole swaths of questions about drug safety.

In another example of the ill-fated twentieth-century use of hormone therapies, physicians prescribed DES (diethylstilbestrol) to women for several seemingly conflicting reasons: to prevent miscarriages, suppress milk production, and, in the 1950s and 1960s, as a morning-after contraceptive. Historian Susan Bell found evidence from the 1940s citing reasons that DES would be harmful to pregnant women. Only decades later did the true injury become evident: the *children* of those who took DES had high rates of cancer (Bell 2009). Only the rarity of the cancer

INJURY FIELDS

Figure 7.1 (continued)

types triggered further investigation; had the DES-exposed babies suffered from common forms of cancer, the correlation would almost certainly never have been made and these cancers would have been simply absorbed into the statistics.[1]

Oncologist Siddhartha Mukherjee notes that doctors have known since the 1960s that the estrogen and progesterone in HRT treatments act as pathological activators of breast cancer. He writes, "A more integrated approach to cancer prevention, incorporating the prior insights of cancer biology, might have predicted this cancer-inducing activity … and potentially saved the lives of thousands of women" (Mukherjee

---

[1] *Sindell v. Abbott Laboratories*, 26 Cal. 3d 588, 163 Cal. Rptr. 132, 607 P. 2d 924 (1980).

2010: 456). Despite this overall critique, Mukherjee doesn't press this observation to note any of the current medical, military, and industrial practices that would benefit from the integrated approach he advocates. Somehow, the amount of time it takes cancer to present, which is so long after the possible triggering exposure, tricks us into a collective forgetting that sees us, each time for a new reason, continuing to use demonstrably dangerous drugs with nearly identical molecular form and biochemical effects.

The market for ova offers a nearly perfect example of the impossibility of enforcing, or even encouraging, better organization of the fields of cancer biology, drug marketing, and medical (or medical-like) protocols. An injured patient cannot bring a legal suit for what the whole practice of medicine "should" or could have known, though she can sometimes bring a lawsuit against a drug manufacturer, asserting that it should have known or disclosed the dangers of a particular drug. As with any critique of large institutions, a delicate balance of power, money, class, and influence affects who gets to speak and who gets heard. The IVF industry offers a financial mainstay to many hospitals and clinics. And big money nearly always brings multiple conflicts of interest.

DATA DUMP

A recent report offers an illustration of how easily the lack of data can be manipulated to sound as though no correlation exists between hormones and cancer. In 2006, the California Institute for Regenerative Medicine initiated a $3 billion program to fund stem cell research, in which the main source of stem cells would be oocytes extracted from young women. Simultaneously, the institute convened a committee through the Institute of Medicine and the National Research Council (NRC) to examine the risks of oocyte donation. Although it acknowledged that the long-term effects of IVF are completely unknown, the committee nevertheless concluded: "The evidence to date ... does not support a relationship between fertility drugs and an increased prevalence of breast or ovarian cancer" (Giudice et al. 2007: 2). The report cites a *lack* of evidence as evidence of *no* danger, rather than acknowledging that no data exist on the long-term effects of IVF drugs on young fertile women.

The scant research on fertility hormones and cancer has tracked infertile women, both those who became pregnant with IVF and those who did not (Dor et al. 1996, Shenfield 1996, Mosgaard et al. 1998,

Pappo et al. 2008, Kramer et al. 2009). Infertile women represent a completely different population than donors. They tend to be ten, twenty, and not uncommonly thirty years older, and often have age or life-related hormonal imbalances related to their infertility that egg donors do not have. Generally, the first wave of research found an increase in cancers among those who took fertility drugs; this was followed by a wave of research that found no significant difference, and a more recent wave that found very significant differences. Most studies have used small subject numbers with short follow-up times to study a narrow range of cancers. To add to the difficulties of studying the effects of IVF on infertile women, the doses and types of hormonal drugs frequently change. Furthermore, while most studies of fertility drugs have focused on cancers of the reproductive organs, both normal and malignant cells in other parts of the body have estrogen receptors. For example, some types of estrogen have effects on the proliferation of normal and malignant colon cells.

One of the very few longitudinal studies tracking infertile women who had ovarian induction treatments found some dire results. Published in 2009, this study tracked 15,030 women who had given birth in 1974–6 (before IVF) and found that those who did not get pregnant within twelve months of taking the ovulation-inducing agent clomiphene citrate, or Clomid (on which long-term animal studies have not been completed), had double the risk of cancer compared to untreated women thirty years after the treatment (Calderon-Margalit et al. 2009). Furthermore, the median age at cancer diagnosis was 49.4, significantly under the median age of diagnosis for the average population. The results of this study may understate the issue, given the more aggressive treatments developed in the 1980s.

The authors of the study conclude that treatment exposure without subsequent pregnancy raises the risk of a variety of cancers, including uterine cancer, breast cancer, malignant melanoma, and non-Hodgkin lymphoma. This makes sense given the increased risk caused by hormonal exposure that is not offset by the "pregnancy break." The authors further point out that the few small trials that have been conducted have been inadequate to study cancer incidence. An adequate study of the cancer risk from hormone exposure would require a registry of thousands of women, which the reproductive industry has actively opposed and which the desire for anonymous donations further complicates. And then there's the money barrier: just who would fund such a study?

Clearly, a definitive answer to any association of hormone exposure and cancer would require more research, as several small studies suggest. For example, a 1994 study published in the *New England Journal of Medicine*, again of infertile women who took clomiphene citrate for more than a year, found that the women had over double the risk of developing invasive ovarian tumors compared with the general population (Rossing et al. 1994). A 2008 study advised further research on finding a connection between IVF therapy and breast cancer (Pappo et al. 2008). A 2011 Dutch study, the first to add a control group of fertile women, found that fertility treatments double the rate of ovarian tumors (van Leeuwen et al. 2011).

Given these studies, combined with what we already know about hormones and cancer from historical examples such as DES and HRT, the connection between hormone exposure and cancer incidence seems utterly undeniable. However, consensus in the medical community is rare. Debate over the 1994 *NEJM* article on infertile women and clomiphene citrate brewed in the subsequent issue of the journal, demonstrating the differing opinions among physicians as to what constitutes adequate evidence. Several letters, criticizing methodological details of the study, dismissed the correlation out of hand, advocating for the continued use of the drug even without counterevidence of its safety (Correspondence 1995). In contrast, another letter cited anecdotal clinical evidence of a threefold increase in invasive ovarian cancer rates for patients who had taken fertility drugs, with a control group of 1,100. The authors of that letter concluded that, regardless of the control group size or other study details, legitimate grounds for concern exist regarding the potentially increased risk of ovarian cancer (Cramer et al. 1995).

In lieu of large randomized control trials, some medical studies focus on case-by-case clinical reports. Two British doctors, K. K. Ahuja and E. G. Simons, collected sixty such reports published in the UK medical literature between 1992 and 1997 on a variety of fatal and life-threatening cancers that followed within a few years of ovarian stimulation (Ahuja and Simons 1998). The authors note the difficulty in systematically correlating these incidents to causation given a variety of factors, including the more potent drugs now used, the difficulty of tracking those who have undergone ovarian stimulation, and the requirement of physician interest in making the correlations, writing them up, and publishing them.

Because of the lack of a registry or follow-up, when cases of cancer pursuant to fertility treatment turn up at all, they do so most often in clinical case reports, blogs, documentaries, and magazine articles, venues that make the incidents easy to dismiss as individual and anecdotal, albeit tragic, cases. Although the lag time of cancer makes it difficult to attribute cause, single adverse outcomes have in the past occasionally led to the discontinued use of experimental drugs (Schneider 2007). Indeed, in the face of negligible research or commitment from the medical industry, informal testimonies in the public sphere may be the only way to turn the tide from silence to disclosure.

The Ahuja and Simons report is a key document in this debate. One of the cases they reviewed involved the death of a thirty-nine-year-old British woman who had undergone oocyte extraction for her sister at the age of thirty-three. The patient file had been closed as a successful procedure after the birth of a baby girl. Five years later, however, the clinic made contact with the mother of the baby girl to inquire whether she wanted to continue to keep the embryos she had frozen at the clinic. At that point the clinic learned – only incidentally – of the donor's terminal colon cancer and death. (This is exactly the kind of information that formal tracking procedures would bring to light.) Upon researching that case and others, Ahuja and Simons concluded that these cases of cancer following egg extraction should not be discounted as insignificant, and that "empirical findings about the actual experiences of parents and children in families created by assisted conception should form the basis of future policy, rather than uninformed opinion" (Ahuja and Simons 1998: 228). Ahuja has since become an active proponent of compulsory embryo donation, a program adopted by several European countries that avails unwanted embryos to would-be parents, thus reducing the need for new rounds of fertility treatments.

Even one of the studies most often cited as evidence of no increased cancer risk with IVF concludes that "given the recent marketing of fertility drugs and the fact that exposed women are only beginning to reach the cancer age range, *further follow-up is necessary.*" Furthermore, since the drugs change slightly all the time, there isn't time to do real follow-up each time (Brinton 2007: 42). With no central registry, making the necessary correlations between drugs and people would require intricate methods, including finding the addresses of donors, figuring out names changed after marriage, and so on. Such a study would cost millions of dollars, though that would be a relatively small fraction of industry profits. Even if a study or registry were to start now, it would take thirty to forty years to collect adequate data, by which time the drugs will surely have changed. Tracking data using population aggregates, as has been done to track the efficacy of population-wide cancer screening, will not work, given the low numbers of donors compared to the variation in potentially resulting cancers, spread among at least four or five types.

Alternatives include procedures, shown to be equally successful, that use fewer hormones or involve the extraction of the usual one egg cell produced each month (Edwards 2007, Holzer et al. 2007).

THE CHOICE PARADOX

The earliest attempts at IVF took place in New York and the United Kingdom in the explosive aftermath of the 1973 U.S. Supreme Court decision on abortion. This may have been coincidence, or may indeed may have had both scientific and social roots in the development of birth control and attempts at women's Lib. At any rate, *Roe v. Wade* balanced the government's two competing interests in protecting a mother's health and also in protecting a potential human life. Based on the Ninth Amendment's right to privacy, the court ruled that a woman can terminate an early pregnancy "in harmony with her own beliefs on the mystery of life," while states maintain the authority to limit abortions as fetuses become viable later in a pregnancy.

Lawyers continue to debate the legal logic of the justices' arguments. Into this miasma about rights and privacy and who gets to have those, the development of IVF just a few years after this decision presented some extremely awkward and confusing questions that threatened the precarious logic of both pro-choice and pro-life positions on abortion. For that reason, many interests led away from even having a discussion about how embryos and fetuses – as potential children – should be experimented on by the IVF industry. This has resulted in a sort of hush code about the creation, storage, and disposal of embryos, to the extent that efforts to track the health of children born as the result of IVF has met with huge resistance.

Pro-choicers may worry that regulating IVF based on concern for future children's health would lead down a slippery slope by setting a precedent for valuing a fetus's right to life over a woman's desire to terminate a pregnancy: the issue at the very core of abortion debates. In this view, any public debate on IVF practices would reopen uneasy questions around abortion. Logically, if regulation of embryo implantation implies that embryos have a right to a healthy life, this right would also apply to the life of an embryo or fetus, thus implying that abortion should be banned. No pro-choicer would want to touch that.

Similarly, a consistent pro-life position would require either that no freezing or destruction of embryos – a seemingly unavoidable aspect of IVF – take place. Pro-lifers have not come out against IVF in any notable way, and IVF has not been on the pro-life platform. Attorney Dena S. Davis writes of this position that, "The continued hostility toward abortion ... coupled with the absence of attacks on IVF, can best be described as a relative indifference to the moral status of the embryo, but rather a great deal of hostility toward economic equality of women, sexual activity outside of marriage, and marriages that are not organized along traditional gender lines" (Davis 2006: 275).

Given the potential implications, perhaps the hush code and lack of regulation over the three decades of IVF isn't surprising, and while concerns of re-opening the abortion debate certainly play in the background, the IVF industry has another card in its pocket, since its clients, who also have an interest in this silence, wield considerable economic power. The average birth mother undergoing IVF is white, married, in the top 10 percent income bracket, educated, thirty-six years old, undertaking a highly visible, acceptable, and widely advertised procedure. To be sure, the gene pool represented by IVF participants is at face value one a nation would want to reproduce, so the debate is also quite different from others that increase a nation's population such as refugees and immigrants.

A unique American politics of reproductive health offers one genealogy of IVF. Organ donation offers another. Medical anthropologists have written extensively on the unknown long-term health consequences for organ donors and the dicey ethical issues of a medical procedure that carries much risk and no benefit. Sharon Kaufman discusses the multiple pressures imposed by family on younger relatives to donate organs within kinship networks (Kaufman et al. 2006). This practice puts families in the excruciating position of having to risk a younger family member's health as a trade-off against the possibility that an aging parent or relative may gain a small increase in lifespan. Complicated issues of gifting, marketing, caretaking, familial economics, inheritance, gender, and interfamilial relationship history play into these heartbreaking decision-making processes.

IVF clinics sometimes suggest that people ask sisters, relatives, and even friends and students for donations without suggesting safer alternatives. A friend of mine was even asked by her professors for a donation. These known-donor stories provide some of the most painful ones, because if the donor suffers from bad health afterward, nobody knows if it is related to the procedure. Price-fixing the gametes to make them seem more gift-like does not change the basic endangerment of actual kinship networks in the name of potential future ones.

If there is already confusion about what – or at least how we should categorize – these little petri dishes contain (African green monkey cells aside) the FDA has jumped into the fray by regulating oocytes not as organs or whatever the abortion debate would name these bits of material. Rather, the FDA defines them as human tissue. This encourages the idea that egg cells and embryos are merely clumps of cells rather than personally invested objects produced with significant effort and technological infrastructure that may one day become people.

The confusion about how, exactly, IVF donorship should be envisaged – in the context of reproductive health? as organ donation? as tissue exchange? as commodity exchange? – has also led to confusing ideas about who should pay for it. Fifteen states currently require that insurers provide coverage for infertility, despite mixed research on whether having children actually improves people's happiness, life satisfaction, and mental well-being (Powdthavee 2009). The notion of health that underpins the inclusion of IVF in health insurance seems to advocate for the notion that reproductive health means choice about whether (and when) to reproduce. The current formation of families reflects broader practices and assumptions about desire, technology, choice, health, economic stability, and consumption. Similar ideas have produced the possibility of IVF, so it's virtually impossible to distinguish them.

CONCLUSION

A recent book aimed at middle school students (yes, *children*) touted egg donation, without reference to the dearth of health research, as a way to save for their college expenses (Lew 2010). (Imagine this one shelved between *Little House on the Prairie* and *Watership Down*.) Ironically, the increasing burden of educational expenses leads some women to wait until their mid-thirties and forties to have children, so they have time to pay off what they owe for their own education and to save for their children's future debts. (Age-related infertility accounts for some 80 percent of IVF cases) (Skoch 2010). In that sense, IVF relies on – one might even say, requires – structural inequities among the generations as well as material differences in the bodies of younger and older people. The injuries then recursively circulate among generations of women, as older women covet the genetic material of younger women, who unknowingly, but likely, put themselves at risk for future infertility and cancer. That doesn't mean that the blame rests on the "older" women, who are also caught within personal and economic webs of desire and hope that lead to many rounds of treatment and often to devastation at the end of it all with the attendant feelings of failure and the individuation of that failure that peculiarly attends the American medical infrastructure.

IVF, with the multiple injuries it produces, sits atop a seemingly indestructible pillar of family. At the same time, misogyny has been at the rotten core of the making of the American family. The depths of that include the way it has used hormones as a catch-all substitute for women's medical care, the unanswered issues about children's health cut short by the abortion debate, and the practice of giving small people identified as girls dolls to play with. Perhaps we won't see the injuries that IVF has wrought until we rethink the very idea and expectations of what a nuclear family is, and what value it has, to whom. Until we do that, Americans remain at the mercy of technologies that can ride a rhetorical apotheosis of family as it employs a method for producing them that is rotten to the core.

However, it's parsed, the children are the real losers in the IVF gamble (and when children lose, their parents lose). The genetic and epigenetic research isn't done. The hormones that are taken by mothers and donors aren't noted in their ongoing health records (remember how important that was to DES, or the FDA thought it might be in the case of the Vero cells used to grow the embryos). Thus, even if someone did want to do that research, there is no historical data. Rosanna Weksberg, a University of Toronto geneticist and epigeneticist found a 1,000-fold increase in genetic diseases among kids born by IVF but couldn't find a clinic that would work with her to track this in-the-making (Kirschner et al. 2000, Blackwell 2011). After a small flurry of attention in the media, the story died out. There is only one player in this morass that wins from this: the clinic.

Then, as the value of genetically related children at any cost increases, quite literally, can we assume that a correlating decrease takes place among orphans and foster children? Ironically, this baby-producing circuit exists *because* America is downright unfriendly to the health and education of actual, existing children. Indeed, it is partly the presumed, and unrealistic, sentimentality about children themselves that forecloses questions about the social and physical costs of how they are produced.

I framed this chapter by asking how we might be able to salvage a critical edge for the term *injury*. I use the term injury as opposed to other designations of human wounding because I want to hark back to the word's etymology and maintain the idea that such wounding is wrong and should be wrong as a matter of law. To think this through, I've presented an example of the nearly indiscriminate introduction of a technology with enormous social, medical, and economic consequences that hit at virtually every level – from the costs of health insurance to the place of the nuclear family in our culture to the pressures on women in their historically policed role as reproducers. The analysis demonstrates the multiple approaches required to begin to grasp the ways in which injuries – known and unknown – circulate just beyond grasp.

I was drawn to study torts in the first place for the tidy but powerful logic that required corporations to pay some heed, in the twentieth century, to the new bodies they were producing with cars and chemicals and guns and cigarettes. With the accelerated scale of bodily reconfiguration, post nuclear-fallout, post-Monsanto, post-pension, post-proximate cause, injury is no longer an event, but a field in which body burdens pass from generation to generation and from smoke-stack to crustacean. The tidy logics need cleaning up.

References

Ahuja, K. K. and E. G. Simons. (1998). "Cancer of the Colon in an Egg Donor: Policy Repercussions for Donor Recruitment." *Human Reproduction* 13:227–31.

Bandera, C. A. (2005). "Advances in the Understanding of Risk Factors for Ovarian Cancer." *Journal of Reproductive Medicine* 50:399–406.

Beatson, G. T. (1896). "On Treatment of Inoperable Cases of Carcinoma of the Mamma: Suggestions for a New Method of Treatment, with Illustrative Cases." Paper presented to the Edinburgh Medico-Chirurgical Society, May 20, 1896. *Lancet* 2:104–7.

Becker, G. (2000). *Elusive Embryo: How Women and Men Approach New Reproductive Technologies.* Berkeley, CA: University of California Press.

Bell, S. (2009). *DES Daughters, Embodied Knowledge, and the Transformation of Women's Health Politics in the Late Twentieth Century.* Philadelphia, PA: Temple University Press.

Berger, J. (1999). "Our Towns: Yale Gene Pool Seen as Route to Better Baby." *New York Times*, January 10.

Blackwell, T. (2011). "In-Vitro Fertilization Linked to Rare Genetic Disorders." *National Post*, September 25.

Bleyer, A. (2011). "Latest Estimates of Survival Rates of the 24 Most Common Cancers in Adolescent and Young Adult Americans." *Journal of Adolescent and Young Adult Oncology* 1(1):37–42.

Brinton, L. (2007). "Long-Term Effects of Ovulation-Stimulating Drugs on Cancer Risk." *Reproductive BioMedicine Online* 15.

Calderon-Margalit, R. et al. (2009). "Cancer Risk after Exposure to Treatments for Ovulation Induction." *American Journal of Epidemiology* 169:365–75.

CDC. (2014). "ART Success Rates." www.cdc.gov/art/artdata/index.html [cited as CDC 2014].

Chlebowski, R. T. et al. (2010). "Estrogen Plus Progestin and Breast Cancer Incidence and Mortality in Postmenopausal Women." *JAMA* 304:1684–92.

Coeytaux, F. (2005). Testimony on Egg Retrieval to California Senate Committee, Joint Oversight Hearing on the Implementation of Proposition 71, the Stem Cell Research and Cures Act, March 9. www.geneticsandsociety.org/article.php?id=180.

Collaborative Group on Hormone Factors in Breast Cancer. (1996). "Breast Cancer and Hormonal Contraceptives: Collaborative Reanalysis of Individual Data on 53,297 Women with Breast Cancer and 100,239 Women without Breast Cancer for 54 Epidemiological Studies." *Lancet* 347:1713–27.

"Correspondence: Risk of Ovarian Cancer after Treatment for Infertility." (1995). *New England Journal of Medicine* 332:1300–2 [cited as Correspondence 1995].

Cramer, D., W. P. Hartge, P. C. Nasca, and A. S. Whittemore. (1995). "Letter to the editor." *New England Journal of Medicine* 332:1300–2.

Davis, D. S. (2006). "The Puzzle of IVF." *Houston Journal of Health Law and Policy* 6: 275.

"Donor Source." (2017). www.fertilitysourcecompanies.com/egg-donation/beginner/.

Dor, J., L. Lerner-Geva, J. Rabinovici et al. (1996). "Cancer Incidence in a Cohort of Infertile Women Treated with In Vitro Fertilization." *52nd Annual Meeting of the American Society for Reproductive Medicine* suppl., 147.

Dumit, J. (2012). *Drugs for Life*. Durham, NC: Duke University Press.

Edwards, R. C. (2007). "IVF, IVM, Natural Cycle IVF, Minimal Stimulation IVF – Time for a Rethink." *Reproductive Medicine Online* 15:106–219.

Ethics Committee of the American Society for Reproductive Medicine. (2007). "Financial Compensation of Oocyte Donors." *Fertility and Sterility* 88 [cited as Ethics Committee 2007].

Family Issue Fact Sheet No. 2010–03 (March 2010), S.B. 1306/H.B. 2651 – Human Egg Provider Protection Act, Center for Arizona Policy [cited as Family Fact Sheet 2010].

FDA. (2017). "Information and Recommendations for Physicians Involved in the Co-Culture of Human Embryos with Non-Human Animal Cells." www.fda.gov/BiologicsBloodVaccines/Xenotransplantation/ucm136532.htm

Giudice, L., E. Santa, and R. Pool, eds. (2007). *Assessing the Medical Risks of Human Oocyte Donation for Stem Cell Research: Workshop Report.* Washington, DC: National Academic Press.

Hamilton, J. (2000). "What Are the Costs?" *Stanford Magazine*, November–December.

Holzer, H. et al. (2007). "In Vitro Maturation of Oocytes Collected from Unstimulated Ovaries for Oocyte Donation." *Fertility and Sterility* 88:62–7.

Jain, L. (2004). "Dangerous Instrumentality (Bystander as Subject in Automobility)." *Cultural Anthropology* 19(1):61–94.

(2006). *Injury: The Politics of Product Design and Safety Law in the United States.* Princeton, NJ: Princeton University Press.

(2013). *Malignant: How Cancer Becomes Us.* Berkeley, CA: University of California Press.

Jordan-Young, R. (2010). *Brain Storm: The Flaws in the Science of Sex Differences.* Cambridge, MA: Harvard University Press.

Kaufman, S. R., A. J. Russ, and J. K. Shim. (2006). "Aged Bodies and Kinship Matters: The Ethical Field of Kidney Transplant." *American Ethnologist* 33:81–9.

Kennard, E. A. et al. (1989). "A Program for Matched, Anonymous, Oocyte Donation." *Fertility and Sterility* 51:655–60.

Kirschner, M. et al. (2000). "Molecular Vitalism." *Cell* 100:86.

Kramer, W., J. Schneider, and N. Schultz. (2009). "U.S. Oocyte Donors: A Retrospective Study of Medical and Psychosocial Issues." *Human Reproduction* 24:3144–9.

Lahl, J. (2009). Eggsploitation: The Infertility Industry Has a Dirty Little Secret, a film by the Center for Bioethics and Culture, dir. *Jennifer Lahl* (Lines that Divide).

Langston, N. (2010). *Toxic Bodies: Hormone Disruptors and the Legacy of DES.* New Haven, CT: Yale University Press.

van Leeuwen, F. E., H. Klip, T. M. Mooij, et al. (2011). "Risk of Borderline and Invasive Ovarian Tumours after Ovarian Stimulation for In Vitro Fertilization in a Large Dutch Cohort." *Human Reproduction*, October 26, 3456–65. http://humrep.oxfordjournals.org/content/early/2011/10/19/humrep.der 322.full.

Levine, A. (2010). "Self-Regulation, Compensation, and the Ethical Recruitment of Oocyte Donors." *Hastings Center Report*, March–April: 25–36.

Lew, K. (2010). *Egg Donation: The Reasons and the Risks.* New York: Rosen Publishing.
Lutjen, P. et al. (1984). "The Establishment and Maintenance of Pregnancy Using In Vitro Fertilization and Embryo Donation in a Patient with Primary Ovarian Failure." *Nature* 307(1984):174–5.
Magnus, D. and M. K. Cho. (2006). "A Commentary on Oocyte Donation for Stem Cell Research in South Korea." *American Journal of Bioethics* 6:W23–4.
Mathias, R. J. and M. H. Clench. (1995). "Placebo Controlled Study Randomizing Leuprolide Acetate." *Digestive Diseases and Sciences* 40: 1405.
Maxwell, K. N., I. N. Cholst, and Z. Rosenwaks. (2008). "The Incidence of Both Serious and Minor Complications in Young Women Undergoing Oocyte Donation." *Fertility and Sterility* 90:2165.
Murphy, M. (2017). Alterlife in the Aftermath of Environmental Violence, talk given at UCSF, February 8, 2017.
Millican, L. (2003). "Testimony before the Subcommittee of Science, Technology, and Space, Committee on Commerce, Science, and Transportation." *U.S. Senate*, March 27.
Mosgaard, B. J., O. Lidegaard, S. K. Kjaer, et al. (1998). "Ovarian Stimulation and Borderline Ovarian Tumours: A Case–Control Study." *Fertility and Sterility* 70:1049–55.
Mukherjee, S. (2010). *The Emperor of All Maladies: A Biography of Cancer.* New York: Scribner.
Myers, J. P. and F. S. vom Saal. (2008). "Time to Update Environmental Regulations: Should Public Health Standards for Endocrine-Disrupting Compounds Be Based upon Sixteenth-Century Dogma or Modern Endocrinology?" *San Francisco Medicine* 81:30–1.
Nader, R. (1965). *Unsafe at Any Speed.* New York: Richard L. Grossman.
National Cancer Institute. (2013) "Adolescents and Young Adults with Cancer." www.cancer.gov/cancertopics/aya/types/quiz.
Norsigian, J. (2005). "Egg Donation Dangers." *GeneWatch* 18(5):6–8, 16.
Oudshoorn, N. (1994). *Beyond the Natural Body: An Archaeology of Sex Hormones.* New York: Routledge.
Pacific Fertility Center. (2017). www.pfcdonoragency.com/egg-donor/egg-donor-testimonials.
Pappo, I., et al. (2008). "Possible Association between IVF and Breast Cancer Incidence." *Annals of Surgical Oncology* 15:1048–55.
Pearson, H. (2006). "Special Report: Health Effects of Egg Donation May Take Decades to Emerge." *Nature* 442:607–8.
Powdthavee, N. (2009). 'Think Having Children Will Make You Happy?' *Psychologist* 22:308–10.

"Prempro Settlement Reached in Lawsuit over HRT Breast Cancer." (2010). *AboutLawsuits.org*, August 31. www.aboutlawsuits.com/prempro-settlement-reached-lawsuit-breast-cancer-12483 [cited as Prempro Settlement 2010].

Roberts, E. (2011). "Abandonment and Accumulation: Embryonic Futures in the United States and Ecuador." *Medical Anthropology Quarterly* 25:232–53.

Rossing, M. A., J. R. Daling, N. S. Weisset, et al. (1994). "Ovarian Tumors in a Cohort of Infertile Women." *New England Journal of Medicine* 331:771–6.

Russo, J., R. Moral, G. A. Balogh, et al. (2005). "The Protective Role of Pregnancy in Breast Cancer." *Breast Cancer Research* 7:131–42.

Sauer, M. V., R. J. Paulson, and R. A. Lobo (1996). "Rare Occurrence of Ovarian Hyperstimulation Syndrome in Oocyte Donors." *International Journal of Gynecology and Obstetrics* 52:259–62.

Schneider, J. (2007). "It's Time for an Egg Donor Registry and Long-Term Follow-Up." *Testimony at Congressional Briefing on Human Egg Trafficking*, November 14.

Seaman, A. M. (2012). "IVF in Young Women Tied to Later Breast Cancer." *Reuters*, June 23. www.reuters.com/article/2012/06/22/us-ivf-breast-cancer-idUSBRE85L1DM20120622.

Shenfield, F. (1996). "Cancer Risk and Fertility Treatments: A Question of Informed Consent." *Journal of Fertility Counseling* 15–16.

Shepard, T. H., ed. (1992). *Catalogue of Teratogenic Agents*, 7th edn, Baltimore, MD: Johns Hopkins University Press.

Silver-Greenbert, J. (2012). "In Vitro a Fertile Niche for Lenders." *Wall Street Journal*, February 24.

Skoch, I. (2010). "Should IVF Be Affordable for All?" *News Week*, July 21.

Sprague, B. L., et al. (2011). "The Contribution of Postmenopausal Hormone Use Cessation to the Declining Incidence of Breast Cancer." *Cancer Causes and Control* 22:125–34.

Stewart, L. K. et al. (2012). "In Vitro Fertilization and Breast Cancer: Is There Cause for Worry?" *Fertility and Sterility* 98:334–40.

Uroz, V. and L. Guerra. (2009). "Donation of Eggs in Assisted Reproduction and Informed Consent." *Medicine and Law* 28:565–75.

Watkins, E. (2007). *The Estrogen Elixir: A History of Hormone Replacement Therapy in America*. Baltimore, MD: Johns Hopkins University Press.

CHAPTER EIGHT

GOOD INJURIES

Anne Bloom and Marc Galanter

INTRODUCTION

Pain is associated with injury, but not all pain signals injury. Consider the following practices: body building, corseting, head/neck-shaping, foot binding, circumcision, dieting, piercing, tattooing, plastic surgery, sterilization, and castration. Each of these bodily practices involves pain, but the results are not always viewed as injurious. Depending on the setting, the results of these practices are sometimes read as "injury" and other times as "enhancement" or cure.

These arguably "good" injuries can be sorted along several dimensions, including temporary/permanent; reversible/irreversible; public/invisible; decorative/restorative; and signifying/masking. Some "good" injuries can also be understood as a formative experience or marker of a stage of life. Not uncommonly, whether injuries are viewed as harmful or enhancing is also influenced by fashion or religious obligation. Where either is at play, we tend to view the result of such practices – like circumcision, piercing, tattooing – as "enhancement" rather than "injury." The key point is that the construction of a particular event as "injury" is very much an interpretive event. Consent or a desire for the result of the ostensibly injurious practice plays a role in this interpretive process, but so do many other factors.

In this chapter, we examine how cultural perceptions of "injury" have changed over time in connection with two practices: tattooing and plastic surgery. We suggest that the increasing frequency of each practice may be associated with a category shift from "injury" to "enhancement." We argue that this shift is influenced by one or more factors: (1) the role of professional gatekeeping; (2) the extent to which the practice is viewed as a form of identity construction/presentation; and (3) the perceived curative aspects of the practice. In the analysis that follows, we demonstrate how these factors have influenced a shift in the perception of "injury" in the realms of tattooing and plastic surgery, such that some practices previously considered "injurious" may now be considered "enhancing."

Although our analysis complicates the notion of injury, we do not mean to minimize the suffering that is experienced by those who are injured. But we do wish to call attention to the role of social and cultural forces, including law, in shaping these experiences. In the setting of tattoo practices and plastic surgery, we are struck particularly by the influential role of professional gatekeepers – the tattoo artists and plastic surgeons – in determining when an injury has occurred. One of the questions raised by this essay is whether practices that emphasize individual construction of identity – like tattooing and plastic surgery – pose a challenge to the role of professionals in determining when an injury has occurred. More broadly, our analysis interrogates legal frameworks that rely on the establishment of an "injury" as a predicate for regulation or compensation.

The well-known dispute pyramid, for example, begins with the perception of injury (Felstiner et al. 1980). As a result, it does not address a significant portion of the interpretive activity that precedes the point at which an individual perceives that an injury has occurred. The root of the word "injury" – injuria – implies a *wrongful* source of pain. As we know from the dispute pyramid, some of these wrongs come to be pursued and others do not. But what the dispute pyramid does not consider is the earlier processes by which some experiences of pain come to be understood as wrongful and others do not. Our analysis suggests that gaining a better appreciation of these interpretive processes may improve our understanding of how disputes come to be litigated.

While our focus in this essay is on the interpretive move from "injury" to "enhancement," it is clear that a categorical shift in the perception of the meaning of inflicted pain may also go in the other direction. The results of the practices of corseting and foot binding, for example, seem to have moved categorically from enhancement to injury as the practices became less common and were no longer viewed as valuable or necessary for the construction or presentation of female identity. We note, too, that some practices seem to be caught in an ongoing injury/enhancement debate. Circumcision, for example, began as a practice of a religious culture, which was then medicalized and became considered enhancement. Today, however, circumcision is increasingly viewed as injury. How law and other cultural discourses intersect to influence these shifts in perception deserves much greater attention.

TATTOOING AS A "GOOD" INJURY

Tattoos provide an excellent example of arguably "good" injuries. The process of obtaining a tattoo is inevitably painful, yet the result of the practice is often viewed as an "enhancement," rather than an "injury" that should be prevented or compensated by law. In contemporary legal practice, however, the distinction between "enhancement" and "injury" remains an important one. Legal regulation of tattoo practices that lead to perceived "enhancement" tends to focus on hygiene, qualifications, and professional standards, as well as age or ability to consent. Legal regulation of tattoo practices that result in "injuries," on the other hand, generally focuses on prohibiting the practices entirely and on awarding tort damages. Our analysis of the history of tattoo practices, however, casts doubt on the meaningfulness of this distinction, suggesting that a different regulatory approach may be in order.

Tattooing has flourished since the final decades of the twentieth century. A Harris Poll of 2,225 US adults, surveyed online in October 2015, found that some 29 percent of Americans reported having at least one tattoo (seven in ten of these reported having two or more) (The Harris Poll 2016). The presence (and number) of tattoos has been increasing with each successive generation, from 10 percent among those aged 70 or more to 47 percent among those 18–35. Acceptance of tattoos in various occupational and social settings has increased correspondingly, if unevenly.

Not only are more people tattooed, but there has been a marked change in the class and gender of who is tattooed. No longer is tattooing confined to working class males. The "tattooed lady" was once a sideshow attraction (Mifflin 1997, Osterud 2014), but now women are the majority of people acquiring tattoos. While reported tattoos among males have increased from 16 percent in 2003 to 27 percent in 2015, the percentage of tattooed females has more than doubled over this period from 15 percent to 31 percent. Women have also become a prominent and growing portion of tattoo artists.

With the increase in tattoo prevalence has come increased regulation. Maine initiated the first statewide tattoo regulation in 1978. By 1995, 29 states regulated tattooing and by 2011, 41 states had least one statute regulating tattooing practice, with the nine states without statutes leaving regulation to local governments (Carlson et al. 2012). This move to regulate followed a 1999 publication of a model code for tattoos by the National Environmental Health Association that was expressly designed to assist state legislatures in developing health regulations for tattooing. Many of the model regulations focused on restrictions on tattooing minors and ensuring that the tattoo recipients have fully consented to the procedure. Soon thereafter, the states began to adopt similar restrictions.

By 2012, fully forty-five states in the United States had regulations controlling the tattooing of minors (National Conference of State Legislators 2012). Of these forty-five states, twenty-eight allowed tattooing of a person under the age of eighteen with the consent of a parent, guardian or custodian, and fifteen states banned tattooing those under the age of eighteen almost completely. Here we see how the age of the tattoo recipient marks a clear transition from "injury" to "enhancement," even when the physical result of the practice is exactly the same. But among adults too, a failure to provide consent can transform the result of the practice from "enhancing" to "injurious."

Many states require tattoo artists to obtain written consent from clients before performing tattoo procedures. Some states also require the client to attest by signature that he or she "is not intoxicated or under the influence of drugs or alcohol."[1] As these regulations make clear, the question of consent is legally significant for purposes of determining whether an injury has occurred in this setting. This is not surprising. But, importantly, consent is just one of many considerations that influence whether tattoo practices are viewed as enhancing or injurious. Even where consent exists, and the tattooing is not of a minor, the regulations convey a great deal of concern about the potentially injurious results of tattoo practices.

A closer look at tattoo regulations, for example, suggests that the consent requirement is a vehicle for warning would-be tattoo recipients about the potential health risks associated with obtaining a tattoo. Most states, for example, require the consent form to include a statement of the risks associated with tattooing and the distribution

---

[1] See, e.g., Ky. Admin. Regs 45:065(8)(3) (2013).

of aftercare instructions. Oklahoma goes even further and requires the consent form to include a list of medical conditions that the clients should disclose, along with recent consumption of food.[2] It is also interesting to note that, of the various categories of tattoo regulation, hygiene and sanitation were the most exhaustive and detailed. Generally, states regulate the minimal hygiene standards for the tattoo procedure itself, the equipment, the tattoo artists, and the building in which the tattooing takes place. This extensive emphasis on health and sanitation in the regulation of tattooing suggests the extent to which public officials view tattooing as a potentially injurious practice and even perhaps believe that it is a practice indulged in by people who are impulsive and require protection.

More than half of the states in the United States also require tattoo artists to register, be certified, or obtain a license before engaging in tattooing. There are various requirements a tattoo artist must meet in order to be registered, certified, or licensed. Generally, artists must complete blood-borne pathogen training, be at least eighteen years of age, complete an application, and pay a fee (usually less than $100). The tattoo artist must typically renew the application each year.[3] Some states also impose educational and training requirements. For example, a high school diploma or equivalent is required to practice tattooing in Iowa, Kansas, Nebraska, and Oregon.[4] And some states, such as Minnesota, require a specific amount of supervised experience.[5] Similarly, almost all states require the tattoo parlor itself to be licensed.[6] This emphasis on regulating the businesses themselves is indicative of the extent to which regulators view tattooing as a consumer choice – not unlike other consumer choices that involve bodily enhancement – that is potentially injurious, if proper protocols are not followed.

With the surge in regulation and the number of people obtaining tattoos, we also see the increased presence of tattoos and tattooing in the media and, with these developments, the expressive component of tattooing has also changed. To some extent, there were always tattoo norms governing the copying of designs, placement of tattoos

[2] Okla. Admin. Code 310:233-3-6(a) (2013).
[3] See, e.g., N.C. Gen. Stat. Ann. § 130A-283(c).
[4] Iowa Admin. Code r. 641-22.9(4) (West 2013); Kan. Admin. Regs. § 69-15-5(c) (2013); 172 Neb. Admin. Code § 44-003-44-003.01(2) (2013); Or. Rev. Stat. Ann. § 690.365(1a) (2013).
[5] Minn. Stat. Ann. § 146B.03(4) (2013).
[6] See, e.g., Ga. Code Ann. § 31-40-2 (2013).

(on the face, etc.), obscenity, and objectionable symbols and slogans. Increasing regulation formalized some of these norms, but also seems to have changed the nature of the practice itself. In the 1960s, professionally educated and trained artists began to enter the field, for example, the now well-known artist Ed Hardy. Both tattoo artists and their clients became better organized, with tattoo conventions and various media devoted to discussing and documenting the practice. Both developments also raised the status of tattoo professionals and may have helped tattooing become more socially acceptable as another normal form of consumption. As one Las Vegas tattoo shop advertised, "You can change your décor ... [d]esign a wall, your car, the appearance of your house, *or your flesh*" (emphasis added) (Benson 2000: 245).

After the 1960s, the location of tattoo parlors also began to change. Instead of being located in the sleazier parts of urban areas, tattoo parlors began to appear in more desirable parts of the communities and even in shopping malls. Some places also became "appointment only" – emphasizing the professionalized and artistic nature of the work. Meanwhile, more women became tattoo artists and, increasingly, tattoo artists have attended art school as part of their training. And of course, at this time, the customer base also began to change, with women and members of the middle class obtaining tattoos in increasing numbers.

The changes in demographics correspond with changing motivations for obtaining tattoos. Historically, tattoo practices were often tied to marking or commemorating specific life cycle events. They have also been employed to mark group identity, as in gangs. Increasingly, however, tattoo practices are closely connected with the individual construction of personal identity. Indeed, contemporary tattoo practices are increasingly understood in terms of self-realization, especially for women (Caplan 2000).

For some, tattooing is a means of enhancing the body to make it more physically attractive in response to cultural demands, much like exercise or plastic surgery. As one tattoo recipient explained:

> I went through plastic surgeries, diets, and exercise programs in the last five years to get my body in the best looking and feeling shape possible ... So I thought, hey, a tattoo artist is a kind of aesthetician. He could help make me beautiful, like the doctor who surgically raised my brow, or the trainer who brought out my stomach [muscles] (Atkinson 2004: 134, quoting "Rachael").

It is important to note, however, that tattoos are quite different from most other forms of bodily expression. Unlike clothing, make-up, henna or even "fake" or temporary tattoos, "real" tattoos demand the commitment of permanence and unerasability. While fashion plays a part, more deep-seated identity aspirations also seem to be at play. For example, some women obtain tattoos as a way of reclaiming their own bodies in response to rape, harassment, or abuse.

Moreover, tattooing continues to have strong links with resistance or rejection of mainstream culture in the minds of tattoo professionals and their clients, and in culture more broadly. To quote another tattoo recipient:

> I put on this armor [tattoos] and show how I won't lie down and be a victim. It's like drawing a line in the sand and saying, I might be at risk but you can't cross this line. Right here is where I make my stand (Atkinson 2004: 138, quoting "Regina").

This is an example of the tattoo serving as both a marker of resistance and as a carapace or protective shell. If anything, the expansion of tattoo practice seems to have expanded the opportunity to engage in this kind of resistance to a much broader audience. There is also a perception, compared with the past, of greater autonomy on the part of the tattooed subject, who now plays a larger role in choosing a designer and proposing or modifying the design, rather than picking from a limited set of options on the wall.

There is also growing recognition of the potential role that tattooing may play in healing injuries. For example, in recent years, tattoo artists have begun to provide nipple tattoos to women who have undergone a mastectomy and reconstruction of a breast. Typically, doctors with very little training or experience with tattooing have performed this procedure. But, increasingly, tattoo artists are sought out to perform the procedure as well. In some instances, tattoo artists have even formed formal partnerships with plastic surgeons to provide the service to the surgeon's patients. This type of alliance suggests a curative dimension of tattooing.

Interestingly, this resonates with older conceptions of tattooing. It appears that the very earliest tattoo practices were engaged in for curative reasons. In 1991, some 57 tattoos were found on the so-called "Tyrolean Iceman," whose bodily tissue is dated as between 5,350 and 5,100 years old (Pabst et al. 2009). Tattoos were also found on female Egyptian mummies dating from around 211 BC. In each instance, the tattooing appears to have been performed for reasons such as healing arthritis or fostering fertility. Historically, tattoos have also been associated with a protective power that helps to guard the recipient against poor physical and spiritual health (Cortez 2013).

In modern times, however, tattoos have frequently been viewed as a form of self-harm. Yet there is also increasing recognition that tattooing may play a therapeutic role, especially for those with psychological or emotional injuries. Some tattoo practitioners, for example, describe tattooing as a way of externalizing or perhaps sealing against internal pain (Benson 2000). Others view the practice as a means of releasing pain or engaging in a self-transformation in response to past injury. In one study of Chicana tattoo recipients, for example, the researcher found that virtually all of the tattoo recipients had obtained one or more of their tattoos during a stressful or traumatic period in their lives and viewed the tattoos as an essential part of their healing (Cortez 2013). As one recipient explained, the tattoo was "a coping mechanism ... because I felt I hadn't healed fully yet[without the tattoo]" (ibid.: 177). Moreover, several recipients associated their tattoos with the eventual release of physical symptoms that they associated with trauma, such as head, neck, or stomach pain (ibid: 184–9).

From this perspective, tattooing may be viewed not simply as enhancement, but as a "good injury" that empowers its subjects by making them feel, and perhaps helping them to be perceived as, less vulnerable. Still, tattooing practices necessarily entail the infliction of pain and wounding. For some, however, this temporary pain can be "restorative" or "healing" and allows them to "make something beautiful" out of far more intense internal pain (Cortez 2013: 193–4). In other words, the practice of tattooing becomes a way of discharging other kinds of pain and allowing the healing process to begin.

Regulations on tattoos arguably interfere with some of these attempts to heal and express the self. On the other hand, increased regulation may have helped to legitimate tattoo practices and, in doing so, made the practices more accessible and culturally acceptable. Thus, the relationship between law and culture in this context seems complex. The increasing frequency of tattoo practices appears to be associated with a categorical shift from "injury" to "enhancement." But, at the same time, the increased regulation may have lessened some of tattooing's transgressive – and perhaps expressive – appeal.

PLASTIC SURGERY AS A "GOOD" INJURY

Like tattoos, the results of plastic surgery are commonly perceived as "good" injuries. The processes involved are often even more painful than tattooing, yet the industry is relatively unregulated, with surgical standards, rather than law, largely determining the parameters of what is permissible. As with tattooing, plastic surgery is on the rise. In the last few decades, the number of plastic procedures performed annually has risen dramatically in the United States. To give a few examples, from 1997 to 2016, liposuction procedures increased 134 percent, breast lifts increased 712 percent and tummy tucks increased 434 percent (American Society for Aesthetic Plastic Surgeons 2016). More men are pursuing plastic surgery than ever before: nearly 1 in 10 procedures in the United States in 2016 were performed on men (ibid.). A greater percentage of young people are also undergoing plastic surgery. According to the latest statistics, people aged 35–50 have more procedures performed than any other demographic, with the 19–34 age group not far behind (ibid.). As with tattooing, "injury" has been transmuted into "enhancement."

In the plastic surgery context, surgeons have played an important role in drawing the line between "injury" and "enhancement," in response to changing cultural attitudes. Indeed, plastic surgery practices began as a technique for correcting bodies with culturally unacceptable differences. Some of the earliest plastic surgeries, for example, were developed to rebuild the noses of sixteenth-century syphilitics so that the symptoms of the disease would be less visible. Because of this history, the surgery was initially viewed as an expedient to repair injury and not as an injury itself. The surge in plastic surgery that took place after the First World War, when surgeons employed the techniques on injured soldiers, was viewed in a similar way. Even when the surgeries did not succeed, they were widely viewed as a response to injury, rather than injurious in themselves (Taschen 2005).

After the First World War, plastic surgeons began to distinguish between performing "plastic" surgeries to repair injured body parts and "cosmetic" surgeries that focus on enhancement. Over time, this distinction became very important. Surgical practices gain more cultural currency, and typically qualify for insurance coverage, when they are characterized as "plastic." In large part, this is because "plastic surgery" is associated with healing. "Cosmetic" surgery, in contrast, has been historically associated with vanity. The distinction between "plastic" and "cosmetic" surgeries, however, is not always clear (Bloom 2014). The history of "eye lifts" (blepharoplasty) provides an interesting example (Shirakabe et al. 1985). Initially developed by a Japanese physician as an admittedly "cosmetic" procedure to make Japanese eyes appear more Western, the same physician later claimed that the procedure was not "cosmetic." According to this new narrative, the lids of his Japanese patients were physical "defects" that needed to be corrected. Today, the procedure may be designated as either "plastic" or "cosmetic," depending on the surgeon's assessment of the patient's pre-surgical condition. Because there is essentially no difference between the actual results or surgical techniques employed, however, cosmetic procedures like eye lifts are now increasingly referred to as "plastic."

For similar reasons, "plastic" surgery today is understood to encompass both cosmetic and reconstructive procedures. In 1999, the American Society of Plastic and Reconstructive Surgeons changed its name to the American Society of Plastic Surgeons to more strongly communicate the message that there is no distinction between the two. At the same time, the terms "plastic" and "cosmetic" continue to play an important role in the demarcation of professionals operating in this field. "Plastic" surgeons are board certified by the American Board of Plastic Surgery, while "cosmetic" surgeons have less training and may include general practitioners. "Cosmetic" surgeons tend to emphasize that "cosmetic" surgery is elective and not medically necessary. "Plastic" surgeons, in contrast, explain their work in terms of ensuring "normal" functioning and appearance. As was the case with eye lifts, however, the standards for what constitutes "normal" functioning and appearance have changed over time.

While plastic surgery was previously a relatively uncommon practice, surgical procedures to address perceived imperfections are increasingly expected, especially for women, almost as a form of bodily maintenance. At the same time, the possibilities for surgical transformation are quite constrained. In the case of aging women, for example, it is not acceptable to undergo surgery to look older (American Society for Aesthetic Plastic Surgeons 2016). Instead, the expectation is that bodies should look "naturally" young, with the help of surgical procedures. Importantly, for the most part, these expectations are determined by men. Some 85 percent of board-certified plastic surgeons are men and the medical standards governing plastic surgery practices are largely determined by these male surgeons' aesthetic preferences (Bloom 2014).

Like tattoos, however, the results of plastic surgery practices can also be considered a form of self-expression. Consider the plastic surgery practices of the French artist Orlan, who uses her body as a medium for her art. Orlan has undergone multiple plastic surgeries to make parts of her body look more like the body parts that are portrayed in famous works of art. Instead of making her look younger, however, Orlan's surgeries were intended to give her the forehead of Leonardo da Vinci's Mona Lisa and the chin of Botticelli's Venus. Instead of trying to look "natural," Orlan views her plastic surgeries as a struggle against nature. In other words, Orlan is deliberately "injuring" herself for artistic reasons that have nothing to do with healing (Davis 2003). In this respect, Orlan might be viewed as a contemporary counterpart of the tattooed ladies of old – a pioneer in the employment of plastic surgery as a form of self-expression (Osterud 2014).

At the same time, Orlan's artistic practice is similar to that of ordinary plastic surgery consumers. Orlan emphasizes that she views the surgeries as a way of becoming more fully herself. Interviews with plastic surgery consumers indicate that they approach their own surgeries in a similar way (Gimlin 2012). Like Orlan, they view their surgeries as vehicles of self-expression and self-determination. As is the case in tattooing, US women, in particular, have historically described their decision to undergo plastic surgery in terms of an expression of autonomy (Gimlin 2012) and freedom (Davis 2003). For example, a schoolteacher in her mid-thirties who underwent facial surgery described her feelings afterward as "It gave me a kick, like, I'll be damned, but I really did it" (ibid.: 79). More recently, US consumers of plastic surgery have begun to emphasize self-improvement as their primary motivation (Gimlin 2012).

Ordinary plastic surgery consumers are not presented with the same array of surgical options as Orlan, however. Most plastic surgeons would not agree to do surgeries like the ones Orlan obtained, even for a well-known artist. This is because the particular aesthetic result that Orlan is seeking to achieve does not correspond with the range of aesthetic procedures that are considered acceptable by most plastic surgeons. Not unlike an earlier point in history, when many plastic surgeons in the United States refused to perform surgeries that might allow an individual to fake "race," today's plastic surgeons refuse to perform surgeries that they consider aesthetically or socially undesirable. Examples of the types of surgeries that plastic surgeons routinely refuse to perform include requests for breasts that are "beyond the normal range," surgery that causes deliberate scarring, and facial surgery to achieve a "feline look" (Taschen 2005: 304, 310).

Plastic surgeons readily acknowledge that their own cultural preferences play a role in their surgical recommendations. Many consider themselves artists and recommend surgeries that reflect their own "style" (Taschen 2005: 92–3). These aesthetic choices are supported by regulations governing plastic surgery – which defer heavily to professional standards set by plastic surgeons themselves – and by legal standards in tort law that determine "injury" in the plastic surgery context by deferring to the judgments of plastic surgeons. These judgments also restrict the self-expressive choices that plastic surgery consumers can make. As one article advising on legal issues in plastic surgery explained, "[t]he patient who ... has unrealistic expectations for surgical results ... should be avoided before performing surgery" (Shiffman 2005: 212). The same piece also explains that patients with a "dysmorphic" personality – who see defects in their appearance when they are none – should be avoided. In other words, it is the plastic surgeon rather, than the consumer, who determines whether one is sufficiently "injured" or in need of "enhancement." This stands in stark contrast to tattooing, where consumer choice and involvement in the design are key parts of the practice.

As with tattooing, many recipients of plastic surgery also view the surgeries as a form of healing (Huss-Ashmore 2000). Most people undergoing plastic surgery, for example, say that they are undergoing surgery to feel more "'at home' in their bodies" (Davis 2003: 110). It is also not uncommon to see the procedures marketed in terms that relate to health. One columnist, for example, referred to plastic surgery as a "great adjunct to the [recipient's] health and fitness regime, improving those areas that diet and exercise won't" (Taschen 2005: 108). Rebecca Huss-Ashmore describes these as "therapeutic" narratives in which the focus is on healing the surgery recipient in ways that allow the individual's true identity to emerge (Huss-Ashmore 2000).

THE INTERSECTING DIMENSIONS OF GOOD INJURIES

Both tattooing and plastic surgery may be viewed as practices implicated in the construction of identity. Tattoos, once an important cultural signifier of group identity, are now widely embraced by individuals as expressive of personal choice. Similarly, plastic surgery is increasingly an expression of identity by younger women and others, for whom the surgery is not culturally mandated in the same way that it is for women of a certain age and class. Thus, both practices are popular tools in the catalogue of options for self-presentation. Perhaps more important, what seems particularly distinctive of our time is this sense that you can construct yourself in this way.

It is also interesting to note that there is a minority of (mostly younger) people undergoing plastic surgery who are less interested in looking natural. Instead, in the spirit of Orlan, they are more interested in using the surgery as a form of open self-expression where the presence of the work is obvious. The aim is not to appear natural. In this respect, plastic surgery may be following the path of tattooing, where the subject of the practice plays a more active role in selecting a designer or directing the design, rather than picking from a limited set of options. When this occurs, the subject has greater autonomy and, under those circumstances, the result of the practice looks even more like "enhancement." At this point in time, however, the medical community exercises much greater control over the enhancement options that are available to plastic surgery recipients than tattoo artists exercise over tattoo recipients.

In any event, the growing cultural emphasis on self-construction – through tattooing, plastic surgery, and other practices – poses a challenge to conventional understandings of injury. Both tattoo practices and plastic surgery necessarily entail wounding and the infliction of pain to achieve the desired transformation. In these contexts, however, the wounding does not result in what we might ordinarily consider "injury." Like many medical procedures, these practices are typically accompanied by consent, which – in most instances – tends to remove them from the scope of legal injury. Nevertheless, this does not resolve the cultural question of whether an injury or enhancement has occurred, particularly in the case of minors. While certain types of plastic surgeries – such as harelip, nose and double eyelid surgery (on Asian children) – are performed routinely, other types of plastic surgeries on minors are more controversial. Plastic surgery to "normalize" the features of children with Down syndrome, for example, has drawn criticism – even when there is parental consent – as has surgery to construct binary (male/female) sex characteristics on intersex infants. In these instances, the debate over whether the procedure results in injury or enhancement is ongoing.

With both tattooing and plastic surgery, the increasing frequency of the practices seems to be associated with a categorical shift from injury to enhancement. In each instance, however, the increasing frequency also appears to correlate with greater regulation of the practices in the form of professional standards and licensing. At least initially, the emergence of a well-regulated profession appears along with a tremendous expansion of access. There remains the possibility, however, that the professionalization of the practices may limit the freedom to shape one's own identity and to participate in practices aimed at challenging dominant cultural norms.

Professionals play a key gatekeeping role in both practices, primarily by limiting choices and shaping what is permissible. Tattoo artists, for example, usually will not tattoo faces and the backs of hands because they view the result as potentially posing too much of an "impairment" for purposes of socializing and employment. Similarly, most plastic surgeons decline to do horns or other modifications that they think are a mistake. Both tattoo artists and plastic surgeons also have signature looks, which tend to emphasize the artistry of the professional more than the distinctiveness of the recipient. Professionals in both fields tend to impart their artistic values to the recipients of their services.

We also note the recent emphasis in both practices on the role of these apparently "good injuries" in promoting healing. For people who have been damaged, physically or psychically, tattoos and plastic surgery seems to take on a curative dimension, especially for women. Specifically, in some instances, the results of the tattooing or plastic surgery seem to help the subject to feel less vulnerable. The emphasis on the potentially therapeutic role of these practices, in turn, may help to facilitate an understanding of these "good injuries" as "enhancement." At the same time, the designation of the practice as "enhancement" seems to generate a different perception of the subject, who is now perceived as less vulnerable as a result of the practice.

Mass media depictions of tattooing and plastic surgery reflect, and perhaps help to construct, these changing perceptions. Indeed, it is notable that, while tattooing and plastic surgery practices have become increasingly normalized in the mass media, other body modification practices, such as piercing, continue to be negatively framed in the media as potentially injurious (Adams 2009). A recent survey of articles about tattooing, for example, suggests that tattooing is now widely associated with fashion, identity and art rather than social deviance (ibid.: 110). Similarly, articles on plastic surgery commonly draw upon the institutional legitimacy of medicine to frame the practice in terms of health and wellness (ibid.: 112). Piercing, in contrast, continues to be portrayed as a health hazard, with an emphasis on the perceived absence of professional oversight and regulation in the piercing industry (ibid.: 116). And, while recipients of tattoos and plastic surgery are now largely portrayed as mentally healthy individuals engaging in self-expression or self-improvement, the pursuit of other kinds of bodily modifications, such as piercing, continues to be viewed as an indicator of antisocial behavior or mental illness (ibid.: 116). These studies highlight the extent to which the construction of a particular body modification experience as "injury" is very much an interpretive event. While consent plays some role, so do many other factors – including the perceived curative aspects of the practice and the perceived legitimacy of the individual's interest in controlling the terms of their own identity presentation.

The relationship between law and cultural perceptions of injuries in the tattooing and plastic surgery contexts is plainly complex. On the one hand, the increasing regulation and resulting professionalization of both practices seems to be associated with a categorical shift from "injury" to "enhancement." On the other hand, the growing cultural emphasis on self-construction and the increasing emphasis on the therapeutic and expressive value of these practices for individuals also seem to pose a challenge to the role of professionals in determining the scope of options to be made available to consumers and the boundaries imposed.

The implications of these developments seem especially significant for women, who are increasingly choosing to undergo plastic surgery at younger ages and have gone from being a tiny minority of the tattooed population to a majority, and the fastest growing demographic of tattoo consumers. While, in some instances, the presentation choices appear to conform to conventional constructions of femininity, the uptick in activity might also be read as an expression of the desire for self-assertion that has accompanied the drive for equality. Many American women, for example, now view plastic surgery as a form of self-improvement that will help them to become more successful in the marketplace (Gimlin 2012). And many women also report that they obtain tattoos as a form of resistance to dominant gender codes (Atkinson 2002: 233). As more and more women engage in these practices, it seems likely that they will also seek to play a larger role in negotiating the terms of regulation.

References

Adams, Josh. (2009). "Bodies of Change: A Comparative Analysis of Media Representations of Body Modification Practices." *Sociological Perspectives* 52(1):103–29.

American Society for Aesthetic Plastic Surgeons. (2016). *2016 Cosmetic Surgery National Data Bank Statistics*. www.surgery.org/sites/default/files/ASAPS-Stats2016.pdf.

Atkinson, Michael. (2002). "Pretty in Ink: Conformity, Resistance and Negotiation in Women's Tattooing." *Sex Roles* 47:219–35.

(2004). "Tattooing and Civilizing Processes: Body Modification as Self-control." *The Canadian Review of Sociology and Anthropology* 41:125–46.

Benson, Susan. (2000). "Inscriptions of the Self: Reflections on Tattooing and Piercing in Contemporary Euro-American." Pp. 234–54 in *Written on the Body. The Tattoo in European and American History*, edited by Jane Caplan. London: Reaktion Books.

Bloom, Anne. (2014). "Plastic Injuries." *Hofstra Law Review* 42(3), Article 3. http://scholarlycommons.law.hofstra.edu/hlr/vol42/iss3/3/.

Caplan, Jane. (2000). "Introduction." Pp. 234–54 in *Written on the Body. The Tattoo in European and American History*, edited by Jane Caplan. London: Reaktion Books.

Carlson, Valeria P., Everett J. Lehman, and Myrna Armstrong. (2012). "Tattooing Regulations in U.S. States, 2011." *Journal of Environmental Health* 75:30–7.

Cortez, Carisa Prieto. (2013). "*Survivors Ink: Self Transformation, Self-Creation and Healing Through Tattoo*." PhD Dissertation, University of California, Santa Barbara.

Davis, Kathy. (2003). *Dubious Equalities*. Oxford: Rowman and Littlefield Publishers.

Felstiner, William L.F., Richard L. Abel, and Austin Sarat. (1980). "The Emergence and Transformation of Disputes: Naming, Blaming, Claiming ..." *Law & Society Review* 15:631–54.

Gimlin, Debra. (2012). *Cosmetic Surgery Narratives, A Cross-Cultural Analysis of Women's Accounts*. London: Palgrave Macmillan, Basingstoke.

Huss-Ashmore, Rebecca. (2000). "'The Real Me': Therapeutic Narrative in Cosmetic Surgery." *Expedition* 42:26–37.

Mifflin, Margot. (1997). *Bodies of Subversion: A Secret History of Women and Tattoo*. New York: Juno Books.

National Conference of State Legislators. (2012). "Tattoos and Body Piercings for Minors." *NCLS.org*. www.ncsl.org/issues.

Osterud, Amelia Klum. (2014). *The Tattooed Lady: A History*, 2nd edn. Lanham, MD: Taylor Trade Publishing.

Pabst, Maria Anna, Ilse Leftosky-Papst, Maximillian Moser, Leopold Dorfer, and Eduard Egarter-Vigl. (2009). "The Tattoos of the Tyrolean Iceman:

A Light Microscopical, Ultrastructural and Element Analytical Study." *The Journal of Archaeological Science* 36:2335–41.

Shiffman, Melvin A. (2005). "Medical Liability Issues in Cosmetic and Plastic Surgery." *Med Law* 24:211–32.

Shirakabe, Y., T. Kinugasa, M. Kawata, T. Kishimoto, and T. Shirakabe. (1985). "The Double-Eyelid Operation in Japan: Its Evolution as Related to Cultural Changes." *Annals of Plastic Surgery* 15:224–41.

Taschen, Angelika. (2005). *Aesthetic Surgery*. Los Angeles: Taschen.

The Harris Poll. (2016). "Tattoo Takeover: Three in Ten Americans Have Tattoos, and Most Don't Stop at Just One." February 10. www.theharrispoll.com/health-and-life/Tattoo_Takeover.html (accessed October 15, 2017).

CHAPTER NINE

PRIVACY AND THE RIGHT TO ONE'S IMAGE
A Cultural and Legal History

Samantha Barbas

After receiving calls from her neighbors, a woman found that her daughter's picture had been used in an ad for a local ice cream store, without the daughter's or the mother's consent. Her daughter had simply "liked" the ice cream store on Facebook. The woman was outraged and embarrassed. People across the country whose photographs had been similarly exploited under Facebook's Sponsored Stories advertising program sued Facebook (Henn 2013).

In 1948, the *Saturday Evening Post* ran a critique of cab drivers in Washington, DC that accused them of cheating their customers. A photograph appeared with the article that depicted a woman cab driver, Muriel Peay, talking to the article's author on the street. The caption did not name her, and the article did not refer to her. Although the woman consented to be photographed, she did not know that the picture would be used in an article on cheating cabbies. She was humiliated, and she sued the magazine.[1]

Angry and insulted, these individuals could have done any number of things to address their sense of injury and violation. They chose to sue. In the past hundred years, in increasing number, Americans have turned to the law to help them defend their reputations and public images. The twentieth century saw the creation of what I describe as a *law of public image*, and the phenomenon of *personal image litigation*.

---

[1] *Peay v. Curtis Pub. Co.*, 78 F. Supp. 305 (D.D.C. 1948).

Under these laws of image, you can sue if you've been depicted in an embarrassing manner, even if no one thinks less of you for it. If a newspaper or website publishes your picture in a way you find offensive, you can, under certain circumstances, receive monetary damages for your sense of affront – for the outrage that someone has taken liberties with your public image and interfered with the way you want to be known to others. These "laws of image" consist principally of the tort actions for invasion of privacy, libel, and intentional infliction of emotional distress.

One's *image* or *public image*, as I define it, is one's public face, the persona one projects to the world through such external signs and attributes as one's gestures, speech, dress, and social behavior. An image is something that one has, and that one creates: it is our conscious externalization of self. Image overlaps with, but is distinct from *reputation*, which is an external judgment – how other people see you. Image law protects both the right to a good reputation and the right to one's image – the right to control one's public image and to feel good about one's public presentation of self.

These laws of image are a modern invention, created to address conceptions of the self and personal injury that have become dominant in the United States in the past hundred years. This essay explores the origins of these laws of image, tracing them to the rise of what I describe as an *image-conscious self*, the modal self of our mass-mediated, mass consumer society. The laws of image are an expression of a people who have become fascinated – even obsessed – with their personal images; who have come to see their images as coextensive with their identities, so that an injury to one's image constitutes an injury to one's self.

***

The story begins at the end of the nineteenth century, with the rise of major urban centers in the United States. In 1860, only 20 percent of the population lived in towns of 2,500 or more. By 1900, a third of the population lived in towns and cities. Between 1860 and 1910, America's urban population increased sevenfold (Hofstadter 1955: 173).

The process of urbanization unsettled long-established ways of creating a social self. In small towns and villages, a person's social identity had been a product of ongoing interactions with a known and familiar community. While reputations and social identities were by no means unchangeable, they were somewhat fixed. The collective memory in small communities was strong, and a person "knows better than to suppose that he can deceive [others] into thinking that he is something radically different from what he is" (Blumenthal 1932: 44).

By contrast, in the cities, surrounded by strangers, one's social identity was more often a function of first impressions rather than continued contact. While in a small community there was little need for an individual to carefully "signal" herself – to display her background, beliefs, and social status on the surface of her appearance – the more socially fluid and fragmented conditions of city life demanded that people externalize their identities. As sociologist George Simmel observed in 1903, the "brevity and rarity" of meetings between individuals on the streets and other urban venues created a desire to "make oneself noticeable" upon first glance, to distinguish oneself through one's manners, looks, and gestures (Simmel 1950: 421).

The heightened importance of surfaces and first impressions led to increased attention to the presentation of self in public. In the cities and large towns of the late nineteenth century, there was a new preoccupation with mastering and perfecting one's social appearance. "Impression management," to use sociologist Erving Goffman's phrase, became an important personal project and goal (Goffman 1955). People began to speak of life in theatrical metaphors – of social existence as an "act" on a "stage." One "performed" one's identity, went out in public to "see and be seen." It was thought that these "presentational performances" required proper costume, diction, and gestures; advice and etiquette books, with elaborate instructions on how to dress, how to greet people, and what to say in public, were issued at an unprecedented rate (Schlesinger 1946: 35).

Technological and industrial developments enhanced this attentiveness to self-presentation in public. Portrait photography was becoming popular, and mass-produced clothing, ubiquitous by the 1890s, put a fashionable appearance within the reach of the ordinary consumer (Schorman 2003: 13). Advertisements encouraged people to scrutinize their appearances and to purchase items that would help them enhance their looks and images. While public visibility had always been an essential part of life for the famous, the notion that "everyone could and should be looked at" was a novel, modern concept (Braudy 1997: 506).

By the late nineteenth century, individuals across the social spectrum were being encouraged to cultivate an attitude toward their bodies, appearances, and feelings that was strategic and instrumental.

They were adopting an external perspective on themselves, considering how they might appear before strangers, and seeing themselves as *images* in the eyes of others (Kasson 1991: 114). There was to be a reward for this scrupulous management of personal image – respect, upward mobility, and the possibility of social and material success. Especially in the new urban centers, where social hierarchies were unstable, it was thought that the "self-made" man could create a new identity and advance socially by appearing more refined and genteel than he really was.

To be clear: people were not becoming "superficial." We can see, nonetheless, a new attentiveness to public images, and to potential threats to those images. John Kasson, in his history of urban life and manners in the nineteenth century, has noted the great fear in this time of being discredited and "exposed" – that nosy neighbors, gossiping houseguests, and whispering co-workers might reveal the "truth" behind one's social façade (Kasson 1991: 114). The mass media were posing especially formidable threats to personal image, threats that the average citizen was seemingly helpless to control, manage, or defend against.

***

In the late 1800s, with urbanization, an expanding audience for publications, and advances in publishing technology, a massive volume of printed material flooded the market. Mass-circulation magazines such as the *Ladies' Home Journal* debuted and became popular (Kaestle and Radway 2009: 57, 60–1). Total national circulation of monthly magazines rose from 18 million in 1890 to 64 million in 1905 – nearly four magazines per American household (ibid.: 103). Newspaper readership increased 400 percent between 1870 and 1900, and the number of newspapers doubled (Pember 1972: 10).

In the early 1800s, the typical subject of press coverage had been the activities of "public figures" – politicians, public officials, captains of industry. Publishers eventually realized that "human interest" stories – "chatty little reports of tragic or comic incidents in the lives of the people" – attracted more readers than dry copy about the comings and goings of officials and statesmen (Hughes 1940, Dicken Garcia 1989: 64). Crimes, love affairs, divorces, holidays, social outings, illnesses, births, deaths – matters of ordinary existence were scooped out of neighborhoods by aggressive "roving reporters" and fed to a curious public. "The interest in other people's affairs in this country is almost measureless," observed the *Outlook* magazine in 1896. "The morning and evening papers make us feel as if we belonged to a great village and ... as if our chief interest lay in what is going on at the other end of the street" (The Passion for Publicity 1896: 738). In the 1880s and 1890s, several states proposed and passed laws providing for civil liability or criminal punishment for sensational press content.[2] There was also a turn to the tort of libel.

For centuries, the twin torts of defamation – libel and slander – had protected reputations against scandalous falsehoods. One's reputation is one's good name among one's peers – the "estimate in which he is held by the public in the place he is known."[3] In order to be legally actionable as a libel or slander, a statement had to be both defamatory and false. A defamatory statement was one that seriously lowered a person's esteem in his community: it "expose[d] a person to hatred or contempt ... injure[d] him in his profession or trade, [and] cause[d] him to be shunned by his neighbors" (Odgers 1887: 19). The rise of the sensationalistic press and "human interest" journalism led to a surge in libel lawsuits. In his study of tort litigation in turn of the century New York, Randall Bergstrom found that the number of libel cases before the New York Supreme Court increased by over twenty times between 1870 and 1910 (Bergstrom 1992: 20). Francis Laurent's study of a trial court in Wisconsin showed a significant increase in libel cases between 1875 and 1914, most of them against local newspapers (Laurent 1959: 49, 164).

Initiating a lawsuit is, inevitably, an assertion of rights. When plaintiffs commenced a libel lawsuit, they were claiming, in effect, that they had a legal entitlement to their reputations. There was nothing novel about this. In theory, the common law had always protected reputation. Yet the fact that more people were claiming the right – that men and women across the social spectrum felt compelled to bring libel lawsuits – suggests not only that people saw their public images and reputations as being especially imperiled, but also that those aspects of the self had become more valuable and treasured. A good reputation was a sign of virtue and rectitude; it was also critical to socioeconomic mobility in the late 1800s, a time of greatly expanding opportunities

---

[2] Several states passed laws that prohibited the publication of "criminal news, police reports ... or accounts of ... bloodshed, lust, or crime." See *Winters* v. *New York*, 333 U.S. 507 (1948).

[3] *Cooper* v. *Greeley & McElrath*, 1 Denio, 347 (N.Y. Sup. Ct. 1845).

for social advancement. There was another reason for this protectiveness of reputation – Americans' increasing image-consciousness, their attunement to social appearances and the impressions they made in the eyes of others.

***

Defamation law dealt with false statements that lowered one's standing among one's peers. It did not always or adequately address the problem of media "gossip" – facts that were often true, and that did not necessarily injure reputation, but nonetheless caused humiliation and distress. The search for legal remedies for the gossip problem led to the invention of the legal "right to privacy," credited to the famous 1890 *Harvard Law Review* article "The Right to Privacy."

The article, by the future Supreme Court justice Louis Brandeis and his colleague Samuel Warren, attacked gossip columns and information about personal affairs "spread broadcast in the columns of the daily papers." "Persons with whose affairs the community has no legitimate concerns" were "being dragged into an undesirable and undesired publicity" (Brandeis and Warren 1890: 193). To a dignified person seeking respect and status, having the details of one's personal life publicized in the press caused embarrassment and "mental pain and distress," "far greater than could be inflicted by mere bodily injury" (ibid.: 214).

The article accused the press of "invading privacy" when it revealed a person's emotions, activities, and personal idiosyncrasies before a public audience, even though such matters were not "private," in the sense of being secret or concealed. Newspapers could "invade privacy" when they published a person's photograph, even if it was taken at a public event, or when they described one's participation in social activities such as weddings or balls. The article discussed the recent case of *Manola v. Stevens*, involving flash photographs of an actress obtained without her permission as she appeared on the stage (Brandeis and Warren 1890: 195). The description of a woman at a social gathering was technically not "private," nor were pictures of an actress performing in public. These publications were nonetheless said to "invade privacy" because in presenting the subject out of context, and before an audience not of her own choosing, they impaired her ability to create her own social identity, to define her public image as she wished.

Brandeis and Warren proposed a common law cause of action that would allow the victims of such "invasions of privacy" to sue and recover monetary damages (Brandeis and Warren 1890: 219). Unlike libel, their tort of invasion of privacy did not protect a person's esteem in the eyes of others so much as one's capacity to define his own public persona: "the right of determining ... to what extent his thoughts, sentiments, and emotions shall be communicated to others" (ibid.: 198). The right to privacy was the right to keep one's personal affairs out of the public eye, and more broadly, to determine one's own public image without undue interference from the mass media. A manifestation of the emerging image consciousness of the time, it was the right to control one's public image and to receive damages for injuries to one's feelings about one's image. By 1910, eight states had recognized a "right to privacy" as a right to control one's public image and to protect one's image against unwanted, humiliating media depictions.[4]

***

As the image-conscious sensibility gained purchase on the popular imagination in the twentieth century, and the mass media posed ongoing threats to people's public images, existing areas of law were expanded and new laws created to protect what was being described as a right to one's public image. In the 1930s and 1940s, a majority of states recognized the tort right to privacy, described as a right to avoid undesirable and "unwarranted publicity."[5] Libel claims increased, and courts expanded libel doctrine to reach a wider range of emotional harms and image-based harms. In a number of different contexts, courts were recognizing a right to one's image, and the *personal image lawsuit* became a fixture of American legal culture.

***

In the first few decades of the twentieth century, the United States became an *image society*, marked by an escalating cultural emphasis on images, surfaces, and social appearances. An especially intense brand

---

[4] At common law: *Pavesich v. New England Life Ins. Co.*, 50 S.E. 68 (Ga. 1905); *Pritchett v. Knox Cty. Bd. of Comm'rs*, 85 N.E. 32 (Ind. App. 1908); *Foster-Millburn Co. v. Chinn*, 120 S.W. 364 (Ky. 1909), *appeal after remand*, 127 S.W. 476 (Ky. 1910); *Schulman v. Whitaker*, 39 So. 737 (La. 1906); *Vanderbilt v. Mitchell*, 67 A. 97 (N.J. E. and A. 1907). By statute: New York, 1903, N.Y. Civ. Rights Law § 50; Utah, 1909, Utah Code Ann. §§ 76-4-8 and 76-4-9; Virginia, 1904, Va. Code Ann. § 8-650.

[5] *Sidis v. F-R Pub. Corp.*, 113 F.2d 806 (C.A. 2d Cir. 1940).

of image consciousness took root in the 1920s, a decade that is often described by historians as the first "modern" decade in US history – one that saw the rise of a mass society, the mass media, mass-marketed products, and increasing cultural standardization and homogeneity (see Dumenil 1995).

In 1920, the census registered, for the first time, more Americans living in cities than in rural areas (McNeese and Jensen 2010: 107). As sociologists Robert Park and Ernest Burgess wrote in their 1925 study *The City*, the contacts of the city might have been face-to-face, "but they are ... superficial, transitory, and segmental" (Wirth 1938: 12). The perceived depersonalization of daily life, and the superficiality of social exchange, produced something of an existential crisis for Americans in this time. American culture became preoccupied with the dilemma of personal distinction – the difficulty of "standing out from the crowd." How could one preserve a sense of self amidst a sea of strangers? The answer posed by advertisers, personnel managers, psychologists and other cultural arbiters lay in *personal image* – a distinctive appearance, "magnetic personality," and pleasing first impression. A "winning image" was one that was so stunning and unforgettable – so charismatic and appealing – as to secure for a person instant notice.

As a practical matter, the cultivation of a positive image had practical application in many areas of life in which the rise of a mass society and constant interaction with strangers posed very real and tangible problems of distinction and recognition. One domain in which the positive image and first impression was coming to be seen a critical asset was the burgeoning white-collar sector of the economy – business, sales, and customer relations. Success in these areas, it was said, hinged on the ability to cultivate a pleasing image – on "salesmanship," "people skills," and brand recognition. The basis of effective selling was the positive first impression – creating a desirable image of a product and, even more, of the salesperson. Before long, the imperatives of the world of sales and service were applied to social relations more generally. The efforts of salespeople to sell products to skeptical customers became a metaphor for the social struggle waged by every person in an effort to distinguish themselves in the modern world. Attracting the attention and positive regard of strangers, the basis of success in any pursuit, demanded that an individual put forth an ideal impression on the first try.

The relatively new advertising industry, in conjunction with the new field of popular psychology, promised individuals that they could use conspicuous consumption and the strategic display of goods to achieve a stunning image, distinguish themselves from the crowd, and "win friends and influence people" (Carnegie, Carnegie, and Pell 1936). Advertisers heightened concerns with personal image; the mission of the ad agency was to create discomforts and dissatisfactions with one's image that could only be assuaged through purchasing goods. Advertisers encouraged consumers to see themselves through the searching gaze of strangers who needed to be persuaded or impressed. "Do you wonder, when you meet a casual friend, whether your nose is shiny?" asked an ad for Woodbury's Soap. "Do you anxiously consult store windows and vanity cases at every opportunity?" (Peiss 1998: 142). Ads played upon popular insecurities with identity and appearance, and they reinforced the perception that images were essential to social advancement (Marchand 1986: 14).

The 1920s gave rise to a new, defining phenomenon of American society, perhaps the single greatest force behind the new culture of images – the entertainment celebrity. The United States became a "celebrity culture." Film actors, who had seemingly mastered the art of "impression management," became role models and cultural heroes. Audiences were fascinated with the way film actors put themselves together – how they created a stunning image and constantly manipulated that image to please, amuse, and fascinate others. In the image-conscious culture, the actor had become the modal self.

***

In the period between the two world wars, the mass media suffused and transformed American life. Daily newspaper circulation increased from 22.4 million copies in 1910 to 39.6 million copies in the 1930s. Ninety percent of Americans were estimated to be newspaper readers (Lee 1947: 731). Nearly 4,500 periodicals were published each year in the 1930s and circulated a combined 180 million copies per issue (Kyvig 2004: 190–1). By the end of the decade, half the homes in the United States contained at least two radios, which were on for about five hours a day (Cashman 1989).

The proliferation of mass communications brought more injuries to public images and reputations, and with them, the continued expansion of libel law and litigation. As soon as radio and motion pictures were popularized, their creators were sued for libel. The threat of libel litigation had become so significant that major newspapers, magazines, and book publishing houses retained libel lawyers for prepublication review, and insurance organizations began writing libel and slander insurance for publishers and broadcasters (Berger 1937, Thayer 1943: 340).

Libel doctrine transformed and expanded to meet the demands of the image-conscious society. In the 1930s and 1940s, courts were broadening the definition of a defamatory publication. A defamatory publication was not only one that cast a person into disrepute. A publication could be defamatory if it tarnished a person's reputation or image *in his own eyes*, causing mental distress (Wade 1962: 1093–5). In 1935, the torts scholar Calvert Magruder noted an increasing number of libel cases where plaintiffs had won damages, not for an objective loss of reputation, but for "the sense of outrage and chagrin that the defendant should have made an attack upon his reputation" (Magruder 1935: 1055). Courts were turning their focus from external, interpersonal relations inward, to the realm of one's self-perception and one's feelings about one's public image.

Thus it was that a court held that a woman had a cause of action for libel when a newspaper said that she had been served with process while sitting in a bathtub – an accusation that did not impute immoral conduct or likely damage her reputation, but nonetheless embarrassed her.[6] In *Zbyszko v. New York American*, from 1930, the newspaper had published an article on the theory of evolution. In one part of the article, the text read: "The Gorilla is probably closer to man, both in body and in brain, than any other species of ape now alive. The general physique of the Gorilla is closely similar to an athletic man of today, and the mind of a young gorilla is much like the mind of a human baby." Near that text appeared a photograph of the wrestler Stanislaus Zbyszko, in a wrestling pose, and under it a caption: "Stanislaus Zbyszko, the Wrestler, Not Fundamentally Different from the Gorilla in Physique."[7] Though it was unlikely that any reader would think worse of the wrestler for this, the jury sympathized with his sense of affront and awarded him $25,000 (A Collect As You Go Tour of the Publisher's Chain 1936: 50).

The major development in image law was the growing recognition of the tort of invasion of privacy. By 1940 the privacy tort, as a right to control one's public image, had been recognized in at least fifteen jurisdictions (Nizer 1940: 526, 536). The *Restatement of Torts* acknowledged the tort in

---

[6] *Snyder v. New York Press Co.*, 137 A.D. 291, 121 N.Y.S. 944 (N.Y. App. Div. 1910).
[7] *Zbyszko v. New York American*, 228 A.D. 277, 239 N.Y.S. 411 (N.Y. App. Div. 1930).

1939: "a person who unreasonably and seriously interferes with another's interest in not having his affairs known to others or his likeness exhibited to the public is liable to the other," read its summation (American Law Institute 1939: 389). At a time of great public criticism of media invasions of privacy, and increasing cultural demands to control and perfect one's public image, there was much popular support for the privacy tort. Media audiences wanted to gawk, to peer in on others' lives, even to be voyeurs, but were upset when the gaze was turned back on them.

It was not total solitude, concealment, or anonymity that people seemed to want, but rather *selective self-exposure*. In an age when actors and other performers were seen as cultural heroes, celebrated for their personal lifestyles, publicity of one's private affairs was not always unwelcome, intrusive, or annoying. In a celebrity culture, being thrust into the spotlight for one's proverbial 15 minutes of notoriety was, for some, an appealing possibility. Many of the "gregarious millions," "crave to be lifted out of the morass of anonymity," and believed that "any publicity, even though unfavorable, is better than none at all" (Ragland 1928: 87).

Regardless of whether one sought fame or was content in the confines of a narrower world, control over one's publicity and public image – the ability to put one's own "spin" on one's persona – was seen as critical. Writers discussed the importance of a broad legal right to control one's image, a right to create one's image on one's own terms. In the face of "multiplying hordes of newsmongers," a "right to privacy" was essential (Levy 1935: 190).

***

A few privacy cases from this time involved the publication of deeply intimate, personal material. In 1939, *Time* magazine published an article titled "Starving Glutton," about a woman who had a metabolic disorder that led her to eat huge quantities without gaining weight. The picture published with the article, taken by a reporter over the woman's protests, showed Dorothy Barber in bed in a long-sleeved hospital gown. She sued for invasion of privacy and won damages at trial. "Certainly if there is any right of privacy at all, it should include the right to obtain medical treatment at home or in a hospital for an individual personal condition ... without personal publicity," an appeals court concluded, upholding the judgment.[8]

[8] *Barber v. Time, Inc.*, 348 Mo. 1199, 159 S.W.2d 291 (Mo. 1942).

The majority of privacy cases did not involve publications that were especially private, however. Truly intimate depictions – deeply personal gossip, explicit stories about people's romantic affairs, lurid photographs – were typically not the subject of lawsuits; legal action would only attract further attention to the sensitive, embarrassing material (Dawson 1948: 39). Instead, most privacy cases involved situations where people had been presented in a manner they found unfavorable, misrepresentative, upsetting, or annoying, even though the activities portrayed were not especially scandalous, personal or secret. A number of privacy suits, for example, involved photographs of a person taken on the street and published without consent. In these cases, the law of privacy had very little to do with "privacy." No exposure of "private life" had occurred. Rather, the right to privacy was a right to not be depicted in a fashion that contradicted one's own, desired self-presentation, "under circumstances which are complimentary as well as those which are critical."[9] "Privacy" was about the right to choose one's own audiences, about shielding people from unwanted publicity that clashed with how they wanted to be known to the public.

In the 1929 case *Jones v. Herald Post*, a woman named Lillian Jones witnessed her husband assaulted and stabbed to death on the street, and tried to fight back against the attackers. She sued for invasion of privacy when the *Louisville Herald Post* published her picture with a truthful account of her heroic efforts. She claimed that the publication was offensive to her. In *Hillman v. Star Publishing*, a woman sued the *Seattle Star* for invasion of privacy when it ran her photo along with an article about her father's arrest for mail fraud. She claimed that this caused her "shame, humiliation, and a sense of disgrace."[10]

The plaintiff in *Blumenthal v. Picture Classics* was an "elderly and respectable" woman, a bread vendor, who sued over newsreel footage that depicted her selling her wares on the streets of the lower East Side. The footage was a candid, unaltered street scene, part of a newsreel titled "Sight Seeing in New York with Nick and Tony." The woman complained that the portrayal was "foolish, unnatural, and undignified," and an "invasion of privacy." A trial court issued an injunction restraining the distribution of the newsreel.[11] In *Sweenek v. Pathe News*,

---

[9] *Hull v. Curtis Pub. Co.*, 182 Pa. Super. 86, 125 A.2d 644 (1956).
[10] *Hillman v. Star Pub. Co.*, 64 Wn. 691, 117 P. 594 (1911).
[11] *Blumenthal v. Picture Classics, Inc.*, 235 App. Div. 570, 257 N.Y.S. 800 (N.Y. App. Div. 1932).

from 1936, a woman claimed that unauthorized newsreel footage taken of her in an exercise course for overweight women – "a group of corpulent women attempting to reduce with the aid of some rather novel and unique apparatus" – was an invasion of privacy because the footage was embarrassing.

Some of these lawsuits – though certainly not all – could be described as fairly petty. The law professor Harry Kalven, Jr believed that most parties who came forward with privacy claims had "shabby, unseemly grievances and an interest in exploitation." "I suspect that the fascination with the great Brandeis trade mark, excitement over the law at a point of growth, and appreciation of privacy as a key value have combined to dull the normal critical sense of judges and commentators and have caused them not to see the pettiness of the tort they have sponsored," he wrote in an article titled "Privacy in Tort Law – Were Brandeis and Warren Wrong?" (Kalven 1966: 332).

Even the most seemingly 'thin-skinned' of these plaintiffs were not necessarily insincere or duplicitous, however. Although we can't know for sure, the men and women presented in an inaccurate or otherwise displeasing manner in various newsreels, comic strips, and articles may well have been hurt. This sense of injury and affront is a testament to the image consciousness of the time. It is only in a culture where people feel deeply possessive and protective of their public images that such misrepresentations, even if objectively benign, will be experienced as serious harms. It is only in a culture that has invested great importance in images, that has freighted public images with such emotional and psychological weight, that the law will recognize such harms and take them seriously. The law tracked the growing cultural focus on personal image, and in recognizing these "privacy" claims as worthy of judicial attention, and in some cases monetary judgments, courts validated, even heightened the image-conscious sensibility.

***

Sympathetic to the importance of public image, and plaintiffs' interests in controlling and shaping their public personae, courts provided relief in a number of these cases. Yet at the same time as the courts were recognizing a right to one's image that made embarrassing or distressing media representations legally actionable, they were also acknowledging another kind of image right: the rights of publishers, writers, and filmmakers to depict people's likenesses and life stories, and the public's right to consume them. In a culture where politics and social life were being transacted through images, where media images had become the common currency of social exchange, the ability to freely depict individuals and public affairs was critical to the "free and robust" public discourse that was beginning to be described as a central value of the First Amendment. By the 1940s, imposing liability for truthful commentary about a person, even if distressing to him, was coming to be seen as a form of state control over expression that smacked of the totalitarian governments in Europe and Asia against which the United States was at war.

Brandeis and Warren and courts adjudicating early twentieth-century privacy cases had recognized a privilege that would exempt the publication of "matters of public interest," or "matters of public concern." Before the 1930s, the definition of a "matter of public concern" had been narrow. What was a matter of "public concern" or "public interest" was not what actually *interested* the public – for then gossip and sensationalism might be immune – but rather, what judges believed that the public *should* know, in its own best interest. In the 1930s and 1940s, courts began to expand the "matters of public interest" privilege. Purely entertaining, titillating publications, such as a highly dramatized account of a criminal trial, gossip columns, and even murder mysteries were said to be matters of legitimate "public interest" or "public concern" that could be written about freely, even if the individuals involved were unwilling to be publicized.[12] For judges to create their own definition of "matters of public interest," one that overrode the media's publishing decisions and implicitly, the public's consumption choices, was to some courts an impermissible censorship of the press.

Because there was great curiosity about public figures' private lives, their personal affairs were usually "matters of public interest," said courts. As such, public figures – defined as those who submitted themselves to "public approval" – had very little in the way of privacy (American Law Institute 1939). According to some courts, even ordinary people "waived" their right to privacy when they went into public places, or were involved in "matters of public interest" (ibid.). In *Jones v. Herald Post*, involving the woman who tried to attack her husband's murderer, the court concluded that the woman had, albeit unwillingly,

---

[12] *Colyer c. Richard K. Fox Pub. Co.*, 162 A.D. 297, 146 N.Y.S. 999 (N.Y. App. Div. 1914); *Elmhurst v. Pearson*, 80 U.S. App. D.C. 372, 153 F.2d 467 (1946); *Middleton v. News Syndicate Co.*, 162 Misc. 516, 295 N.Y.S. 120 (N.Y. Misc. 1937).

become an "innocent actor in a great tragedy in which the public had a deep concern," and as such, it was not an invasion of privacy to publish her photograph.[13] Insofar as they generated public interest or curiosity, there was "no invasion of a right of privacy in the description of the ordinary goings and comings of a person or of weddings, even though intended to be entirely private."[14]

Not everyone in the legal world endorsed this expansive view of privileged material. To some, the public's interest in learning about people and public affairs, and the right of the press to convey that information, did not justify interfering with a person's public image when that interference created serious emotional or psychic harm. There was a battle underway. The ideals of modern expressive freedom cut both ways: liberty meant the right to express oneself through one's image, and at the same time, the freedom to make images of others. This tension would trouble courts, lawyers, legal theorists, and the public in the coming decades. When were the media justified in overriding people's right to create their own images? Could *the right to one's image* and *the freedom to image* be reconciled?

***

In the post-Second World War era, courts imposed further limitations on the image torts in the name of freedom of speech and the public's "right to know." Despite this, the proliferation of the media, new communication technologies, and a cultural focus on personal images and "image management" led to the significant growth of image law and personal image litigation. There was deep cultural confusion around image laws and image rights. At the same time that the laws of image were being narrowed, they expanded to accommodate people's increasing protectiveness of their public images in an image-saturated society, what was being described as an "age of images" (Boorstin 1962).

***

In postwar America, images – of affluence, desire, mobility, and fame – "reached ... into every corner of our daily lives," observed historian Daniel Boorstin (1962: 249). The Second World War had brought

---

[13] *Jones v. Herald Post Co.*, 230 Ky. 227, 18 S.W.2d 972 (Ky Ct. App. 1929).
[14] *Barber v. Time, Inc.*, 348 Mo. 1199, 159 S.W.2d 291 (Mo. 1942).

with it unprecedented prosperity, and the middle-class lifestyle came within the reach of millions. By the end of the 1950s, most families owned their homes, their cars, and a television set. It was a culture of appearance and aspiration; advertising in glossy magazines and on television spread bright pictures of consumer products and their happy users for envy and emulation.

In his landmark work *The Lonely Crowd*, sociologist David Riesman wrote of the rise of a new personality type that was emerging as an "influential minority" in "contemporary, highly industrialized, and bureaucratic America," particularly among "the upper middle-class of our larger cities" (Riesman 1950: 19). He called this the "other-directed" personality (ibid.: 9). The "other-directed" individual – the product of an affluent, mobile, consumerist society – was deeply concerned with his image and appearance; he continually reinvented and adjusted his public persona in an effort to please and impress others. Riesman noted the manifestations of this other-directed orientation in various cultural practices and texts of the time, from children's novels to stories and ads in women's magazines that dealt with "modes of manipulating the self in order to manipulate others," for the attainment of such "intangible assets" as prestige, acceptance and affection (ibid.: 106).

This "other-direction" – an orientation toward appearances, surfaces, packaging, glamour, and perfecting and controlling one's image in the eyes of others – should be familiar to us, with its origins in the pre-Second World War era. There were, however, significant developments in postwar culture that escalated the emphasis on personal image and image management. By the 1950s, the number of white-collar workers outnumbered blue-collar workers for the first time in US history. Labor power, more than ever, took the form of "personality" and "people skills." The burgeoning service occupations placed on their participants intense requirements for managed self-presentation – in sociologist Erving Goffman's words, that "one give a perfectly homogeneous performance at every appointed time" (Goffman 1955: 56). The phrase "personal image" first entered popular culture in the 1960s. With willpower and focus, advised a 1962 business success manual titled *The Magic Power of Putting Yourself Over with People*, "you can have the kind of personal image you want," and through your image, "sell yourself" to others (Arnold 1962).

The guiding theme of postwar advertising was that everyone and everything had an image that could be successfully marketed to anyone if presented convincingly enough. Advertising surged in the 1950s.

By the mid-1950s, the United States was spending $9 billion annually to sell products (Moskowitz 2001: 157). As ever, product advertisements encouraged consumers to view themselves with the critical gaze of spectators, as performers under the constant scrutiny of friends and strangers. Other "image industries" flourished; the affluent society generated and consumed media images in unprecedented volume. Newspaper circulation reached historic highs (Young and Young 2004: 153). A paperback "revolution" in the 1950s made books available for only 25 cents (Burress 1989: 73). The cosmetics industry was selling over $1 billion a year, and the garment industry was producing $2 billion dollars' worth of goods annually (Koshetz 1952: F1; Breines 2001: 95).

Celebrity culture flourished, and it spread beyond the realm of entertainment to virtually every other area of endeavor. The mass-mediated "superstar" was emblematic of the age, obsessed as it was with images, entertainment, and fame. Celebrities knit together a national culture based on shared images – "Jackie's hairdo, Marilyn Monroe's pout, Marlon Brando's swagger" (Farber and Foner 1994: 49). As ever, the essence of celebrity remained style rather than substance. Modern celebrity rewarded those who had appealing lifestyles and personalities, and who could project those personalities in an alluring fashion. Since media attention – and little else – was the basis of fame, it remained an eminently democratic aspiration. Celebrities continued to serve as role models of successful self-presentation, and there was great fascination with the ways that stars publicized themselves, how they transformed, manipulated, and spun their images. The public was enthralled with "backstages," with the activities of publicists and press agents, and the inner workings of Hollywood and other image-making "factories" (Boorstin 1965: 194).

In his widely acclaimed 1962 book *The Image: A Guide to Pseudo Events in America*, Daniel Boorstin observed that the United States had entered an "age of images." Like Riesman, Boorstin lamented what he saw as the alienating effects of mass communication and mass consumption, the vaunting of surfaces over depth, and the centrality of simulated, vicarious experiences to cultural life (Pells 1985: 225–56). Politics had become a form of shadow theater, enacted through television clips, sound bytes, press conferences, and other staged "pseudo-events," Boorstin (1965: 194) wrote. It was becoming a matter of faith that the right image could "elect a President or sell an automobile, a religion, a cigarette, or a suit of clothes" (ibid.: 192). "Before the age of images, it was common to think of a conventional person as one who strove for an ideal of decency or respectability." Now one tried to "fit into the images found vividly all around him." "We have fallen in love with our own image, with images of our making, which turn out to be images of ourselves" (ibid.: 192).

***

The state of image law and litigation reflected the growth of the media, its heightened sensationalism, and the image consciousness in the culture of the time. Legal protections for personal image, and one's right to control one's image, increased in the postwar era, as did Americans' use of the law to protect those interests. Libel assumed increasing prominence in legal and popular culture, and privacy law and litigation expanded.

At its 1953 meeting, the American Newspaper Publishers' Association noted that libel claims against newspapers were on the rise. Arthur Hanson, counsel for the ANPA, claimed that the number of libel suits had grown by several 100 percent in the 1950s (Rosenberg 1995: 247). According to one torts treatise, libel suits had been far "more numerous" in the 1950s than in previous years (Miller 1952: 191). There was great inflation in the size of judgments and claims; some plaintiffs were claiming that their reputations were worth millions (Rosenberg 1995: 247; Forde 2008: 113).

Courts continued to expand the definition of a defamatory publication to include representations that were not necessarily harmful to a person's social relations, but that were nonetheless injurious to his feelings about his image (Developments in the Law of Defamation 1956: 881). As the law professor Edward Bloustein summarized in 1964, there was an "increasing tendency" in the law of defamation to go "beyond the traditional reaches" of the protection of reputation to protect "personal humiliation and degradation" (Bloustein 1964: 993). Law professor John Wade noted that "the law of defamation has been expanded to include certain situations where there was no real injury to plaintiff's reputation but he was held up to ridicule or otherwise subjected to mental disturbance" (Wade 1962: 1094).

By the late twentieth century, the bulk of the money paid out in damage awards in defamation suits went to "compensate for psychic injury, rather than any objectively verifiable damage to one's reputation," observed law professor Rodney Smolla (1986: 24). The tort's protected interest broadened from "extrinsic, community-based reputation" to "freedom from psychic or emotional harm to the individual" (Bezanson 1988: 541). The focus of the action, in many instances, is the "decline in self-reputation" suffered by the plaintiff. The actions for defamation and privacy were converging; courts were "assimilat[ing] defamation cases to privacy" (Kalven 1966: 334).

***

In the 1950s, the privacy tort came into its own. The number of privacy cases more than doubled that of any previous decade (Pember 1972: 147). By the 1960s, there were more than 300 reported privacy cases, most of them involving the media (Kalven 1972: 361). "How many more (privacy cases) are settled in lower courts or out of court cannot even be estimated," wrote *Journalism Quarterly* in 1953. "The number of cases can be said to be definitely increasing" (Davis 1953: 187). By 1960, the invasion of privacy tort was "declared to exist by the overwhelming majority of American courts" (Prosser 1960: 389).

In 1963, a forty-four-year-old mother, Flora Bell Graham, the wife of a chicken farmer from rural Cullman County, Alabama, attended the county fair with her sons, and she went with them into a fun house. As she left, her dress was blown up by air jets – part of the "fun." A photographer from the local paper got a snapshot, and the picture of the woman ran on the front page. Even though the picture was taken in a public place, the trial court made an award of several thousand dollars, upheld by the state's Supreme Court. "Not only was th[e] photograph embarrassing to one of normal sensibilities," the court concluded, but was "offensive to modesty or decency" to the point of being "obscene" (County Fair Picture 1964).[15]

It was not only suggestive or explicit portrayals that invaded privacy. Courts found invasions of privacy in all manner of media depictions that plaintiffs claimed to be embarrassing, offensive, or otherwise injurious to their public images. The film industry was a real "target for invasion of privacy lawsuits," noted one publishing trade journal in 1953 (Davis 1953: 187). A California trial court issued a $290,000 judgment against the film company Loew's Inc over a complaint by a woman who was the model for an Army nurse in the film *They Were Expendable*. The court found that depicting her romance with a Navy lieutenant on screen was an invasion of her privacy (ibid.).

---

[15] *Daily Times Democrat* v. *Graham*, 276 Ala. 380, 162 So2d 474 (Ala. 1964).

Privacy cases continued to be brought – and won – over publications that were benign in most people's eyes, in some cases even complimentary, albeit displeasing to the subjects of publicity. In the early 1960s, Warren Spahn, the famous baseball player, sued over an unauthorized biography that he claimed was too flattering. The biography depicted him as a war hero who had been awarded the Bronze Star. Spahn had served in the Army, but had not been decorated. The book also inaccurately portrayed his relationship with his father, who appeared in the story as a kind mentor and coach, and it incorporated false, invented dialog. Spahn found all this to be offensive, sued for invasion of privacy, and was successful at trial. Spahn later told an interviewer that he was embarrassed at the way his military experience had been glorified and was concerned that people would think he planted the account to make himself look heroic (Yasser 2008: 49). The publication was enjoined and Spahn awarded damages.[16]

The "privacy" right to one's public image was widely supported, in both popular culture and in the legal world. The idea of a legal right to protect one's public image against unwanted or distorted media depictions resonated with the cultural ideals in the image-conscious society. Privacy was the individual's "rightful claim ... to determine the extent to which he wishes to share himself with others," in the words of one legal scholar. Everyone had a right to "choose those portions of the individual which are to be made public" (Breckenridge 1970: 1–3). Wrote one federal judge, "in a society predicated on individual rights, each person should be entitled to choose the face he or she wishes to present to the public unless that right is waived or some other right is paramount" (Forer 1987: 19).

***

The privacy right to control one's personal image was prized in postwar America, but freedom of speech had also become a core cultural and legal value. The student movement of the 1960s had begun with the famous Berkeley free speech protests, and the right to dissent, question authority, and challenge the status quo was a critical demand of the counterculture (Farber and Foner 1994: 196–8). In the era of Vietnam, the Pentagon Papers, anticommunist purges, and the public revelation of extensive government spying, political criticism was being described

---

[16] *Spahn v. Julian Messner, Inc.*, 18 N.Y.2d 324, 221 N.E.2d 543 (N.Y. 1966).

as a "public duty".[17] The "crusading journalist," risking punishment to expose injustice, was romanticized in the popular culture of the time (Gajda 2009: 1039).

The Supreme Court's protection of free speech was unprecedented. Between the end of the Second World War and the 1970s, the Court issued decisions that protected a wide range of previously proscribed material (Hale 1987: 3, Strossen 1996: 71–2). Almost three-fourths of the free speech cases that came before the Court in the 1950s and 1960s were decided in favor of free expression (Strossen 1996: 69). The Court's opinions described free expression as an important personal liberty, furthering "self-fulfillment," and the "right to autonomous control over the development and expression of one's intellect, tastes, and personalities."[18] The ability to freely express one's thoughts, beliefs, and personal identity was seen as essential to the growth and enhancement of the individual (Sandel 1998: 80). Decisions also emphasized the importance of freedom of speech and press to democratic self-governance through "public discussion" (*New York Times v. Sullivan* [1964]). With the public dependent on the mass media as a source of information about public affairs, "a broadly defined freedom of the press" was necessary to "assure the maintenance of our political system and an open society."[19]

In this free speech zeitgeist, courts often dismissed privacy suits against the media under the common law "matters of public interest" privilege. Fearing a "judicial censorship" of the press, courts continued to define the content of the popular media as synonymous with the "public interest." In this view, if something appeared in the "press" – a film, novel, television episode, or even tabloid or detective magazine – by definition, it was a matter of public interest, and "newsworthy." The public had a "right to be informed," whether the information was material about a politician's home and family life or a sensationalistic article about a homicide in *Official Detective Stories* magazine.[20]

Every person, celebrity or not, surrendered one's right to privacy by becoming part of an event that was a "newsworthy" matter of public concern, whether voluntarily or involuntarily, in the view of some

---

[17] *New York Times Co. v. Sullivan*, 376 U.S. 254 (1964).
[18] *Doe v. Bolton*, 410 U.S. 179 (1973).
[19] *Time, Inc. v. Hill*, 385 U.S. 374 (1967).
[20] *Blount v. T.D. Pub. Corp.*, 423 P.2d 421 (N.M. 1967); *Kapellas v. Koffman*, 1 Cal. 3d 20, 31, 459 P.2d 912 (Cal. 1969).

courts. A newspaper that ran a large picture of a murdered boy's decomposed body was not liable to the boy's parents. The court concluded that the boy, albeit unwillingly, became part of an event of "public interest" by virtue of being murdered and waived his right to privacy.[21] Likewise, given live television coverage, the paparazzi, and the increasing presence of cameras in public, people were said to "assume the risk" of unwanted publicity whenever they went outside their homes. The dominant rule was that "photographers on public property may take pictures of anyone they want to, objection or not" (The Press: Freedom to Photograph 1954).

In the seventy years after the famous Brandeis and Warren invention, the legal action for invasion of privacy, as the right to one's public image, had developed, flourished, and been pruned back by courts that could not reconcile that right with American society's dependence on media images, and its commitment to freedom of expression. The history of American image law is a saga of simultaneous expansion and limitation – the increasing recognition of personal image rights over the course of the twentieth century, and at the same time, their restriction by legal doctrines and concepts of freedom of speech.

***

By the 1970s, the modern doctrines of the tort laws of image had been established, as had the "image-conscious sensibility." As this chapter has illustrated, the twentieth century witnessed the rise of a cultural attitude or outlook, rooted in the middleclass but not limited to it, in which the self is conceptualized in terms of images. Influenced by a variety of cultural forces, from the "image industries" to celebrity culture to the mobile and fluid conditions of modern, urban life, Americans became aware of having public images and *being* images: one's identity was embedded, at least in part, in the image or persona one strategically constructed and presented to others. In a world of crowds, surfaces, and distant and impersonal social relations, the ability to perfect and manage one's image came to be regarded as critical to social mobility, public recognition, and material success. Individuals from a variety of backgrounds and circumstances asserted that they owned their images, that they had an entitlement to their images and a right to control them, and that this prerogative was critical to their ability to live and

[21] *Bremmer v. Journal-Tribune Pub. Co.*, 247 Ia 817, 76 N.W.2d 762, 766-67 (Ia, 1956).

function as free and self-determining individuals, and to pursue the fabled American Dream.

The law both responded to and contributed to this focus on images and the rise of the image-conscious self. By the 1940s, as we have seen, a body of tort law protected the individual's public image, their ability to control this image, and their feelings about their image. We saw the expansion of litigation in these areas, and despite doubts and resistance among some sectors, widespread support for these laws – in the judiciary, among academics, in the public at large. Tort law became a venue for, and participant in, modern America's intense concerns with personal image.

Personal image was *legalized*: images, and people's feelings about their images, came to be viewed as appropriate matters for legal intervention, regulation, and supervision. This is not to say that every person who was insulted, maligned, or misrepresented undertook legal action – far from it. Most libels, "invasions of privacy," and other image-based harms never made it to a lawyer, never made it to court. They were endured, or dealt with informally. I am not suggesting that Americans have been litigious around their reputations and public images in any absolute sense. We can see, nonetheless, a growing "claims consciousness" around personal image (Kalven 1966: 338). As the law expanded its authority over image-based harms and emotional harms, as privacy and libel litigation gained publicity and apparent social approval, there was a popular awareness that affronts to one's public persona could be dealt with legally, if one chose – that legal recourse was one avenue, among many, that could be pursued, and perhaps should be pursued.

The effect of this legalization of image, I suggest, was to validate and reinforce the sense of possessiveness and protectiveness toward one's public image and persona. In acknowledging a right to control one's image and one's feelings about one's image, the law affirmed the image-conscious sensibility. As in so many other areas of conduct, the law marked out a terrain of normative, socially acceptable behavior and feeling, through the reasonableness, or "reasonable person" standard (Green 1968: 241). Particularly in the latter half of the twentieth century, courts and juries often defined the reasonable person with respect to image as an individual who was conscious of, and quite sensitive to, their social appearance; who was likely to be hurt, perhaps deeply so, when publicized in a false, misleading, miscontextualized or humiliating manner – or in any fashion that sharply clashed with their own self-image. While there was much disagreement as to the thickness of the normal person's skin, and the free speech limitations on image rights, the law recognized emotional distress as a reasonable response to a tarnished or distorted public persona, and deemed such injuries significant enough to merit recognition and recompense, although perhaps less so than some may have wished. This legal affirmation legitimated the seriousness toward personal image that was being cultivated and urged upon the public by the other cultural forces we have seen. Free speech limitations notwithstanding, American culture embraced the idea of a legal right to be vindicated and compensated for image-based harms, part of a broader, fundamental right to possess and control the self.

References

"A Collect as you Go Tour of the Publisher's Chain." (1936). *Newsweek*, February 22.

Arnold, Stanley Norman. (1962). *The Magic Power of Putting Yourself Over with People*. Englewood Cliffs, NJ: Prentice-Hall.

Berger, M. Marvin. (1937). "Detecting Libel Before It Appears." *Editor and Publisher*, May 29.

Bergstrom, Randolph E. (1992). *Courting Danger: Injury and Law in New York City, 1870–1910*. Ithaca, NY: Cornell University Press.

Bezanson, Randall. (1988). "The Libel Tort Today." *Washington and Lee Law Review* 45:535–56.

Bloustein, Edward. (1964). "Privacy as an Aspect of Human Dignity: An Answer to Dean Prosser." *New York University Law Review* 39:962–1007.

Blumenthal, Albert. (1932). *Small-Town Stuff*. Chicago: University of Chicago Press.

Boorstin, Daniel J. (1992). *The Image: A Guide to Pseudo-Events in America*. New York: Vintage Books.

Brandeis, Louis and Samuel Warren. (1890). "The Right to Privacy." *Harvard Law Review* 4:193–220.

Braudy, Leo. (1986). *The Frenzy of Renown: Fame and Its History*. New York: Oxford University Press.

Breckenridge, Adam Carlyle. (1970). *The Right to Privacy*. Lincoln, NB: University of Nebraska Press.

Breines, Wini. (1992). *Young, White, and Miserable: Growing Up Female in the Fifties*. Boston, MA: Beacon Press.

Burress, Lee. (1989). *Battle of the Books: Literary Censorship in the Public Schools, 1950–1985*. Metuchen, NJ: Scarecrow Press.

Carnegie, Dale, Dorothy Carnegie, and Arthur R. Pell. (1981). *How to Win Friends and Influence People*. New York: Simon and Schuster.

Cashman, Sean Dennis. (1989). *America in the Twenties and Thirties: The Olympian Age of Franklin Delano Roosevelt*. New York: New York University Press.

"County Fair Picture." (1964). *Editor and Publisher*, May 30.
Davis, Norris. (1953). "Invasion of Privacy: A Study in Contradictions." *Journalism Quarterly* 30:179–88.
Dawson, Mitchell. (1948). "Law and the Right of Privacy." *American Mercury* 39:397.
"Developments in the Law of Defamation." (1956). *Harvard Law Review* 69:876–959.
Dicken Garcia, Hazel. (1989). *Journalistic Standards in Nineteenth-Century America*. Madison, WI: University of Wisconsin Press.
Dumenil, Lynn. (1995). *The Modern Temper: American Culture and Society in the 1920s*. New York: Hill and Wang.
Farber, David R. and Eric Foner. (1994). *The Age of Great Dreams: America in the 1960s*. New York: Hill and Wang.
Forde, Kathy Roberts. (2008). *Literary Journalism on Trial: Masson v. New Yorker and the First Amendment*. Amherst, MA: University of Massachusetts Press.
Forer, Lois G. (1987). *A Chilling Effect: The Mounting Threat of Libel and Invasion of Privacy Actions to the First Amendment*. New York: Norton.
Gajda, Amy. (2009). "Judging Journalism: The Turn Toward Privacy and Judicial Regulation of the Press." *California Law Review* 97:1039–105.
Goffman, Erving. (1959). *The Presentation of Self in Everyday Life*. Garden City, NY: Doubleday.
Green, Edward. (1968). "The Reasonable Man: Legal Fiction or Psychosocial Reality." *Law and Society Review* 2:241–57.
Hale, Dennis. (1987). "Freedom of Expression: The Warren and Burger Courts." *Communications and The Law* 9:3.
Henn, Steve. (2013). "Facebook Users Question $20 Million Settlement Over Ads." NPR, May 13. www.npr.org/sections/alltechconsidered/2013/05/14/182861926/facebook-users-question-20-million-settlement-over-ads.
Hofstadter, Richard. (1955). *The Age of Reform: From Bryan to FDR*. New York: Vintage Books.
Hughes, Helen McGill. (1940). *News and the Human Interest Story: A Study of Popular Literature*. Chicago, IL: University of Chicago.
Kalven, Harry. (1966). "Privacy in Tort Law – Were Brandeis and Warren Wrong?" *Law and Contemporary Problems* 31:332.
Kasson, John F. (1990). *Rudeness and Civility: Manners in Nineteenth-Century Urban America*. New York: Hill and Wang.
Koshetz, Herbert. (1952). "Garment Industry Has No Complaint." *New York Times*, April 6.
Kyvig, David E. (2002). *Daily Life in the United States, 1920–39: Decades of Promise and Pain*. Westport, CT: Greenwood Press.
Laurent, Francis W. (1959). *The Business of a Trial Court: 100 Years of Cases: A Census of the Actions and Special Proceedings in the Circuit Court for*

Chippewa County, Wisconsin, 1855–1954. Madison, WI: University of Wisconsin Press.

Lee, Alfred McClung. (1937). *The Daily Newspaper in America: The Evolution of a Social Instrument*. New York: Macmillan Co.

Levy, Newman. (1935). "The Right to Be Let Alone." *American Mercury*, June.

Magruder, Calvert. (1936). "Mental and Emotional Disturbance in the Law of Torts." *Harvard Law Review* 49:1034–67.

Marchand, Roland. (1985). *Advertising the American Dream: Making Way for Modernity, 1920–1940*. Berkeley, CA: University of California Press.

McNeese, Tim and Richard Jensen. (2010). *World War I and the Roaring Twenties, 1914–1928*. New York: Chelsea House.

Miller, Vernon X. (1960). *Selected Essays on Torts*. Buffalo, NY: Dennis.

Moskowitz, Eva S. (2001). *In Therapy We Trust: America's Obsession with Self-Fulfillment*. Baltimore, MA: Johns Hopkins University Press.

Nizer, Louis. (1940). "The Right of Privacy: A Half Century's Developments." *Michigan Law Review* 39:526–96.

Odgers, William Blake and Melville Madison Bigelow. (1881). *A Digest of the Law of Libel and Slander: With the Evidence, Procedure, and Practice, both in Civil and Criminal Cases, and Precedents of Pleadings*. Boston, MA: Little, Brown.

"The Passion for Publicity." (1896). *Outlook*, April 25.

Peiss, Kathy Lee. (1998). *Hope in a Jar: The Making of America's Beauty Culture*. New York: Metropolitan Books.

Pells, Richard H. (1985). *The Liberal Mind in a Conservative Age: American Intellectuals in the 1940s and 1950s*. New York: Harper and Row.

Pember, Don R. (1972). *Privacy and the Press: The Law, the Mass Media, and the First Amendment*. Seattle, WA: University of Washington Press.

"The Press: Freedom to Photograph." (1954). *Time*, August 9.

Prosser, William L. (1960). "Privacy." *California Law Review* 48:383–423.

Ragland, George. (1928). "The Right of Privacy." *Kentucky Law Journal* 17:85–122.

"Restatement of Law Torts." (1939). Volume IV, Division 10, Chapter 41, As Adopted by the American Law Institute. St. Paul, MN: American Law Institute Publishers.

Riesman, David. (1950). *The Lonely Crowd: A Study of the Changing American Character*. New Haven, NJ: Yale University Press.

Rosenberg, Norman L. (1986). *Protecting the Best Men: An Interpretive History of the Law of Libel*. Chapel Hill, NC: University of North Carolina Press.

Sandel, Michael J. (1998). *Democracy's discontent: America in Search of a Public Philosophy*. Cambridge, MA: Belknap Press of Harvard University Press.

Schlesinger, Arthur M. (1946). *Learning How to Behave, A Historical Study of American Etiquette Books*. New York: Macmillan Co.

Schorman, Rob. (2003). *Selling Style: Clothing and Social Change at the Turn of the Century*. Philadelphia, PA: PENN/University of Pennsylvania Press.
Simmel, George. (1950). "The Metropolis and Mental Life." In *The Sociology of George Simmel*, edited by Kurt H. Wolff. New York: The Free Press.
Smolla, Rodney A. (1986). *Suing the Press*. New York: Oxford University Press.
Strossen, Nadine. (1996). "Freedom of Speech in the Warren Court." In *The Warren Court: A Retrospective*, edited by Bernard Schwartz. Oxford: Oxford University Press.
Thayer, Frank. (1943). "The Changing Libel Scene." *Wisconsin Law Review* 1943:331–51.
Wade, John. (1962). "Defamation and Privacy." *Vanderbilt Law Review* 15:1093–5.
Wirth, Lewis. (1938). "Urbanism as a Way of Life." *American Journal of Sociology* 4:2–24.
Yasser, Ray. (2008). "Warren Spahn's Legal Legacy: The Right to Be Free from False Praise." *Seton Hall Journal of Sports and Entertainment Law* 18:49–84.
Young, William H. and Nancy K. Young. (2004). *The 1950s*. Westport, CT: Greenwood Press.
"Zbyszko v. Ape." (1930). *Time Magazine*, February 24.

PART III

INEQUALITY AND/AS INJURY

CHAPTER TEN

INJURY INEQUALITY
Mary Anne Franks

INTRODUCTION

Social and legal understandings of injury play a key role in structuring society. They shape our sense of moral obligations to each other, help us assign blameworthiness, and govern how our collective resources – economic, psychological, and political – are to be distributed. In particular, judgments about injury determine allocations of risk and responsibility in society. Accordingly, distorted assessments of the quality, nature, and significance of injury can have serious consequences.

In social and legal systems characterized by what I call "injury inequality," injuries affecting the powerful are exaggerated, while those affecting the vulnerable are downplayed. This is serious cause for concern for several interconnected reasons: first, overinflated claims of injury do violence to the concept of injury itself, warping society's collective understanding of harm. Injury inequality also preserves the lion's share of resources for addressing the injuries of the privileged, leaving little for those already less equipped to cope with injury. While elites can expect that their injuries will be accommodated in the structure of law and society itself, the marginalized must make do with self-help. The effect is not limited to economic, legal, or physical resources, but extends to psychological resources. Injury inequality discourages empathy and compassion to the harms suffered by the less powerful. This results in legal and social practices that reinforce an unjust and perverse allocation of risks, burdens, and benefits. Such practices send social messages that directly conflict with a commitment to equality across race, gender, and class. At a minimum, outsized solicitude for elite injuries creates indifference to marginalized injury. In the worst case, such solicitude affirmatively promotes marginalized injury as a sacrifice necessary to preserve the interests of the powerful.

Injury inequality and its consequences can be illustrated and examined in numerous contexts. Here, my focus will be on three categories of legal and social norms in the United States: justifiable use of deadly force, freedom of speech, and sexual assault. In a very literal sense, the legal and social framework of each of these categories in the United States was unequal from the start: the vast majority of laws governing self-defense, constitutional rights, and bodily autonomy were written by white, property-owning men, at a time when nonwhites and women were prevented from participating in civic discourse and policymaking (Franks 2015b). The fact that the elites in power were self-serving in their development of legal and social norms is arguably unremarkable, were it not for the fact that these same elites characterized their project as one committed to equality and justice. It is worth interrogating how well the professed values of the "Founding Fathers" have been expressed throughout history and in the present day.

JUSTIFIABLE USE OF DEADLY FORCE

The evaluation of potential injury is crucial to legal and social norms surrounding the use of deadly force. Broadly speaking, deadly force is supposed to be justified only when the harm to be prevented outweighs the harm that will be inflicted. Accordingly, judgments about justifiable force are judgments about relative injury. Currently, our legal and social norms about deadly force frequently weigh potential injury to white men more seriously than actual injury to women and racial minorities. This is true with regard to deadly force used by both private citizens and by law enforcement.

For much of US history, criminal law formally discouraged private citizens' use of deadly force. The law of self-defense in most states, until very recently, reflected the judgment that human life should generally be preserved, and that punishment for wrongdoing (even serious wrongdoing) was best handled by the state rather than by individual victims. This discouragement of deadly self-help is reflected in the "duty to retreat" doctrine, some version of which could be found in the law of every US state: if a threatened person can escape a conflict in complete safety without resorting to the use of force, she has an obligation to do so.

One important historical exception to the duty to retreat is the so-called "castle doctrine." According to this doctrine, if a person is threatened in his home (his "castle"), he has no duty to retreat, even if he could do so in complete safety. This doctrine made clear that a man's right to be secure in his home is so precious that it outweighs the otherwise prevailing preference for the preservation of human life.

The use of "his" and "man" in this context is deliberate. It is men who have been considered lords of the "castle," and, thus, men who have the privilege of using deadly force to protect it. Rarely has the castle doctrine been invoked at all, to say nothing of successfully, on behalf of women who defended themselves from attack by violent intimate partners in their own homes. More often than not, in fact, the castle doctrine has been used to defeat the proposition that anyone other than the man of the house had the right to use deadly force within it. Women who refuse to leave their homes when faced with violence should be ideal beneficiaries of the castle doctrine, yet the most common question they face from police officers, judges, and juries is "Why didn't you leave?." Battered spouses who have killed their abusers are rarely viewed as engaging in justifiable self-defense. They are lucky if they can convince courts that their actions should be excused because of distress or trauma; their chances of being found justified in using force are extremely slim (Franks 2014). In other words, legal and social norms impose a *de facto* duty to retreat on women facing violence in their homes, while the men who perpetrate this violence continue to enjoy the privilege of the castle doctrine.

One could say, then, that the law of defensive force is ripe for reform. But the kind of reform it has undergone in the twenty-first century has actually aggravated both gender and racial inequalities in the use of force. This has been accomplished through so-called "Stand Your Ground" laws, increasingly permissive gun laws, and aggressive law enforcement practices.

Florida passed the first Stand Your Ground law in 2005, and more than thirty other states have since followed suit (Franks 2015a). These laws expand both the number and nature of exceptions to the duty to retreat. The right that was once limited to "castles" now applies not only to homes, but to vehicles, "dwellings" (including tents), and, most controversially, to public spaces. Many of these laws also expand the type of threat that can permissibly be addressed with deadly force. Before the rise of Stand Your Ground laws, it was widely agreed that deadly force could only be used in confrontations that threatened great bodily injury or death; several of the new laws allow for the use of deadly force against a range of nonviolent felonies, including robbery. Stand Your Ground laws thus, fundamentally alter the calculus that has historically defined self-defense law, including the assessment that property never outweighs life.

What these laws do not do, however, is address the gender inequality at the heart of the castle doctrine. In fact, many of the sponsors and supporters of these laws have expressly specified that the new provisions are not meant to apply to domestic violence situations. These include Marion Hammer, the former president of the National Rifle Association (NRA), who emphasized that Stand your Ground laws weren't meant to be used to, "… take action against an estranged spouse who breaks into the home if they own the home" (Franks 2014: 1115–6). While promoters of Stand Your Ground and expansive gun laws have often attempted to appropriate the plight of victimized women, cases, such as that of Marissa Alexander, illustrate the hollowness of their commitment.

In 2012, Marissa Alexander fired what she characterized as "warning shots" at her estranged husband after he became aggressive and refused to let her leave the home (Amber 2015). Alexander had previously obtained a protection order against Grey because of his physical abuse. Grey himself testified that he had been physically violent with all of his intimate partners and that Alexander never pointed the gun at him on the day of the shooting.[1] The Stand Your Ground narrative would suggest that Alexander's situation is exactly the kind of scenario the laws are meant to address. Alexander was defending herself in her own home from someone that she *knew* – not merely assumed – to be a threat: Grey had in the past threatened to kill her if she ever cheated on him, and had beaten her seriously enough on a prior occasion to put her in the hospital. But not only did police arrest her on the spot after Grey called 911, but Alexander was denied Stand Your Ground immunity at a special hearing. The judge based the ruling on the fact that Alexander had apparently been angry, not afraid, when she shot at Grey, and that she had other options to exit the situation. Alexander was convicted and sentenced to twenty years (Piggot 2015). Though she was later granted a retrial because of an error in the trial court jury instructions, she was again denied Stand Your Ground immunity.[2]

It is illuminating to compare Alexander's treatment by the criminal justice with George Zimmerman's. It took two months along with extensive media coverage and public outcry for Zimmermann to be arrested for

---

[1] Though he later recanted these statements.
[2] Alexander eventually accepted a plea deal of three years in prison, which she had already served, as well as two years of house arrest.

shooting an unarmed black teenager, Trayvon Martin, to death (Andrews 2016). After entertaining the idea of advancing a Stand Your Ground defense, Zimmerman proceeded to trial with a conventional self-defense claim and was acquitted of all charges. How could the outcome for a man who killed an unarmed black teenager following a confrontation he had himself had initiated in a semi-public space be so different from the outcome for a woman who fired a warning shot against a known abuser in her own home? As Florida Congresswoman Corrine Brown wrote in response to the verdict in the Alexander case, "The Florida criminal justice system has sent two clear messages today. One is that if women who are victims of domestic violence try to protect themselves, the Stand Your Ground law will not apply to them ... the second is that if you are Black, the system will treat you differently" (Amber 2015).

Largely due to the efforts of the NRA, the rhetoric of self-defense and the rhetoric of gun rights have become almost inextricable. The NRA pushes the false narrative that crime is increasing and that average citizens are constantly confronted by threats to themselves and their property. That is, the NRA urges the public as well as legislators to believe that the potential injury to average citizens is so great that it warrants changing legal and social norms about the use of violence. The executive vice-president of the NRA, Wayne LaPierre, is known for speeches detailing long lists of things that people should fear and take up arms against: riots, terrorists, hurricanes. This rhetoric has fueled the passage of what have been called "guns everywhere" laws in several states, encouraging the open carry of weapons in place such as bars, parks, and daycare centers. The same rhetoric is used to lower the standards for obtaining concealed carry licenses and to make it easier for domestic abusers to keep their weapons even after it is clear that they pose a threat to a current or former partner. It is no coincidence that the membership of the organization setting the standards for self-defense for all Americans is predominantly white and male (Winkler 2015). The evolution in self-defense law – and its conflation with gun rights – is based on a grotesque distortion of injury that exaggerates the potential harm to the most privileged members of society while downplaying the potential harm to the most vulnerable members.

The claim that Stand Your Ground and permissive gun laws protect the public against injury is demonstrably false. States with such Stand Your Ground laws experience *increases* in homicides (Li 2014). To take Florida as an example, a 2017 study found that the implementation of the Stand Your Ground law was associated with a 24.4 percent increase in homicides (Humphreys, Gasparrini, and Wiebe 2017). States with permissive gun laws are no safer – and are arguably in fact less safe – than states with more restrictive gun laws (Parker 2014). Women, in particular, suffer when weapons are more accessible (DeFilippis and Hughes 2016). There is considerable evidence that both kinds of laws increase the tendency of people to shoot strangers over minor altercations or misunderstandings. What is more, the burden of this increased violence is not shared equally across the population: a shooter is far more likely to prevail on a Stand Your Ground defense when the victim is black than if the victim is white (Li 2014).[3]

The 2012 shooting of Jordan Davis, an unarmed black teenager, was similar in many respects to the shooting of Trayvon Martin by George Zimmerman earlier that year, but received less media attention (Zook 2015). Michael Dunn, a white man, was sitting in the passenger side of a vehicle in the parking lot of a gas station in Florida while his girlfriend was inside buying snacks. An SUV was parked in the next spot that was playing loud music – "thug music," or "rap crap," as Dunn would later call it. Dunn was offended by the music and ordered the young men in the vehicle to turn the music down. A heated verbal exchange followed. At some point, Dunn took out his gun from the glove compartment and shot at the SUV three or four times before the driver backed up the vehicle to exit the parking lot. Dunn shot at the fleeing vehicle another five or six times. When the panicked teenagers reached safety, they discovered that Davis was dead. Dunn later claimed that he started firing because he saw a gun emerge from the back seat. No evidence of any weapon was ever found. Dunn never mentioned seeing a weapon to his girlfriend or anyone else – not at any point the night of the shooting as they drove back to their home, or the next morning after he learned that one of the passengers was dead. Dunn's first mention of the gun came after he was arrested.

In this case, a man sitting in a vehicle with a deadly weapon within reaching distance considered the injury of loud rap music to be reason enough to initiate a confrontation. At some point, Dunn was so convinced that the young men in this vehicle posed a threat to him that he either actually hallucinated a weapon or decided the young men's disobedience alone warranted the use of deadly force. Either version tells us that Dunn perceived enough injurious potential in these

---

[3] "The task force found that in instances where a white shooter kills a black victim, that homicide was 350 percent more likely to be ruled as justified than if a white shooter killed a white person" (Li 2014).

young men – whom he did not know and who had not initiated contact with him – to believe he was justified in shooting them.

Depressingly similar stories abound: Theodore Wafer, who shot an unarmed, black, female teenager named Renisha McBride after she knocked on his door looking for help following a car accident; Randall Kerrick, who shot Jonathan Ferrell, an unarmed black man seeking assistance after a car accident; Rodney Black, who shot two black men near his property because he thought they were trespassing, when in reality one of the men had bought the property next to Black and was coming to take a look at it.

The injury inequality at work in the use of deadly force is not limited to private citizens. On August 9, 2014, a young, unarmed black man named Michael Brown was shot and killed by police on a street in Ferguson, Missouri (Mejia 2014). His body was left in the street, uncovered, for more than four hours. The Ferguson police department refused to name the officer who killed Brown for several days, citing concerns for *his* safety. The day they released the name, the department also released a video purporting to show Michael Brown stealing cigarillos at a local convenience store. The implication of this information, along with the report that Brown had marijuana in his system the day he died, is clear: that Brown was not an innocent victim, that he was responsible for his own death. The actions taken by police in the days and nights following Brown's murder were further exercises in injury inequality. Police confronted unarmed, largely peaceful protestors with riot gear, tear gas, and rubber bullets (Reilly 2015). They brazenly and lawlessly stripped citizens of their constitutional rights to free assembly and speech, imposing curfews, ordering protestors to disperse, and threatening to shoot and mace journalists attempting to report on the events.

Since Michael Brown's death, there has been a seemingly endless series of incidents involving police using deadly force against unarmed black men, black women, and the mentally ill, even as there have been numerous examples of law enforcement managing to peacefully resolve situations involving visibly armed white men. The differences between how the police handle a disturbance call involving black teenagers at a pool party (Srivastava 2015) or the traffic stop of a black woman who failed to signal while changing lanes (Ohlheiser and Phillip 2015) and the way they have handled open-carry demonstrations by white men (Broderick 2014) and armed resistance on government-owned property (Friedman 2014) is telling.

The injury inequality at the heart of self-defense reform is clear: Stand Your Ground laws, expansive gun laws, and militarized law enforcement generally prioritize the interests of white men over minority men, and of men over women. The narrative surrounding deadly force – the law of self-defense and the accompanying rhetoric of gun rights and social order – capitalizes on and appropriates the notion of injury: danger is everywhere, around every corner, so "we" have to make sure that we are well-armed and well-prepared to respond to them. But, as we can see from these cases, this rhetoric revolves around a thoroughly exaggerated sense of injury to those who have the least to fear, and a dismissal of the injury to those who are truly threatened.

FREE SPEECH

Self-proclaimed free speech defenders are fond of claiming that all speech is by default protected by the First Amendment. Those with knowledge of constitutional doctrine will concede that some speech can permissibly be regulated, but that these exceptions are exceedingly narrow. Speech that does not fall into one of the "historically recognized" exceptional categories (often considered to be limited to obscenity, true threats, incitement, and fighting words) is presumptively protected. Many proponents of this view maintain that the injury caused by virulently racist, sexist, and homophobic expression is simply not that serious; others concede that such expression is harmful, but that regulating such speech would inflict a far more serious harm on society.

The view that the First Amendment presumptively protects all expression, with the exception of a small number of categories explicitly spelled out in recent Supreme Court decisions, is, however, inaccurate. First, even the purportedly small number of those categories is in fact not that small: in addition to obscenity, true threats, incitement, and fighting words, the Supreme Court has held that child pornography, defamation, and invasions of privacy are not entitled to full First Amendment protection. In addition, the Supreme Court has also indicated that laws prohibiting discrimination, including sexual harassment laws, comport with the First Amendment. A recent law review article puts the number of other forms of expression that various courts have found not to receive First Amendment protection at 43 (Collins 2013: 417–23). Far more than this, as First Amendment scholars such as Frederick Schauer point out, are excluded not explicitly, but implicitly, from First Amendment protection. As Schauer puts it, the First Amendment does not even "show up" when the expressive conduct in question has to do with property and business rights, including copyright, fraud, trade secrets law, product liability, and nondisclosure agreements (Schauer 2004: 1766). The regulation of information to preserve privacy and confidentiality, especially with regard to financial and health disclosures, is also rarely challenged on First Amendment grounds. The same is true of laws regarding perjury and privileged communications between fiduciaries.

The selective deployment of the First Amendment is one of the barest expressions of injury hierarchy. Speech harms that implicate financial, business, and judicial interests are viewed as extremely serious. Speech harms that implicate other interests, such as racial or gender equality, are viewed as trivial.

Injury inequality in the free speech context is demonstrated in the resistance to the regulation of sexual harassment, hate speech directed at women and racial and sexual minorities, and most recently, nonconsensual pornography, also known as "revenge porn." This is despite the fact that discriminatory speech, in addition to inflicting grave harms on individual victims – ranging from the loss of employment or educational opportunities to severe psychological trauma to suicide – inflict harm on society as a whole by discouraging and inhibiting the contributions of its less privileged members. Groups disproportionately targeted for harassment and abuse often remove themselves from public forums – from workplaces to social media – as a way to cope. That allows elites to replicate and reinforce the status quo, shutting down possibilities for diversity and evolution.

Self-styled free speech defenders frequently invoke the concept of "chilling effects." *Webster's Dictionary* defines a chilling effect as the "inhibition or discouragement of the legitimate exercise of a constitutional right, especially one protected by the First Amendment to the United States Constitution, by the potential or threatened prosecution under, or application of, a law or sanction." The conventional wisdom about laws regulating harassment or other forms of abuse is that they will chill protected speech. As powerful as this concept is intuitively, empirical evidence that laws regulating speech create chilling effects is thin (Kendrick 2013). Empirical evidence of how *harassment* chills expression, mobility, and association, however, is abundant.

In her in-depth article on street harassment, Cynthia Bowman observed that "the continuation and near-general tolerance of street harassment has serious consequences both for women and for society at large. It inflicts the most direct costs upon women, in the form of fear, emotional distress, feelings of disempowerment, and significant limitations upon their liberty, mobility, and hopes for equality" (Bowman 1993: 542). According to a 2014 study on street harassment, nearly a third of women who experienced street harassment stopped going to certain places alone. Twenty-nine percent of women changed the way they walked or behaved in an attempt to deter harassers; 15 percent tried to avoid harassment by changing the way they dressed; while others gave up an outdoor activity, such as exercising, because of harassment or made life-changing decisions like quitting a job or moving because of harassment (Stop Street Harassment 2014: 20–1).

New technology has amplified the reach, scope, and power of harassment. Women are disproportionately singled out for vicious, sexualized harassment online, as detailed by Amanda Hess in her award-winning 2014 article, "Why Women Aren't Welcome on the Internet" (Hess 2014). From Twitter mobs to doxxing to revenge porn to offline "SWATting," women are being driven out of their jobs, schools, and homes due to harassment (Citron 2014, Chemaly 2015). Yet calls for even the most modest regulation of life-destroying behavior have been met with staunch resistance in the name of "free speech." Attempts to hold even the worst online actors accountable for the abuse they solicit and promote are overshadowed by absolutist and inaccurate interpretations of the Communications Decency Act Section 230, which provides broad immunity to information service providers for content provided by third parties (Franks 2013). Critics of regulation gravely warn that any attempt to hold individuals accountable for their expression, no matter how destructive or unjustified, will destroy free speech as well as the Internet as we know it. There is generally no evidence for this claim provided beyond insinuations and grim speculation.

In other words, the mere possibility of imagined injury to an abstract concept of speech outweighs actual, severe, in many cases irremediable injury to vulnerable individuals. This distortion of injury is not limited to debates over harassment, but also stalking, protection orders, discrimination laws, and advertisements for sex trafficking.

SEXUAL ASSAULT

The potential injury of false rape claims, as well as the perceived reputational injury of actual rape convictions, is frequently weighted more heavily than the actual injury inflicted upon rape victims and upon women generally. Even though the chances of a man being falsely accused of rape are extremely low, the mere possibility of a false rape claim is often used to justify or at least mitigate the failure of the state to adequately investigate and prosecute sexual assault. This exaggerated fear is also used to justify extreme skepticism by law enforcement, the media, and mainstream society regarding reports of rape.

Common narratives about rape often center on the potential damage that falsely accused men may face, rather than on the injury inflicted upon women who have been raped or who are forced to navigate their lives around the fear of rape. The percentage of supposed "false claims" of rape is similar to that of other crimes, somewhere between 2 and 8 percent, but given that the vast majority of rapes – as much as 84 percent – are never reported, the actual percentage of false claims is far lower than that. According to a study by the Centers for Disease Control and Prevention, there were nearly 1.3 million rapes of women in the United States in 2010, nearly all of them committed by men. In other words, rape is a very real epidemic, whereas false accusations of rape are barely even statistically significant. Yet "false claim" cases such as the one involving the Duke lacrosse team in 2006 (Luther 2016) and *Rolling Stone*'s "Jackie" debacle in 2014 (Sisario, Spencer, and Ember 2016) are better known than any of the millions of sexual assaults that occur each year.

The supposedly devastating impact of false rape claims on innocent individuals is often offered as a justification for the outsized attention paid to such cases. While there is no doubt that some people who are falsely accused of rape suffer serious consequences, there is little hard evidence to demonstrate that the majority of such individuals experience long-term damage to their reputation or careers (see Luther 2016). In fact, many receive tremendous support in their communities and from the public at large. It is also significant that in many cases, men who have actually been *convicted* of rape receive more sympathy and support than their victims. Even straightforward cases of rape that result in convictions have a tendency to be framed in terms of the impact of the convictions on men's lives, as opposed to the impact on victims' lives. As just a few examples of the injury inequality animating the legal and social norms of sexual assault, let us consider the 2012 Steubenville, Ohio rape verdict, the 2016 "Stanford swimmer" rape case, and the rehabilitation of famous rapists in popular culture.

The Steubenville trial was unusual not least because it presented an unambiguous case of nonstranger rape. Photographic evidence clearly showed that two young men sexually assaulted an incapacitated teenage girl at a party. Yet CNN and other major media outlets covering the trial when the guilty verdict and sentence was read – a sentence, incidentally, that was mere one to two years in a juvenile detention facility – focused on the impact of the verdict on the rapists' futures in football. CNN's Poppy Harlow commented, "These two young men who had such promising futures – star football players, very good students – literally watched as they believed their life fell apart" (Shapiro 2013). Hardly a mention was made of the injury to the rape victim (Wemple 2013). One of the two convicted rapists was released early and returned to play football in the fall of 2014 (Warsinskey 2014).

In January 2015, Brock Turner sexually assaulted an unconscious woman behind a dumpster (Stack 2016). Turner was a swimmer at Stanford University; the victim remains anonymous. Turner was convicted of three counts of sexual assault. He faced a maximum of fourteen years in jail; the prosecution asked for six. The judge in the case sentenced Turner to six months in jail, expressing his concern that a lengthier sentence would have a "severe impact" on Turner (Miller 2016). After the sentence, it was revealed that Turner's father had written a character witness letter arguing that his son should have received no jail time at all, calling the sentence, "a steep price to pay for 20 minutes of action." The father's letter detailed his son's athletic skills, blamed alcohol for the assault, and bemoaned the negative impact of the case on his son, including the fact that Turner no longer seemed to enjoy eating his favorite foods. It made no mention of the suffering that Turner had inflicted on his victim. The victim published the statement that she had read aloud in court, which quickly went viral. In it, she highlights Turner's evasion of responsibility and the elevation of his self-interest over all: "Do not talk about the sad way your life was upturned because alcohol made you do bad things. Figure out how to take responsibility for your own conduct" (Baker 2016).

In 1992, boxer Mike Tyson was convicted of raping an eighteen-year-old woman in a hotel room. After the judge pronounced his sentence – ten years, with the last four suspended – Tyson said, "I've been crucified, humiliated worldwide" (Shipp 1992). Tyson's defense attorney, Harvard Law School professor Alan Dershowitz, wrote a column about the case in the hardcore pornography magazine *Penthouse*, entitled, incredibly, "The Rape of Mike Tyson" (De Los Reyes 1993). Since his release from prison, Tyson has appeared in successful Hollywood films such as *The Hangover* and now performs a one-man show about his life for large audiences (Seitz 2010).

Director Roman Polanski admitted to drugging, raping, and sodomizing a thirteen-year-old girl in 1977. Polanski fled to France after serving barely more than a month in prison, and attempted to have the case dismissed several times. In 2009, Polanski traveled to Switzerland to receive a Lifetime Achievement Award at the Zurich Film Festival.

He was detained at the airport in connection with the outstanding arrest warrant stemming from the 1977 sexual assault. More than a hundred members of the film community, including directors, actors, and producers, signed a petition demanding his release (Knegt 2009). The petition referred to Polanski's act of child rape as "a case of morals" and noted the "dismay" of filmmakers: "It seems inadmissible to them that an international cultural event, paying homage to one of the greatest contemporary filmmakers, is used by the police to apprehend him" (ibid.). In 2010, Swiss authorities declined the United States's request to extradite him (Associated Press 2014). In 2011, Polanski received his Lifetime Achievement Award at the Zurich Film Festival to a standing ovation (Roxborough 2011).

Despite the fact that women and girls face extremely high probabilities of being sexually assaulted, and the fact that men and boys face infinitesimally low odds of being falsely accused of rape and even lower odds of suffering lifelong consequences even for actual rape convictions, it is women and girls who are expected to bear the burden of preventing sexual assault. Every rape victim's actions are scrutinized for what she could have done to avoid the assault, while the perpetrator's choice to rape – and the indulgences and the habits of the society that led to his choice – is often passed over without comment. This is despite the fact that no amount of precautions a victim takes can ever ensure that she will not be raped, and no reasonable precaution even results in an appreciable lowering of their risk. For years, women and girls have been given, and have dutifully obeyed, a near-endless list of steps they should take to avoid sexual assault: watching what they wear, where they walk, how much they drink, which parties they go to, who they talk to, what they say – none of which has made even the slightest impact on rates of sexual assault, but which does have a serious impact on women's freedom, autonomy, and equality with men. But that impact is not counted or even recognized as an injury, and to the extent that rape itself is counted as an injury, it is viewed at least in part as a failure of the victim to be appropriately careful.

CONCLUSION: WHO MUST TAKE CARE?

These are just a few demonstrations of the damage caused to society by distorted conceptions of injury. They illustrate how social and legal resources are drained by exaggerated claims of injury by powerful groups, leaving little or no resources for vulnerable groups. Injury inequality, moreover, does violence to the concept of injury itself, measuring harm according to the status of the putative victims rather than on objective evaluation.

One way of understanding the impact of injury inequality is to consider who is expected to "take care." Who is expected to bear the burden of risk or resolve ambiguous interactions? If the necessity of using deadly force, calculating chilling effects on expression, or determining the existence of sexual consent is often ambiguous, who is expected to shoulder the burden of getting it wrong? Who is expected to prevent injury, whether to herself or to society, and who is allowed to take risks and make mistakes? Whose actions do we scrutinize, and whose do we accept without comment? Who is presumed worthy of respect, and who must constantly demonstrate respectability? Whose vulnerability and fallibility are accommodated by the very structures of law and society, and whose are treated as a matter of "personal responsibility"?

The cases outlined in this chapter are only some of the alarming, unjust, and deadly consequences of injury inequality. When we are not careful to recognizing distortions of injury, we not only allow society to be structured around the imagined harms of the privileged, but we also shift the burden of risk entirely to vulnerable populations. Those with power are provided every opportunity to make mistakes and are shielded from the consequences of their recklessness, whereas the marginalized are subjected to hyper-scrutiny of even their most innocuous actions. Injury inequality is at odds with the values of fairness and justice, and stands in the way of true social evolution.

References

Amber, J. (2015). "In Her Own Words: Marissa Alexander Tells Her Story." *Essence*, March 4. www.essence.com/2015/03/04/marissa-alexander-exclusive (last accessed: December 13, 2017).

Andrews, T. (2016). "George Zimmerman's many, many controversies since the Trayvon Martin case." *Washington Post*, May 12. www.washingtonpost.com/news/morning-mix/wp/2016/05/12/george-zimmermans-many-many-controversies-since-the-trayvon-martin-case/?utm_term=.18a98ed3971f (last accessed: December 13, 2017).

Associated Press. (2014). "Court denies Polanski's motion to dismiss 1977 statutory rape case." *The Guardian*. www.theguardian.com/us-news/2014/dec/24/court-denies-motion-polanskis-rape-case (last accessed: December 13, 2017).

Baker, K. J. M. (2016). "Here Is The Powerful Letter The Stanford Victim Read Aloud To Her Attacker." *Buzzfeed*, June 3. www.buzzfeed.com/katiejmbaker/heres-the-powerful-letter-the-stanford-victim-read-to-her-ra?utm_term=.hoE4nm55O#.ddbPpaEEL (last accessed: December 13, 2017).

Bowman, C. (1993). "Street Harassment and the Informal Ghettoization of Women." *Harvard Law Review* 106:52.

Broderick, R. (2014). "A Bunch of Gun Activists Wore Assault Weapons While Walking Around the Baby Clothes Aisle at Target." *Buzzfeed*, June 4. www.buzzfeed.com/ryanhatesthis/moms-versus-assault-weapons-in-target (last accessed: December 13, 2017).

Chemaly, S. (2015). "A Primer on Online Misogyny." *Huffington Post*, June 29. www.huffingtonpost.com/soraya-chemaly/a-primer-on-online-misogyny-revenge-porn-is-only-one-dimension_b_7691900.html (last accessed: December 13, 2017).

Citron, D. K. (2014). *Hate Crimes in Cyberspace*. Cambridge, MA: Harvard University Press.

Collins, R. K. L. (2013). "Exceptional Freedom – The Roberts Court, the First Amendment, and the New Absolutism." *Albany Law Review* 76:418.

DeFilippis, E. and Hughes, D. (2016). "Gun-Rights Advocates Claim Owning a Gun Makes a Woman Safer. The Research Says They're Wrong." *The Trace*, May 2. www.thetrace.org/2016/05/gun-ownership-makes-women-safer-debunked/ (last accessed: December 13, 2017).

De Los Reyes, G. (1993). "Dershowitz Wages Media War for Tyson, The Crimson." *The Crimson*, April 13. www.thecrimson.com/article/1993/4/13/dershowitz-wages-media-war-for-tyson/ (last accessed: December 13, 2017).

Franks, M. A. (2013). "The Lawless Internet? Myths and Misconceptions About CDA Section 230." *Huffington Post*. www.huffingtonpost.com/mary-anne-franks/section-230-the-lawless-internet_b_4455090.html (last accessed: December 13, 2017).

(2014). "Real Men Advance, Real Women Retreat: Stand Your Ground, Battered Women's Syndrome, and Violence as Male Privilege." *Miami Law Review* 68:1099.

(2015a). "How Stand Your Ground Laws Hijacked Self-Defense." Pp. 141–70 in *Guns and Contemporary Society: The Past, Present, and Future of Firearms and Firearm Policy*, vol. III, edited by Glen Utter. Santa Barbara, CA: ABC-CLIO.

(2015b). "Where the Law Lies: Constitutional Fictions and Their Discontents." Pp. 32–80 in *Law and Lies: Deception and Truth-Telling in the American Legal System*, edited by Austin Sarat. New York: Cambridge University Press.

Friedman, B. (2014). "Cliven Bundy v. Ferguson's Peaceful Demonstrators: A Tale of Two Protests." *Salon*, August 18. www.salon.com/2014/08/18/cliven_bundy_vs_fergusons_peaceful_demonstrators_a_tale_of_two_protests/ (last accessed: December 13, 2017).

Hess, A. (2014). "Why Women Aren't Welcome on the Internet." *Pacific Standard*. www.psmag.com/why-women-aren-t-welcome-on-the-internet-aa21fdbc8d6#.qupzzujtk (last accessed: December 13, 2017).

Holly, K. (2014). "Stop Street Harassment." *Unsafe and Harassed in Public Spaces: A National Street Harassment Report*, September 20–1.

Humphreys, D. K., Gasparrini, A., and Wiebe, D. J. (2017). "Evaluating the Impact of Florida's 'Stand Your Ground' Self-defense Law on Homicide and Suicide by Firearm: An Interrupted Time Series Study." *JAMA Internal Medicine* 177(1):44–50. doi:10.1001/jamainternmed.2016.6811.

Kendrick, L. (2013). "Speech, Intent, and the Chilling Effect." *William and Mary Law Review* 54:1633.

Knegt, P. (2009). "Over 100 In Film Community Sign Polanski Petition." *Indie Wire*, September 29. www.indiewire.com/article/over_100_in_film_community_sign_polanski_petition (last accessed: December 13, 2017).

Li, V. (2014). "States with Stand-Your-Ground Laws Have Seen an Increase in Homicides, Reports Task Force." *ABA Journal*, August 08. www.abajournal.com/news/article/states_with_stand_your_ground_laws_have_more_homicides/ (last accessed: December 13, 2017).

Luther, J. (2016). "'I'm Broken': The Duke Lacrosse Rape Accuser, 10 Years Later." *Vocativ*, March 10. www.vocativ.com/295731/im-broken-the-duke-lacrosse-rape-accuser-10-years-later/ (last accessed: December 13, 2017).

Mejia, P. (2014). "Altercation Between Michael Brown and Darren Wilson Unfolded in 90 Seconds: Report." *Newsweek*, November 15. www.newsweek.com/altercation-between-michael-brown-and-officer-darren-wilson-unfolded-90-284728 (last accessed: December 13, 2017).

Miller, M. (2016). "'A Steep Price to Pay for 20 Minutes of Action': Dad Defends Stanford Sex Offender." *Washington Post*, June 6. www.washingtonpost.com/news/morning-mix/wp/2016/06/06/a-steep-price-to-pay-for-20-minutes-of-action-dad-defends-stanford-sex-offender/?utm_term=.6271891d8d5c (last accessed: December 13, 2017).

Ohlheiser, A. and Phillip, A. (2015). "'I Will Light You Up!': Texas Officer Threatened Sandra Bland with Taser During Traffic Stop." *Washington Post*, July 22. www.washingtonpost.com/news/morning-mix/wp/2015/07/21/much-too-early-to-call-jail-cell-hanging-death-of-sandra-bland-suicide-da-says/ (last accessed: December 13, 2017).

Parker, C. B. (2014). "Right-to-carry Gun Laws Linked to Increase in Violent Crime, Stanford Research Shows." *Stanford News*, November 14. news.stanford.edu/2014/11/14/donohue-guns-study-111414/. (last accessed: December 13, 2017)

Piggot, J. (2015). "Judge: Marissa Alexander Released to House Arrest." *News 4 Jax*, January 27. www.news4jax.com/news/marissa-alexander-expected-to-be-released/30947974 (last accessed: December 13, 2017).

Reilly, R. (2015). "'Provocative' Police Tactics Inflamed Ferguson Protests, Experts Find." *Huffington Post*, September 2. www.huffingtonpost.com/entry/ferguson-protests-police-tactics-report_us_55e622a3e4b0aec9f35506ad (last accessed: December 13, 2017).

Roxborough, S. (2011). "Roman Polanski Receives Standing Ovation at Zurich Film Festival." *Hollywood Reporter*, September 27. www

.hollywoodreporter.com/news/roman-polanski-receives-standing-ovation-240825 (last accessed: December 13, 2017).

Schauer, F. (2004). "The Boundaries of the First Amendment: A Preliminary Exploration of Constitutional Salience." *Harvard Law Review* 117:1765.

Seitz, M. (2010). "'The Hangover 2's' Mel Gibson Hypocrisy." *Salon*, October 22. www.salon.com/2010/10/22/mel_gibson_mike_tyson_hangover_2/ (last accessed: December 13, 2017).

Shapiro, R. (2013). "Poppy Harlow, CNN Reporter, 'Outraged' Over Steubenville Rape Coverage Criticism: Report." *Huffington Post*, March 20. www.huffingtonpost.com/2013/03/20/poppy-harlow-cnn-steubenville-rape-coverage-criticism_n_2914853.html (last accessed: December 13, 2017).

Shipp, E. (1992). "Tyson Gets 6-Year Prison Term For Rape Conviction in Indiana." *New York Times*, March 27. www.nytimes.com/1992/03/27/sports/tyson-gets-6-year-prison-term-for-rape-conviction-in-indiana.html?pagewanted=1 (last accessed: December 13, 2017).

Sisario, B., Spencer, H., and Ember, S. (2016). "Rolling Stone Loses Defamation Case Over Rape Story." *New York Times*, November 4. https://www.nytimes.com/2016/11/05/business/media/rolling-stone-rape-story-case-guilty.html (last accessed: December 13, 2017).

Srivastava, R. (2015). "How Fox News Is Justifying Police Conduct In McKinney, In Three Steps." *Think Progress*. www.thinkprogress.org/how-fox-news-is-justifying-police-conduct-in-mckinney-in-three-steps-e0b92478942c#.hks491y4s (last accessed: December 13, 2017).

Stack, L. (2016). "In Stanford Rape Case, Brock Turner Blamed Drinking and Promiscuity." *New York Times*, June 8. www.nytimes.com/2016/06/09/us/brock-turner-blamed-drinking-and-promiscuity-in-sexual-assault-at-stanford.html (last accessed: December 13, 2017).

Warsinskey, T. (2014). "Steubenville Rape Case: Ma'Lik Richmond Returns to Football Field and Hears Cheers." *The Plain Dealer*, August 28–9. www.cleveland.com/metro/index.ssf/2014/08/steubenville_rape_case_malik_r.html (last accessed: December 13, 2017).

Wemple, E. (2013). "CNN is Getting Hammered for Steubenville Coverage." *The Washington Post*, March 18. www.washingtonpost.com/blogs/erik-wemple/wp/2013/03/18/cnn-is-getting-hammered-for-steubenville-coverage/ (last accessed: December 13, 2017).

Winkler, A. (2015). "The NRA Will Fall. It's Inevitable." *Washington Post*, October 9. www.washingtonpost.com/posteverything/wp/2015/10/19/the-nra-will-fall-its-inevitable/?utm_term=.b886c98f4ea8 (last accessed: December 13, 2017).

Zook, K. B. (2015). "The Lessons of Jordan Davis's Murder, Revisited." *The Nation*, November 23. www.thenation.com/article/the-lessons-of-jordan-daviss-murder-revisited/ (last accessed: December 13, 2017).

CHAPTER ELEVEN

THE UNCONSCIONABLE IMPOSSIBILITY OF REPARATIONS FOR SLAVERY; OR, WHY THE MASTER'S MULES WILL NEVER DISMANTLE THE MASTER'S HOUSE

Kaimipono David Wenger

> The islands from Charleston south ... are reserved and set apart for the settlement of the negroes now made free by the acts of war and the proclamation of the President of the United States ... each family shall have a plot of not more than forty acres of tillable ground ...
>
> Gen. William T. Sherman[1]

> It is beyond debate that slavery caused tremendous suffering and ineliminable scars throughout our Nation's history. However, Plaintiffs' claims, as alleged in their Complaint, fail based on numerous well-settled legal principles ... Plaintiffs' Complaint fails to state a claim upon which relief can be granted, a serious defect the court cannot overlook regardless how egregious the circumstances giving rise to the claims.
>
> In re African-American Slave Descendants Litigation[2]

> It was in these early years that Ross began to understand himself as an American – he did not live under the blind decree of justice, but under the heel of a regime that elevated armed robbery to a governing principle.
>
> Ta-Nehesi Coates (2014)

> The master's tools will never dismantle the master's house. They may allow us to temporarily beat him at his own game, but they will never enable us to bring about genuine change.
>
> Audre Lorde (1984: 12)

Associate Professor of Law, Thomas Jefferson School of Law. Thanks to Kath Rogers for excellent feedback.

[1] Gen. William T. Sherman, Special Field Order No. 15.
[2] In re African-American Slave Descendants Litigation, 304 F. Supp. 2d 1027, 1075 (2002).

UNCONSCIONABLE IMPOSSIBILITY OF REPARATIONS FOR SLAVERY

INTRODUCTION

The history of legal advocacy for slavery reparations is a history of failure. Slaves and their descendants have repeatedly sought compensation for the horrific harms inflicted on them. These efforts, beginning even before the end of slavery and continuing to the present day, have often employed the language and tools of law. And yet, over the 150 years since the end of slavery, no compensation has been paid; the fabled "forty acres and a mule" were never delivered.

On the surface, it is astounding that millions of people can be subjected to the most horrible abuses, with not a penny in compensation ultimately paid. After all, the structure of the legal system is designed to address wrongs, and slavery combines many of the most terrible wrongs imaginable – theft, imprisonment, assault, murder. How is it that an uncompensated wrong of this magnitude can continue to exist?

This chapter discusses the curious unwillingness of the legal system to provide compensation for the harms of slavery. Ultimately, the chapter concludes that the failure of law in this area – the impossibility of reparations – is no accident. Rather, the legal system is doing what it was always designed to do. Law itself is a social construct designed by societal elites to protect elite interests, and the master's tools will never dismantle the master's house.

THE HORRORS OF SLAVERY

The harms of slavery are impossible to fully catalog; existing historical scholarship can and does fill volumes (e.g., Berlin 1998, Franklin [1947] 2000) and a full discussion is well beyond the scope of this chapter. However, it is crucial to keep in mind the extent of these harms while discussing reparations, and so this chapter begins with a powerful snapshot of the human cost of slavery, from Ta-Nehisi Coates' article "The Case For Reparations" (2014). Coates notes that:

> Forced partings were common in the antebellum South. A slave in some parts of the region stood a 30 percent chance of being sold in his or her lifetime. Twenty-five percent of interstate trades destroyed a first marriage and half of them destroyed a nuclear family.
>
> When the wife and children of Henry Brown, a slave in Richmond, Virginia, were to be sold away, Brown searched for a white master who might buy his wife and children to keep the family together. He failed:

> The next day, I stationed myself by the side of the road, along which the slaves, amounting to three hundred and fifty, were to pass. The purchaser of my wife was a Methodist minister, who was about starting for North Carolina. Pretty soon five wagon-loads of little children passed, and looking at the foremost one, what should I see but a little child, pointing its tiny hand toward me, exclaiming, "There's my father; I knew he would come and bid me good-bye." It was my eldest child! Soon the gang approached in which my wife was chained. I looked, and beheld her familiar face; but O, reader, that glance of agony! May God spare me ever again enduring the excruciating horror of that moment! She passed, and came near to where I stood. I seized hold of her hand, intending to bid her farewell; but words failed me; the gift of utterance had fled, and I remained speechless. I followed her for some distance, with her hand grasped in mine, as if to save her from her fate, but I could not speak, and I was obliged to turn away in silence.
>
> In a time when telecommunications were primitive and blacks lacked freedom of movement, the parting of black families was a kind of murder. Here we find the roots of American wealth and democracy – in the for-profit destruction of the most important asset available to any people, the family (Coates 2014).

These passages shock the conscience. "O, reader, that glance of agony! May God spare me ever again enduring the excruciating horror of that moment! … I could not speak, and I was obliged to turn away in silence" (Coates 2014, quoting Henry Brown). It is impossible to read this language without shuddering; and of course this is just one anecdote from a system that created many thousands of such interactions, most of them unrecorded. A true measure of the human costs of slavery is impossible, the magnitude of aggregate harm is simply incomprehensible.

However, legal tools exist to measure and categorize injury, and, from the legal perspective, this vast ocean of harms can be distilled and broken down into a still-vast and horrifying list of concrete and very serious torts and crimes, including kidnapping, theft, assault, false imprisonment, sexual assault, and murder (Westley 1998, Wenger 2010). Slavery was not only a moral outrage, it was also a set of specific legal harms; that is, from the legal perspective, it is not only the case that something horrible and incomprehensible happened; it is also the case that very concrete instances of assault, kidnapping, rape, and so forth, took place, with enumerated legal elements clearly satisfied. In addition, the history makes clear how law participated in these harms. Slavery was not a minor wrinkle or a quirky anomaly; rather, it was, "deeply embedded in the social, political and legal structure of the nation" (Finkelman 1997).

A VERY BRIEF HISTORY OF REPARATIONS ADVOCACY (ESPECIALLY LAWSUITS)

Even before the end of slavery, slaves and freed slaves sought compensation from their former owners; these early reparations attempts were universally rebuffed (Magee 1993, Brophy 2006, Bell 2008). During the Civil War and then, following emancipation, advocates advanced a variety of compensation proposals through different avenues, typically focused on state-provided compensation. The most well-known proposal is General Sherman's Field Order No. 15 (and its follow up orders), providing that freed slaves were to be given "forty acres and a mule" from seized confederate lands and surplus Army animals. However, that decision was countermanded by President Andrew Johnson, who instead directed that compensation be handled by the Freedmen's Bureau; the Bureau in turn was not effective in providing compensation to freed slaves (Brophy 2006). In the following century, a number of African-American leaders argued for some kind of reparations, including the repatriation movement led by Marcus Garvey and the Black Manifesto published by James Forman during the civil rights era; those claims were also unsuccessful (Magee 1993, Wenger 2011).

In recent years, legal experts, beginning with Boris Bittker, began to explore in detail the idea of *legal claims* for reparations (Bittker 1973). Following and in connection with that conversation, activists also brought lawsuits seeking reparations and proposed legislation on the topic (Brophy 2006, Wenger 2010). At the same time, broader cultural conversations and advocacy continued as well (see, e.g., Robinson 2000, Coates 2014). But the legal cases offered unique and intriguing possibilities. They seemed to open the door to potential remedies. They also provided opportunity to illustrate the reach and meaning of the law. And perhaps inadvertently, they did just that.

The major reparations lawsuits of the modern era are *Cato v. United States*[3] and *In re African-American Slave Descendants Litigation*[4]

---

[3] *Cato v. United States*, 70 F.3d 1103 (9th Cir. 1995).
[4] *In re African-American Slave Descendants Litigation*, 375 F. Supp. 2d 721 (N.D. Ill. 2005); *In re African-American Slave Descendants Litigation*, 471 F.3d 754, 763 (7th Cir. 2006).

(Brophy 2006, Wenger 2010). *Cato* highlights the legal claims against government defendants. Government involvement in slavery was extensive, as state and federal governments and their officials were involved in the creation, enforcement, and application of slave laws for many decades. These government entities derived substantial financial benefit from slavery, while passing the cost along to enslaved persons.

Cato plaintiffs sought redress from the United States government for, "damages due to the enslavement of African Americans and subsequent discrimination against them, for an acknowledgement of discrimination, and for an apology" (Brophy 2006, Wenger 2010). In particular, the complaint in the *Cato* lawsuit sought:

> compensation of $100,000,000 for forced, ancestral indoctrination into a foreign society; kidnapping of ancestors from Africa; forced labor; breakup of families; removal of traditional values; deprivations of freedom; and imposition of oppression, intimidation, miseducation and lack of information about various aspects of their indigenous character. [Plaintiffs] also request that the court order an acknowledgment of the injustice of slavery in the United States and in the 13 American colonies between 1619 and 1865, as well as of the existence of discrimination against freed slaves and their descendants from the end of the Civil War to the present. In addition, [Plaintiffs] seek an apology from the United States.

The case was brought in federal district court in 1994. However, the District Court ultimately dismissed the complaint, and the Ninth Circuit affirmed. The court found the complaint deficient for a number of substantive reasons. The major problem was sovereign immunity: The complaint "does not refer to any basis upon which the United States might have consented to suit" and, "neither identifies any constitutional or statutory right that was violated, nor asserts any basis for federal subject matter jurisdiction or waiver of sovereign immunity." In addition, the court found several other flaws in the complaint, such as lack of standing. The court concluded with a broad assessment that "the legislature, rather than the judiciary, is the appropriate forum for this relief" (Brophy 2006, Wenger 2010). *Cato* effectively closed the door on reparations lawsuits against government entities; no successful slavery reparations claims have been brought against government actors since.

The 2002 *Slave Descendants* litigation targeted private companies. Many private companies benefitted financially from the institution of slavery, including insurance companies, banks, railroads, and newspapers (Brophy 2006, Wenger 2010). The *Slave Descendants* complaint was not barred by sovereign immunity, as *Cato* had been, because it was brought against private defendants, rather than government entities. Plaintiffs also sought to avoid problematic causation-based defenses by bringing their claims against long-lived corporate defendants who had existed at the time of slavery and profited directly from it. In addition, the *Slave Descendants* lawsuit drew on recent innovations in legal strategy which had resulted in an eventual settlement and reparations for Holocaust victims, employing both tort and unjust enrichment arguments (ibid.).

The district court in *Slave Descendants* dismissed the case based on the lack of causal connection between defendants' actions and plaintiffs' harms. The court wrote, "Plaintiffs cannot establish a personal injury sufficient to confer standing by merely alleging some genealogical relationship to African-Americans held in slavery over one-hundred, two-hundred, or three-hundred years ago." Ultimately, the district court was unwilling to find liability where causation was this attenuated. The appellate court agreed, writing that, "this causal chain is too long and has too many weak links for a court to be able to find that the defendants' conduct harmed the plaintiffs at all, let alone in an amount that could be estimated without the wildest speculation" (Wenger 2006, 2010).

The statute of limitations was also a fatal barrier. The *Slave Descendants* court noted:

> Many of the torts set out in the instant complaint occurred prior to the formal end of chattel slavery in the United States of America. These claims would have accrued by 1865 at the latest. The longest limitations period for any of Plaintiffs' claim is ten years, which would have run well over a century prior to the filing of the instant Complaint. If cognizable claims ever existed, those claims were owned by former slaves themselves, and became time-barred when the statutes of limitations expired in the nineteenth century. As such, Plaintiffs' century-old claims are barred by the statutes of limitation in every jurisdiction.

Ultimately, the court ruled that plaintiffs were entitled to no legal remedy (Brophy 2006, Wenger 2006, 2010). Claims against both private companies and government actors had failed.

This failure occurred despite the best efforts of reparations advocates to model their claims after successful litigation from other cases. In fact, as advocates noted, a major factor in the renewed focus on legal claims for reparations was the success of similar claims in other arenas (Brophy 2002, Wenger 2010). Litigation, using both tort and unjust enrichment theory, had resulted in successful settlement and recovery in Holocaust cases. Meanwhile, Japanese-American internees had successfully sought compensation through legislative channels. As Brophy noted, "advocates of reparations for slavery have drawn from other reparations precedents" (Brophy 2002).

Reparations advocates employed both tort and unjust enrichment arguments. Tort claims are relatively straightforward. Slavery clearly involved a large number of actions that meet the standard definitions of intentional torts (Finkelman 1997, Hylton 2004b). Tort law is the primary vehicle that ensures that victims of harm receive compensation (Weinstein 1995, Hylton 2004b). It is not difficult to frame the harms of slavery in terms of tort (Westley 1998, Brophy 2006). If the kinds of actions that took place in slave times were to happen today, they would certainly be torts.

Unjust enrichment claims offer a different path to legal remedy, requiring only that claimants show that a defendant unjustly obtained some benefit from the claimant and that the benefit should be refunded. This legal tactic was successfully used in Holocaust and tobacco cases, although not all advocates agreed about this strategy in the reparations context (Sebok 2004, Brophy 2006).

Scholars had suggested other potential legal avenues for compensation. For instance, Bittker argued that desegregation claims might be brought under civil rights laws, and I argued that a takings clause remedy might be available; other advocates proposed using human rights law approaches (Bittker 1973, Wenger 2003, Brophy 2006). Reparations litigants also struggled with policy questions about the goal of reparations litigation. Was the goal based on social welfare and equitable distribution of wealth, or a more narrow desire to correct specific historic injustices? (Hylton 2004a, b). Ultimately, reparations lawsuits focused only on the most narrow issues of tort and unjust enrichment, the clearest paths to liability. And even then, they failed.

Advocates also tried legislative strategies. The major legislative push for reparations has come through the efforts of congressman John Conyers (D-Mich) and proposed bill H.R. 40.[5] This bill would establish a commission to "examine the lingering negative effects of the institution of slavery and the discrimination ... on living African-Americans and on society in the United States," to

---

[5] Commission to Study Reparation Proposals for African-Americans Act, H.R. 40, 114th Cong. (2015).

"recommend appropriate ways to educate the American public of the Commission's findings," and to "recommend appropriate remedies in consideration of the Commission's findings." H.R. 40 is a strategic move based on the experience of Japanese-American internees, where a commission was formed to study the internment, issue a report, and make recommendations. The commission ultimately recommended that interned individuals receive compensation, and Congress then passed legislation which granted some internees compensation for their time in camps (Brophy 2006). Envisioning a similar arc for slavery reparations, Congressman Conyers has introduced H.R. 40 every session of Congress since 1989, but it has never even been voted on (ibid.).

Advocates also sought apology for the harms of slavery, often in the context of a larger reparations proposal (Brooks 2004, Wenger 2009). A number of state and municipal governments, as well as the federal government, have passed legislation apologizing for their roles in slavery. The state-level apologies are a highlight of the "microreparations" movement, including apologies from states, cities, and private entities (Wenger 2010). In addition to state apologies, a number of corporations and universities have apologized for their role in slavery, and sometimes created commissions to study and discuss their history (ibid.).

The federal government's apology is complicated. The House of Representatives passed an official apology on July 29, 2008. The Senate formally apologized for slavery on June 18, 2009. In general, the apologies are a welcome move forward. They typically describe the harms of slavery and express regret and sorrow. For instance, the Senate apology stated that slaves were "brutalized, humiliated, [and] dehumanized" and "apologizes to African-Americans on behalf of the people of the United States, for the wrongs committed against them and their ancestors who suffered under slavery and Jim Crow laws."

However, unlike the House apology, the Senate apology also contained additional limiting language, specifically stating that it could not be used as a ground for monetary compensation: "Nothing in this resolution – (A) authorizes or supports any claim against the United States; or (B) serves as a settlement of any claim against the United States." Because of that language, I have called it a sort of "apology lite" which failed to express true contrition (Wenger 2009). Ironically, the apology lite provides an excellent illustration of the limits of legislative approaches to reparations.

THE REPARATIONS DILEMMA

Legal claims for reparations create a sort of dilemma. As I have written elsewhere, they "are neither easily granted nor easily denied, and serious problems arise for either answer" (Wenger 2010).

Problems with Denying Restitution

There are serious problems with denying claims for slavery reparations. Slavery was a massive and systematic violation of the rights of millions of individuals. Normally, society contemplates that the legal system will address serious rights violations – even relatively minor violations are subject to law. Of course, legal avenues vary depending on the specifics of a particular case. However, an overarching theme of the legal system is that serious wrongs will receive some kind of legal response (Weinstein 1995, Wenger 2007). Tort law has been the traditional avenue to obtain remedies in these kinds of cases (Weinstein 1995).

Slavery is multiple orders of magnitude more serious than the minor violations which tort law often addresses. As such, it seems all the more unacceptable for society to fail to address the harms it caused. Tort law is in part about accountability, and a failure to address the harm of slavery would be a major blow to accountability. The moral intuition underlying tort law is that it is morally unacceptable not to address harms of this magnitude. Advocates have argued that a government that commits an atrocity incurs a moral obligation to apologize and provide compensation (Brooks 2004). In contrast, if mass harms go uncompensated, citizens may lose faith in the rule of law (Wenger 2007).

Tort law is not designed only to address minor violations. Instead, it includes potential avenues for relief for various kinds of massive harms. For instance, class action lawsuits are designed to provide some level of restitution for large numbers of people who have been injured by another party's bad actions (Weinstein 1995). These cases often result in some sort of mass distribution, where mass tort claims become the vehicle for holding defendants accountable for harms to large groups of victims (ibid.). In theory, the same legal system that addresses small harms should also be able to accommodate even large cases. Indeed, not only would one expect the same rules to apply to these cases, but a contrary policy of not applying them would be seriously problematic. If the law can only address minor scrapes and bruises, what good is it? Thus, one might reasonably expect a system of corrective justice under the rule of law to have some remedy in place for a set of egregious wrongs like slavery (Wenger 2010).

Yet reparations claims have already been denied for well over a century. Despite repeated attempts to secure redress over the past 150 years, neither courts nor legislatures have ever made restitution in any meaningful way. As Westley (1998) notes:

> If there is a substantive view of oppression embedded in the claim for slavery reparations, it is that state-sponsored transgenerational private and public expropriation of labor and wealth accumulation potential through force and violence is unjust, that those who suffer such a fate deserve material and symbolic redress from perpetrators, and that the obligation of corporate or government wrongdoers to make redress is not extinguished so long as they continue to exist (Westley 1998).

Thus, very good arguments can be made to show that restitution claims should not be denied. Given these arguments, the lack of compensation is a significant outlier – and the repeated court and legislative punting is an outrage. The law has figured out ways to address other harms, so why not this one?

Problems with Granting Restitution
On the other hand, it is also true that reparations cases are not a particularly good fit for courts. They are complicated and raise difficult legal issues, and courts are not particularly well equipped to address claims for slavery reparations using either tort or unjust enrichment legal frameworks (Wenger 2010).

Courts in the private law context traditionally focus on private actions, such as tort and contract claims. A variety of requirements in those contexts – such as tort law's causation rules – do not map well onto reparations claims. This is a problem that advocates have known about for some time, and have tried to address. As noted above, some advocates have argued that traditional tort rules on causation should be modified given the unique harms and context of slavery; this might include recognition of group harms, an expanded framework for proximate causation, or new approaches to showing causation statistically (Matsuda 1987, Wenger 2006). However, that discussion concedes the initial problem, which is that reparations claims are highly challenging under existing legal frameworks. They bring multiple kinds of attenuated causation, which makes them a difficult fit for courts accustomed to more basic tort claims (Wenger 2006).

Reparations claims also fit imperfectly with tort law's corrective focus. Advocates like Randall Robinson have written that reparations should be viewed as payment due on a debt, a corrective framing which dovetails with tort law approaches (Robinson 2000). However, the corrective approach clashes with reparations claims in many places. Corrective justice typically demands a close link between victim and defendant – exactly the characteristic that reparations claims lack. In addition, corrective justice seeks to put people in the position they would be in if the wrong had not occurred. However, it is unclear how to apply this rule in the case of slavery. True compensation for these kinds of harms is impossible because the value of the damage done is incalculable. Reparations are always dealing in the realm of fundamentally inadequate responses because money cannot truly compensate victims (Wenger 2010). Symbolic gestures may help fill this gap, but they could also backfire. Symbolic or token remedies may create a perception, for instance, that a horrible harm has been reduced to a simple commodity that can be purchased with a small amount of money (ibid.).

Reparations claims, in many ways, seem more distributive than corrective. However, distributive justice remedies are difficult to receive through the judiciary and are often legislated instead. When they do show up in tort law, distributive justice ideas most often manifest in settlement. But reparations claims are nowhere near settlement. This is in part because of the basic problem: Reparations claims do not fit well into the court system, so there is little incentive to settle (Wenger 2010).

Finally, it is not clear that tort law or unjust enrichment has the moral heft to handle reparations claims. Writing about the lack of moral dimension in unjust enrichment, Anthony Sebok notes that unjust enrichment provides "an impoverished understanding" of reparations claims, because it merely turns them into claims that slaves were not paid (Sebok 2004). Similarly, Brooks writes with regards to tort claims that "[t]he final problem with the tort model" is "its moral deficiency … [T]he tort model clouds the black redress movement's identity with international human rights movements" (Brooks 2004). The limits of legal solutions sometimes frustrate not only courts, but also reparations advocates.

Because of these problems, it is no surprise that courts have rejected legal claims for reparations. It is correct that there are many ways in which the tort system does not fit well with reparations claims. It is also true, however, that lack of redress is unacceptable. The result is a paradox of sorts – the reparations dilemma. Tort compensation is a poor fit, but nonremedy is a moral outrage (Wenger 2010).

THE IMPOSSIBILITY OF REPARATIONS

Tort compensation is a poor fit because of the limitations of the legal system. But that creates a follow up question: Why do those limits exist in the first place? After all, law is a human creation meant to serve specific purposes. It can address the theft of 10 dollars or 10 billion dollars; it can comprehend thefts of obscure intellectual property or corporate interests. But it cannot address the mass enslavement of an entire people. *Why not?* Who builds a system that addresses minor cuts and bruises but not horrendous injuries? The omission of a remedy for this kind of harm is a mind-boggling oversight.

Unless it isn't.

Unless this omission is, in fact, a feature of the way that the law was designed and created in the first place. And if that is the case, then the impossibility of reparations is not some unfortunate coincidence. Reparations are impossible because the legal system was built to make them impossible.

Certainly, the law frequently reflects the overt racism and prejudices of legal elites. Court decisions have often been based on overt stereotypes about women, people of color, and other marginalized groups (Wriggins 2005, Chamallas and Wriggins 2010). The Constitution itself was created through a series of conversations that were punctuated and riddled with overt expressions of racism (Bell 2008). It is in fact quite routine that the most vulnerable groups find themselves excluded and marginalized in legal structures designed by societal elites; this exclusion then reinforces their vulnerability (Fineman 2010).

Less obvious and overt racial biases and assumptions also shape the law. These may be manifest through structures of privilege and subordination, where the rights of dominant elites are protected while the rights of more marginalized groups are not (Wildman 1996). Law often builds on and reinforces existing structures of privilege. As Franks notes, it is common under law that "injuries affecting the powerful are exaggerated while those affecting the marginalized are downplayed" (Franks, Chapter 10).

Tort law is one such locus of privilege, a site where existing structures of power are exercised and maintained. This may occur explicitly. For instance, tort law damage calculations may rely on gender- and race-based wage tables in damage calculations, an approach that systematically undervalues harms to minority groups, which are underrepresented in higher-wage jobs (Chamallas 2005, Wriggins 2010). In addition, as the Black Lives Matter movement highlights, tort compensation or criminal liability may depend on subjective and biased beliefs about the worthiness of the victim.

Bias also affects the many unstated value judgments and assumptions underlying tort law and the scope of injury. What is a normal amount of risk for a worker to assume? What is a safe driving speed? Who is the "reasonable man?" Tort law reflects the assumptions of the majority. That approach tends to systematically undervalue and downplay the harms suffered by marginalized groups.

And above all, tort law relies on assumptions about the meaning of injury – that is, what kinds of harms will count as "injury" for the law to address, and what kinds of losses will simply be chalked up as unfortunate and passed along to the victim to absorb (Engel 2010). In this process, injury and remedy make up a sort of "moving frontier" in constant conversation with one another, where injuries do not exist in a vacuum, but against a backdrop of societal expectations (Galanter 2010).

Those societal expectations in turn manifest through legal doctrines. For instance, the concept of causation is not a neutral judgment of objective facts. Rather, it is a "value-laden inquiry that cannot be separated from considerations of social policy" because "assessments of causation are influenced by the identity of the injured parties and that causal attribution is a dynamic process, the product of cultural as well as intellectual developments" (Chamallas 1994).

The effects of these underlying biases become evident when we attempt to place reparations within tort frameworks. Matsuda (1987) articulated an early legal argument for reparations under tort law, arguing for extending current tort doctrines to cover instances where an entire group of people had been harmed. She noted that traditional tort law failed to account for the possibility of group harms and intergenerational harms, and urged an approach of "looking to the bottom" to recognize the validity of such claims. Matsuda framed reparations claims in a way that would allow for tort recovery, using a model of victim group, perpetrator group, and a causal connection to show group harm. Similarly, some advocates urged using a mass tort model to show causation through statistical methods (Wenger 2006). However, no courts have accepted these theories, which are seen as novel.

But why is this an unusual or novel idea to begin with? Matsuda's article starts out with the correct descriptive point that existing tort law does not easily extend to cover the types of harms of slavery. *Why not? Because tort law was designed by legal and societal elites.*

Tort law is a set of created legal rules, developed over time, by elites. As such it was created to cover the variety of harms that could be imagined by people like Blackstone. As a well-off citizen, Blackstone could imagine a number of potential harms: He could imagine being a victim of private theft, for instance, or property damage, or arbitrary action by a constable toward him as an individual. And so the legal system was developed with those harms in mind.

But that system has structural blind spots, because "rules created within a predominantly white, male-dominated system often fail to take into account the differing experiences of more marginalized groups in society" (Chamallas 1994). The blind spots line up with the power gaps: "The limits society places on legal tools reflect the assumptions and privileges of the majority" (Wenger 2010).

It is *because of* these built-in limitations, based on privilege, that tort law is not a good fit for reparations claims brought by an entire people disenfranchised and enslaved. Mr Blackstone did not build in a remedy for that kind of harm because he did not contemplate suffering it. As I wrote previously, "The tort system does not contemplate some types of mass harm because the parties in power – those who create the rules of tort law – do not face those types of harm." When we consider how gaps in tort coverage come into being, we see that these gaps "reflect a particular set of societal values and choices. When we say that reparations claims fail, we are reflecting certain societal values" (Wenger 2010).

This is not an accidental omission. Rather, the entire system of law and politics was designed to protect the interests of the elites. In rejecting reparations claims, tort law is not failing; it is exactly fulfilling its design. *This is how the system is supposed to work.*

THE MASTER'S MULES

Can law ultimately provide a path to reparations? Or is law itself inextricably bound to the structures of privilege and oppressions from which it originated? The question calls to mind Audre Lorde's observation about how some social structures function as "the master's tools." Writing about how mainstream white feminists excluded the voices of queer women and women of color, Lorde noted that:

> Those of us who stand outside the circle of this society's definition of acceptable women; those of us who have been forged in the crucibles of

difference – those of us who are poor, who are lesbians, who are Black, who are older – know that survival is not an academic skill. It is learning how to take our differences and make them strengths. For the master's tools will never dismantle the master's house. They may allow us temporarily to beat him at his own game, but they will never enable us to bring about genuine change. And this fact is only threatening to those women who still define the master's house as their only source of support (Lorde 1984, emphasis added).

Lorde's comments were made in the context of feminist activism and ways that mainstream white feminism excluded outsider voices. Her metaphor illustrates how such exclusion reinforces the same sorts of hierarchy and structures of power that underlie patriarchy and racial oppression to begin with. The metaphor can extend far beyond its initial context; broadly speaking, it calls into question the very possibility that activists can ever really redeploy structures of power in ways that fight subordination.

Is law itself one of the master's tools? If so, and if we believe Lorde, then it follows that any attempt to combat subordination or secure reparations under law is inevitably doomed.

But hasn't law provided an avenue for other civil rights victories? Yes, but as Derrick Bell has written, decisions like *Brown* v. *Board of Education* came about only when white political elites felt that they were necessary to achieve the "economic and political advances at home and abroad that would follow abandonment of segregation." That is, these actions are often the product of interest convergence – they do not spring from altruism, but rather occur when elite interests converge with the interests of African-Americans. The same can be said about abolition itself – it only happened when it was in whites' interests to do so, that is, when the white benefit from freeing slaves outweighed the white loss in doing so (Bell 1980).

Bell illustrates the concept by parable, with the story of the space traders. In that story, fictitious space aliens trade gold, resources, and technology for Blacks in America, who are led away in chains. The moral is clear: majority society will gladly betray the interests of minority groups if this benefits the majority (Bell 2000). And Bell specifically argued that white self-interest would block reparations (Bell 1974). Magee similarly noted the lack of white self-interest in reparations (Magee 1993).

Law has existed as one of the master's tools for centuries. It is occasionally employed to advance minority interests when those converge with elite wishes. Meanwhile, law was fundamental in creating and maintaining the system of slavery. In doing so, "Racial law became an important conduit for the preservation and legitimation of the established order" (Bell 2008). To see the way that even noble-sounding laws are employed as the master's tools, we need look no further than the Reconstruction amendments with their high-sounding guarantee of equality; today they are used by wealthy white college applicants attacking affirmative action programs. Sometimes, society moves forward, but even those forward moves are often followed by periods of regression.

The entire concept of property is a tool of the masters, designed to protect elite interests. The property framework defined Native American claims as outside the scope of its protection, through the Supreme Court's openly elitist ruling in *Johnson v. M'Intosh* that Native Americans had no property rights in their land. Once that baseline was established, then property was given a very high level of protection, sometimes higher than individual protections. For instance, trespass to property requires only a general intent, as compared to wrongs against an individual (i.e., one need not intend to trespass). So, property gets the higher protection – *after* the claims of Native Americans have been excluded in their entirety. The result is a self-reinforcing process, where property is the measure of society, and society then creates structures that protect that property. Native American attempts under law to recover their lands only enmesh them deeper in the structure that dispossessed them to begin with. Property rights in law are an example of the master's tools.

The same phenomenon explains the failure of reparations lawsuits. The structures of tort, of settlement, are all part of the master's tools; they are legal and power structures designed to remedy certain kinds of harms – the kinds of harms that Blackstone imagined himself, or someone like him, suffering. As a tool of the master, law focuses on protecting the settled expectations of elites, the status quo. And this leads inevitably to the failure of reparations lawsuits.

Any change would require significant rethinking of the meaning of injury, of the meaning of law. But this is unlikely to occur and there is considerable cultural inertia against it. Concepts like *stare decisis* build in a stability which benefits those who already have privilege. Law is not interested in unsettling the settled. White Americans resent reminders of racial injustice, like the Black Lives Matter movement. Most white Americans like to think of slavery as something that happened a long time ago and ended, having little effect today (Gross 2008, Waterhouse 2011). Reparations are a highly contested topic in the culture wars, and the gap between white and black responses to surveys is incredibly high (Brophy 2004, 2006). Meanwhile the existing narrative reinforces itself. As I wrote previously:

> Because remedy and injury are mutually constitutive, people will to some extent define injury backward from the existence of a legal remedy. Under that definition, an injury is something that the legal system addresses. Thus, if there is no legal harm, then there was no foul to begin with ... When a society decides that an injury really needs to be compensated, it will generally find a way to provide restitution ... Ultimately, then, society makes policy choices about what exactly is too big to remedy (Wenger 2010).

Which brings us back to Sherman's field order granting 40 acres and a mule. The 40 acres account starkly illustrates just how law functions as one of the master's tools. Sherman's order was itself an act of violence, a gunpoint redistribution of property away from temporarily powerless whites. Its evocative language of 40 acres and a mule painted a picture of acceptance and respectability for newly freed slaves, and it sparked hope for some kind of substantive change; but ultimately it failed because there are structural obstacles to any sort of progress, especially when that progress relies on the master's tools. And, like Sherman's order, reparations lawsuits have failed as well.

Can the master's mules ever dismantle the master's house? Time will tell.

References

Bell, Derrick. (1974). "Dissection of a Dream." *Harvard Civil Rights-Civil Liberties Law Review* 9:156–65.

(1980). "*Brown v. Board of Education* and the Interest-Convergence Dilemma." *Harvard Law Review* 93:518.

(2000). "After We're Gone: Prudent Speculations on America in a Post-Racial Epoch." Pp. 3–5 in *Critical Race Theory, The Cutting Edge*, 2nd edn, edited by Richard Delgado and Jean Stefancic. Philadelphia, PA: Temple University Press.

(2008). *Race, Racism and American Law*, 6th edn. New York City: Aspen.

Berlin, Ira. (1998). *Many Thousands Gone: The First Two Centuries of Slavery in North America*. Cambridge, MA: Harvard University Press.

Bittker, Boris. (1973). *The Case for Black Reparations*. Boston, MA: Beacon Press.

Brooks, Roy. (2004). *Atonement and Forgiveness: A New Model for Black Reparations*. Berkeley, CA: University of California Press.

Brophy, Alfred. (2002). "Some Conceptual and Legal Problems in Reparations for Slavery." *New York University Annual Survey of American Law* 58:497–556.

(2004). "The Cultural War Over Reparations for Slavery." *DePaul Law Review* 53:1181–213.

(2006). *Reparations: Pro and Con.* Oxford: Oxford University Press.

Chamallas, Martha. (1994). "Questioning the Use of Race-Specific and Gender-Specific Economic Data in Tort Litigation: A Constitutional Argument." *Fordham Law Review* 63:73.

(2005). "Civil Rights in Ordinary Tort Cases: Race, Gender, and the Calculation of Economic Loss." *Loyola Los Angeles Law Review* 38:1435.

Chamallas, Martha and Wriggins, Jennifer B. (2010). *The Measure of Injury: Race, Gender and Tort Law.* New York: New York University Press.

Coates, Ta-Nehisi. (2014). "The Case for Reparations." *The Atlantic*, June.

Engel, David. (2010). "Lumping as Default in Tort Cases." *Loyola Los Angeles Law Review* 44:33.

Fineman, Martha. (2010). "The Vulnerable Subject and the Responsive State." *Emory Law Journal* 60:251–76.

Finkelman, Paul. (1997). *Slavery and the Law.* Madison, WI: Rowman and Littlefield Publishers, Inc.

Franklin, John Hope and Alfred A. Moss Jr. ([1947] 2000). *From Slavery to Freedom: A History of African Americans*, 8th edn. New York: Knopf.

Galanter, Marc. (2010). "The Dialectic of Injury and Remedy." *Loyola Los Angeles Law Review* 44:1–10.

Gross, Ariela. (2008). "When is the Time of Slavery – The History of Slavery in Contemporary Legal and Political Argument." *California Law Review* 96:283.

Hylton, Keith. (2004a). "A Framework for Reparations Claims." *Boston College Third World Law Journal* 24:31–44.

(2004b). "Slavery and Tort Law." *Boston University Law Review* 84:1209–67.

Lorde, Audre. (1984). "The Master's Tools Will Never Dismantle the Master's House." In *Sister Outsider: Essays and Speeches.* Trumansburg, NY: Crossing Press.

Magee, Rhonda V. (1993). "The Master's Tools, from the Bottom Up: Responses to African-American Reparations Theory in Mainstream and Outsider Remedies Discourse." *Virginia Law Review* 79:863–916.

Matsuda, Mari. (1987). "Looking to the Bottom: Critical Legal Studies and Reparations." *Harvard Civil Rights-Civil Liberties Law Review* 22:323–400.

Robinson, Randall. (2000). *The Debt: What America Owes to Blacks.* New York: Penguin.

Sebok, Anthony. (2004). "Two Concepts of Injustice in Reparations for Slavery." *Boston University Law Review* 84:1405–44.

Waterhouse, Carlton. (2011). "Total Recall: Restoring the Public Memory of Enslaved African-Americans and the American System of Slavery Through Rectificatory Justice and Reparations." *Journal of Gender, Race and Justice* 14:703–42.

Weinstein, Jack. (1995). *Individual Justice in Mass Tort Litigation*. Chicago, IL: Northwestern University Press.

Wenger, Kaimipono David. (2003). "Slavery as a takings clause violation." *American University Law Review* 53:191–259.

———(2006). "Causation and Attenuation in the Slavery Reparations Debate." *University of San Francisco Law Review* 40:279–326.

———(2007). "Reparations Within the Rule of Law." *Thomas Jefferson Law Review* 29:231–50.

———(2009). "Apology Lite: Truths, Doubts, and Reconciliations in the Senate's Guarded Apology for Slavery." *Connecticut Law Review CONNtemplations* 42:1–12.

———(2010). "'Too Big to Remedy?': Rethinking Mass Restitution for Slavery and Jim Crow." *Loyola Los Angeles Law Review* 44:177–232.

———(2011). "From Radical to Practical (and Back Again?): Reparations, Rhetoric, and Revolution." *Journal of Civil Rights and Economic Development* 25:697–738.

Westley, Robert. (1998). "Many Billions Gone: Is It Time to Reconsider the Case for Black Reparations?" *Boston College Law Review* 40:429–76.

Wildman, Stephanie. (1996). *Privilege Revealed: How Invisible Preference Undermines America*. New York, NY: New York University Press.

Wriggins, Jennifer B. (2005). "Torts, Race, and the Value of Injury, 1900–1949." *Howard Law Journal* 49:99–141.

———(2010). "Automobile Injuries as Injuries with Remedies: Driving, Insurance, Torts and Changing the Choice Architecture of Auto Insurance Pricing." *Loyola Los Angeles Law Review* 44:69–90.

CHAPTER TWELVE

INFLICTING LEGAL INJURIES
The Place of the "Two-Finger Test" in Indian Rape Law

Pratiksha Baxi

INTRODUCTION

In this chapter, I focus on the earliest forms of truth-technologies inscribed on women's bodies – what has been popularly characterized as the "two-finger test" (clinically known as the bimanual examination) in rape cases. During my fieldwork in the rural District and Sessions Court in Ahmedabad, Gujarat (1996–8), I found that it was commonplace to find in medico-legal certificates (MLCs) alongside the case history, age and descriptions of injuries, the information: "P/V (Per Vagina): two fingers admissible or inadmissible." The interpretation of the findings of the two-finger test provided in these certificates provided insight into how these are further translated as – "habituated to sexual intercourse," "habitual" or "used to sex." The category of the habitué or the habituated woman is deployed to transform a testimony to rape into a statement of consensual sex. I characterize this movement through the technique of the two-finger test, which enables the transformation of coercion into consent, as the medicalization of consent. I suggest that the movement of the colonial category of *habituated to sex* in rape cases to the everyday vocabulary of legal and medical experts is mediated by the canonical space inhabited by medical jurisprudence textbooks, which bear the signature of scientific authority. I argue that all raped victims – irrespective of age – are subjected to an

This chapter is based on excerpts from: Pratiksha Baxi. 2014. *Public Secrets of Law: Rape Trials in India*. Delhi: Oxford University Press.

invasive mimicry of the act of sexual violence via the technique of the two-finger test. This is the cost that is exacted from the raped survivor for testifying against rape.

THE PLACE OF MEDICO-LEGAL LANGUAGE IN RAPE TRIALS

Medico-legal categories mediate everyday conversations amongst lawyers about rape, influence lawyerly readings of briefs and frame the structure of the testimony. To illustrate how the language of the courtroom is suffused by medico-legal categories, I recall the originary moments of my fieldwork. Initially, none of the lawyers I met were willing to speak to me about ongoing rape trials in the District and Sessions Court in Ahmedabad (Gujarat, India), where I followed rape trials from 1996 to 1998. I had yet to learn the vocabulary of how to speak about rape in the court. Just as I had begun to despair, the additional public prosecutor (APP), whom I call Hirabhai, told me about a statutory rape and kidnapping case he was to prosecute. He then took me to the courtroom, where he requested the case papers from the bench clerk.

We sat at the far end of the lawyer's table and he turned to the medico-legal aspects of the case. Turning to the accused's medical certificate, in his booming voice which echoed in the half-empty courtroom, Hirabhai said "You know what a man's primary sexual organs are, don't you?" A little taken aback, I nodded. Then he turned to the victim's medical certificate. After going over the other details about bodily development and superficial injuries, he asked me, "Do you know what a hymen is?" I responded in the affirmative. Rather theatrically, he drew a vagina on a small piece of paper to explain the technical terms for injury on the *labia minora* or *labia majora*. The discussion carried on in the chamber, where he instructed his woman junior, whom I call Beenaben, to explain "it" to me. After he had left she said, "Pratiksha, do you know that a man cannot rape a woman by simply touching her, or kissing her." I nodded even more puzzled and curious now. She carried on "Well, how do I explain how a man rapes?" I replied, "Beenaben, do you mean partial or complete penetration?" She nodded in relief.

In performing a specific revelation of the public secrets of rape, Hirabhai directed my attention to the vocabulary by which I could research rape in the court. Insisting that medical jurisprudence separates the social from the clinical, Hirabhai maintained that a "decent" legal practice could coexist with frank discussions on the topic of rape.[1] As he put it, the vocabulary allowed for a "frank" space that enabled him to teach his woman juniors how the prosecution could more freely disregard rape allegations in many cases. At the same time, this "frank" space created an opening for the initiation of my research.

Toward the last phase of the research (fifteen months after the preceding conversation), I decided to ask direct questions, which may have been thought of as talking about secrets men do not share with women, even when they are equals in a professional setting. I cite here a discussion with another public prosecutor, whom I call Mr Rajput, who believed that women could not be raped unless there is grievous violence; and that women who were habituated to sex without marks of injury frequently lied about rape. These were not uncommon views in the court. Mr Rajput pursued these points in the privacy of his chamber, explaining to me why he thought that "habituated" women were liars. He asked me to sit in a chair besides him and lowered his voice so that his colleagues could not overhear him, through the wooden partitions that separated the chambers of the public prosecutors. And he spoke in English.

R: That day you were saying about habituated. I did not say anything because other people were around. A woman cannot really be raped.
PB: Why?
R: It becomes quite large. The opening in a habituated woman therefore becomes quite large therefore habituated.
PB: You mean the vaginal canal.
R: Yes, that's why two fingers go in quite easily
PB: But that's what I was discussing with Dr B (a forensic expert) – that is, the finger test is quite unreliable. What about masturbation?
R: That is there. But see if two fingers go in easily (shows vertically and horizontally by way of a gesture) it means that she is habituated, the entire hole, that's why I say a woman cannot really be raped.

---

[1] Yet another viewpoint is insistent that the disciplinary location configures desire and gaze in specific ways that de-sexualizes male gaze. As Hirabhai said to me, "Baxi, if I were to look at a naked dead woman in a morgue I would be dispassionate. Even though I am a man. I would not see her with the same kind of gaze. Same is with doctors. One does not gaze at a nude dead woman as if she were a woman."

PB: But that was not my point of view. I was trying to say that why must her past sexual history be linked to her credibility?
R: But it must.
PB: Why? Why should it be considered against morality?
R: Because it is. Because with married women rape is not possible, and in our society sex before marriage is not allowed.
PB: Why do women have to experience rape as worse than death or shameful that they will kill themselves? I am arguing for another point of view.
R: But a woman cannot be raped unless ... how do I explain? Do you know what secondary sexual organs are? Do you know why doctors write secondary sex organs are well developed?
PB: You mean?
R: The organ develops after a woman has an erection, that's why they are well developed, that's how they find out she is habituated. How do I explain this to you?
R: The woman becomes wet. The penis cannot go in unless the woman is not willing. She cannot be willing unless she is wet – like a machine – a rod cannot go in without lubrication (gestures).[2]
PB: But what about cases in which there is partial penetration?
R: I have not found such cases, they all claim complete penetration, that is why I am saying that a woman cannot be raped.

Mr Rajput stopped speaking, when a colleague walked in. He added:

R: You see I am MSc in Biochemistry. We were taught all of this. I have worked in a hospital for one year. Come again we will discuss this.

This lesson in "biochemistry" was a lesson in alterity – of how men experience pleasure while talking about rape and women's bodies (Jong 2004: 257). The prosecutorial body itself becomes a subject of desire, inserting in talk about rape male fantasies to possess and objectify. During a trial, a survivor knows that the testimony gives pleasure and experiences the questions put to her as sexual harassment, yet since such talk is staged under the judicial stare, it is imbued with the values of objectivity and classified as evidence. Something very similar took place as Mr Rajput lectured me on how a woman could not be raped.

[2] Note here that the use of the category of "lubrication" conflates biological changes with pleasurable sex. Lees has rightly argued that "sexual arousal may cause the vagina to lubricate but this does not mean that a moist vagina necessarily implies sexual arousal" (Lees 1997: 97–8).

The language of cross-examinations in Indian rape trials, which divides the body into sexual parts, calibrates duration, maps ejaculations, charts marks of resistance and choreographs postures, resounds with cacophony. The architecture of doctrinal law is built on the scaffold of courtroom talk, which situates humiliation at the heart of the testimony. The metaphoric judicial gavel is not always raised to regulate such ways of talking to rape survivors. Excited declarations of extreme habituation, voyeuristic judicial directives to enact postures or breathless recording of states of ejaculations all suggest that doctrinal law is necrophilic in relation to courtroom talk, in the sense that legal actors take a certain pleasure in developing the law on the emotional corpses of rape victims.

The frequent references to Modi or Lyon (both medico-legal texts) in Gujarat courts illustrated the critical role of medical jurisprudence textbooks, which acted as a medium of both pedagogy and prescription, often imparting the structure of the questions posed in a trial. A typical medico-legal textbook is disconcerting to read, since the techniques and frameworks deployed by medical jurists during the colonial period exist alongside newer additions about forensic techniques and approaches to victims of violence. Standard medico-legal textbooks, such as Modi, Lyon or Taylor, run into numerous editions, which are revised and updated by different editors, but continue to be published under the name of the original author, even posthumously. Modi's textbooks, for example, are an authoritative source of medical jurisprudence in law courts today. The first edition came out in 1920.

Recent editions of medical jurisprudence manuals are marked by different temporalities retaining sexist and racist colonial constructions of the lying, colonized, female subject alongside more contemporary discussions on the trauma of rape. It seems likely that change will be possible only when "at each juncture of writing newer editions, the experts ... abandon the trend of slavishly copying from the older texts, [including the] outdated examples and the archaic sexist presumptions" (Agnes 2005: 1866). In the meantime, the simultaneity of temporalities creates a puzzle for researchers attempting to read the construction of women's biographies in rape trials, as the women's biographies are effectively emptied of historical contexts. At the same time, as illustrated below, historical temporalities – including the colonial era two-finger test – shape both the discourse of rape trials and how rape survivors are perceived by legal actors in Indian courts.

THE TWO-FINGER TEST: THE VOICES OF MODI AND THOINOT

During the nineteenth century, British medical experts debated whether rape, i.e., the complete penetration of the vagina by the penis, was possible by an adult man in the case of a girl child below the age of ten years. This debate coincides with the emergence of partial penetration as a diagnostic category. Observations of rape on Indian children played a significant role in these debates, which ultimately led to the development of the two-finger test that, until recently, was central to the determination of evidence in Indian rape trials.

One of the more influential British medical experts was Chevers (1856), who argued that young female children could be completely penetrated, resulting in severe laceration. In support of his argument, Chevers pointed to instances of the brutality and frequency with which rape was committed on children, especially young girls during the "first act of connexion" in India (ibid.: 479). Among the cases and exhibits he cites, Chevers tell us that "the museum of Calcutta Medical College contains a preparation, sent by Mr G Evans, displaying the uterus, vagina [and other bodily parts] ... of a young Mahomedan female, showing laceration of the perineum and a considerable portion of the vaginal sheath" (ibid.: 481). Chevers further explains that the injuries were "the effects of violence done to the parts on the first act of copulation, by which a violent hemorrhage, to the destruction of the child (barely two years old) was occasioned" (ibid.: 481). As we can see from this report, colonial medical jurisprudence treated raped bodies of native children as specimens in a laboratory. The resultant medico-legal knowledge that it was possible to rape a child *in nature* then circulated back to the metropolis, while also stating the adult brown man's difference – marked by his sexual brutality toward female children.

Subsequently, Taylor (1865) cited Chevers's observations of rape on Indian children to repudiate the idea that the hymen might be treated as physical proof, since this model was unable to account for rape on female children where the hymen may remain intact. Nor was it able to account for the absence of the hymen due to reasons of pathology. For example, in some cases the hymen might remain intact despite repeated instances of penile penetration, as in the case of prostitutes in Paris (Thoinot 1911). As Lyon noted, "as a general rule, when sexual intercourse takes place, the hymen is lacerated or ruptured ... if, however, the aperture in the hymen is larger than usual or membrane itself be lax, repeated intercourse may take place without rupture or even laceration" (Lyon 1918: 262). As a result, Lyon held that in rape cases virginity "is not an essential question, seeing that vulval penetration is all that is necessary to constitute the offence of rape; and this may not be effected without destruction of signs of virginity" (ibid.: 261).

We find that that "anatomical examination became more detailed in the second third" of the nineteenth century "the forms of the hymen, in particular, were definitely classified and sketched in the treatises in their labial, diaphragmatic, half-moon and annular versions" (Vigarello 2001: 142). This led to the development of a technique – what is popularly known as the "two-finger test" today – to ascertain whether a woman's vagina could have been penetrated or not, irrespective of the presence or absence of the hymen. In Lyon's work, for example, we find references to the medico-legal technique of inserting glass pipettes, measuring cones or two fingers into the vagina as a means of determining penetration (Lyon 1918, see also Modi and Bahadur 1922).

The insertion of glass rods, cones, pipettes or fingers into the vagina of the raped survivor may be thought of as an early and enduring form of "truth-technology." This "truth-technology" was introduced in colonial India in the late nineteenth century, alongside "new 'truth-technologies' such as medical jurisprudence, criminal photography, fingerprinting and blood – and semen-stain analysis," which "became increasingly significant in a wide variety of colonial criminal prosecutions and especially critical in rape cases" (Kolsky 2010: 112, also see Singha 2000).

How then is the woman's body re-made into a legal artifice through medical technique? We can trace the elaboration of the two-finger test in Modi's medical jurisprudence textbooks. In the sixth edition, which was well established by 1940, he says:

> In cases where the hymen is intact and not lacerated, it is necessary to note the distensibility of the vaginal orifice. The possibility of sexual intercourse having taken place without rupturing the hymen may be inferred, if the vaginal orifice is big enough to admit easily the passage of two fingers. In virgins under 14 years of age the vaginal orifice is so small that it will hardly allow the passage of one little finger through the hymen (Modi and Bahadur 1940: 337).

Similarly, the 2002 edition of Modi holds:

> In cases where the hymen is intact and not lacerated, it is absolutely necessary to note the distensibility of the vaginal orifice, in the number of fingers passing into the vagina without any difficulty. The possibility

> of sexual intercourse having taken place without rupturing the hymen may be inferred if the vaginal orifice is capacious enough to admit the passage of two fingers easily (Modi and Bahadur 2002: 503).

Irrespective of the age of the victim, medical jurists continue to uphold the validity of the two-finger test, since the presence of the hymen is not considered to be a reliable indicator of virginity. In 2002, the validity of the two finger-test in relation to children and young girls is presented as follows:

> ... the circumference of the hymen can also be measured by a measuring cone. A circumference of 9 to 10 cm is considered the least necessary for coitus. In girls below fourteen years of age, the vaginal orifice is usually so small that it will hardly allow the passage of the little finger through the hymen. It is often difficult to distinguish between an indentation in a fimbriated hymen and a tear, unless the hymen is stretched by a fingertip, glass rod or Brittan's hymenscope, which also give excellent transillumination of hymen when a tear is found to extend up to the vaginal wall (Modi and Bahadur 2002: 503).

The 1969 edition of Modi's manual promulgates the necessity for medical experts to determine the difference between a "true" and a "false" virgin, since the hymen, as a "particular anatomical structure" was no longer considered an absolute proof of virginity. I quote,

> It is seen that the presence of an intact hymen is not an absolute sign of virginity. With an intact hymen there are true virgins and false virgins. The necessary points for distinguishing between the two are as follows: If in a woman with an intact hymen, the edges of the membranes are distinct and regular, with an orifice of small dimension, which allows the terminal phalanx of a finger to penetrate and the hymen is well stretched, all the presumptions are in favor of non-penetration of the penis into the vagina. On the other hand, if in a woman who has an intact hymen, the hymeneal orifice lets one, two or more fingers easily, if the hymen is relaxed as to undulate and allow itself to be depressed, one can conclude that the woman can most certainly be a virgin, but also that a body of the size of the penis in erection could perfectly well pass through the hymeneal orifice without rupturing it once or several times. A true virgin or a false virgin, both are possible and one cannot be certain of either nor can one express such certainty. (Modi and Bahadur 1969: 319, also see Modi and Bahadur 1972: 305)

The references to "true" and "false" virgins follow medical texts almost exactly. The passages cited above in the different editions of

Modi's textbooks are sourced from a French medical jurist, Léon-Henri Thoinot.[3] With an intact hymen there are true virgins and false virgins. How shall we distinguish them? Here are the necessary points in this respect:

> If, in a woman with an intact hymen, you find the edges of the membrane distinct and regular, with an orifice of small dimensions, which scarcely allows the extremity of the finger to penetrate; if, when the thighs are separated, the hymen is well stretched, all the presumptions are in favour of a true virginity, or, to express it better and not go beyond what ought to be stated, all the presumptions are in favour of a non-penetration of the penis into the vagina.
> On the other hand, if, in a woman who has an intact hymen, the hymenial orifice lets one, two or more fingers pass through easily; if the hymen is relaxed in such a way as to undulate and allow itself to be depressed easily, you will conclude that the woman can most certainly be a virgin, but *also that a body of the size of the penis in erection could perfectly well pass through the hymeneal orifice without rupturing it, once or several times*. A true virgin or a false virgin, both are possible, and you cannot be certain of either, nor can you express such certainty (Thoinot 1911: 55, emphasis in original).

It is stunning that the 1969 edition of Modi repeats Thoinot almost word for word, as if repetition itself produces its own truths.[4]

Why is the technique of the two-finger test so important to the medicalization of consent? I argue that the substitution of the two-finger test allows for medical experts to engage in a practice that imitates penile penetration in its diagnosis of rape. In other words, the relationship that is drawn between the clinical test and the erect penis is one of mimesis. The substitution here is performed by a technique that is in a mimetic relationship to the act of penile penetration. Hence, the two-finger test replaces the notion that the presence or absence of the hymen can by itself signify virginity or its absence. The two-finger test is a technique that verifies whether the hymen is broken or not, and whether it is distensible or not, through a medical practice that

---

[3] His book, entitled *Medico-legal Aspects of Moral Offences*, was first published in French in 1898.

[4] The 1969 edition – published after Modi's death – cites Thoinot more extensively than Modi did himself, although Modi based his assertion that the presence or absence of the hymen by itself cannot testify to sexual experience or sexual violence on Thoinot's findings.

imitates penile penetration. The substitution rests, however, on the precarious de-sexualization of the clinical practice.

The line between the medicalized two-finger test (*as if* it were a surgical procedure) and assault is a thin one, which is determined by whether the medical examination is carried out with or without the consent of the patient. Medical jurists have been aware of the mimesis in their emphatic recommendation that doctors secure the patient's consent for this test. Consent then converts assault into a medical test. For example, Modi cautions that a rape victim

> ... should never be examined without her written consent taken in the presence of a witness if she is of and over 12 years of age and is capable of understanding the nature and implication of the examination, or without the written consent of her parent or guardians if she is under the age of 12 years or a feeble minded person. The examination of a female without her consent is regarded in law as an assault. It must be remembered that the police court has no power of compelling a woman to submit the private parts of her person to the examination of a medical man (Modi and Bahadur 1940: 336).

It is not clear what the victim ought to consent to. Consent is an empty category from the point of view of the woman. It separates technique as the medically sanctioned "do-ing" of the law from sexual assault.

POLITICS OF "PENISTRATION"

I now describe the way the medico-legal textbook imparts structure to testimony. I analyze below the testimony of the gynecologist who treated Noornissa ("Noor"), a child who was raped by her stepfather when she was twelve years old. In the ethnographic vignettes below, I juxtapose excerpts from various editions of Modi's textbook with excerpts from Dr Kadam's testimony, the gynecologist who verified the injuries of rape inflicted on Noornissa.[5] I argue that medico-legal categories are treated as if these exist in the experience of the rape survivor.

---

[5] I use a later edition of Modi's textbook. While the changes in the editions retain the original emphasis on procedure, medical examination and false cases in almost exactly the same words, the newer sections that have been added on in the recent editions are cited here to indicate that while recent additions have been made in response to the growing awareness about rape, such textbooks do not historicise medical conventions.

I maintain that underlying the statutory rape provision is an inherent anxiety, which finds a clear expression when statutory rape is translated as "technical rape." Hence, Noornissa was constructed as a child-adult capable of inflicting injuries on her own body.[6]

> The hymen is deeply situated, and as the vagina is very small, it is impossible for the penetration of the adult organ to take place. Usually the penis is placed either within the vulva or between the thighs.
> (Reddy 1990: 298, also see Modi and Bahadur 1922, 2002)

Figure 12.1

I begin with an account of the prosecution's examination of the medical expert. The prosecution elicited the case history narrated to the doctor by the patient. Following this, the gynecologist testified that Noornissa had suffered a number of injuries. Dr Kadam testified that he found a 7 × 1 × 1 cm abrasion on her chin, a bruise on the left side of her nose, a bruise on her right side of her breast, on her left hand a 4 × 2 cm long bruise and many long and thin scratches on both sides of her thighs. He testified that on her fourcette there was a 1 cm deep laceration in the six o'clock direction and on the left labia minora there was a 1 cm long cut wound. He testified that Noornissa could not be older than fourteen years at that time of the crime. Dr Kadam (referred to as Dr in the excerpts below) testified in Gujarati and English. The excerpts from the textbooks cited alongside excerpts of court proceedings illustrate how medico-legal norms frame courtroom talk. Consider the following excerpts from the examination-in-chief, which the defense lawyer constantly interrupted.

---

[6] The efforts of women's groups and child rights groups had resulted in the enactment of *The Protection of Children from Sexual Offences Act, 2012 (No 32 of 2012)* [hereafter POCSO], which came into force on 14 November 2012. For the first time, the law distinguished between adult and child survivors of sexual violence. Until November 2012, rape was seen as an adult crime, denying children's voices a rightful place in judicial discourse. The POCSO Act envisages newer ways of architecting children's testimony in special courts for children, adjudicated by special prosecutors, by adopting distinct courtroom procedures. Yet how the potential of this Act will be actualized remains to be seen. This essay allows insights into the difficulties of displacing the rape culture that inhabits our courtrooms, wherein the disqualification of rape survivor's voices in courts of law remains routine.

APP:	In case of A GIRL OF TENDER YEARS THE INNER PART (REFERRING TO THE HYMEN) IS HIGHER – IS THAT RIGHT?
DR:	YES, IT is higher.
DL (INTERRUPTS):	The inner part.
DR:	I am saying that.[7]
J (D):	In the case of a small girl the hymen (*yoni patal*) in the inner part is higher.

If the law is clear that vulval injury is sufficient to establish the fact of rape in law, then why is it important that the hymen is deeply situated in the case of children? I argue that underlying this line of questioning is the assumption that a virile young man should ordinarily be able to destroy the membrane. Taylor states:

> To constitute the offence of rape, it is not necessary that there should be complete penetration of penis with emission of semen and rupture of hymen. Partial penetration of the penis within the Labia majora or the vulva or pudenda, with or without emission of semen, or even attempt at penetration is quite sufficient for the purpose of law.
> (Modi and Bahadur 2002: 495)

Figure 12.2

> In the case of an old man or of weak virile power, vulval intercourse might be had without destroying the membrane; but such a case could have only been decided by the special circumstances, which accompanied it. The presence of an unruptured hymen affords a presumptive but not an absolute proof that a woman is a virgin; and if of the ordinary size and shape, and in the ordinary situation, it shows clearly that although attempts at intercourse may have been made, there can have been no vaginal penetration (Taylor 1866: 610, emphasis added).

I wish to draw attention to two important points from the excerpt cited above. First, when the child's body is distinguished from an adult body, it is read from the viewpoint of ascertaining whether it is possible to penetrate the vagina without causing severe damage to or breaking the hymen. Second, the underlying assumption is that ordinarily a young and virile man would be able to destroy the hymeneal membrane. Here, the defense sought to establish that Noornissa was not a

---

[7] This means that the doctor meant to say that the hymen is situated deeper in a child's vagina.

child of "tender years" and Shakeel, the accused, as a young and virile man could not have raped her without destroying her hymen.

Consider the set of questions that followed as the examination-in-chief continued. In this excerpt, the defense lawyer attempted to characterize the doctor as unprofessional as if he were embarrassed about answering the question about partial penetration. The words in italics were spoken in English.

APP: The injury in the *fourcette* and *labia minora* has happened due to *partial penetration*.

...

J TO DL: What is Gujarati for *penistration* (pronounced in court and spelt as such in the Gujarati transcript)?
DL: Due to *penetration* (correcting the pronunciation)
J (D): The injury on Noornissa's vagina (*yoni*) on seeing that according to my experience the injury is caused by the entry of the penis into her vagina and due to *penistration* (emphasis added).

We find here a slippage between penetration and "penistration" – the latter combining into a singular category the meaning encased in the concept of penile penetration. The question about how to translate penetration in Gujarati is important. In the above-cited excerpt, the word "penetration," pronounced and spelt as "penistration," is retained in the court transcript. I emphasize this usage since it vividly communicates how rape is defined in legal discourse. When penetration is translated in Gujarati, words like "entry" and "insertion" are used interchangeably. The objective is to establish that injury was caused due to the entry or insertion of the penis into the vagina. The language that translates penetration into the legal vernacular does not embody the idea that such an act is violent. It concentrates on the idea of entry (by *penistration*), where lack of consent then is technically assumed.

The examination-in-chief continued to determine medical opinion on whether the hymen of a child who has been raped could remain intact. Note here the confusion between the judge, prosecutor and the defense lawyer about which body part the question alludes to.

APP: Aye, Doctor, supposing there is partial penetration in vulva then can the hymen remain intact? If there is injury on the *fourcette*, can the hymen remain intact?

J: Which part?
APP: Hymen.
DR: Hymen.
J: No, no. Hymen is intact.
DR: *Fourcette, labia majora?*
J (D): If the penis (*ling*) enters partially then there can be injury on the vagina's *fourcette* and *labia minora* part and despite that the hymen can remain intact (*akhband*).

The medical expert's testimony defines partial penetration as vulval injury caused by forcible penile penetration and the presence of a wholly closed hymen. The experience of rape is translated as what the penis does to the vagina. It penetrates the vagina forcibly, leaving marks of injury, yet it is partial. It is partial penetration because the hymen, which according to the medico-legal textbooks is situated higher in children compared to pre-adolescent girls, is not destroyed.[8]

The complexity of the category of partial penetration becomes more clear when we refer to Noor's testimony in cross-examination. From Noor's testimony, we learn that the category of partial penetration does not describe the experience of rape. Yet the defense lawyer, who in the cross-examination had subjected Noornissa to repeated questions asking her how she "knew" that the accused had fully penetrated her, converted the medico-legal category into an "experiential" category. I cite an excerpt from Noor's testimony here.

DL: Look here you were lying down, then what did he do, how much did he do that you do not know. How much did he put his place of urination, half-full?
N: Full (*akhi*).
DL: How did you see, you were saying that you were lying down then how did you come to know?
N: Blood came out.
J: He inserted that's why blood came out?
N: Yes.
DL: How do you know that he had inserted?
N: (quiet initially) Because he penetrated me, that's why.

---

[8] In the case of rape on a twelve-year-old, the Supreme Court in *Wahid Khan* v. *State of Madhya Pradesh* held that 'it has been a consistent view of this Court that even a slightest penetration is sufficient to make out an offence of rape and depth of penetration is immaterial' (MANU/SC/1850/2009, para. 25).

The word partial means unfinished, incomplete, limited, and half-done. It also means biased, one-sided, unfair, and inequitable. The category of partial penetration is translated here as placing half of the penis in the vagina. We have seen that partial penetration may mean that the penis has not been able to damage the hymen, but nowhere is the suggestion made that partial penetration must be calculated in proportion to how much a penis penetrates a vagina. Yet questions about how deeply the vagina is penetrated animate the trial. In the phallocentric translation of the category of partial penetration as "half" or "full" penetration, the defense tries to introduce doubt that Noor did not actually know if she had been raped. Noor's insistence that she experienced full penetration is questioned over and over again.

From Noor, we learn that partial penetration is *not* an experiential category. Yet the defense translates it as such. The defense lawyer "by his power to raise and enforce topics" leads Noor to accept the assumption that full or half penetration is relevant to the true testimony to her experience of rape (Taslitz 1999: 83), such that she has to insist that she *knew* that she was fully penetrated, showing how "the rape trial silences and discredits the complainant's voice, using medical and legal discourses to distort their testimony" (Lees 1997: 84). The politics of "penistration" encodes statutory rape as "technical rape" in the defense lawyer's attempts to deny that Noornissa is a child.

TECHNICAL RAPE

It bears repetition that technical rape is a term used by lawyers to refer to statutory rape. The anxiety produced by the category of technical rape may be traced back to the construction of female children as seductive. According to Taylor:

> It may be observed, that the consent of the female does not excuse or alter the nature of the crime where she is under ten years of age, since consent at this period of life is invalid; and the carnal knowledge of the female is rape in law. Even the solicitation of the child does not excuse it (Taylor 1845: 458).

We are told that no matter what provocation the solicitation of a child may cause, it is the law that deems such expressions of consent invalid. I argue that the characterization of statutory rape as technical rape is not a simple matter of the use of folk categories in law. Rather, it masks the construction of the child as provocative and seductive to uphold the view that a child witness is not actually a child; thus, making a gesture toward the desires of the provoked. Moreover, the twin categories of false cases and self-inflicted injuries as a medico-legal norm naturalize the idea that it is possible to read signs of falsity from the feminine body. I show the centrality of these arguments by detailing the cross-examination of the expert witness below. I argue that the construction of the child as provocative and seductive underlies the defense argument that the child witness is not a child actually in a technical rape case

> Excerpt 1 illustrates the defense argument that Noor inflicted the external injuries on herself.

> To substantiate false charges, marks of violence are sometimes self-inflicted. Modi saw a young woman of twenty years alleged to have been raped by a man. She had several marks simulating scratches made with a *kankar* (pebble) on the forearms and chest, which could be wiped off by rubbing them with a piece of wet cloth.
> (Modi and Bahadur 2002: 502)

Figure 12.3

DL: If I do it myself then can I injure myself (gestures)? Judge explains the question.

DR: Multiple scratches are not possible, others are possible but multiple scratches are not possible.

J (D): It is true that the bruises on N's chin, the wound on her nose and bruise on the left side of her breast could have been self-inflicted. It is not true that the multiple scratches on N's right and left thighs could have been self-inflicted.

> Excerpt 2 illustrates the defense argument that the internal injuries were superficial injuries. Note that the judge mediated the tension between the defense lawyer and the prosecutor in the exchange cited below.

DL: ... injury over *labia majora*; the skin had peeled?

DR (TO J): There was no CLW (cut long wound) – muscle too was injured. It is more than superficial, sir (*saheb*).

J (D): It is not true that on N's *labia majora* the skin had peeled off because of which there was injury but I am saying that the injury was more than the skin having been peeled off. And the injury extended to the muscle. Only the skin had not peeled off. And the injury was up to the muscle. It is not true that the aforesaid injury was not peeled off but I am saying that the aforesaid wound was peeled off and the muscle below the skin was also lacerated, which was more than superficial wounds.

Excerpt 3 illustrates the defense argument that Noor had inflicted injury on her vagina by herself.

DL: Can she do it by herself, inflict the injury on herself by her nails?
DR: No. She can cut herself superficially but inflict such wounds on herself – a child cannot do these.
DL: She is not a child (*balak*)!!
J (D): It is not true that the current matter is such that the injury could have been inflicted on the *labia minora* with nails. But I am saying that if nails inflict such injury then only the skin will peel and such deep injury cannot take place.

Modi saw a case in which the father thrust his thumb forcibly into the vagina of his six-year-old daughter in order to bring a false charge of rape against his neighbour, who was his enemy and lacerated the posterior part of the vagina and the posterior commissure.

(Modi and Bahadur 2002: 506)

Figure 12.4

Excerpt 4 illustrates the argument that the vaginal injury was caused due to the forcible insertion of a thumb.

DL: If thumb is inserted then?
DR: No. I do not agree with you.
J (D): It is not true that the aforesaid injury on Noornissa's *labia minora* was such an injury that could have been caused by the insertion (*pravesh*) of a thumb.

Excerpt 5 illustrates how injury is differentiated from psychological complications that follow rape.

Some victims may need professional psychological help. The medical officer should be ready to offer reassurance and advice to the victim or her parents.

(Modi and Bahadur 2002: 507)

Figure 12.5

DL: If there is no treatment then in this case can there be complications?
DR: What complications?
DL: Greater bleeding, greater swelling
DR: Yes, and psychological complications
J: That depends on the person. Those (psychological complications) can happen even when according to her wishes (*iccha*), he is talking of injury.
DR: There would be difficulty in passing urine, swelling on the vulva. Greater injury, person may also be in shock.
J (D): It is true that in this case on seeing the kind of injury on the vagina if there is no immediate treatment then other kinds of complication can take place. On the kinds of complications that can happen in that context I am saying that there can be greater bleeding and in the practice of passing urine pain be experienced.
DR: I want to tell that such patients can contract AIDS.

Everyone in the courtroom laughed.

J TO DL: Do you want to submit this?
DL: Patients can contract AIDS or gonorrhoea.
J: Sexual diseases (*Gupt rog* – literally, secret diseases)
DR: Gonorrhoea
J (D): And if the concerned person suffers from AIDS and sexual diseases (*gupt rog*) then the victim can also get such a disease.

The relationship between courtroom talk and the medico-legal archive then remains relevant to our understanding of courtroom talk in as much as the archive sets the limits on what can be said in the courtroom. The first four excerpts cited above demonstrate how self-inflicted injuries or the medico-legal discussion on false cases structure the cross-examination. Modi's assertion that he examined a case in which the father had inserted his thumb in the child's vagina to lodge a false case has been generalized into a medico-legal norm. This medico-legal norm is impervious to the public discourses on child sexual abuse that name such forms of forcible penetration as rape. The emphasis on falsity exists alongside the suggestion that the child is not really a child. In saying that Noor is not a child, the defense lawyer actualizes the implicit assumption that underlies the construction of technical rape. Technically, while the consent of a child remains irrelevant, the idea of a solicitous child is actualized in the way the entire cross-examination is framed. It is the category of nature that is the unspoken category, evoked in the defense lawyer's continual assertion that Noor is not a child. The translation of statutory rape as technical rape marks this movement from the legal to the natural. Such an articulation is expressed to the gynecologist suggesting that he cannot see the work of desire in the legal subject who is not really a child. Noor, then, is not a child, for children by this argument cannot be raped and those who are cannot be labelled children.

The excerpts cited above are instructive in understanding how the court denies the possibilities of therapeutic jurisprudence (Cattaneo and Goodman 2010). Therapeutic jurisprudence is broadly defined as those approaches to law that attempt to institute policies and procedures that do not re-victimize the victim. In Indian courts, however, the moment expert opinion leans toward therapeutic jurisprudence, be this in terms of treatment for trauma or other risks to health,[9] we find that the expert opinion is belittled and treated as if it were not relevant to the purposes of law.

By situating excerpts from medico-legal manuals side-by-side with a segment of the rape trial of a twelve-year-old child, I demonstrate how medico-legal manuals provide a script to the defense lawyer, structuring his cross-examination frame by frame. I contend that defense lawyers feign ignorance by treating diagnostic categories *as if* these are experiential categories. Even in the instance of statutory rape, medico-legal textbooks provide the resources to defense lawyers to suggest that the child is actually a child-adult, a seductive child who really could not have been raped in nature.

I have argued that a gynecological examination cannot really prove habituation and the two-finger test is state-sanctioned assault. This is the cost a patriarchal society extracts from rape victims for speaking out against the violence of rape. The penetrative practice of clinicians escapes a charge of violence precisely because it is signified under another domain of scientific rationality that is sanctified by the state. State-sponsored medical jurisprudence then invents such a clinical test precisely because it measures injury against itself, rather than injury to

---

[9] In the 2002 edition of Modi, a new section on AIDS has been added. It follows the medico-legal discussion of unnatural sexual offences.

the victim. The object of diagnosis here is not the harm caused to the injured woman, but how society is injured by the act of rape.

THE FICTION OF THE HABITUÉ: PROTESTS, REFORM, AND COURTS

Despite several petitions by different women's groups to protest against the sexist and racist assumptions that underlie the medical jurisprudence of the two-finger test, change was slow. It began when the Centre for Enquiry into Health and Allied Themes (CEHAT), an NGO based in Mumbai, took the lead in developing protocol for forensic examination and an instruction manual, which have been adopted in hospitals in Mumbai (CEHAT 2010, also see Pitre 2005, HRW Report 2010). The new protocol forbids doctors from deploying the two-finger test. Yet Indian courts were initially reluctant to strike the two-finger test. Moreover, even though many appellate courts issued guidelines[10] to various agencies, including the police and hospitals, to deal with rape survivors with sensitivity and dignity, none of these focused on the legality and constitutionality of the two-finger test. And debate continues over the appropriate place for the two-finger test in contemporary medical jurisprudence.

Following CEHAT's initial efforts, in 2009, the Delhi High Court issued guidelines outlining the required response from police, medical experts, and prosecutors in rape cases.[11] A committee was formed headed by Justice Gita Mittal to oversee the implementation of these guidelines. Ironically, many of these initial moves to improve the medical response to rape survivors resulted in the reassertion of the test.[12]

---

[10] *Hanuman son of Mahadeo Kuchankar Versus State of Maharashtra, through P.S.O., P.S. Gadchandur*, Bombay High Court, Nagpur Bench, Criminal Appeal No. 368 of 2007, decided on February 25, 2009.

[11] *DCW v. Delhi Police*, Writ Petition (Criminal) 696 of 2008, order dated April 23, 2009.

[12] The Maharashtra State Government, whilst issuing guidelines on how forensic examinations should be conducted on rape survivors, noted that the medico-legal report should specify the state of the hymen and how many fingers may be inserted in the vagina (HRW Report 2010: 9). CEHAT opposed this move on the grounds that neither was this test legally admissible nor was it in keeping with international health norms on how rape survivors should be treated. Likewise, the office of the Director General of Health Services, Delhi "introduced a template for the forensic examination of rape survivors at government hospitals that seeks information about the size of the hymeneal orifice and asks doctors to comment on whether the victim is habituated to sexual intercourse" (ibid.).

In July 2010, Justice Kannan, who co-authored the 2011 edition of Modi's medical jurisprudence with Dr K Mathiharan, wrote that he had revised the chapter on rape in light of the critique of the medico-legal discourse on rape. Modi 2011 names rape as an act of sexualized violence and grievous crime. The infamous sections on false cases and self-inflicted injuries were now removed. New case law was introduced to instruct doctors about the new directions that courts have taken. By insisting that vulval injury is sufficient to constitute rape, the new jurisprudence clarified that the two-finger test should not be read to characterize some women as habituated to sex and that a lack of injuries does not mean that the victim has not been raped.

Still, the legacy of Thoinot continued to haunt Indian medical jurisprudence on rape. In 2010, the *Human Rights Watch Report* (2010), condemned the two-finger test as a colonial, sexist, and injurious procedure, just as the 2011 version of Modi went to print. Two months later, Additional Sessions Judge Dr Kamini Lau challenged the medicalization of consent in Indian rape trials, in what is now considered an historic judgment.

In August 2010, Justice Lau expressed surprised concern in a Delhi trial court after noticing that medical examination of rape victims included the two-finger test and characterized the victim as "habituated to sex."[13] Making a distinction between a "hymen test" and the "two-finger test," Justice Lau opined that a limited vaginal examination in the case of unmarried women, which notes "if the hymen cord is intact" and "use of force [including] any signs of tearing or bruising of or near the vagina" ought to be sufficient.[14] Apart from such "hymen tests," Justice Lau was unable to "understand why the Per Vagina (PV) test, which is normally called the Finger Test, [was] being carried out in routine on victims of sexual offences."[15]

Justice Lau ruled that "the manner in which this medical test (PV Test) is carried out by inserting a finger inside the vagina of a woman irrespective of age or marital status is violation of her body and, in the absence of her consent, would be violative of Constitutional dictates of right to Life as enshrined under Article 21 of the Constitution of

---

[13] *St. v. Umesh Singh and Anr*, FIR No.1135/06, PS Uttam Nagar, Rohini Delhi District Court.
[14] Ibid., page 23 of 27.
[15] Ibid.

India."[16] This test, the court held, violates the woman's right to privacy since it makes public her private sexual life. In any case, the court concluded that "the PV Test/Two finger test, medically has no scientific or conclusive basis and the opinion rendered by the doctor to the extent of congestion of vestibule is subjective."[17]

The next major development was the *Criminal Law (Amendment) Act 2013*, which came into force retrospectively from February 3, 2013, following unprecedented and sustained protests in the aftermath of the brutal gang-rape and subsequent death of a twenty-three-year-old woman on a bus in Delhi. As the details of the brutality on the young woman and her male friend who boarded a private bus after watching a film at a mall hit the media, it seemed as if the threshold of toleration of sexual violence had broken down. International and national publicity for the protestors demanding an abolition of the archaic and patriarchal unscientific two-finger test generated public interest in looking at rape as a public health issue at long last.

In response to the Delhi protests of 2012–13, the government set up a committee under the chairpersonship of the late Justice Verma to recommend to the government how to amend the law on issues relating to "extreme sexual assault" and questions of stricter punishment. Amidst televised debates on castration and the death penalty, many went to work furiously detailing major and minor reforms in the laws, courts, city planning, and governance that could be put in place, even though at the time it was unclear whether or not these constituted the terms of reference of the Justice Verma Committee (JVC). Women's groups, feminist lawyers, disability rights groups, and queer activists were given the chance to appear before the JVC only a couple of days before the report was released, after much effort by feminist lawyers. This was an unparalleled time, when we saw the emergence of a public intimately engaged in the project of judicial reform.

The JVC recommended the abolition of the two-finger test; and put forward a protocol for medical examination of rape survivors. And then followed *Lillu @ Rajesh & Anr. v. State of Haryana* (2013), wherein the Supreme Court held that:

> ... medical procedures should not be carried out in a manner that constitutes cruel, inhuman, or degrading treatment and health should be of paramount consideration while dealing with gender-based violence.

---

[16] Ibid., page 24 of 27.
[17] Ibid., page 25 of 27.

The State is under an obligation to make such services available to survivors of sexual violence. Proper measures should be taken to ensure their safety and there should be no arbitrary or unlawful interference with his privacy. Thus, in view of the above, undoubtedly, the two finger test and its interpretation violates the right of rape survivors to privacy, physical and mental integrity and dignity. Thus, this test, even if the report is affirmative, cannot ipso facto, be given (sic) rise to presumption of consent.[18]

Subsequently, the government abolished the two-finger test and introduced a medical protocol in March 2014 after concerted efforts by several women's and health rights groups and feminist lawyers (Government of India 2014). Whilst there is a shift to standardizing the medical protocol and aligning it with WHO guidelines, the practice of the two-finger test remains contested. In 2015, the Delhi government issued a circular permitting the P/V test. A sharp media response followed claiming the Delhi government had reinscribed the now infamous two-finger test.

Critiquing the media, noted lawyer and activist Flavia Agnes argued that the media had conflated the clinical examination of the vagina at times necessary for noting injuries and collating evidence with the two-finger test when used as a "chastity test" to determine marks of habituation. While Agnes (2015) critiqued the medicalization of consent, she noted that

> ... it is time to abandon the sensational and titillating term "two-finger test" which has a negative connotation and instead use the more scientific, accurate and non-judgmental term, P.V. test. It is time to delink moral assumptions from medical examinations and use medical procedures to assess the extent of injuries and to provide treatment ... Rather than banning the test, it would be more prudent to ban the term "two-finger test" from our medical and legal vocabulary.

In response, CEHAT argued that while P/V examination is routine for therapeutic and forensic purposes, the two-finger test is a specific gynecological practice that directs medical gaze to elasticity and habituation. CEHAT argued that simply banning the term "two-finger test" (and not the practice as well) would not have the desired effect of displacing the clinical practice of medicalizing consent by noting habituation or elasticity.

---

[18] *Lillu @ Rajesh and Anr. v. State of Haryana*, MANU/SC/0369/2013, paras 12–1.

This debate takes us back to Thoinot, who categorically linked the insertion of two or more fingers to a clinical mimesis of an erect penis. The two-finger test was invented as a test intended to be mimetic of penile penetration to determine whether or not the elasticity of the hymen could be made to speak the truth under scientific gaze. While Agnes's (2015) argument could be read to mean that we must only abandon the language used by Thoinot to displace this clinical practice, the counter argument by CEHAT (2015) is that the category of two-finger test must be retained in order to displace the practice. In the latter argument, the two-finger test as a historically specific colonial and sexist medico-legal practice must be named, displaced, and stigmatized.

Both positions – Agnes' and CEHAT's – critique the conflation of the clinical examination of the vagina with the two-finger test. However, we also need to note how clinical practices of routine gynecology inherit sexist genealogies inserting bias toward sexually active single women or queer bodies, naming them as *deviant* bodies. Clinical categories, when located in the histories of sexist, racist, and colonizing medical practices, diagnose and interpret symptoms of pathology or injury in ways that deploy phallocentric standards of the normal and the pathological. While the figure of the habitué may have been evacuated from doctrinal law, it is resurrected in practice at different sites of the law, be this in police stations, courtrooms, hospitals, or forensic laboratories. The cunning of judicial reform lies in folding in feminist critique without displacing the rape trial as a sexualized spectacle.

References

Agnes, Flavia. (2005). "To Whom do Experts Testify? Ideological Challenges of Feminist Jurisprudence." *Economic and Political Weekly* 40(18): 1859–66.

(2015). "'Two-Finger Test': Truth and Hype." *Asianage*, June 23.

Cattaneo, Lauren Bennett and Lisa A. Goodman. ([2009] 2010). "Through the Lens of Therapeutic Jurisprudence: The Relationship Between Empowerment in the Court System and Well-Being for Intimate Partner Violence Victims." *Journal of Interpersonal Violence* 25(3):481–502.

Centre for Enquiry into Health and Allied Themes (CEHAT). (2010). *Manual for Medical Examination of Sexual Assault*. www.cehat.org/go/uploads/Publications/R83Manual.pdf (last accessed: December 13, 2017).

Chevers, Norman. (1856). *A Manual of Medical Jurisprudence for Bengal and the North Western Provinces*. Calcutta: F Carbery, Bengal Military Orphan Press.

Government of India (GOI). (2014). *Guidelines and Protocols–Medicolegal Care for Survivors: Victims of Sexual Violence*. New Delhi: Ministry of Health and Family Welfare, Government of India.

Human Rights Watch (HRW). (2010). *Dignity on Trial: India's Need for Sound Standards for Conducting and Interpreting Forensic Examinations of Rape Survivors*. New York: Human Rights Watch.

Jong, Ferdinand de. (2004). "The Social Life of Secrets." Pp. 248–76 in *Situating Globality: African Agency in the Appropriation of Global Culture*, edited by Wim Van Binsbergen and Rijk Van Dijk. Leiden and Boston: Brill.

Kolsky, Elizabeth. (2010). "The Body Evidencing the Crime: Rape on Trial in Colonial India, 1860–1947." *Gender & History* 22(1):109–130.

Lees, Sue. (1997). *Ruling Passions: Sexual Violence, Reputation and the Law*. Milton Keynes: Open University Press.

Lyon, J.B. (1918). *Medical Jurisprudence for India*, 6th edn (with illustrative cases). Calcutta: Thacker, Spink and Co.

Modi, Jaising Prabhudas and Rai Bahadur. (1922). *A Text-Book of Medical Jurisprudence and Toxicology*, 2nd edn. Calcutta: Butterworth.

(1940). *A Text-Book of Medical Jurisprudence and Toxicology*, 6th edn. Bombay: Butterworth.

(1969). *Modi's Textbook of Medical Jurisprudence and Toxicology*, 17th edn, edited and revised by Natwar J. Modi. Bombay: N M Tripathi.

(1972). *Modi's Textbook of Medical Jurisprudence and Toxicology*, 18th edn. Bombay: N M Tripathi.

(2002). *Modi's Medical Jurisprudence and Toxicology*, 22nd edn (Reprint), edited and revised by B. V. Subrahmanyam. Delhi: Lexisnexis Butterworths.

Reddy, Narayan K.S. (1990). *The Essentials of Forensic Medicine and Toxicology*. Hyderabad: Sri Lakshmi Art Printers.

Singha, Radhika. (2000). "Settle, Mobilize, Verify: Identification Practices in Colonial India." *Studies in History* 16:151.

Taylor, Alfred Swaine. (1845). *Medical Jurisprudence*. Philadelphia, PA: Lea and Blanchard.

(1856). *Medical Jurisprudence*, 4th American from the 5th and improved London edition, edited with additions by Edward Hartshorn. Philadelphia, PA: Lea and Blanchard.

(1865). *A Manual of Medical Jurisprudence*. Philadelphia, PA: Lea and Blanchard.

(1866). *Medical Jurisprudence*. Philadelphia, PA: Lea and Blanchard.

Thoinot, L. (1911). *Medicolegal Aspects of Moral Offenses*, translated from the original French and enlarged by Arthur W. Weysse. Philadelphia, PA: F.A. Davis Company.

Vigarello, Georges. (2001). *A History of Rape: Sexual Violence in France from the 16th to the 20th Century*, translated by Jean Birell. Cambridge: Polity Press.

CHAPTER THIRTEEN

THE STATE AS VICTIM
Ethical Politics of Injury Claims and Revenge in International Relations

Li Chen

Scholars of various disciplines, including contributors to this book, have extensively analyzed the meanings of injury claimed by individuals or local communities. In contrast, injury claims of state actors have received far less critical attention outside the often technical treatment in diplomatic history or international law and relations. A cursory glance through the chronicle of modern global history reveals that injury claims were and continue to be crucial for the policies and ideologies of numerous states over the last few centuries. By reexamining some of the injury claims made in the history of Sino-foreign relations and other international contexts, this chapter seeks to explore why states have found injury claims to be so useful, and how they have made use of such claims to rationalize foreign policies and political agendas. I argue that the claim of victim status provides unique and much-needed moral and political legitimation for state actors in their efforts to consolidate power at home and achieve strategic goals abroad, especially when the means or motives of such efforts are otherwise questionable or hard to justify. Instead of treating the injury claims of different states as just a matter of legal adjudication, we have to attend to the power politics and discourses that operate to render certain injuries more worth recognizing, grieving and avenging than others. This hierarchy of injuries, constructed often on the basis of perceived political, cultural or racial differences between nations or states, has had a lot to do with the serious inequities and endless violence that continue to plague the modern system of international relations. The associated victim/wound politics and its underlying discourses must be interrogated rather than taken for granted if we hope to address the problems with the modern world order.

Sixty years after South Asia had been decolonized, Indian historian Ranajit Guha still lamented the painful legacy of British colonialism: "Whenever I read or hear the phrase colonial India, it hurts me. It hurts like an injury that has healed and yet has retained somehow a trace of the original pain linked to many different things – memories, values, sentiments" (Guha 1998: 85). His experience testified to the considerable traumatizing power of the narrative of colonial injury on the people of former colonies. Likewise, foreign invasion and domination from 1839 through 1945 has left the national psyche of modern China deeply scarred. The unequal treaties with Britain, France and the United States after the First Opium War in 1839–42, the killing and pillaging by the foreign powers during the Second Opium War of 1856–60 and during the Boxer Uprising around 1900, and the Japanese occupation in 1937–45 combined to turn that century into one of humiliation and injury in China's collective memory (Wang 2015, Zhang, Deng, and Zhao 2001). As exemplified by the influential work of postcolonial scholars such as Guha, Frantz Fanon, Edward Said and others, these feelings of injury and indignation could generate most effective criticism of colonial or imperial violence and oppression (Fanon [1952] 2008, [1961] 1963, Said 1993, 1994). It is also true that former colonies have often mobilized these sentiments to serve their political agendas. For instance, in *Wronged by Empire*, Manjari Miller has argued that colonialism was such a "transformative historical event" and "collective trauma" for countries like India and China that the two nations' ideologies and foreign policies have been driven by a primary "goal of victimhood" as well as two subordinate goals of securing "maximum territorial sovereignty" and "maximum international status" in the postcolonial era (Miller 2013). However, we would be mistaken to think that only the vulnerable or subjugated countries were eager to play the victim (see, e.g., Gelber 2004). In fact, as this chapter shows, claiming injuries or victimization has been unusually popular among the dominant powers over the last few centuries. One of my goals in this chapter is to explore how victimization becomes a source of empowerment or serves to justify action and violence that victimize others.

In the pages that follow, I will first sketch out the moral and legal implications of injury claims or victimhood in international relations. Then, I will draw examples from the history of Sino-Western relations to demonstrate why and how dominant empires frequently made claims of injury against a militarily weaker state. The third section will analyze the victim politics that has conditioned the differential representation and treatment of injury claims. The chapter concludes with a brief discussion of the victimhood claimed by postwar Japan and more recently the United States as (former) dominant powers to offer some reflections on why it is time to stop justifying the infliction of greater violence and injury on the grounds of one's own suffering.

MORAL AND JURIDICAL IMPLICATIONS OF CLAIMING INJURY OR VICTIMHOOD

In his provocative book titled *A Nation of Victims*, Charles Sykes in 1992 already saw the United States as a "society of victims" characterized by "a readiness not merely to feel sorry for oneself but to wield one's resentments as weapons of social advantage and to regard deficiencies as entitlement to society's deference" (Sykes 1992: 12). Two decades later, political philosopher Diane Enns again wondered aloud "why victims are currently invested with a moral authority that many feel unable or unwilling to challenge" (Enns 2012). This rising culture of victimhood in contemporary societies testified to the postmodern excesses of injury claims that turned the victim status into moral innocence, legal entitlement and an excuse for shirking individual or collective responsibility. But the rationale underlying this politics of victimhood or injury has a long genealogy and history.

The orthodox interpretation of the familiar imagery of Jesus Christ dying on the Cross illustrates this point. The suffering and sacrifice enabled Jesus not only to redeem the sinned humanity, but also to prove the boundless love and virtue of God. The cruelty and wickedness of his persecutors established the goodness of Jesus and all the victims he stood for. The message for Christian believers is clear enough: If my oppressor or injurer "is already evil, I cannot not be good, [and] I am therefore good" (Eze 2011: 5–6). Hence, the victim status serves to presumptively establish the moral righteousness and superiority of the injured, whose legal and political rights are in turn justified on the ground of past suffering or injustice. This dichotomy between the injurer and the injured is the key to deciphering the victim politics and the assumed moral justification of revengeful violence.

Although Jesus himself never responded to violence by revengeful violence, a secular discourse of injury that presumed the moral hierarchy between the injurer and the injured and the natural justice of revenge prevailed in the context of interstate relationship from early on and was codified by the founding texts of the modern law of nations (and later known as international law). For instance, Spanish theologian and jurist Franciscus de Victoria (c. 1483–1546) held that "injury" is the sole just cause of war and that a belligerent state can lawfully take all actions incidental to a just war for self-preservation, reparation of damages or prevention of injury (Victoria [1557] 1917, Wheaton 1845: 48). Likewise, in *The Rights of War and Peace*, Hugo Grotius (1583–1645), a Dutch lawyer and diplomat and another founder of international law, cited classical and medieval authorities in the 1620s to conclude that "there is no other reasonable cause of making war, but an injury received" or threatened. Echoing Victoria, he also noted that self-defense, recovery of loss and punishment for past injuries to prevent future ones constitute the three "just causes" of war in international relations (Grotius [1625] 2005: 393–5). A just war would allow the injured to dispossess the injurer of its rights, property, liberty or even life if necessary. Unlike individuals, whose right of defense is "momentary, and ceases as soon as one can apply to a judge," as Grotius pointed out, a state can continuously exercise the right of self-defense (as long as fresh injuries and damages are received) and is entitled to avenge the injury (ibid.: 416–7, [c. 1604] 2005: 102–7). Recognizable injuries include the (threatened) damages to the interests and property and to the reputation, dignity and honor of a nation or state. The idea that such an injury is the foundation or cause of "every just war" was confirmed by leading authorities of international relations of later times, including Emmer de Vattel (1714–67), a prominent eighteenth-century Swiss jurist (Vattel [1758] 2008: 483–4, 288–9).

In the canons of international law, therefore, it had been well established by the mid-eighteenth century that injury claims have the legal and moral effects of transforming a preventive or retaliatory war into a natural right, or even an obligation, for the injured. Principles were developed over time to restrain the potential abuses of the just war doctrine by emphasizing, *inter alia*, the proportionality between the original injury and the harm caused by a consequent just war. But over the last few centuries, the above-mentioned ideas of injury and revengeful justice have remained the logical linchpin for modern treatises of international law regarding whether and when a state can lawfully launch a war against another state. The resulting discourse of injury and just war shaped Western colonial expansion, starting from the fifteenth century, and subsequent international relations in general.

Early modern colonial powers such as Portugal, Spain, France, England and Holland frequently justified their overseas colonial expansion by claiming a set of assumed natural rights to free trade, travel and preaching in the non-Christian world. Local resistance to their exercise of such "rights" was construed as an injury to them and thus a cause of just war (Williams 1992, Pagden 1995, 2003, Anghie 2004). As I have recently analyzed elsewhere, it was not the dominant powers' military or political domination, but their alleged victimization or injury that often became the most effective means for securing colonial expansion and subjugation. Besides claiming *direct injury*, the colonial powers also developed the doctrine that an injury to humanity in general and thus an *indirect injury* to a presumably sympathetic and philanthropic Christian nation created a legal right and duty for the latter to interfere. For instance, leading jurists such as Victoria, Grotius and Henry Wheaton (1785–1848) all agreed that a Christian nation had the right to wage a just war to save the people of a pagan state from the injury and oppression of their "tyrannical" or "barbaric" governments in the interest of humanity. This concept of indirect injury later evolved into the modern principle of humanitarian intervention by a third party or the international community in the name of humanity and natural rights. Claiming direct or direct injuries, while capitalizing on the affective power of these often sentimental claims, became a major technology of empire to win public sympathy and support for controversial foreign policies in the nineteenth and twentieth centuries (Chen 2017, see also Moyn 2010). Nonetheless, as shown below, the liberal ideas of natural rights, justice and rule of law that made the injury discourse so valuable for colonial empires had the potential of enabling the dominated people to claim injury and injustice against the foreign powers for violating their rights accorded by these presumably universal principles. Besides, the same ideas could and often did inspire domestic and international criticism of unjustifiable wars and violence.

INJURY CLAIMS AND VICTIM POLITICS IN SINO-WESTERN ENCOUNTERS, 1500S–1900S

Unsurprisingly, the injury discourse also played a significant role in the history of Sino-Western relations. When the Portuguese, Spanish,

Dutch, English and French arrived in southern China in the sixteenth and seventeenth centuries, China posed a very different challenge to them than the smaller states that they had dominated elsewhere. In contrast with their privileged status in other colonies, European (and later American) empire builders in South China were placed under a variety of legal restrictions that were designed to minimize the foreign threat to China's interest and security. Neither was late imperial China willing to recognize these strangers' self-assumed "natural rights" to trade, travel and preaching Christianity freely within its territory (Chen 2016: 17–25).

From the very beginning, the more aggressive European explorers viewed these restrictive Chinese policies as injurious to their rights and interests and thus a cause of just war. After the first Portuguese embassy in 1521 failed to obtain free trade or colonial settlement in China, its members urged the Portuguese Viceroy of India to send an expedition of 2,000 or 3,000 troops to storm South China and capture the provinces of Guangdong, Fujian and Zhejiang. By waging a ruthless war, the expeditionary force would terrorize that vast and rich empire into *a tributary state*, which then had to send "a ship laden with silver" to Portugal every year and let the Portuguese control the lucrative China trade.[1] After local Chinese officials had allowed the European traders and missionaries to enter Macao and Guangdong, Jesuit superior Francisco Cabral (1533–1609) and others continued to press for more privileges and freedom in China by force.[2] In 1584, Alonso Sánchez (1547–93), procurator-general of Manila, assured King Philip II of Spain that the latter had a perfect legal right to conquer China (Doyle 2005: 266). Three years later, on behalf of the Iberian interests in the East Indies, he submitted a long memorial to the king and then had an audience with him, providing detailed advice on a large-scale expedition against China. Invoking Victoria's natural-law arguments as Cabral did, Sánchez contended that Chinese

---

[1] About the embassy and the letters of Cristóvão Vieira and Vasco Calvo that urged the China expedition, written in the 1520s–30s, see Ferguson (1902: 115–66, 24–51). Also see Jin (2005: 93–120 (1536), 258–70 (69–87)).

[2] Cabral urged King Philip II (1527–98) to send a fleet with 7,000–10,000 troops to conquer and evangelize China and obtain its annual revenue of 150 million dollars. Cabral justified the invasion on the ground that local officials had injured and insulted the Portuguese in Macao. See Francisco Cabral to Philip II, June 25, 1584, at Archivo General de Indias (Seville) (cited as AGI), Patronato, 25/21, Doc. 11; also see Jin (2005: 259–65).

hostilities to or restrictions on European missionaries and traders violated the European nations' rights under the law of nations and justified military retaliation. China's vast territory and population, immense treasures and infinite variety of products would make this "the greatest occasion and the grandest beginning that ever in the world was offered to a monarch" and a "Christian heart" desirous of "riches and eternal fame."[3] By turning China into a "hispanized and christianized" colony through Spanish schooling and by controlling its resources and trade, Spain, which had recently annexed Portugal, would be in a position to defeat European rivals such as France and England, subjugate all the countries around China, and make the Spanish king the "lord of all the world" (Blair and Robertson 1903: 214–28, Jin 2005: 261). Although these ambitions became even less realistic after the Spanish Invincible Armada was defeated by the English navy in August 1588, the rationale for invading or colonizing China, as articulated by Sánchez and his contemporaries, illustrated how much the injury discourse could have remade the Sino-Western relationship or, by extension, modern world history.[4] As discussed below, Britain and other Western powers would invoke the discourse of injury to wage a series of wars to force China open in the nineteenth century.

However, this discourse of injury and just war had internal contradictions from the outset. For instance, citing the same theory of universal justice and natural law as Sánchez did, José de Acosta (1539–1600), another Spanish Jesuit missionary, found no sufficient grounds for invading China to preach the Gospel. In his view, China's restrictive policies were justified because the Europeans had earned the reputation as "a warlike people who are eager to dominate" other countries after entering them in the name of free "communication and trade" since the 1490s, and the military expeditions

---

[3] Alsonso Sánchez, "The Proposed Entry into China, in Detail," at Blair and Robertson (1903: 197–233); also see "De la entrada de la China en particular," at AGI, Patronato, 24/66. On the resources of China, see Alsonso Sánchez, "Relación de las cosas particulares de la China [read to King Philip II]," Madrid, 1588, at Biblioteca Nacional (Madrid), MS 287, ff.198–226. Also see Doyle (2005: 255–64) and Ollé (2000: 129–34).

[4] His lobbying at Rome in the next few years only succeeded in getting Popes Gregory XIV and Innocent IX in 1591 to approve his effort to convert the Chinese and authorize Spain to protect the missionaries by force (see Bourdon 1960, Doyle 2005: 271–2, Ollé 2000: 141–56). On the Anglo-Spanish wars, see Parker (2000).

advocated by Sánchez and others only confirmed that. Like Victoria and Grotius, Acosta questioned the Pope's universal jurisdiction over non-Christian nations. He also noted that the Chinese were far more civilized than the "savages, barbarous or even bestial" natives elsewhere and should thus be treated differently from the Amerindians or the infidel Muslims as enemies of the faith. He concluded that the Chinese might have actually suffered enough injuries for a just war against the Europeans (Acosta 1954a: 331–3, 1954b: 337–41, Doyle 2005: 267–70). His rebuttal pointed to the potentiality of the injury discourse serving to justify completely opposite arguments and claims.

Although the sixteenth-century Iberians' plan to subjugate China never materialized, the injury discourse acquired momentum among the Western powers in the next two centuries. China's policies on the foreign trade and missionaries continued to generate a growing sense of resentment among the Westerners. By the late eighteenth century, partly thanks to the influential writings of Montesquieu and others, Chinese law and government had come to be represented as so arbitrary, barbaric or incompatible with the Western ideas of law and justice as to retrospectively justify the European empire builders' *a priori* demand for extraterritoriality and other privileges in China. China's attempts to enforce its sovereign power and law against foreign lawbreakers only further scandalized the Western community, who decried the Chinese policies and practices as injurious and insulting (Chen 2016: 18–68, 156–200).

For instance, when a French officer killed a British seaman in an affray near the anchorage of Whampoa, about twelve miles from the city of Guangzhou, in 1754, the British representatives urged the Chinese officials to punish the French offender because they knew that a European would almost certainly escape the due punishment for a homicide in China if he were sent back to Europe for trial as the French suggested. The French representatives in China warned their European counterparts: "We considered it would be doing you an injury as also ourselves and all the European nations in delivering him up to [the Chinese] because it would be to acknowledge their tribunal [as] a competent judge in our differences." Once China claimed jurisdiction over disputes between the Europeans, according to the French, the Westerners could no longer preserve the liberty and legal immunity that they had hitherto enjoyed in China. The recognition of Chinese law and jurisdiction thus constituted an injury and "dangerous evil" to the Western nations, and the Dutch, Portuguese and Swedish officers agreed with the French.[5]

Although they rejected the French plea in this case because a British person was the victim therein, the British officials made the same kind of argument in other cases to justify resisting Chinese jurisdiction. In the famous *Lady Hughes* case of 1784, where a British gunner was executed by the Chinese for having killed two Chinese in a nearby boat at Whampoa, the British officials denounced the Chinese judicial proceedings in this case and the Chinese legal system in general as capricious and cruel. They proposed what amounted to an imposition of British extraterritoriality in China on the grounds that voluntary submission to Chinese law would appear to all that the British had given up "every moral and manly principle" and would bring an everlasting national disgrace to the foreigners involved. These sentiments were shared by many other Euro-Americans then in China and beyond (IOR/G/12/79: 170–1, Chen 2016: 25–68). After an Italian seaman on board the American ship the *Emily* was strangled by the Chinese authorities for having killed a Chinese woman vendor at Whampoa in 1821, the Americans made similar complaints about Chinese law and injustice and cited this incidence as a major reason for insisting on extraterritoriality in China in 1844 (ibid.: 188–9, Askew 2004). Together, with the other stories of Chinese insults of foreigners, sensational reports of these disputes turned them into what may be called in our time "moral injuries" and enduring "cultural traumas" for the foreign nations involved, prompting many to urge military actions to change the status quo of Sino-Western relations (Chen 2016: 185–92).

The two Opium Wars in the mid-nineteenth century were both represented as necessary for redressing the indignities and injuries that the British, as well as other Westerners, had suffered in China. Besides citing earlier examples of unacceptable Chinese practices, the British Government and its supporters argued that the First Opium War was made inevitable also by the Chinese officials' arbitrary destruction of British "property" and detention of British Chief Superintendent of Trade Charles Elliot. In reality, Elliot made himself a "prisoner" of the Chinese anti-opium officials because he wanted to turn the Chinese

---

[5] "To the Gentlemen Supracargoes of the English East India Company of Canton," October 1754, Indian Office Records, British Library, London, IOR/R/10/3 (1742–55): 297.

legal action against British smugglers into an international dispute for the purpose of protecting the enormous British economic and political interests linked to the contraband opium trade. Representing the opium traders and Elliot as victims of Chinese despotism and violation of international law helped displace or suppress the vexing questions of the illegal and immoral nature of the opium trade that had become crucial to the British Empire and had been officially sanctioned by the legislators and governments in London and British India. These injury claims allowed many of the British decision-makers and public to feel legally and morally justified for forcing China not just to pay for the destroyed contraband drug and the war expenses, but also to reverse its foreign policies and concede privileges (Chen 2016: 204–40).[6]

Likewise, to further open China up for foreign opium, products and exploitation, Britain and France launched the Second Opium War in 1856 by again claiming to be victims of Chinese injustice. The Chinese seizure of a local smuggling boat with expired registration from the British colony of Hong Kong was considered an insult to British national honor and a breach of the 1842 Sino-British Treaty of Nanjing, while the French joined the British expedition supposedly to avenge Chinese persecution of Catholic missionaries. Local resistance to the foreign forces during the war then became new grounds for foreign brutalities, including the bombardment of the densely populated city of Guangzhou in 1856 and the plundering and destruction of the old Summer Palace (Yuanmingyuan) in Beijing in 1860 (Wong 1998, Hevia 2003). After the two Opium Wars, the defeated China made many concessions through a series of treaties with the foreign powers and had become a so-called semi-colony by the late nineteenth century (see Mayers [1877] 1901 for the treatises).

DIFFERENTIAL TREATMENT OF INJURIES, GRIEVABILITY, AND RIGHTS

The tendency in much of the earlier scholarship to reduce the causes of nineteenth-century Sino-Western conflicts to a matter of avenging Chinese mistreatment or injury of foreigners has for too long distracted us from investigating the questionable foundation of the foreign powers'

---

[6] See Elliot to Palmerston, April 13, 1839, FO17/31: 124–35, and April 3, 1839, FO17/31: 113–14, Foreign Office Records, National Archives, London. For more generally about the war, see Chang (1964).

policies and actions. Orientalizing the Chinese as cruel and barbarian injurers led many to assume the justice of Western actions, while making it unnecessary to apply the supposedly universal principles of natural rights, equal sovereignty or international law to China. In this process, the foreign violations of Chinese rights and interests were seldom recognized as such in this dominant colonial discourse of injury. As critical scholar Sarah Ahmed has put it, "[t]he differentiation between forms of pain and suffering in stories that are told, and between those that are told and those that are not, is a crucial mechanism for the distribution of power" (Ahmed 2004: 33). That was particularly true in the age of empire.

The discriminatory treatment of injuries did not go unnoticed in the nineteenth century. As the London-based *Daily News* observed at the time of the Second Opium War, it is a "monstrous fact, that in order to avenge the irritated pride of a British official, and punish the folly of an Asiatic governor, we prostitute our strength to the wicked work of carrying fire and sword, and desolation and death, into the peaceful homes of unoffending men, on whose shores we were originally intruders." The same newspaper found the British bombardment of Guangzhou and the current war with China to be "a bad and a base one – a reckless and wanton waste of human life at the shrine of a false etiquette and a mistaken policy" (quoted in Marx 1857a). After plowing through the published British official records of this conflict, Karl Marx likewise concluded in a letter to the *New York Daily Tribune* in April 1857: "[T]his most unrighteous war has been waged. The unoffending citizens and peaceful tradesmen of Canton [i.e., Guangzhou] have been slaughtered, their habitations battered to the ground, and the claims of humanity violated, on the flimsy pretence that 'English life and property are endangered by the aggressive acts of the Chinese!'" Marx was particularly harsh on the hypocrisy of waging the two Opium Wars in the name of repairing the foreigners' injuries. Although most British politicians and commentators knew, or should have known, that the official charges against the Chinese were "baseless," according to Marx, they took pains to "divert investigation from the main issue, and to impress the public mind with the idea that a long series of injuries" constituted "a sufficient *causus belli*" of the wars. As far as Marx could tell from the English records, "the Chinese have at least ninety-nine injuries to complain of to one on the part of the English" (Marx 1857c, see also Marx 1857a, b, 1859a, b, 1860).

As Judith Butler has recently pointed out, framing one's pain or loss as more "grievable" and thus more worthy of reparation or revenge than those of the cultural, racial or social Other has often had the strategic effect of desensitizing people and making them more willing to condone otherwise reprehensible violence toward the latter (Butler 2006, 2010, Sontag 2003). Different representations of injury and grievability often allowed the dominant to manipulate the injury discourse at the expense of the dominated. This explains why so many modern empires invoked this discourse to justify aggression against weaker countries over the past few centuries. Historical anthropologist Ann Stoler has described this popular tendency to ignore or refuse to care about the suffering of others as an imperial practice and disposition of "disregard" (Stoler 2009: 256). In another 1857 commentary on the Second Opium War, Karl Marx succinctly captured the political and moral economy that conditioned the imperial disregard of the pain of others:

> How silent is the press of England upon the outrageous violations of the treaty daily practiced by foreigners living in China under British protection! We hear nothing of the illicit opium trade, which yearly feeds the British treasury at the expense of human life and morality. We hear nothing of the constant bribery of sub-officials, by means of which the Chinese Government is defrauded of its rightful revenue on incoming and outgoing merchandise. We hear nothing of the wrongs inflicted 'even unto death' upon misguided and bonded [Chinese] emigrants sold to worse than Slavery on the coast of Peru, and into Cuban bondage. We hear nothing of the bullying spirit often exercised against the timid nature of the Chinese, or of the vice introduced by foreigners at the ports open to their trade. We hear nothing of all this and of much more, first, because the majority of people out of China care little about the social and moral condition of that country; and secondly, because it is the part of policy and prudence not to agitate topics where no pecuniary advantage would result. Thus, the English people at home, who look no further than the grocer's where they buy their tea, are prepared to swallow all the misrepresentations which the Ministry and the Press choose to thrust down the public throat (Marx 1857c).

As seen earlier, such silence and disregard of the local people's suffering was in sharp contrast with the voluminous and ceaselessly recycled expressions of indignation, grieving and commemoration about the injuries and insults suffered by Westerners in China and other "Oriental" countries. These differential valuations and treatments of injuries and rights also made it appear more reasonable to demand excessive retaliation for what oneself had suffered ('Demand Punishment of China' 1900, Martin 1870). For instance, the sensational tales of

Indian cruelty toward the 100 or so European prisoners in the Black Hole of Calcutta in 1756 served not only to call for the British war and killings in the next year but also to naturalize the origin of British colonization of the Indian subcontinent that lasted until 1947 (Chatterjee 2012).

Dominant empires in this period so frequently resorted to brutal violence to avenge their "injuries" that they often believed the best defense of their behavior was to draw attention to the equally or more deplorable conduct of other empires. For this reason, the London *Times* reprinted a letter from a German solider in Beijing in 1900 to counter the recent German criticism of British brutalities in South Africa. This solider recounted how Chinese prisoners of war were treated when the foreign allies attacked North China to avenge the Boxer rebels' violence toward Chinese Christians and foreigners: "Today we were called at dinner time to the aid of German sailors. We took 76 Chinamen prisoners, tied them together by their pigtails and placed them in our midst. Some of our rough fellows beat them cruelly so that their bodies were all covered with blood. It was dreadful. After dinner they were ordered to be shot ... We stood at 12 to 15 paces, four men to a Chinaman, and at the word of command they all whined for mercy. But then came Fire! and all was over." Eager to prove German cruelty beyond doubt, the *Times* also included a letter from another German solider in China. The latter lamented to his mother at home that all the "murdering and butchering" that he witnessed was "simple madness." But he also found that inevitable "because the Chinese [were] outside the law of nations." As a result, no Chinese was taken prisoner but were all shot or else stabbed to "spare our cartridges." Having recently had to bayonet 74 prisoners on a Sunday afternoon, he wrote: "It was horrible. Let us hope this will not last long or we shall forget we are human" ('German Treatment of the Chinese' 1900). By excluding China from the pale of civilization and international law except for holding it responsible for protecting the foreign powers' treaty rights under international law, the colonial discourse of injury and justice refused to take cognizance of injuries caused by the dominant empires (Chen 2016: 206–36). The pain and death of the European prisoners at the Black Hole of Calcutta were turned into a key to the British Empire in India, but the suffering and decimation of many more people in China and elsewhere became the *unremarkable* collateral damage of the revengeful colonial forces or of the price paid for the global spread of the European "civilizing mission."

LEGACY OF THE INJURY DISCOURSE IN THE MODERN ERA

While the discourse of injury had helped advance the interests of the foreign empires in China during the nineteenth century, twentieth-century Chinese revolutionaries or reformers, like their counterparts in other former (semi)colonies, also became adept at appropriating and deploying this discourse to mobilize their compatriots to fend off foreign domination. Through government media, history books, school education and family story-telling, memories of the humiliating century from 1842 through 1945 became a national cultural trauma over the past century. Strategic use of the memories and the related patriotic sentiments provided much-needed legitimacy for the Republican governments in 1911–49 and the People's Republic of China afterwards. In the late twentieth century, famous sites such as the relics of the old Summer Palace (destroyed by the Anglo-French forces in 1860) and the mass graveyard of the tens of thousands of victims of the Nanjing Massacre (committed by the Japanese army in late 1937 and early 1938) were transformed into grand national memorials to remind people of all the atrocities and injuries that the nation has suffered in the hands of the foreign powers (Lee 2008, Wang 2012).

By selectively retelling and monumentalizing memories of the historical wounds and injuries, the Chinese authorities sought to claim a new historical agency for the modern nation state or the ruling party. What was once a powerful weapon of the foreign powers became an effective instrument for the Chinese government and ruling elites to reconstruct national identity, consolidate domestic power and secure international support. In the process, the tendency to stress the *collective* pain or injury of the body politic in opposition to the foreign oppressors operated to marginalize the suffering of individuals in concrete moments and circumstances. In the meantime, this nationalist discourse helped divert attention from the people's suffering caused by domestic policies and politics since the end of foreign colonialism (Lim 2014). Therefore, like the colonial discourse of injury, the postcolonial discourse of injury or victimhood can also "exclude and conceal": It often fails to recognize the actual victims, who do not fit neatly into the authorized official narrative of national history, while it also tends to conceal "the agency of victims in their own victimhood (not to mention in making others suffer)" (Ochs 2006: 357). The modern citizenry has thus claimed victimhood of past injuries, and the implied moral righteousness, by association or inheritance, a practice that is called "allusive victimhood" (Ochs 2006: 357). By fixating the people's attention on the injustice of the past and foreign, the "[i]njury claims thus produce and maintain the citizen-victim that transforms the wound into an identity" of the modern nation (Rice 2012: 82).

Some scholars contend that memories of the "century of humiliation" have become "the prime raw material for constructing China's national identity," which has in turn defined its national interests and informed its foreign policy and international conduct (Wang 2012: xiii, 1–5). Wendy Brown has recently cautioned us against the peril of seeking "sovereign subjectivity" in the present through "fetishisation" of the wound of the past or "through eternal repetition of pain" (Brown 1995: 76). But our critical reflections here should not be taken to suggest that all past injustices be forgotten or written off. The current Lord Elgin, descendant of the Eighth Lord Elgin who led the British forces in the Second Opium War and authorized the looting and burning of the Summer Palace in 1860, might have meant well when he remarked to a BBC reporter in 2015 of what his ancestor did in Beijing: "These things happen. It's important to go ahead, rather than look back all the time." The fact that his family still hold on to some of the valuable Chinese artworks taken from the Summer Palace (just as numerous Anglo-American and French museums do) suggests that history cannot simply be willed away (Bowbly 2015). In Brown's words, the "counsel of forgetting … seems inappropriate if not cruel" for those previously oppressed people whose pain has not yet been recognized (Brown 1995: 74). Indeed, as Sarah Ahmed has put it, "To forget would be to repeat the forgetting that is already implicated in the fetishsation of the wound," and our purpose of remembering is not to turn the historical wound into what defines our identity and political goals, but to break the hold of the past and take actions to prevent the recurrence of similar injustice (Ahmed 2004: 32, 34).

It is true that a deep-rooted sense of injury and victimhood is still noticeable in many countries that suffered foreign occupation or domination in the nineteenth and twentieth centuries (see, e.g., Jensen and Ronsbo 2014). But it is not just previously dominated countries like China or India that have sought to make use of injury claims in the modern era. For instance, even though China and various other countries in East and Southeast Asia still resent imperial Japan as the perpetrator of horrendous brutalities and crimes against humanity in the Second World War, Japan has tried to portray itself as the victim over the last few decades. Right-wing politicians and ultranationalists denied even the existence of the Nanjing Massacre, in which as many as 200,000–300,000 civilians and prisoners of war were mass-murdered and tens of thousands of women were gang-raped during a short span of six weeks (Chang 2014). As Yukiko Koga's chapter in this book and other recent studies have shown, a combination of international and domestic politics led to widespread amnesia in postwar Japan toward this dark chapter of the nation's history and the sufferings experienced by people at home and abroad. As recently as 2013, Japanese Prime Minister Abe Shinzo still publicly questioned whether Japanese occupation and pillaging of China in the 1930s–40s could even be called invasion (Buruma 2015).

While disputing or glossing over the suffering of other nations invaded by imperial Japan, the postwar Japanese government took various means to appeal to the discourse of injury in its attempts to refashion a modern national identity and regain international respectability. Among the two and a half million "war dead" memorialized by the government in the imperial shrine of Yasukuni in Tokyo (established in 1869) are also the Japanese soldiers and officers who were said to have "sacrificed" their lives for Japan during the Second World War, including the fourteen class A war criminals since 1978. The fact that many senior Japanese officials, including several prime ministers, paid tribute to these convicted war criminals at the shrine in a widely broadcast ceremony every year has added insult to injury of the neighboring countries whose memories of Japanese atrocities are kept alive by their own governments (Yoneyama 1997, Eykholt 2000, Yang 2000).

Besides commemorating the killed members of the military, the Japanese government also built memorial museums at Hiroshima in 1955 and at Nagasaki in 2002 to honor the Japanese victims of the atomic bombs detonated by the American forces over those two cities in August 1945. Instead of situating these tragic events in the larger context of war, Japanese imperialism, and the suffering of other nations during this period, the official discourse of the atomic bombings represented the Japanese almost as a special category of victims, who symbolized a suffering and threatened humanity and could be compared only to the Jewish victims of the Holocaust. In so doing, the experiences of the Japanese victims were isolated from the rest of imperial Japanese history and from the pain of other nations victimized by Japan (Shan 2005, Yoneyama 1997). As Lisa Yoneyama pointed out, the

Japanese way of "remembering the atomic destruction of Hiroshima and Nagasaki as events in the history of humanity has significantly contributed to the forgetting of the history of colonialism and racism in the region" (Yoneyama 1999: 12). These ways of claiming injury and victimhood have helped deflect domestic and foreign criticism of the right-wing denial of Japanese war crimes, while providing the Japanese politicians with a sense of moral innocence and righteouness in international relations.

Although many Japanese see their nation as the victim of imposed historical guilt or of the inhumane decision of the American government to drop the atomic bombs to kill tens of thousands of civilians in 1945, the United States, even as the sole hegemon of the world since the early 1990s, has not shied away from claiming victimhood either. One of the more recent examples would be how the American government justified its "global war on terrorism" after Al-Qaeda suicide bombers crashed four passenger planes and killed about 3,000 Americans on September 11, 2001. Instead of reflecting on past foreign policies and trying to end the vicious cycle of hatred and violence, American politicians and mainstream media immediately called for both retaliatory and preemptive attacks on Afghanistan and other countries suspected of harboring or supporting terrorist groups. In the next seven years, the Bush administration invoked the time-honored doctrine of just war to launch a series of military campaigns in South Asia and the Middle East, purportedly to avenge the deaths of the American victims, often in spite of protests of the victims' relatives (Seidler 2013: 74–6). Influenced by the discourse of injury and revengeful justice promoted by the government and media, many American people and politicians for years dwelled on the pain and suffering of their compatriots while showing little regard for the people in regions targeted by American military actions.

According to a report published in March 2015, at least 1.3 million people had been killed in Iraq, Afghanistan and Pakistan directly or indirectly by the United States' war on terrorism during the twelve years since its inception. This figure is almost ten times more than has been reported or generally known. In Iraq alone, 1,000,000 people or 5 percent of the country's population had perished, and 3,000,000 people had been displaced. The tally included neither those killed by American drone strikes in Yemen, Somalia and elsewhere nor those who survived but were seriously injured by American military operations or bombs ("Body Count" 2015). The millions of people who were killed or injured by the American troops have often been treated as "unmarkable and ungrievable" in American media and public discourses. The lives of the foreign casualties are not recognized as such and hence are deemed less worth respecting or mourning (Butler 2006: 34–5, Giroux 2004).

The danger of claiming injuries to justify preemptive war for eliminating a suspected enemy or feared threat was recognized long time ago. An ancient Roman author, Aulus Gellius (c. 125–after 180 CE), already observed that "[t]hat a gladiator's condition is such, that he must either kill or be killed; but human life is not under such unhappy circumstances" (Grotius 2005: 399). Quoting Gellius, Cicero (106–43 BCE), and Thucydides (460–395 BCE), Grotius thus declared in the 1620s: "to pretend to have a right to injure another, merely from a possibility that he may injure me, is repugnant to all the justice in the world" (ibid.: 417).[7] As we can never be "in perfect security" in this world, he counselled, it "is not in the way of force, but in the protection of providence, and in innocent precautions, that we are to seek for relief against uncertain fear" (ibid.). However, over the last two decades, this uncertain fear and the *gladiator's mentality* have driven the United States to wage a "total war on terrorism" – a war without border, without targeted enemy, and without end – while turning the country into "a security state" in which the rule of law and civil rights and freedom are dramatically curtailed in the interest of national security (see, e.g., Clarke 2004, Greenberg 2016). In the process, the American people themselves have become victims of the hardline policy they supported in the aftermath of 9/11.

While the United States went on the offensive supposedly as a victim of terrorism, its military actions against Muslim countries created a breeding ground for even more radical Muslims to join terrorist organizations which, ironically or not, have also claimed it as their primary mission to fight against the "injurious" discrimination and aggression of the United States and its allies (Clarke 2004). Thus, nearly all parties to this ongoing global struggle make claim to injury or victimhood as the reason for their killing and violence. If a culture of victimhood has indeed prevailed in many contemporary societies, it can be argued that a similar culture has long influenced state actors,

---

[7] As Grotius paraphrased it, Cicero stated to the effect that "one frequently commits injustice, by attempting to hurt another, in order to avoid the evil which he apprehends from him" (Grotius 2005: 399–400, quoting Thucydides).

as illustrated by the historical examples in this chapter. When Donald Trump repeatedly described China's favorable trade balance with the United States as "killing" and "raping" the latter during his presidential campaigns in 2016, he invoked the discourse of injury/victimhood in both domestic civil society and international relations (Diamond 2016). His defeat of Hillary Clinton, who had been the clear favorite of most polls and political pundits, in the general election was to a great extent attributable to the efficacy of his strategy of convincing millions of American voters that they were indeed *victims* of manipulative Chinese and illegal Mexican immigrants, free trade, globalization and incompetent American Democratic politicians. The Trump administration's widely criticized policies on international trade and immigration (including the so-called Muslim ban, allegedly to prevent terrorism) in early 2017 once again demonstrated the staying and possibly growing power of victim politics in both national and international contexts.

The history of the discourse of injury has shown that, perhaps counterintuitively, a dominant state or empire has the capacity "not only to injure but also of being injured and making claims to the effect." As Lydia Liu reminds us, "the strong and the powerful can be the first to lay legal and moral claims to injury against the disfranchised and retain an enormous stake in maintaining the political structure of resentment in the larger imperial order." The discourse of injury can be "a dangerous and productive force in the making of the modern world," since it provides the legal and moral justifications for imperial ambitions when military or political power alone falls short (Liu 2009: 214–5). If Anne Stoler is right in thinking that "imperial states by definition operate as states of exception that vigilantly produce exceptions to their principles and exceptions to their laws" (Stoler 2006: 140), then the discourse of injury shall be understood as one of the most important means for these states to make such exceptions without officially abandoning their fundamental values and ideologies. Given that their evolution was so intimately related to the imperial discourse of injury, the modern (Western) liberal ideas of rights, law, freedom, property and sovereignty "ought no longer to serve as the sole lens through which we examine the question of suffering." To end the vicious cycle of violence and retaliation, it is important to remember that "alternative articulations of injury existed in the past and continue to exist in the present" (Liu 2009: 215–6). A main task of this chapter has been to recover and make sense of some of these alternative articulations.

When pondering these issues in *Precarious Life*, Butler pointed out that "it is one matter to suffer violence and quite another to use that fact to ground a framework in which one's injury authorizes limitless aggression against targets that may or may not be related to the sources of one's own suffering" (Butler 2006: 4). She suggested that instead of using our loss or injury to justify war and violence (which inevitably leads to more violence and injury), our suffering and grieving should "yield an experience of humility, of vulnerability, of impressionability and dependence." This recognition of shared precariousness and destructibility of all human beings may discourage us from dehumanizing and thus attacking the suspected injurer for our vengeance and encourage us to seek "non-military political solutions" (ibid.: 29–35, 128–51). Critics might dismiss Butler's pacifist proposal as utopian and irrelevant to the real politics of the world today, but her proposal at least leads to more hope and less injury than what the realist or neoconservative politicians have offered. Our reexamination of the genealogy and moral economy of states' injury claims and victimhood, even in a highly selective manner, may help draw more critical attention to the power politics underlying the discourse of injury and revengeful justice that has profoundly shaped the modern history of international law and relations over the last few centuries.

References

Acosta, J. D. ([1587] 1954a). "Parecer sobre la guerra de la China [March 15, 1587]." Pp. 331–4 in *Biblioteca de Autores Españoles*, Vol. 73, edited by F. Mateo. Madrid: Ediciones Atlas.

——— ([1587] 1954b). "Respuesta a los fundamentos que justifican la guerra contra la China." Pp. 334–45 in *Biblioteca de Autores Españoles*, Vol. 73, edited by F. Mateo. Madrid: Ediciones Atlas.

Ahmed, S. (2004). *The Cultural Politics of Emotion*. New York: Routledge.

Anghie, A. (2004). *Imperialism, Sovereignty, and the Making of International Law*. Cambridge: Cambridge University Press.

Askew, J. (2004). "Re-visiting New Territory: The Terranova Incident Re-examined." *Asian Studies Review* 28(4):351–71.

Blair, E. H., and Robertson, J. A. eds. (1903). *The Philippine Islands, 1493–1898*, Vol. 6. Cleveland, OH: Arthur Clark Co.

Body Count: Casualty Figures after 10 Years of the "War on Terror", Iraq, Afghanistan, Pakistan (2015). Washington, DC, Berlin, Ottawa: Physicians for Social Responsibility. www.psr.org/assets/pdfs/body-count.pdf (last accessed: December 13, 2017).

Bourdon, L. (1960). "Un Projet d'Invasion de la Chine par Canton à la fin du XVI siècle." *Actas do III Colóquio Internacional de Estudos Luso-Brasileiros* 1:97–121.

Bowlby, C. (2015). "The Palace of Shame That Makes China Angry." *BBC News*, February 2. www.bbc.com/news/magazine-30810596 (last accessed: December 13, 2017).

Brown, W. (1995). *States of Injury: Power and Freedom in Late Modernity*. Princeton, NJ: Princeton University Press.

Buruma, I. (2015). *The Wages of Guilt: Memories of War in Germany and Japan*. New York: New York Review of Books.

Butler, J. (2006). *Precarious Life: The Powers of Mourning and Violence*. New York: Verso.

(2010). *Frames of War: When is Life Grievable?* New York: Verso.

Chang, H. P. (1964). *Commissioner Lin and the Opium War*. Cambridge: Harvard University Press.

Chang, I. (2014). *The Rape of Nanking: The Forgotten Holocaust of WWII*. New York: Basic Books.

Chatterjee, P. (2012). *The Black Hole of Empire: History of a Global Practice of Power*. Princeton, NJ: Princeton University Press.

Chen, L. (2016). *Chinese Law in Imperial Eyes: Sovereignty, Justice, and Transcultural Politics*. New York: Columbia University Press.

(2017). "Affective Sovereignty, International Law, and China's Legal Status in the Nineteenth Century." Pp. 421–39 in *The Scaffolding of Sovereignty: Global and Aesthetic Perspectives on the History of a Concept*, edited by Z. B.-D. Benite, S. Geroulanos, and N. Jerr. New York: Columbia University Press.

Clarke, R. A. (2004). *Against All Enemies: Inside America's War on Terror*. New York: Free Press.

Demand Punishment of China. (1900). *New York Times*, August 4, p. 2.

Diamond, J. (2016). Trump: "We Can't Allow China to Continue to Rape Our Country". *CNN*, May 2. www.cnn.com/2016/05/01/politics/donald-trump-china-rape/ (last accessed: December 13, 2017).

Doyle, J. P. (2005). "Two Sixteenth-Century Jesuits and a Plan to Conquer China: Alonso Sánchez and Jose de Acosta: An Outrageous Proposal and Its Rejection." Pp. 253–73 in *Rechtsdenken: Schnittpunkte West und Ost: Recht in den Gesellschafts-und Staatstragenden Institutionen Europas und Chinas*, edited by H. Holz and K. Wegmann. Münster: LIT Verlag.

Enns, D. (2012). *The Violence of Victimhood*. College Station, TX: Pennsylvania State University Press.

Eykholt, M. (2000). "Aggression, Victimization, and Chinese Historiography of the Nanjing Massacre." In *The Nanjing Massacre in History and Historiography*, edited by J. A. Fogel. Berkeley, CA: University of California Press.

Eze, C. (2011). *Postcolonial Imagination and Moral Representations in African Literature and Culture*. Lanham, MD: Lexington Books.
Fanon, F. ([1961] 1963). *The Wretched of the Earth*, translated by C. Farrington. New York: Grove.
——— ([1952] 2008). *Black Skin, White Mask*, new edition translated by R. Philcox. New York: Grove.
Ferguson, D., ed. (1902). *Letters from Portuguese Captives in Canton, Written in 1534 and 1536*, Vol. 30. Bombay: Education Society's Steam Press.
Gelber, H. G. (2004). *Opium, Soldiers and Evangelicals: Britain's 1840–42 War with China, and Its Aftermath*. New York: Palgrave Macmillan.
"German Treatment of the Chinese." (1900). *The Times*, p. 6.
Giroux, H. A. (2004). *The Terror of Neoliberalism: Authoritarianism and the Eclipse of Democracy. Boulder, Colorado: Paradigm, 2004*. Boulder, CO: Paradigm.
Greenberg, K. J. (2016). *Rogue Justice: The Making of the Security State*. New York: Crown Publishers.
Grotius, H. (2005 [1625]). *The Rights of War and Peace*. Indianapolis, IN: Liberty Fund.
——— (2005 [c. 1604]). *Commentary on the Law of Prize and Booty*, translated by G. L. Williams. Indianapolis, IN: Liberty Fund.
Guha, R. (1998). "A Conquest Foretold." *Social Text* 54:85–99.
Hevia, J. L. (2003). *English Lessons: The Pedagogy of Imperialism in Nineteenth-Century China*. Durham, NC: Duke University Press.
Jensen, S., and Ronsbo, H. (2014). *Histories of Victimhood*. Philadelphia, PA: University of Pennsylvania Press.
Jin, G., ed. (2005). *Xifang Aomen shiliao xuancui (Western Historical Sources on Macao in the 15th–16th Centuries)*. Guangzhou: Guangdong renmin chubanshe.
Lee, H. (2008). "The Ruins of Yuanmingyuan; Or, How to Enjoy a National Wound." *Modern China* 35(2):155–90.
Lim, L. (2014). *The People's Republic of Amnesia: Tiananmen Revisited*. Oxford: Oxford University Press.
Liu, L. H. (2009). "Injury: Incriminating Words and Imperial Power." Pp. 199–218 in *Words in Motion: Toward a Global Lexicon*, edited by C. Gluck and A. L. Tsing. Durham, NC: Duke University Press.
Martin, W. A. P. (1870). "The Tientsin Massacre." *New York Evangelist* 41(36):1.
Marx, K. (1857a). "The Case of the Lorcha Arrow." *The New York Daily Tribune*, June 23.
——— (1857b). "Parliamentary Debates on the Chinese Hostilities." *The New York Daily Tribune*, March 16.
——— (1857c). "Whose Atrocities." *The New York Daily Tribune*, April 10.
——— (1859a). "The New Chinese War." *The New York Daily Tribune*, October 1.
——— (1859b). "Trade with China." *The New York Daily Tribune*, December 3.

(1860). "British Politics." *The New York Daily Tribune*, February 14.
Mayers, W. F. (1901 [1877]). *Treaties Between the Empire of China and Foreign Powers: Together with Regulations for the Conduct of Foreign Trade, Conventions, Agreements, Regulations, etc. and the Peace Protocol of 1901*, 3rd edn. Shanghai: North-China Herald Office.
Miller, M. C. (2013). *Wronged by Empire: Post-Imperial Ideology and Foreign Policy in India and China*. Stanford, CA: Stanford University Press.
Moyn, Samuel. (2010). *The Last Utopian: Human Rights in History*. Cambridge: Harvard University Press.
Ochs, J. (2006). The Politics of Victimhood and Its Internal Exegetes: Terror Victims in Israel. *History and Anthropology* 17(4):355–68.
Ollé, M. (2000). *La invención de China: percepciones y estrategias filipinas respecto a China durante el siglo XVI*. Wiesbaden: Harrassowitz.
Pagden, A. (1995). *Lords of All the World: Ideologies of Empire in Spain, Britain and France, c. 1500–c. 1800*. New Haven, CT: Yale University Press.
  (2003). "Human Rights, Natural Rights, and Europe's Imperial Legacy." *Political Theory* 31:171–99.
Parker, G. (2000). *The Grand Strategy of Philip II*. New Haven, CT: Yale University Press.
Rice, J. (2012). *Distant Publics: Development Rhetoric and the Subject of Crisis*. Pittsburgh, PA: University of Pittsburgh Press.
Said, E. (1993). *Culture and Imperialism*. New York: Alfred A. Knopf.
  (1994). *Orientalism*. New York: Vintage Books.
Seidler, V. J. (2013). *Remembering 9/11: Terror, Trauma and Social Theory*. London: Palgrave.
Shan, L. (2005). "Implicating Colonial Memory and the Atomic Bombing: Hayashi Kyoko's Three Short Stories." *Southeast Review of Asian Studies* 27. (Online Version of the Paper Presented at the Southeast Conference of the Association for Asian Studies in 2005).
Sontag, S. (2003). *Regarding the Pain of Others*. New York: Picador.
Stoler, A. L. (2006). "On Degrees of Imperial Sovereignty." *Public Culture* 18(1):125–46.
  (2009). *Along the Archival Grain: Epistemic Anxieties and Colonial Common Sense*. Princeton, NJ: Princeton University Press.
Sykes, C. J. (1992). *A Nation of Victims: The Decay of American Character*. New York: St. Martin's Press.
Vattel, Emer de. ([1758] 2008). *The Law of Nations, or, Principles of the Law of Nature*. Indianapolis, IN: Liberty Fund.
Victoria, F. d. ([1557] 1917). *De Indis et de ivre Belli Relectiones, Being Parts of Relectiones Theologicae XII*, translated by J. P. Bate, edited by Ernest Nye. Washington, DC: Carnegie Institution of Washington.
Wang, J. (2015). *Unequal Treaties and China*. Hong Kong: Enrich Professional Publishing.

Wang, Z. (2012). *Never Forget National Humiliation: Historical Memory in Chinese Politics and Foreign Relations*. New York: Columbia University Press.

Wheaton, H. (1845). *History of the Law of Nations in Europe and America: From the Earliest Times to the Treaty of Washington, 1842*. New York: Gould, Banks and Co.

Williams, R. A. (1992). *The American Indian in Western Legal Thought: The Discourses of Conquest*. Oxford: Oxford University Press.

Wong, J. Y. (1998). *Deadly Dreams: Opium, Imperialism, and the Arrow War (1856–60) in China*. Cambridge: Cambridge University Press.

Yang, D. (2000). "The Challenge of the Nanjing Massacre: Reflections on Historical Inquiry." Pp. 133–80 in *The Nanjing Massacre in History and Historiography*, edited by J. A. Fogel. Berkeley, CA: University of California Press.

Yoneyama, L. (1997). "Memory Matters: Hiroshima's Korean Atom Bomb Memorial and the Politics of Ethnicity." In *Living With the Bomb: American and Japanese Cultural Conflicts in the Nuclear Age*, edited by L. Hein and M. Selden. Armonk, NY: M.E. Sharpe Publishers Inc.

(1999). *Hiroshima Traces: Time, Space, and the Dialectics of Memory*. Berkeley, CA: University of California Press.

Zhang, H., Deng, H., and Zhao, Y. (2001). *Guochi baitan (A Hundred Talks on National Humiliation)*. Beijing: Zhonghua shuju.

CHAPTER FOURTEEN

LAW'S IMPERIAL AMNESIA
Transnational Legal Redress in East Asia

Yukiko Koga

INTRODUCTION

Legal efforts seeking official apology and compensation for Japanese imperial violence have become a prime site of Chinese and Japanese attempts to come to terms with the past since the 1990s, when Chinese victims of Japanese imperialism from the first half of the twentieth century filed scores of lawsuits against the Japanese government and corporations within Japanese courts. Coming to terms with the past takes many forms, yet legal redress has gained momentum in the past

An earlier and more extended version of this chapter was first published as "Between the Law: The Unmaking of Empire and Law's Imperial Amnesia," *Law & Social Inquiry*, vol. 41, no. 2 (Spring 2016): 402–34. Field research in China and Japan over the last fifteen years was made possible by the generosity of the Chinese plaintiffs, Japanese lawyers, Chinese lawyers, and advocates and activists who allowed me to participate in and observe their involvement in the transnational legal redress movements. I would also like to thank the National Endowment for the Humanities, Japan–U.S. Friendship Commission, Association for Asian Studies Northeast Asia Council, and Hunter College for their financial support for my field research in China and Japan. Any views, findings, conclusions, or recommendations expressed in this article do not necessarily reflect those of the National Endowment for the Humanities or the Japan–U.S. Friendship Commission, or those of the Association for Asian Studies. My gratitude also goes to Waseda University in Japan for library access, and, for institutional support, to the People's Law Office in Tokyo, the University of Tokyo Interfaculty Initiative in Information Studies, Hunter College of the City University of New York, and fellowships at the Cogut Center for the Humanities and the Department of East Asian Studies at Brown University and the Harvard Academy for International and Area Studies at Harvard University.

two decades, not only in East Asia, but also elsewhere in the world to account for violence and injustice committed during the Second World War.[1] This chapter examines what it means to account for past violence through legal means, especially after decades have passed since the demise of the Japanese empire in 1945. It looks specifically at a series of postwar compensation lawsuits filed in Japan by Chinese victims in the past two decades that underscore the unfinished project of the unmaking of empire, which formally ended with Imperial Japan's defeat in the Second World War.[2] These lawsuits have also brought to the fore both the potential and challenges for juridifying historical responsibility transnationally through the use of the domestic law of the former perpetrator nation. Unlike the Tokyo Tribunal that took place immediately after the war to criminalize wartime violence, these recent postwar compensation lawsuits use the Japanese Civil Code to seek monetary compensation and official apology for deaths and injuries caused by the Japanese government and corporations. Combining legal analyses of these postwar compensation lawsuits with ethnographic observation inside and outside the courtroom, this chapter explores the role of law in this belated project of the unmaking of empire.

Since the early 1990s, the Japanese court system has processed more than a dozen lawsuits filed by Chinese victims, represented by a group of nearly 300 Japanese lawyers working *pro bono*. These lawsuits – referred to in Japan as "postwar compensation lawsuits" (*sengohoshōsaiban*)[3] –

---

[1] For a global context in which postwar compensation for Japanese wartime violence is motivated by Holocaust compensation attempts, see Yoneyama (2003).

[2] This chapter is based on my field research in China and Japan (2003–4, 2012–13, and follow-up research in summers). During my field research in Asia, I worked with Japanese lawyers representing Chinese war victims *pro bono* in their lawsuits against the Japanese government and corporations. I observed weekly court proceedings of various postwar compensation trials; participated in meetings with lawyers, plaintiffs, and civic support groups; accompanied the lawyers on investigative trips to China; and participated in the activities of victim groups in China. Since I speak both Japanese and Chinese and have formal training in law and experience living in Northeast China (where many victims were from), I ended up playing the role of interpreter and mediator among Chinese victims, Japanese and Chinese lawyers and citizen supporters, and media. During my year-long field research in 2012–13, I was affiliated with the People's Law Office in Tokyo, where I had access to the relevant legal documents and ample opportunities to discuss the cases with the lawyers involved on a daily basis. In some cases in the text I have altered the names and identifying details of individuals to protect their identity.

[3] In China, these lawsuits are often referred to as "compensation lawsuits against Japan" (*dui Ri suopeisusong*).

range from the wartime use of forced labor (abduction of male Chinese to be enslaved in Japan), the so-called "comfort women" (victims of wartime sexual slavery), the 1932 Pingdongshan and 1937 Nanjing Massacres, and air raids, to human experiments for biological and chemical warfare perpetrated by Japanese Army Unit 731. Four landmark rulings by the Supreme Court of Japan in 2007 rejecting the compensation claims filed by the former comfort women and survivors of wartime forced labor came to mark the end of an era for the decades-long legal redress movements.[4] Analyses of these lawsuits, predominantly by legal scholars, primarily make normative claims accusing the Japanese government and corporations of irresponsibility and thus shift the discussion of these cases to the realm of political will, leaving the law and legal space themselves underexplored.[5] Furthermore, by focusing on the intersection of law and politics, these legal analyses often leave out exploring the intersection of law and economy, which I argue is the crux of the incomplete project of the unmaking of empire.

This chapter explores this post-imperial legal space and examines the place and role of law within it. The first section, "Before the Law," ethnographically sketches the emergence of a particular kind of *transnational legal space* for historical redress through a transnational legal redress movement that was propelled by the underlying moral and financial debts arising from the lack of accountability for Japan's imperial violence. We shall see how Chinese plaintiffs crossed their own jurisdiction and came to stand before the Japanese law. The second section, "Between the Law," explores this legal space by examining the three primary arguments developed over more than a decade of legal processes. I demonstrate how the deployment of these legal doctrines effectively created a legal lacuna, which positioned the plaintiff not *before the law*, as they had expected, but *between the law*, by declaring the Law's irrelevance in belatedly accounting for historical violence.

I argue that this legal lacuna points to two significant but underexplored areas in unmaking of empire in the legal sphere. In the first, the legal lacuna highlights the persistently imperial nature, albeit in a

---

[4] Heisei 16 (ju) No. 1658 (forced labor case) and Heisei 17 (ju) No. 1735 (comfort women case). On the basis of these rulings, the Supreme Court dismissed the appeals of other cases on the same day (Heisei 17 [o] No. 985 [comfort women case], Heisei 14 [ne] No. 511 and Heisei 8 [wa] No. 5435 [forced labor case]).

[5] See, e.g., Askin (2001), Shin (2005), Gao (2007), and Levin (2008).

disguised form, of the post-imperial Japanese legal framework after Japan's "rebirth" as a democratic state, raising the question of what happens to the legal landscape when the empire disappears. At stake here is the assumed radical discontinuity between the imperial and post-imperial Japanese legal systems, which is often oddly absent from otherwise robust debates about latent continuity in political and cultural spheres due, in part, to the symbolic status that the postwar Japanese Constitution (the so-called Peace Constitution) holds not only in Japan, but also elsewhere in Asia. In the second, the legal lacuna points to an underexplored absence of law in addressing deimperialization within the legal sphere. I explore this simultaneous persistence and absence of law, the revelation of which itself is integral to the belated efforts to redress the past. Through the optic of *between the law*, this chapter elucidates *post-imperial legal space* as an underexplored aspect of transitional justice.[6] I demonstrate how, at the intersection of law and economy, post-imperial reckoning is emerging as a new legal frontier, putting at stake what I call *law's imperial amnesia*, produced through the erasure of former colonial and imperial subjects within the postwar legal framework.

BEFORE THE LAW

(For)given Time
In his parable "Before the Law," Franz Kafka ([1924] 1988: 213–15) describes a countryman in front of the gate of Law, which is guarded by a doorkeeper. Despite the countryman's repeated plea to enter the gate to stand before the Law, the doorkeeper suggests the difficulty in reaching the Law and answers the plea by telling him, "Not yet." Time passes by, and the aged and weakened countryman eventually dies at the foot of the doorkeeper without ever going through the gate of Law. Whereas Kafka's story is silent about how the countryman arrived *before* the gate

---

[6] The post-imperial transition is an underexplored area of inquiry within the rich literature on transitional justice. In the East Asian context, the tectonic shift that took place in the region in 1945 with the demise of the Japanese empire is often framed within the rubric of postwar transition, with a focus on war tribunals as the primary sites of transitional justice. This chapter builds on recent works that challenge this framework of postwar transition and instead locates post-imperial transitional justice within the larger process of the unmaking of the Japanese empire within East Asia. See, e.g., Asano (2013), Hahm and Kim (2015), Kushner (2015), and Yoneyama (2016).

of Law, it is important not to underestimate the enormous efforts and historical constellation that brought Chinese victims before the Law in the 1990s.

As I have demonstrated elsewhere (Koga 2016b), the diplomatic framework that I call *(for)given time*, in which the Chinese government renounced its reparation claims against Japan in exchange for economic cooperation in the 1972 Joint Communiqué that established their diplomatic relations after twenty-seven Cold War years, privileged wealth accumulation over repayment of moral and financial debts to the victims of Japanese imperial violence. By renouncing reparation claims, which the Japanese side feared that the Chinese would demand, the Chinese government in effect gave a "gift" to Japan. Instead of reparations, the new Sino-Japanese relations centered on Japan's Official Development Assistance (ODA) to China, at a time when other countries were reluctant to invest in China, which was just beginning to recover from the turmoil of the Cultural Revolution. But the Japanese ODA was never declared the replacement for war reparations, and the "gift" from China came with the expectation that Japan not revert to its imperialist past. As anthropological studies have shown, a gift demands reciprocity, and thereby becomes a debt to be repaid (Mauss [1924] 1990). In 1972, the Japanese received a gift – China's renunciation of war reparation claims – and in turn incurred a debt that they would find difficult to repay, since it was measured in their attitude toward the past rather than in currency or concrete demands. The 1972 agreement gave the Japanese not forgiveness but the gift of time to repay this moral debt. It is this *(for)given time* that set the stage for the new phase in Sino-Japanese relations against the background of unpaid compensation for the victims: the robust development of the formal economy, initially through Japanese ODA, which started in 1979, and increasingly through Japan's direct investment in China.

The complicity of the Chinese state in privileging formal economy over moral economy has expressed itself in small and large gestures, ranging from their reluctance to support the victim initiatives to seek redress, to outright intimidation of those involved in the legal redress movement, to the judicial refusal to accept lawsuits by its own citizens. Since 2000, the Chinese courts in various provinces had refused to accept the past five attempts by the victims to file compensation lawsuits until a notable shift took place in February 2014, when the Beijing No. 1 Intermediate People's Court decided to accept a forced labor case, to which I will return later.[7] In one of these five cases, involving a prominent Japanese corporation, after the court refused to accept the case the lead Chinese lawyer and the leading figures among the plaintiffs were browbeaten by a high-ranking local government official, who expressed strong concerns that such a lawsuit would jeopardize ongoing negotiations with this corporation looking to invest in the region.

My use of parenthesis in *(for)given time* expresses this ambiguous location of moral debt, which the Chinese state has used as a political leverage for both domestic and diplomatic maneuvering. *(For) given time* is a temporal framework produced through the Japanese and Chinese governments' shared project of deferring the pursuit of redress while seeking wealth accumulation. Structurally it is a silencing mechanism that forced many Chinese victims to maintain their long years of silence.

Yet, at the same time, *(for)given time* functions as a reminder of the gift relations and attendant moral debt that have fueled the redress movements in China and Japan.[8] While a full analysis of the emergence of these legal redress movements requires a separate essay, their genesis highlights how these simultaneous movements opened up a *transnational legal space* for redressing Japan's imperial violence. The following montages of various participants will give you a sense of what it took for disparate sentiments – deep-seated anger, hope, and responsibility – and global contexts to collide in order to create the historical constellation that brought Chinese victims before the law.

THE SURVIVOR

When I visited one survivor of wartime forced labor, seventy-eight-year-old Li Guoqiang, in his modest, lower-middle-class apartment on the outskirts of Beijing in 2008, he had just come back from a trip to Chengdu, in central China, where he and fellow survivors were guests of honor at the Jianchuan Museum, a privately run cluster of museums

---

[7] These compensation lawsuits were submitted to Hebei High Court on December 27, 2000 (forced-labor case), Zhejiang High Court on May 12, 2003 (biological-warfare case), Shanghai High Court on September 5, 2003 (forced-labor case), Shandong High Court on September 16, 2010 (forced-labor case), and Chongqing High Court on September 10, 2012 (air-raid case).

[8] Elsewhere I have explored more in detail the relationship between formal and moral economies in relation to *(for)given* time, and examined how the unpaid moral and financial debts drove silence into redress movements (Koga 2013).

established in 2004 by a local millionaire. Li is among the few surviving members of the roughly 40,000 Chinese men who were abducted and forcibly brought to Japan in the 1940s to be enslaved, mostly in mines, factories, and shipyards. Subjected to brutal labor conditions, only about 32,000 survived to see the Japanese defeat in 1945.[9] While offering me watermelon to cool off from the heat of a nearly three-hour journey from the center of Beijing to his home, he proudly showed me pictures of the trip to the museum.

One picture captured the moment when the museum staff took imprints of the ailing men's hands to be set into the pavement of the museum plaza, among life-size statues of revolutionary heroes of modern Chinese history and significant political figures in the Chinese Communist Party (CCP). "We are also part of China's history," Li proudly declared, while showing me a picture of the group standing among the statues. The weight of his utterance "We are also part of China's history" only became clear to me later, when he finished recounting his wartime ordeal in Japan and his thoughts drifted back to his life in China after repatriation.

He invited me to his bedroom-turned-study, which was filled with books. While proudly showing me his large collection of books on the Japanese invasion of China, Li explained, "I left my family, my wife, and six children, to learn why China was invaded by Japan, and why I almost died three times in Japan during the war." In his thick accent, he recounted how, after repatriation to civil-war-torn China, he was first recruited by the Kuomindang army and then eventually made his way to the Chinese Communist People's Liberation Army, in which he built a career and earned numerous medals for his outstanding service. But, then, in the early 1950s, he was cast out of the Liberation Army, suspected of having been a spy because of his wartime experience in Japan and because he had been repatriated to China on a US ship after the Japanese defeat.[10] With nowhere else to go, he returned to his village to become a farmer. Li explained to me why he remained silent

---

[9] For an overview of the mobilization of Chinese forced laborers, see Nishinarita (2002) and He (2005). In English, see Kratoska (2005).

[10] Both the Japanese government and the Supreme Commander of the Allied Powers (which occupied Japan after the Second World War, from 1945 to 1952) had growing concerns about the labor movements emerging as a result of coalitions between the Chinese, particularly CCP members, and the Japanese laborers in occupied Japan. It became in their respective interests to repatriate the Chinese, which took place from October 9 to December 11, 1945.

about his wartime experience: "My wife didn't want me to tell my wartime story to our children for fear of harming them. I hadn't told my story to anybody else until the Japanese lawyers contacted me in the 1990s to file a lawsuit. It was only after being contacted by the Japanese lawyers that I learned about other survivors of the wartime forced labor now living in Beijing."

Li appreciated that the new historical museum in Chengdu recognized his and fellow forced laborers' wartime ordeals as an integral part of China's national history, that their sacrifice was recognized as part of communist nation-building. His elation, captured in the group pictures taken at the museum, also underscores the postwar silencing that took place not only in Japan but in China as well. The Jianchuan Museum is the only historical museum in China to date that devotes a section to wartime forced labor, although the memorial in Tianjin Martyr Cemetery on the outskirts of Tianjin enshrines the repatriated remains of forced laborers who perished in Japan. The legal process not only made the survivors' voices audible, but also brought this silencing mechanism to the fore.

Li and others like him had to travel a long road before they became the face of Chinese suffering under Japanese imperialist aggression in China. Various factors had to align before these gray-haired victims could stand in front of Japanese judges. What prompted Li to break his silence, he recounted to me as we sat for lunch at a restaurant in Beijing in 2013, was a Chinese media report about emergent historical revisionism in Japan: "I felt the need to take action in the face of Japan's unwillingness to repent. The media reported the Japanese history textbook censorship, which forced the textbook author to remove his descriptions of the Japanese invasion of China. Seeing how the Japanese didn't acknowledge what they did in China forced me to change my mind about keeping my silence." Li first went to the Japanese Embassy in Beijing, but the young Chinese guard did not let him in. But as soon as Li showed the guard his ID indicating his retirement status from the People's Liberation Army, the guard became extremely

---

As I discuss later in this chapter, hurried repatriation of Chinese was followed by what I call "inverted compensation," in which the involved Japanese corporations received large sums of compensation from the Japanese government in 1946 against the background of unpaid wages to the victims, who were shipped back to civil war-torn China without a penny. This took place during the US occupation of Japan following the Japanese defeat, indicating tacit US approval at the advent of the Cold War.

polite. The guard then told Li to ask for help at the local municipal government, who, in turn, suggested that Li seek out GengZhun, the former leader of the forced labor uprising, known as Hanaoka Uprising, which took place in one of the mines a few months before the Japanese defeat in 1945.[11] Although GengZhun had told him upon meeting him, "Don't even think about filing a lawsuit, it'll be difficult (*Bu yao da, buhao da*)," Li could not let it go. After he returned to Beijing, Li saw a television news report on Zhang Jian, a Chinese lawyer working with a group of Japanese lawyers on behalf of several former comfort women to file lawsuits in Japan. This media reporting prompted him to contact Zhang Jian, to whom he expressed his desire to file a lawsuit. "The bottom line is," Li punctuated his recounting, "every time that our government negotiated with Japan, they didn't bring up the issue of reparations in favor of getting trade deals from Japan."

THE CHINESE LAWYERS

Chinese lawyer Zhang Jian was drawn into the legal redress movement through a chance encounter with one of the Japanese lawyers at the 1995 Fourth World Conference on Women in Beijing. When Morita Noriko, a veteran female Japanese lawyer, contacted her after the conference to work with a group of Japanese lawyers to file lawsuits in Japan on behalf of victims of sexual slavery by the Japanese Army, Zhang was taken by surprise. She had never heard of comfort women, she told me in her modest law office in Beijing in spring 2013. While she usually maintains a cool composure, her eyes sparkled and her voice became animated as she started to recount her early days of getting involved in the lawsuits. "I couldn't help asking why these Japanese lawyers were starting these lawsuits on behalf of Chinese victims, I mean, as Japanese," Zhang shook her head laughing and continued, "I was skeptical of their motives, you know." "But then, after reading the legal document submitted to the court, I realized that these Japanese were serious and conscientious. They'd put so much effort into studying the issue. I came to realize that for these Japanese lawyers, working for Chinese victims *pro bono* is a way of redeeming their own nation. I came to understand that they were the real patriots." Zhang thus agreed to help the Japanese lawyers' ambitious, if not "reckless" project (as many colleagues of the Japanese lawyers described it, well

[11] On the Hanaoka Uprising, see Seraphim (2015).

aware of the tremendous difficulty ahead, both legally and politically), by identifying some former comfort women to get their stories. "I told them that there was no problem working with them *pro bono* because I thought it would be easy," Zhang laughed again, and pulled out photo albums from her field trips to rural Chinese villages in the mid-1990s. "It was really hard for a city girl like me. For me, it was a discovery of rural China. Going hours and hours on a cart pulled by a horse on unpaved roads in this dry, mountainous landscape to find a level of poverty never seen before … And the stories these women told me. They were nothing like the stories recounted in the legal document. They didn't tell the Japanese lawyers their whole stories. I was in shock."

THE CHINESE ACTIVIST

In the early 1990s the Chinese media started to pick up on sentiments like those of Li. Tong Zeng, a young legal scholar who holds a Masters' degree from Beijing University, wrote an essay in 1990 entitled "China should not wait to seek compensation from Japan," suggesting a possibility for ordinary individuals to pursue compensation by separating the reparation issue between states from the compensation issue for individuals. Tong later wrote another essay entitled "New concept in international law: victim compensation" in *Fazhiribao [Legal daily]* (Beijing) (Tong 1991), which was then reprinted in various other newspapers in China.

While he was studying economic law at Beijing University between 1986 and 1989, Tong was mesmerized by various global tectonic shifts – the fall of the Soviet Union, the unification of Germany, and the end of the Cold War. Hearing about how former Eastern Bloc countries such as Poland were seeking compensation from Russia, Tong started to look into the issue of compensation, which resulted in the aforementioned essay. After this essay was reprinted in various other newspapers, an avalanche of letters from victims or victims' bereaved families started to arrive. Many letters were simply addressed to "Tong Zeng, legal scholar in Beijing." He keeps the more than 10,000 letters that made it to him in cardboard boxes. When I visited him in his sleek office in spring 2013, he pulled out some of these boxes for me. Many letters were written with such intense force that the subsequent sheets of paper had imprints. Many letter writers recounted their sufferings in details over many pages. And many came from bereaved family members written on work-unit letterheads from all around China. The time was ripe, it seemed, for their voices to come out.

But when more than 10,000 victims and their family members showed up in front of the Japanese embassy in Beijing in 1993, the Chinese government started to put pressure to suppress this emerging movement. Tong was followed by the Public Security Bureau police. When Hayashi Toshitaka, one of the lead Japanese lawyers visited Beijing to meet Tong, the police watched over their meeting and the assembled victims were sent away. The second time around, Tong managed to introduce one of the victims to Hayashi by arranging a secret meeting in the basement of a hotel. While leafing through scrapbooks containing newspaper articles reporting on his activities, Tong recounted his involvement at that time:

> When I wrote the essay in 1991, I originally thought of it as an intellectual exercise and that was it – I didn't think about anything beyond it. But then after receiving more than ten thousand letters, I started to feel responsibility. Chinese courts at that time were not open (*bukaifang*) and didn't accept victims' claims. While it is undeniable that these compensation lawsuits filed in Japan would never have happened without the Japanese lawyers' initiatives, these thousands of letters demonstrated that the lawsuits in Japan were based on real demands from the Chinese. And until I received these letters, the predominant sentiments in China had been all about "friendship with Japan!". But these voices demanding justice, which became public through these letters, shifted the sentiments, I think.

The Chinese government saw these growing sentiments as potential political threats, and they exerted pressure large and small on victims as well as their supporters, such as Tong, to curtail or abandon their efforts.

THE JAPANESE LAWYERS

Many plaintiffs in the compensation lawsuits shared with me how until very recently they had received various forms of threats from the Chinese authorities, so much so that they felt the need to change their cell phone numbers frequently. Yet the Japanese lawyers, unaware of the tense and suppressive atmosphere in China in response to growing public sentiments for seeking redress, were upbeat. They were driven to represent Chinese victims by a newly discovered urge to redeem Japan as well as their own professionalism through their *pro bono* work. These were elite and highly accomplished lawyers, who, one way or another, came to the shockingly embarrassing recognition that, despite their famed career as human rights lawyers, they had never given any thought to one of the most gruesome and systematic forms of injustice – Japan's imperial violence.

It started with a chance encounter with a prominent Japanese lawyer Hayashi Toshitaka, who was visiting Beijing in 1994 as part of a Japanese delegation of lawyers to participate in a conference. The meeting was set up by the Chinese Academy of Social Sciences in order to promote interactions among Chinese and Japanese lawyers. During their stay in Beijing and only a few days after their emotional visit to the Nanjing Massacre Museum, the Japanese lawyers heard the media reports on the public remarks made by the newly appointed Japanese Minister of Justice, Nagano Shigeto, at a press conference on May 6, 1994. Minister Nagano expressed his view that "the Nanjing Massacre is made up" and that it was a mistake to consider the Asia-Pacific War as invasion. He instead claimed that the war was a liberation of colonized countries.[12] Nagano's remarks triggered fierce responses in China. The Japanese lawyers' delegation in Beijing delivered a statement to the Chinese media, expressing their protest against the Justice Minister's remarks. At this occasion, Hayashi was confronted by a Japanese journalist, who had been stationed in Beijing and who had been following the growing public sentiments to seek belated redress, as to why he had never considered taking up a compensation case on behalf of Chinese war victims. This was, as Hayashi put it, "a slap in my face. His challenging words totally shattered my confidence and sense of achievement as a human rights lawyer with several landmark cases under my belt."

One by one, Japanese lawyers were drawn into this mission, on the one hand to seek belated compensation and official apology for the Chinese victims, and on the other to re-present historical facts to the public to remedy the pervasive historical amnesia within Japanese society that the lawyers saw as the source of Japanese inability to come to terms with its own imperialist past. Tanaka Makio, a passionate, articulate lawyer and a man of action, explained to a group of Chinese victims how he felt the need to repay the debt that he had inherited from his parents' generation:

> When I started working as a lawyer many years ago, I was not interested in Japan's imperial past. But the news about the discovery of human

---

[12] Justice Minister Nagano was forced to resign within eleven days of his appointment as a result of these remarks.

remains [which many suspected belonged to victims of wartime human experiments] at the former site of the Japanese Army Medical College near Shinjuku [a downtown Tokyo skyscraper area] led me to start interviewing the surviving families of the victims of human biological experiments at the Japanese Imperial Army Unit 731 in Harbin [in Northeast China; the unit was the headquarters of the Japanese Imperial Army's biochemical development units], which shocked me tremendously. Since then, I have strongly felt the weight of perpetration (*kagai no omosa*). As the postwar generation, we inherit the burden of the past. This is my lifework, and I cannot simply consign these events to the past.

The "Chinese postwar compensation lawyers team" was thus formed in August 1995 on the occasion of the fiftieth anniversary of the Japanese defeat in the Second World War.[13] Since its official inception, the Japanese lawyers' team has grown to nearly 300 members. How this lawyers' movement emerged reflects a larger historical context – China's transition to a market-oriented economy, the end of the Cold War, and Japanese society's revisionist swing, to name a few – that aligned the sentiments of varying actors involved in these transnational legal redress movements. All in all, the actors involved felt the need to challenge *(for)given time* and the underlying economy of debt that their respective governments had set as their organizing principle for dealing with the contested pasts stemming from the Japanese imperial violence in China.

THE WITNESS

When Wang Aimei, one of the first former comfort women that the Chinese lawyer Zhang Jian contacted, went to Japan as a witness, she was terrified at both the idea of going to Japan and of testifying in court. Zhang related to me how she was quite shocked when she first visited Wang in rural Shanxi Province in 1996. The story Wang told Zhang about her wartime experience – a story that she had never shared with her own family and that she had asked Zhang to keep secret from them – was much more brutal than what Zhang had read in the legal document prepared by the Japanese lawyers. Asked why she had not told the full story to the Japanese lawyers, Wang told Zhang, "If I tell the Japanese too much, they would kill me, wouldn't they?" She had never left her

---

[13] The lawyers team published a book illustrating their engagement with the lawsuits (see Chūgokujin sensō higai baishō seikyū jiken bengodan 2005).

remote village before, but she, along with three other women, became one of the first women to testify in the Japanese court.

The distrust of the Japanese was so strong that one plaintiff had to deceive her son to get her passport to make the trip to Japan. Her son was afraid that the Japanese would kill his mother if she appeared in court. Testifying in court on only the third day of their arrival in Japan was torturous for these women, and Zhang was concerned about them: "They were in so much pain testifying in court and they were under such distress that I seriously worried that they might fall apart," Zhang recalled. Yet, by the time they were about to leave Japan, Wang whispered to Zhang: "There are good Japanese, actually. They are different from Japanese devils (*Ribenguizi*, a Chinese term often used to describe Japanese during and after the war)."

What Wang Aimei probably did not quite realize, when she waved at the assembled Japanese citizen supporters with a big smile at Narita airport on her way back to China, is how her courageous trip opened up a new legal space for other victims to follow.[14] Out of the series of postwar compensation lawsuits emerged a *transnational legal space*, where Chinese victims came to attain a form of *transnational legal agency* to seek belated justice for the deaths and injuries inflicted by the Japanese government and corporations in Japanese courts. The countryman in Kafka's "Before the Law" never gained the courage to go through the gate of Law; we as readers never know what kind of legal space awaited the man. The man was, temporally, before the Law, but never spatially before the Law. In contrast, our protagonists from China now finally stood before the law.

BETWEEN THE LAW

What I am calling *transnational legal space* entitles plaintiffs to full participation in legal performances in courts, yet simultaneously subjects them to the law's absence as they enter the gate of Law to account for Japan's imperial violence, which is at once both transnational and irreducibly local. What is described in Kafka's "Before the Law" assumes spatial and temporal homogeneity within unspecified time and place in the manner of a fable. Chinese plaintiffs standing before Japanese

---

[14] The term "accidental activists," which Arrington (2016) uses to describe the development of legal activism in the Hansen's disease cases as well as the cases involving the hepatitis C-tainted blood products in South Korea and Japan, is apt here.

judges, however, negotiate a much more complex and heterogeneous temporality and spatiality. An exploration of this emergent transnational legal space tells a story of those who actually enter the gate but find themselves *between the law*, where Law remains as elusive as Kafka's "Before the Law" to account for the past violence.

The compensation cases filed by Chinese victims take place within a space of fundamental disjuncture between law and society: the plaintiffs' society (China) is not governed by the law under which their claims are judged (Japan). They are appealing to the legal system of the country that originally inflicted violence against them. Added to this geographical disjuncture in jurisdiction is the legal standing of individuals under what is loosely termed "international law" – international legal agency of individuals – which remains a disputed point among legal scholars. Plaintiffs' claims based on Article 3 of The Hague Convention of 1907, which sets out compensation liability for wartime damage, were all rejected in the various Japanese courts, based on the argument that this article is not meant for defining individual rights. Put simply, the courts have repeatedly refused to engage international law by denying the international legal agency of individuals. Instead, the legal discussion primarily revolved around the deployment of codified Japanese law (Civil Code).

This situation has led to the emergence of what I call *transnational legal agency* and *transnational legal space*, not as neutral and homogeneous in-betweenness, but as an embodiment of geographical and temporal disjuncture, rupture, and asymmetry that reflect the historical constellation of the region. Transnational legal *agency* emerges from crossing over one's own jurisdiction to stand before another, in order to make transnational claims. A particular form of transnational legal *space* emerges out of the necessity to juridify transnational claims using a domestic legal system.[15] The makeshift nature of this legal space itself indicates how the unmaking of empire in the legal sphere through legal redress for imperial violence appears as an afterthought. Or was it part of the original plan not to address such issues within the legal sphere?

---

[15] The transnational legal space that this chapter analyzes points to dynamics different from those discussed under the rubric of "transnational law." The starting point of the discussion on transnational law is the absence of what is traditionally considered "law," as Roger Cotterrell's concise overview of the literature sums up (2012). In contrast, the series of compensation lawsuits analyzed in this chapter starts with a public recognition of the presence of codified law, which, as the legal process makes visible, is not as firmly engraved in stone as it may initially appear.

In order to answer this question, we shall first look at how this legal space emerges as an uncharted legal frontier and examine the place of law within this space.

Since the Japanese legal system does not allow class action lawsuits, these postwar compensation lawsuits have taken place in a series of localized and simultaneous cases across Japan, with varying results. But all those involved in these cases – Chinese plaintiffs, lawyers, the Japanese government and corporations, the judges, and citizen supporters – saw these cases as a linked whole that addresses historical responsibility for Japan's imperial violence. Looking at the series of compensation lawsuits as a whole, therefore, gives us a better sense of how the legal redress processes developed over two decades and what kind of role that law played.

THREE LEGAL DOCTRINES AND THE LEGAL LACUNA

Hayashi Toshitaka, the Japanese lawyer whose chance encounter in Beijing set in motion the legal redress movement across national boundaries, recounted to me in May 2004 how "reckless" the whole idea of starting lawsuits like theirs seemed at the time:

> If you are not an insane lawyer, you wouldn't join lawsuits like these postwar compensation lawsuits. Lawyers' common sense tells you that there is no way of winning cases like these. I contacted many of my colleagues – all highly accomplished and with a strong sense of pursuing justice – and they looked at me like I'm insane. All of them immediately pointed out the impossibility of breaking the twin legal barriers of the statute of limitations and the sovereign immunity doctrines, with which I concurred. You know the article 724 of Civil Code, which defines the twenty-year statute of limitations. When we filed the first lawsuit in 1995, fifty years had already passed since the end of Japanese empire in 1945.[16] And the sovereign immunity doctrine. The Imperial Constitution of Japan [prewar constitution] exempted the Japanese state from taking responsibility for exercise of state power, and we were dealing with state violence that officially ended in 1945. We were really reckless, if you think about it. But, then, we were much younger, you know, and we felt that we had nothing to lose by being creative and

---

[16] Due to the lack of diplomatic relations between the PRC and Japan until 1972, individual Chinese were not allowed to travel to Japan until 1979. And even after 1979, for most plaintiffs, who are mostly impoverished and illiterate farmers in rural China, filing a lawsuit in Japan was beyond their means and imagination.

thinking outside of box. And we felt like we were stepping into the legal frontier.

Legal frontier it was. The Cold War and other historical factors, including *(for)given time* between China and Japan, had effectively prevented postwar compensation lawsuits from taking place earlier. Legal redress for individuals that should have happened immediately after the demise of the Japanese Empire in 1945 (thus avoiding expiration of the statute of limitations) was deferred for fifty-Cold War years. Just as many frontier studies reveal the manufactured nature of "frontiers," the legal frontier that the Japanese lawyers saw in front of them was thus a product of the post-1945 world – it became a frontier when the long-deferred attempts to account for historical responsibility emerged in the 1990s as a belated project of the unmaking of empire in the legal sphere.

The three legal doctrines deployed over the course of two decades that the plaintiffs' lawyers recognized as legal frontiers – expiration of the statute of limitations, sovereign immunity, and the rejection of individual legal rights to claim compensation – denied the Chinese plaintiffs' claims in succession. These legal developments have effectively presented a legal lacuna, where the plaintiffs found themselves not *before the law*, as they had expected, but *between the law*, an extralegal space devoid of law.[17] It is to this lacuna that we now turn.

THE FIRST LEGAL FRONTIER: THE STATUTE OF LIMITATIONS

In the majority of cases relating to Chinese victims, the court deployed the statute of limitations to deny the Chinese plaintiffs' legal standing. The plaintiffs were perplexed by the temporal space of exception, which denied them the benefit of the law's blessing. It is ironic that many plaintiffs expected the law's ability to deliver justice, since, as many put it, they were in "a society with the rule of law (i.e. Japan), unlike ours here in China."[18]

---

[17] While the seemingly makeshift nature of the transnational legal space created through the postwar compensation cases and the legal lacuna that the legal process produced may at first glance resemble what Fleur Johns calls "non-legality in international law" (Johns 2013), the legal space that has emerged through the redress movement points to different dynamics, as we shall see.

[18] These comments reflect many Chinese plaintiffs' perception of the Japanese court as "a utopic institutional site" (Comaroff and Comaroff 2006: 33), in contrast to their perception of their own society.

Yet the development of the lawsuits resulted in turning this temporal barrier upside down by effectively extending the temporal scope of what counts as violence inflicted by the Japanese. The lawsuits brought to the fore not only violence and injustice during wartime, but also in the postwar era. In the landmark Fukuoka Regional Court decision in 2002 on the forced labor case,[19] the dramatic courtroom disclosure of the supposedly destroyed Japanese government archives (Gaimushōkanrikyoku 1946a, b) revealed what I call the "inverted compensation": In 1946, the Japanese corporations that enslaved the Chinese received large sums of compensation from the Japanese government for the "losses" incurred through the wartime use and postwar loss of Chinese labor. The Japanese government allocated compensation to 135 corporate offices, which amounted to approximately 57 million Japanese yen. Through this *inverted compensation*, the involved corporations were rewarded against the background of unpaid wages to the victims, who were shipped back to civil war-torn China without a penny. This revelation was followed by another courtroom disclosure of the Japanese government archives (Gaimushōkanrikyoku 1952–72), which document Japanese government's decades of active involvement in concealing this wartime practice. The courtroom revelation was a vivid illustration of injustice inflicted *after* the demise of the Japanese Empire.[20]

The statute of limitations rests on the notion of radical discontinuity, which equates the end of injury with the end of original violence. The story of inverted compensation posed a sharp critique of this assumption by demonstrating the persistent *and* new forms of injury brought by systematic injustice *after* the Japanese defeat and the demise of the Japanese Empire. The courtroom discussion around the statute of limitations thus came to highlight the question of *postimperial* responsibility by shifting the focus from wartime violence to postimperial injustice. The case thus raises a new set of questions: Where and when do violence and injustice actually end? Where and when does injury from violence end?

By shifting the terms of debate to consider such questions, the courts' deployment of the statute of limitations – meant to limit the temporal

---

[19] Heisei 12 (wa) No. 1550; Heisei 13 (wa) No. 1690; Heisei 13 (wa) No. 3862, April 26, 2002.

[20] On the inverted compensation and the courtroom drama surrounding the disclosed Japanese government archives, see Koga (2016a).

scope of the law's applicability – ironically resulted in expanding the temporal scope of accountability to encompass the post-1945 actions and inactions of the Japanese government and corporations. Indeed, winning cases for the plaintiffs came through a detailed accounting of postimperial violence and injury. In several forced labor cases, the courts ruled that the deployment of the statute of limitations is "against the principle of justice and fairness." The 2002 Fukuoka Regional Court decision made this point crystal clear and brought a winning ruling for the plaintiffs against Mitsui Corporation. Yet even in this landmark case, which broke the legal barrier of the statute of limitations, the judges continued to deny the legal responsibility of the Japanese state by using the second doctrine, that of sovereign immunity.

THE SECOND LEGAL FRONTIER: SOVEREIGN IMMUNITY

"Ghostly" is how many Japanese lawyers involved in the postwar compensation cases often describe the doctrine of sovereign immunity. They liken the deployment of this doctrine to the apparition of prewar imperial Japan. What the deployment of sovereign immunity does in effect is to declare the present Japanese Constitution irrelevant for deciding the cases because the cases involve actions that took place under the 1899 Meiji Imperial Constitution of Japan. The plaintiffs had thought that they were standing before the law of the present, yet they found themselves standing before the law that no longer exists. Under this doctrine, a legal void is created through the declaration of the law's absence (the current Japanese "Peace" Constitution) and apparitional presenting (the Imperial Constitution), leaving the Chinese plaintiffs between the two temporalities of prewar and postwar, raising questions about the assumed radical discontinuity between imperial and postimperial legal systems.

As the legal processes developed, however, it became clearer and clearer to the parties involved that somebody was doing the work of conjuring up the ghost: As the plaintiffs' lawyers dug deep into the historical literature on the prewar legal system, they discovered, to their surprise, that there was no codified legal foundation to this doctrine. Instead, a close reading of prewar legal practice actually showed that even the Imperial Japanese state did not enjoy automatic exemption from legal responsibility for state actions. They learned how, even under the Imperial Constitution, sovereign immunity became effective through precedents that conjured up the illusory image of the state devoid of accountability, without a codified legal basis, but often in response to political pressures.[21]

In a "good news, bad news" scenario, the 2004 Fukuoka High Court dramatically acknowledged in the forced labor case that the doctrine of sovereign immunity was a product of precedents without legal grounds, and declared that deployment of this doctrine went against "the principle of justice and fairness." Yet while this High Court decision overcame the second legal barrier, it simultaneously restored the first one, overturning the lower court decision (to demand that the Mitsui Corporation pay compensation) by deploying the statute of limitations.[22]

In effect, these two doctrines were deployed to create a legal space of exception in which the law becomes irrelevant by bringing to the fore the layers of temporal legal terrains, which destabilizes the presentness of law in the present.

THE THIRD LEGAL FRONTIER: INDIVIDUAL LEGAL RIGHT TO CLAIM COMPENSATION

In the last doctrine to be deployed, this time in the 2007 Supreme Court decision, the judges ruled that the plaintiffs lacked the legal right to claim compensation (*saiban-jōseikyūsurukinō wo ushinatta*, which literally means "lost the function to claim compensation through legal means") due to the 1972 Joint Communiqué in which the Chinese government renounced the right to claim reparations from Japan.[23] While standing before the Japanese law, this doctrine put the plaintiffs

---

[21] For detailed historical and legal analyses of the ghostly nature of sovereign immunity doctrine, see Matsumoto (2003) and Okada (2013).

[22] Fukuoka High Court ruling on May 24, 2004 (Heisei 14 [ne] No. 511). Judges Minoda Takayuki and Komatani Takao signed the judgment document, but Judge Fujimoto Hisatoshi did not sign due to his objection ("*sashitsukae no tame*") to the decision.

[23] Heisei 16 (ju) No. 1658. For an overview of the Supreme Court decision in English, see Levin (2008). While this Supreme Court decision concerned a forced-labor compensation case originally filed in Hiroshima, often referred to as the Nishimatsu case (as it involved Nishimatsu Construction Company), the Court used it as the basis for dismissing the appeals filed in the Fukuoka and other related cases on the same day.

in a transnational space between China and Japan, a space in the form of a legal void due to the agreement between the two governments.

What needs to be underlined, however, is that the court refused to recognize the plaintiffs' *legal* right to claim compensation, a detail often overlooked in commentaries on this landmark case. In order to understand the importance of this detail, we have to look into the supplementary paragraph (*fugen*) of the ruling. *Fugen*, or supplement, plays an interesting role within the Japanese legal lexicon. *Fugen* follows *shubun* (summary of the decision) and "facts and reasons" (the main argument of the ruling), often as a paragraph or two at the end of the ruling. The function of *fugen* is disputed among legal professionals. Some call it extra-legal, a nonintegral part of the decision and therefore not having the same legal effect as the preceding text. Some call it the essence of the conscience of the judges, which is expressed outside of the constraints of law. In either case, both views share an understanding that *fugen* is something external to the actual ruling, something that goes beyond the boundary of Law.

In *fugen* written for the forced labor case, the Supreme Court judges' deeply emotional and strong language emphasized the sufferings that the plaintiffs endured not only during the war but also over the ensuing years. They contrasted the plaintiffs' psychological and physical sufferings to the economic benefits that the defendant, Nishimatsu Construction Corporation, enjoyed through their wartime use of forced labor *and* through the inverted compensation they received from the Japanese government after the war ended. The judges further reminded the defendant and the Japanese government that the Chinese plaintiffs' lack of individual legal rights to claim compensation did not prohibit the Nishimatsu Corporation and the Japanese government from making their own voluntary arrangements for redress, and strongly encouraged them to make such efforts to provide compensation for the Chinese.[24]

Fugen, this extra-legal supplementary text, declares the Law's irrelevance for seeking redress. Yet in its extra-legal authority, the court strongly suggests that the moral and financial debt be paid back to the

---

[24] Of the Japanese corporations implicated in the lawsuits, Nishimatsu Construction was among the first to settle out of court. On September 23, 2009, Nishimatsu agreed to pay 250 million Japanese yen to 360 Chinese men who were enslaved at the Yasuno power plant in Hiroshima, and on April 26, 2010, to pay 128 million Japanese yen to 183 Chinese enslaved at the Shinanogawa power plant in Nīgata.

Chinese. The voices of the judges are tucked into this supplementary space between the law. In other words, the supplementary space is supposed to supplement or provide what the law itself cannot. Indeed, in creating this space, the judiciary declares itself incapable of providing justice through the law. Instead, yet again, Law defers the arrival of justice, this time by suggesting the appropriate sphere for its arrival is outside of Law.

When we began this section, it was the Chinese plaintiffs who stood before the law. Or so it seemed. As the legal processes progressed, we found these plaintiffs not *before the law* but *between the law*, as the successive deployment of legal doctrines made their legal standing questionable, and, in turn, made Law irrelevant to them. Temporal and geographical disjunctures, which effectively locate the plaintiffs between the imperial and postimperial Japanese legal systems and between the Chinese and Japanese jurisdictions, made the transnational legal space for individuals devoid of itself. At the end of the story, culminating in the 2007 Supreme Court decision, we realize that it was a story of how Law made itself irrelevant through various doctrinal measures. Law absented itself by declaring itself irrelevant to the case.

The gate of Law opened, it seemed, yet, as in Kafka's story, one gate led to another in succession, and in the end, Law did not seem present after all.[25] What does this legal lacuna indicate? The revelation of the *inverted compensation* underscores the unfinished project of unmaking of empire in the *economic* sphere by illuminating the underlying moral and financial debts to the victims. When Law perpetually defers justice in cases that confront this unfinished project, how are we to understand this legal development?

An answer, I suggest in the next and last section, lies in the moment of Japan's deimperialization in 1945 and the place of law at that historical juncture. As we shall see, this lacuna reflects a much less discussed moment back in history – the moment of the Japanese empire's demise in 1945 and the birth of a new legal framework that publicly announced Japan's rebirth as a democratic nation-state. Law's absence reveals the unfinished project of unmaking of empire within the *legal* sphere.

---

[25] My analysis of these legal doctrines in this section is inspired by Derrida (1992a), who, through his reading of Kafka's fable, points to the law's lack of presence in the here and now.

LAW'S FOUNDATIONAL VIOLENCE

Once again, we need to go back in time to the foundational moment of the 1946 Japanese Constitution, the symbol of Japan's rebirth as a democratic and peace-seeking nation devoid of its imperial ambition, commonly referred to in Japan as the Peace Constitution. The Preamble of the Japanese Constitution declares to the world in an idealistic and poetically powerful language that the Japanese people seek to establish themselves as "peace-seeking" people. The Constitution was written in the form of an official pronouncement of Japan's rebirth as a democratic and peace-seeking nation. In order to mark this new beginning as a radical departure from its imperialist past, Japanese society embraced the term "Japan's rebirth" along with the Japanese Constitution, which literally marks this rebirth through inscription. The most emblematic and championed text is Article 9, which many see as the symbol of Japan's deimperialization. In it, Japan renounces war as well as the possession and the use of military forces.

But there are other significant moments in the Constitution that squarely announce Japan's radical shift to a democratic society. Article 1 proclaims that the Japanese people are sovereign, not the Emperor, as was the case under the 1899 Imperial Constitution. To reinforce this point, Article 17 declares that the Japanese state is accountable to the people for state actions and that individuals can seek compensation for wrongful acts, which is a direct rejection of the imperial doctrine of sovereign immunity. The State Redress Act was enacted in 1947 to articulate this Article 17. The message that this Peace Constitution proclaims to the world is that Japanese society embraces the democratic ideal through the determination not to resort to another war while making the state accountable for its exercise of state power. It seemed as if nothing could be missing from this seemingly progressive new legal system.

Yet the legal lacuna, made visible through the successive deployment of the three legal doctrines, directs us to the foundational violence contained within the seemingly innocent pronouncement of "we, the Japanese people" in the newly adopted Peace Constitution. What is excluded through this pronouncement of "we, the Japanese people" are the former colonial and imperial subjects of Japanese Empire, who "disappeared" from the postwar Japanese legal consciousness. Japan's deimperialization in the legal sphere took the form of erasing the empire by the declaration of *kokumin* (Japanese people) as the holder of the subject position and by *abandoning* the former colonial and imperial subjects from the protection of the new democratic and peace-seeking legal system.[26] Yet this erasure, which took place during the drafting of the Peace Constitution (another instance of "before the law"),[27] leaves no trace within the Preamble. Despite the stated determination to seek peace spelled out poetically in the Preamble, any sense of repentance is located in the war experience of the Japanese people: "We, the Japanese people, ... resolved that never again shall we be visited with the horrors of war through the action of government." The oft-used phrase, "*postwar* Constitution" is apt here: the Peace Constitution was a post-*war* Constitution, not a post-*imperial* Constitution. The origin story of Japan's rebirth is thus silent about Japan's imperialist history. Moreover, in portraying the Japanese people as the passive recipient of "the horrors of the war," the Preamble evades the responsibility of the Japanese people while making the state solely accountable for the war. This historical amnesia – the silencing of its imperial violence – forms the foundational violence of the Japanese Constitution, which is championed as the embodiment of postwar peace and democracy.[28]

The abandonment of the former colonial and imperial subjects in the legal sphere – a fact that is often neglected, forgotten, or unspoken in the mainstream scholarship of the Japanese legal system – manifests itself today in the form of the legal lacuna, a transnational legal space

[26] A Japanese sociologist Eiji (1995) provides a sharp analysis of the creation of what he calls "the myth of a single ethnic nation" in postwar Japan. See also Kang (1996). From a legal perspective, see Gotō (2012, 2013), and Ōnuma (1986, 2004, 2007). For a detailed historical study of the movement of people and properties in the process of dissolving the Japanese empire and how such post-1945 arrangement shaped the reparation issues, see Asano (2013).

[27] The draft Constitution written by Government Section of the General Headquarters (GHQ) was completed and approved by General Douglas MacArthur on February 12, 1946. In this GHQ draft in English, the subject position was held by those referred to as "people," "person," and "all natural persons." Furthermore, Article XVI explicitly states the inclusion of foreign nationals under the legal protection by stating that "Aliens shall be entitled to the equal protection of law." Yet in the finalized version of the Constitution in Japanese, the subject position is reduced to "*kokumin*" (Japanese people) and no article is devoted to state the equal protection of foreign nationals spelled out in the GHQ draft Article XVI. For a concise analysis of this erasure in the process of drafting the Constitution of Japan, see Gotō (2012, 2013), Hahm and Kim (2015), and Koseki (1989).

[28] Jacques Derrida (1992b: 13–4) directs our attention to such amnesia embedded in the origin of law by pointing out how "a silence is walled up in the violent structure of the founding act."

of exception, where the victims stand *between the law*. Despite the nationwide obsession with Japan's wartime past (which often expresses itself in amnesic practices), the structure of justice in Japan is deeply embedded in the structure of erasure that I call *law's imperial amnesia*. This abandonment is inscribed even more explicitly in the 1947 State Redress Act, which symbolizes Japan's deimperialization alongside the Peace Constitution. The legal grounds for not recognizing the legal agency of the Chinese plaintiffs in various compensation lawsuits, for example, drew on Article 6 of the State Redress Act, which excludes foreigners from benefiting from this law unless their home countries offer reciprocal legal protection.[29] The court's use of this Article 6 in these cases sheds light on the oft-neglected inscription of exclusion.

The legal lacuna thus ironically points to this silent abandonment and erasure that took place at the moment of Japan's rebirth. The legal lacuna, which leaves the Chinese plaintiffs *between the law*, is thus not only created through the deployment of legal doctrines today. Rather, I argue, it also reflects postwar Japan's foundational violence, in which the unwillingness to provide a legal space to address Japan's imperial violence became inscribed as an integral part of the process of the unmaking of empire. This is what I call a *post-imperial legal space*, which is created through *law's imperial amnesia* – erasure of empire and imperial and colonial subjects in the post-imperial legal consciousness.

CONCLUSION

Law's Imperial Amnesia and the Persistence of Redress

The *post-imperial legal space* that I bring to light in this chapter directs our attention to a slightly different terrain than is explored through the concept of legal imperialism in such forms as the law's role in colonialism, American legal imperialism after the Second World War, or international law as an expression of legal imperialism of the West.[30] What I have highlighted instead is the foundational violence inscribed onto the radically new legal system: legal abandonment through the erasure of empire at the moment of its demise. This imperial amnesia manifests

---

[29] How this exclusionary clause entered into this law calls for further investigation, especially given the timing of its enactment in 1947, when Japan was under US occupation and the world saw the deepening of the Cold War.

[30] On legal imperialism, see, e.g., Gardner (1980), Schmidhauser (1992), Buchanan and Pahuja (2004), and Anghie (2004).

itself today as a legal lacuna, made visible through the deployment of legal doctrines. We have found in the compensation cases – the formal and belated process of the unmaking of empire in the legal sphere – a refusal to legally complete this long-deferred task of imperial reckoning.

Analytically, "between the law" is an optic that allows us to access the uneven terrain of legal space that embodies temporal and spatial disjuncture, rupture, and asymmetry, and, in doing so, to capture the role and place of law. In the compensation cases examined in this chapter, *between the law* elucidates the legal dynamics that defy the assumed presence of law by disclosing the etched erasure within it. We have seen how the legal process revealed the absence of law hidden behind the appearance of law. I have argued that this lacuna reflects the institutional memory of the legal abandonment of former colonial and imperial subjects after the demise of the Japanese empire. Lacuna is the sign and manifestation of this historical erasure, which is inscribed onto the existing codified law, but which nevertheless remains illegible to the public. This legal lacuna, then, captures the place of law different from that explored under the rubric of "transnational law" (where nontraditional "law" presides)[31] or "non-legality" (a legal vacuum that is often recognized as illegal or outside of the purview of law).[32] The discussion on transnational law or nonlegality revolves around the

---

[31] Echoing the conceptualization of "transnational law" laid out by Jessup (1956), Zumbansen (2008: 10–1) contends that transnational "law" emerges out of norm-generating mechanisms, broadly speaking. Zumbansen writes that "transnational law invites a fundamental reflection of what is to be considered *law*" (Zumbansen 2011: 3) For a concise overview of "transnational law," see Cotterrell (2012).

[32] Through the concept of "non-legality in international law," Johns (2013) explores places where international law is considered absent, and she shows that the seeming legal "vacuum" (which is often recognized as illegal or outside of law) is actually an integral part of international law. In contrast, law's presence is not only recognized, but also assumed within the transnational legal space that the compensation lawsuits filed by Chinese war victims have opened up, in the form of codified Japanese law. Yet, as my ethnographic analysis of the three doctrines deployed in these cases demonstrates, the plaintiffs found themselves standing *effectively* in the absence of law. The legal proceedings that I have examined in this chapter illustrate how the courtroom *became* a site for extra-legality as law declares itself absent or irrelevant *through* the legal proceedings.

As we have seen, law's absence only becomes visible through a careful reading of the legal proceedings. The secret of the foundational violence – law's refusal to deliver imperial reckoning to former colonial and imperial subjects – remains less visible and much less discussed even with these cases. To reduce the failed delivery of justice in these lawsuits to the lack of political will, as many commentaries on

question of how to recognize the seemingly law-less space as a legal space. In contrast, *between the law* makes visible the concealed absence of law, *despite* the assumed presence of law. In so doing, *between the law* points to the inscribed erasure within the law in the present.

Empirically, my ethnographic study has demonstrated a curious absence of law – or to put it more accurately, absenting of the law – despite the acknowledged presence of codified domestic Japanese law that is deployed within this emergent transnational legal space. I have shown how law absents itself through legal practices, and with what consequences.[33] The ethnographic reality of "between the law" as a product of legal practices directs us to the unfinished project of the unmaking of empire in the legal sphere at the intersection of law and economy. This is produced not by accident, deferral, or inertia but the *erasure* of empire from the post-imperial legal consciousness in East Asia in pursuit of postwar reconstruction, economic development, and wealth accumulation. The task of unmaking of empire within the legal sphere was framed within the concept of post-*war* while consciously erasing that of post-*imperial*.

The *postimperial legal space* explored in this chapter follows the dissolution of empire, and captures the process of the unmaking of empire in the legal sphere. I have crossed out "imperial" (post-~~imperial~~ legal space) to call attention to the imperial amnesia embedded in this legal space, captured through the concept of *between the law*. I have shown how the task of post-imperial reckoning was reduced to post-*war* reckoning of the Japanese within the Cold War framework. Post-~~imperial~~ legal space, then, points to the structural unwillingness within the legal domain to engage with imperial reckoning. Deimperialization – transition from an empire to a nation-state – is an essential part of the

---

these cases have done, misses this imperial amnesia that characterizes the postwar Japanese legal structure.
[33] As Merry (2006) maintains, an ethnographic analysis of the practice of law is crucial for capturing the presence and absence of law within this transnational legal space. As I have demonstrated ethnographically in this chapter, law's presence (and absence) emerges through the practice of law, not through the positivist understanding of law. The way in which I "read" the legal doctrines in the cases I study is also ethnographic, and I have presented these doctrines as an integral part of the theatrical performance within the courtroom. I shed light on the ethnographic realities of the heterogeneous legal space, where for some law remains absent as a result of the erasure of empire without accountability for its violence.

process of unmaking of empire, but this process has received less attention than its counterpart of decolonization.

The East Asian experience that I explored in this chapter brings to light the new dynamics emerging within this *post-imperial legal space*, which is not unique to East Asia. Postimperial legal redress remains an uncharted legal frontier, as seen in the 2013 British apology and compensation for the Kenyan victims in the Mau Mau Uprising following an historic legal victory for the victims in London's High Court, which spurred interests among the Caribbean nations to seek legal redress for slavery, or a more recent development in the US court in which Namibian victims of large-scale massacres committed by the Germans have filed a class action lawsuit in 2017 to demand reparations for Germany's colonial violence.[34] Yet there is a noticeable lack of analyses on how former imperialist nations have dealt with deimperialization within their respective legal framework within the literature on East Asia, postcolonial studies, or the legal literature on transitional justice, transnational law, or legal imperialism. The ghostly absence of post-imperial legal space within the transitional justice discourse is particularly telling of this glaring omission in our understanding of law's role in colonialism, imperialism, and globalization.[35] Post-imperial legal space remains a legal frontier both as practice as well as academic inquiry.

In this chapter, I have attempted to capture this deliberate and systematic legal lacuna in redressing imperial violence. The cases in East Asia present a particularly revealing form of post-imperial ethos in the legal sphere precisely because the Japanese legal system went through

---

[34] For an overview of the Mau Mau Uprising case, see Elkins (2005, 2011).

[35] How the post-imperial legal space is underexplored intellectually corresponds to the belatedness in addressing such post-imperial reckoning in practice, which is epitomized in Ruti G. Teitel's historical overview of modern transitional justice (2003). She shows how the first phase starts immediately after the Second World War with various war tribunals to account for wartime violence. The second phase is the post-Cold War period, when the world witnessed a wave of post-Socialist and post-authoritarian transitions and reckoning. The third phase is the belated accounting for long-past wrongs at the end of the twentieth century, such as slavery, colonialism, or the Second World War. Teitel's genealogy of modern transitional justice curiously skips the era of decolonization and deimperialization, leaving these double processes of major political transitions outside the analytical realm of transitional justice.

By drawing a link between the transitional *injustice* immediately following the demise of the Japanese empire and the recent attempt to belatedly seek imperial reckoning, my study suggests that incorporation of deimperialization transitional injustice into the analysis of transitional justice allows us to see hidden dynamics.

formal deimperialization, replacing the prewar Imperial Constitution with the postwar Constitution, and enacting the State Redress Act. What I have illustrated in this chapter is how post-imperial injustice – of erasure, silencing, and inaction – found an alibi in the logic of economy built on debt – that is, the economy of debt endorsed by the Japanese, Chinese, and US governments in their common pursuit of economic prosperity at the expense of accounting for individual losses. At the intersection of economy and law we thus found this debt-driven form of the unmaking of empire, perpetually deferring justice while privileging wealth accumulation.

In Kafka's parable, the countryman eventually dies while waiting to go through the gate to stand in front of the law. This may well be the image that guides the Japanese government in their persistent deferral of the arrival of legal justice. They might be hoping that the last of the surviving witnesses will eventually die in front of the gate, even though the gate of Law remains open, as the numerous compensation lawsuits filed within Japan since the 1990s attest. Yet persistence of redress is starting to shift the legal frontier itself.

Ever since the landmark decision by the South Korean Constitutional Court in 2011 to declare unconstitutional the South Korean government's prohibition on individual compensation claims by its citizens against Japan within Korean jurisdictions, some Korean plaintiffs who lost in the forced labor cases in Japan have filed and won cases in the South Korean courts in quick succession in the past several years, and more cases are yet to come.[36] A different gate of Law is now open to

---

[36] See the South Korean Constitutional Court decision, 23-2[A] KCCR 366, *2006Hun-Ma788*, August 30, 2011, which recognized the individual rights to claim compensation in the so-called comfort women cases. Similar to the 1972 Joint Communiqué between the PRC and Japan, the South Korean government renounced its right to claim reparation from Japan in exchange for future economic cooperation arrangements in the 1965 Treaty on Basic Relations between Japan and the Republic of Korea.

The landmark decision by the Supreme Court of Korea on May 24, 2012 (*2009Da22549*) echoed the 2011 South Korean Constitutional Court decision in recognizing the individual rights to claim compensation from Japan, and remanded the lower court case against Mitsubishi Heavy Industries (Busan High Court decision *2007Na4288*, February 3, 2009) involved in the wartime use of forced labor. Following this Supreme Court decision, on July 10, 2013 the Seoul High Court ordered Nippon Steel & Sumitomo Metal Corporation (formerly Nippon Steel Corporation, which merged with Sumitomo Metal Industries in October 2012) to pay 100 million Korean won each to the four plaintiffs for the wartime use of

South Korean victims in their home country, allowing them to stand before the law.[37]

This new development in South Korea is spurring renewed interest among Chinese victims, lawyers, and activists to seek legal redress within Chinese jurisdiction. On March 18, 2014, the Beijing No. 1 Intermediate People's Court officially accepted the lawsuit submitted on February 26, 2014 by a group of forty wartime forced labor victims and their bereaved family members, who seek compensation and apologies from Mitsubishi Materials Corporation and Nippon Coke & Engineering Company (formerly Mitsui Mining). With the emergent pressure to shift the legal frontier to the jurisdiction of victims, the 2007 Japanese Supreme Court decision to deny legal rights to Chinese forced labor victims while suggesting extra-legal forms of redress to repay moral and monetary debts may not be the end of the legal redress movement, as many have suggested. Indeed, some of the forced labor victims reached a historic out-of-court settlement with Mitsubishi Materials in June 2016, while others, dissatisfied with the terms of settlement, are considering further legal action. It may actually signal the opening of a new phase – the belated project of the unmaking of empire in the legal sphere within *post-imperial* legal space – in which the particular form of *post-war* legal space, a product of the Cold War, itself is being challenged.

References

Anghie, Antony. (2004). *Imperialism, Sovereignty, and the Making of International Law*. New York: Cambridge University Press.

Arrington, Celeste. (2016). *Accidental Activists: Victim Movements and Government Accountability in South Korea and Japan*. Ithaca, NY: Cornell University Press.

---

forced labor. On July 30, 2013, the Busan High Court ordered Mitsubishi Heavy Industry to pay 80 million won each to the five plaintiffs. In addition to these cases remanded by the 2012 Supreme Court decision, the decision prompted other cases to be filed against Japanese corporations. Of those new cases, the Gwangju District Court was the first one to rule on November 1, 2013. The court ordered Mitsubishi Heavy Industries Ltd to pay 150 million won each in compensation to four surviving Korean women who were enslaved during the war and 80 million won to the bereaved family of two victims.

[37] Through a conflict-of-laws approach, Knop and Riles (2017) elucidate the heterogeneity of legal time that has played out in the South Korean comfort women case. They show how shifts in jurisdictions bring to the fore uneven terrains of temporalities.

Asano, Toyomi. (2013). *Sengo Nihon no baishōmondai to Higashi Ajiachiikisaihen: seikyūken to rekishininshikimondai no kigen [Japanese Postwar Reparation and Reconfiguration of the East Asia Region: The Right to Claim Reparation and the Origin of the Historical Consciousness Problem]*. Tokyo: Jigakushashuppan.

Askin, Kelly D. (2001). "Comfort Women: Shifting Shame and Stigma from Victims to Victimizers." *International Criminal Law Review* 1(1/2):5–32.

Buchanan, Ruth, and Sundhya Pahuja. (2004). "Legal Imperialism: Empire's Invisible Hand?" Pp. 73–96 in *Empire's New Clothes: Reading Hardt and Negri*, edited by Paul Andrew Passavant and Jodi Dean. New York: Routledge.

Chūgokujin sensō higai baishō seikyū jiken bengodan, editor. (2005). *Sajō no shōheki: Chūgokujinsengohoshōsaiban 10 nen no kiseki [The Barrier Built on the Sand: The Ten-Year Trajectory of the Postwar Compensation Lawsuits by Chinese War Victims]*. Tokyo: Nihon hyōronsha.

Comaroff, John L., and Jean Comaroff. (2006). "Law and Disorder in the Postcolony: An Introduction." Pp. 1–56 in *Law and Disorder in the Postcolony*, edited by Jean Comaroff and John L. Comaroff. Chicago, IL: University of Chicago University Press.

Cotterrell, Roger. (2012). "What is Transnational Law?" *Law & Social Inquiry* 37(2):500–24.

Derrida, Jacques. (1991). *Given Time: I. Counterfeit Money*, translated by Peggy Kamuf. Chicago, IL: University of Chicago Press.

(1992a). "Before the Law." Pp. 191–200 in *Acts of Literature*, edited by Derek Attridge. New York: Routledge.

(1992b). "Force of Law: 'The Mystical Foundations of Authority.'" Pp. 3–29 in *Deconstruction and the Possibility of Justice*, edited by Drucilla Cornell, Michel Rosenfeld, and David Gray Calson. New York: Routledge.

Elkins, Caroline. (2005). *Imperial Reckoning: The Untold Story of Britain's Gulag in Kenya*. New York: Henry Holt and Company.

(2011). "Alchemy of Evidence: Mau Mau, the British Empire, and the High Court of Justice." *The Journal of Imperial and Commonwealth History* 39(5):731–48.

Gaimushōkanrikyoku. (1946a). *Kajinrōmushashūrōjijōchōsahōkokusho [Field Reports on the Work Condition of the Chinese Laborers]*. Tokyo: Diplomatic Record Office of the Ministry of Foreign Affairs of Japan.

(1946b). *Kajinrōmushashūrōtenmatsuhōkoku (yōshi) [Reports on the Work Condition of the Chinese Laborers (Summary)]*. Tokyo: Diplomatic Record Office of the Ministry of Foreign Affairs of Japan.

(1952–72). *Taiheiyōsensōshūketsuniyorunaigaijinhogohikiage (gaikokujin) [Protection and Repatriation of Japanese and Foreigners at the End of the Pacific War (Foreigners)]*. Tokyo: Diplomatic Record Office of the Ministry of Foreign Affairs of Japan.

Gao, William. (2007). "Overdue Redress: Surveying and Explaining the Shifting Japanese Jurisprudence on Victims' Compensation Claims." *Columbia Journal of Transnational Law* 45:529–50.

Gardner, James A. (1980). *Legal Imperialism: American Lawyers and Foreign Aid in Latin America*. Madison, WI: The University of Wisconsin Press.

Gotō, Mitsuo. (2012). "Nihonkokukenpōseiteishiniokeru 'Nihon kokumin' to 'gaikokujin'" ["'Japanese People' and 'Foreigners' in the Drafting of the Japanese Constitution"]. *Hikakuhōgaku [Comparative Law Review]* 45(3):1–28.

——— (2013). "Nihonkokukenpō 10-jō: kokusekihō to kyūshokuminchishusshin-sha" ["Japanese Constitution Article 10: Japanese Nationality Law and Former Colonial Subjects"]. *Wasedashakaikagakusōgōkenkyū [Waseda Studies in Social Sciences]* 13(3):19–39.

Hahm, Chaihark, and Sung Ho Kim. (2015). *Making We the People: Democratic Constitutional Founding in Postwar Japan and South Korea*. New York: Cambridge University Press.

He, Tianyi, editor. (2005). *Erzhanlu Ri Zhongguolaogongkoushushi [Oral History of Japanese-Captured Chinese Forced Laborers during the Second World War]*. 5 vols. Jinan, China: Qilushushe.

Jessup, Philip C. (1956). *Transnational Law*. New Haven, CT: Yale University Press.

Johns, Fleur. (2013). *Non-Legality in International Law: Unruly Law*. New York: Cambridge.

Kafka, Franz. ([1924] 1988). *The Trial*. Definitive Edition, translated by Willa and Edwin Muir. New York: Schocken Books.

Kang, Sang-jung. (1996). *Orientarizumu no kanata e: kindaibunkahihan [Beyond Orientalism: Critique of Modern Culture]*. Tokyo: Iwanami shoten.

Knop, Karen, and Annelise Riles. (2017). "Space, Time and Historical Injustice: A Feminist Conflict-of-Laws Approach to the 'Comfort Women' Agreement." *Cornell Law Review* 102(4):853–928.

Koga, Yukiko. (2013). "Accounting for Silence: Inheritance, Debt, and the Moral Economy of Legal Redress in China and Japan." *American Ethnologist* 40(3):494–507.

——— (2016a). "Between the Law: The Unmaking of Empire and Law's Imperial Amnesia." *Law & Social Inquiry* 41(2):402–34.

——— (2016b). *Inheritance of Loss: China, Japan, and the Political Economy of Redemption after Empire*. Chicago, IL: University of Chicago Press.

Koseki, Shōichi. (1989). *Shin-kenpō no tanjō [The Birth of the New Constitution]*. Tokyo: Chūōkōronsha.

Kratoska, Paul H., editor. (2005). *Asian Labor in the Wartime Japanese Empire: Unknown Histories*. Armonk, NY: M. E. Sharpe.

Kushner, Barak. (2015). *Men to Devils Devils to Men: Japanese War Crimes and Chinese Justice*. Cambridge, MA: Harvard University Press.

Levin, Mark A. (2008). Supreme Court of Japan Decision 2008/04/27: Nishimatsu Construction Co. v. Song Jixiao et al. *American Journal of International Law* 102:148–54.
Matsumoto, Katsuyoshi. (2003). "Kokkamutōseki no hōri" to minpōten [The Doctrine of State Immunity and the Civil Code]. *Ritsumeikanhōgaku* 292:317–82.
Mauss, Marcel. ([1924] 1990). *The Gift: The Form and Reason for Exchange in Archaic Societies*, translated by W. D. Halls. New York: W. W. Norton.
Merry, Sally Engle. (2006). "New Legal Realism and the Ethnography of Transnational Law." *Law & Social Inquiry* 31(4):975–95.
Nishinarita, Yutaka. (2002). *Chūgokujinkyōseirenkō [Chinese Forced Labor]*. Tokyo: Tokyo Daigakushuppankai.
Oguma, Eiji. (1995). *Tanitsuminzokushinwa no kigen: "Nihonjin" no jigazō no keigu [The Origin of the Myth of the Single Ethnic Nation: The Genealogy of the Self-portrait of "Japanese"]*. Tokyo: Shinyōsha.
Okada, Masanori. (2013). *Kuni no fuhōkōisekinin to kōkenryoku no gainenshi: kokkabaishōseido-shikenkyū [Wrongful Conduct of the State and the Intellectual History of Governmental Authority: Legal History of the State Redress System]*. Tokyo: Kōbundō.
Ōnuma, Yasuaki. (1986). *Tan'itsuminzokushakai no shinwa o koete: zainichiKankokuChōsenjin to shutsunyūkokukanritaisei [Beyond the Myth of a Single Ethnic Society: Koreans in Japan and the Emigration and Immigration Administration]*. Tokyo: Tōshindō.
———. (2004). *Zainichi Kankoku Chōsenjin no kokuseki to jinken [Nationality and Human Rights of Koreans in Japan]*. Tokyo: Tōshindō.
———. (2007). *Tōkyō saiban, sensō sekinin, sengo sekinin [Tokyo Tribunal, War Responsibility, Postwar Responsibility]*. Tokyo: Tōshindō.
Schmidhauser, John R. (1992). "Legal Imperialism: Its Enduring Impact on Colonial and Post-Colonial Judicial Systems." *International Political Science Review* 13(3):321–34.
Seraphim, Franziska. (2015). Introduction to "Hanaoka Monogatari: The Massacre of Chinese Forced Laborers, Summer 1945" by Richard Minear and Franziska Seraphim. *Japan Focus: The Asia-Pacific Journal* 13(7):1 (April 27).
Shin, Hae Bong. (2005). "Compensation for Victims of Wartime Atrocities: Recent Developments in Japan's Case Law." *Journal of International Criminal Justice* 3:187–206.
Teitel, Ruti G. (2003). "Transitional Justice Genealogy." *Harvard Human Rights Journal* 16:69–94.
Tong, Zeng. (1991). G"uozhifa de xingainian: shouhaipeichang" [New Concept in International Law: Victim Compensation]. *Fazhiribao [Legal Daily]* (Beijing), May 20, 3.

Yoneyama, Lisa. (2003). "Traveling Memories, Contagious Justice: Americanization of Japanese War Crimes at the End of the Post-Cold War." *Journal of Asian American Studies* 6(1):57–93.

(2016). *Cold War Ruins: Transpacific Critique of American Justice and Japanese War Crimes*. Durham, NC: Duke University Press.

Zumbansen, Peer. (2008). "Transitional Justice in a Transnational World: The Ambiguous Role of Law." Osgoode CLPE Research Paper No. 40/2008.

(2011). "Transnational Law, Evolving." Osgoode CLPE Research Paper No. 27/2011.

CONCLUSION
Jonathan Goldberg-Hiller

Injury takes us to the heart of the liberal imagination. To enjoy rights to life, property, or happiness means that there is an expectation of state-sanctioned remedy for injury to any of these liberal goods. This study of injury, culture and the law, however, moves us beyond a simple liberal image of rights claiming in response to injury. Not only do these authors find limits to the rationally autonomous subject who frequently does not apprise herself of, or act on injury, but they also show us that states, whether through a not-so-benign neglect or through aggressive acts of sovereign authority, injure as much as they might protect. The proto-liberal Thomas Hobbes noted many of these complex cultural and political dynamics of injury when he wrote,

> every particular man is Author of all the Sovereaigne doth; and consequently he that complaineth of injury from his Soveraigne, complaineth of that whereof he himself is Author; and therefore ought not to accuse any man but himself; no nor himselfe of injury; because to do injury to ones self, is impossible (*Leviathan*, Pt. II, Ch. 18).

To understand one's implication in a world where injuries abound, to accept injuries as part of a mystical foundation of authority, is to put one's experiences of harm and one's sense of justice forever into doubt.

In these concluding remarks, I want to ask how we can make this doubt beneficial in our scholarship. In our efforts to displace a simplistic legal liberal framework for comprehending the culture of injury, I am drawn toward an immunitary model, implicit in some of Hobbes' and early liberals' arguments. The contemporary philosopher Roberto

Esposito (2011, 2015) has pointed out that immunity, long before it became a conceptual foundation for biology and medicine, was first a Roman legal concept. Legal immunity was then and still remains a form of protection against the myriad social obligations Esposito argues to be actually constitutive of community.

Esposito argues that immunity is a broader concept than our common ideas of legal immunity that protect some officials or corporations from legal challenge to their authorized duties. This familiar form of legal immunity allows those given protections to fulfill expected roles, but also to do injury without the usual consequence. Yet immunity can also be seen in the political fiction of the legal person dominating our understandings of citizenship, belonging and injury. From this perspective, how we think about the organism who is injured and marshals its forces against dis-ease has a parallel in the legal idea of how we think about those persons who are granted – or successfully demand – the paradoxical privilege to complain of a legally cognizable injury. To make legally credible a threat to one's bodily integrity in this view simultaneously implicates the integrity of valued stations and ways of life. However, because legal personhood is not universally distributed (reflecting political agreements on who counts rather than on the intricate roles foundational for actual lived community), our political communities effectively rely upon legal exclusions. Moreover, as Esposito helps us to see, these exclusions are often imagined in the dangerous form of biological threats to self and community.

While all legal persons are by definition entitled to some degree of immunity, Esposito argues that excessive immunity is corrosive of the political communities we have constructed. Excessive immunity is akin to an auto-immune disorder that perishes the organism in overreaction to perceived environmental threats, or to the lethal antibiotic resistance generated by overuse of antibiotics, or even a genocidal politics that cleanses the body politic of human vermin. The American epidemic of police killings of black men and boys illustrates this problem of excessive immunity, where police, designated to protect a community, instead eliminate some of the community's most vulnerable members in the name of security, making death and injury an integral aspect of the continuity of social and political life, with seeming immunological impunity.

Esposito argues that this immunitary framework – injury and death serving political and biological life – runs beneath our liberal democratic foundations and complicates our appeals to justice (2008, 45 and ff.).

Hobbes' idea of the artificial sovereign who held one's life in its hands was a necessary invention to cease the endless "war of all against all" that he imagined as the passionate backdrop to all agreement and security. For Locke, it is not subordination to the sovereign, but the individual liberty to own property that sustains life, necessitating the immunitarian idea of the ownership of one's person. Yet slaves did not own their persons, nor did Indians own property in a way that entitled them to personhood, and punishment could include the diminution or loss of personhood and property; the person was something you precariously *had* (and could lose) rather than something you *were*. Security against threats to dominant notions of property was Locke's guarantee of life. It is with the utilitarians that this emphasis on security reaches its apex, according to Esposito. Security, for Bentham, is necessary to realize our capacities, making liberty necessarily imbricated with coercion. The biopolitical dimensions of this relationship between liberty and coercion form the underpinnings of liberal community.

This biopolitical idea of an immunitary politics acknowledges many of the complex and likely ineliminable tensions between injury and legality that the previous chapters have addressed. It suggests, most generally, that injury be seen as a measure of belonging in societies and polities constitutively divided against themselves, in which security depends upon suppressing or ignoring those whose injuries are deemed not worth attending. It also brings to the surface the question of the qualitative differences between the quotidian or "slow" forms of injury (Nixon 2011, Povinelli 2011) and *excessive* injury that crosses the immunitary threshold and poses a threat to dominant forms of life. If states can be seen to injure as a condition of their being, then the significant cultural and political dimensions of injury might be found in the distinction between pain and injury and *excessive* pain and injury, or vulnerability and *excessive* vulnerability.

This boundary is set by many authorities and contested in numerous ways. As Bloom and Galanter show here, professional gatekeepers – doctors and tattoo artists, in their examples – are made responsible for policing the line between injury and *excessive* injury in their judgments about which painful bodily experiences are beneficial, and which are medically or socially harmful. Lawyers and judges do similar work in Barbas's chapter when they build concepts to immunize privacy and public image from community interests, or cause public figures to forfeit their immunity in favor of community interests. Although immunitary relationships of this kind appear homeostatic, the frontier between what degree of discomfort, pain or injury is necessary and what is excessive is never neutral. The substrate of suffering is the very condition of possibility for our conversations about, and explorations into, the cultural practices of injury in legal discourse and justice.

In what follows, I extend the immunitary model to highlight new research directions for the study of sociolegal culture and injury that these chapters reveal to us, and to speculate where future research might take us. I look primarily at the interrelated issues of subjectivity, power and inequality, and causation and responsibility.

SUBJECTIVITY

One new focus suggested by reading these chapters in light of an immunitary theory framework is the importance of affect in our thinking about the subject. Affect may be pre-personal, in that it demonstrates the intensities and sensations that exceed institutional norms (such as our ideas of the legal person), or it may be personal in that it traverses feelings and emotions through which we come to know ourselves. In either case, as experiences that challenge boundaries of self and society, affect can make the community's thresholds of protection and injury more apparent. As Elaine Scarry's (1985) work on pain has shown us, translating affect into emotion and word is complex and sometimes impossible, but the acceptable thresholds of protection and injury are still communicated. In these essays, for example, affect helps us understand the barriers embedded in the disputing pyramid that Engel helps unpack in his chapter, and the complicated motivations some have for either discounting pain and injury, or finding a way to climb the pyramid's legal heights.

In order to move beyond the expected role or common interpretations of the legal person rationally vigilant for her rights, everyday expectations of discomfort and pain must transform into the sensation of excessive injuries, either in the amount of pain experienced, or the kinds of emotional experiences that can be called injurious. Rather than simply a psychophysiological process, however, these essays show us that the affective experiences of the subject have sociological dimensions, and socio-legal dimensions as well. What counts as excess, who gets to claim excess, and where such claims can be heard have always been unequal propositions, sometimes controlled in distinctive ways by the law. Wada, for example, shows that the power of emotional feeling has the potential to drive some Japanese litigants to use courts as platforms from which the overwhelming pain of loss can be voiced. In order to do so, however, the litigants must break through the constraining rules of tort law that project onto plaintiffs the denigrated affect of greed, because the law allows them only to ask for monetary compensation.

The link between affect and the emotional subject may lead systems of law to harness some aspects of affect to recreate stable and controllable subjects. Wada draws our attention to this process in his description of the possibilities for courtroom pluralism, where multiple narratives of what constitutes a tort can be allowed to intermingle. This plural space would ostensibly integrate emotion with the formal tort law, expanding the reach of legal remedy with this incorporation. Along similar lines, Osanloo explores the Iranian legal system's creation of an "affective space" and an "emotive domain," notable for their intermingling of pre-legal custom with law, in which emotions are usually processed within a bureaucratic shell. In this criminal system, the convicted murderer faces death unless the victim's family grants mercy. As a result, family members psychically injured by another's violent or murderous act experience what Osanloo calls the double agony of loss and decision-making over the fate of the perpetrator. But I think it is also notable that these Iranian affective spaces also seem to harness feeling and affect in order to reintegrate and reimmunize the injured subject into the social and political community through this individual act of decision-making about the fate of another. Thus, these chapters show the potential of further research into other legal systems' mechanisms for harnessing affect and recreating legal subjects.

Mor suggests in her chapter that one such mechanism we can look for is the potential separation of the moral stigma of injury from the pain and suffering that lies behind it. Tort law too often encourages a spectacle of misery, she argues, in an effort to augment compensation. Yet this spectacle and its resulting stigma desensitizes others to the actual experiences and pains of life-altering injuries. Mor argues that the legal construction of disability as personal tragedy is neither the necessary nor actual lived experience of disability where the challenges of living in a disabling society take many different forms. The idea that alternative ways of life can be legally comprehended without losing the moral wrong of injury is a call to rebuild legal subjects and their immunities in ways more grounded on plural ways of life.

A challenge for further exploration is how we might come to understand and compensate for profound injuries where ways of life are no longer apparent or communicable. The captivating 2005 case of Terri Schiavo, who was in a persistent vegetative state and was caught between a spouse who wished to stop artificial sustenance and parents who did not, demonstrates this difficulty. With brain-injured people in mind, the philosopher Catherine Malabou (2012, xii and ff.) asks whether it is possible to imagine a suffering "in the form of indifference to suffering? In the form of the inability to experience suffering as one's own? Could it be that there is a type of suffering that creates a new identity, the unknown identity of an unknown person who suffers?" Malabou's philosophical challenge is to think injury without affect, and without recreating a stigmatized projection of the subject that is marginalizing or bearing a self.

Malabou's suggestion that new identities might emerge where injury is no longer consciously experienced (as may happen with brain injuries affecting memory or Alzheimer's disease) raises the question of whether biological experiences are the only site where social force or control are absorbed as we think about injury and its cultures. Might the bodily subject, under these circumstances, have an ability to resist and repair itself – like the ways that the injured brain rewires itself – and how might legal culture respond to the new identities and potentialities that can emerge in injury's wake?

This question may have broader political implications than first appear. Fineman's arguments in her chapter for grounding rights not in a set of characteristics or capacities, but as an ethical response to a common if not explicitly universal sense or feeling of biological vulnerability, commits her to a notion of resilience by which essential resources for counterbalancing vulnerability are distributed by the state. This theory of resilience provides an important purchase on seeing state *inaction* as injury, as Fineman argues. But, in its sensitivity to the vital relationship between community and a more inclusive sense of immunity – or protection – does this notion of state inaction as injury also escape the dangers of excess where community priorities manipulate individual resilience?

In answering this question, one conceptual task may be to establish a difference between the idea of resilience and that of flexibility, which has been a hallmark neoliberal demand (Harvey 2007, Malabou 2008). The flexible worker is one who is given "opportunity" by employer and government to take care of – hence, take responsibility for – her own needs in order to be able to conform and adapt to the sudden shifts in economic markets on which the economy now depends. Can a notion of resilience, such as that expressed in Fineman's argument, sufficiently express the hidden injury in this arrangement? Or might we gain a more critical perspective by approaching the biological as capable of resisting incessant calls for change and flexibility, and might this, in turn, allow us to rethink legal norms of injury in even more useful ways?

A related question is whether the idea of vulnerability, and the kinds of care that this framework extols, can provide a balanced form of immunity that avoids producing unnecessary exclusions and violence. The answer to the question of whether vulnerability is a "primal human condition," as Fineman frames it, isn't always clear because "human" has always been a political category, often granted to those who care for others correctly (and rarely universally). As Jeremy Bentham argued, and as Samera Esmeir (2012) has shown in the case of Benthamite British control of Egypt in the nineteenth century, the colonial concern to make "humans" of those considered "savage" and unworthy was dependent on colonial administrators and colonized individuals' proper treatment of prisoners and draft animals, which meant minimizing the degree of injury and inflicted pain on both. While this utilitarian formula does little for the liberty of prisoners or animals, it does suggest that the reconstitution of legal subjectivity may cohere around the humanistic idea of the caregiver rather than the vulnerable – especially the most vulnerable – around us. And this might create its own set of moral problems.

Rasmussen's chapter about animal rights reaches a similar conclusion. Animals who are in our care help us see vulnerability, she argues, and take us beyond the autonomous subject. As we acknowledge that animals can suffer and as we include their pain into our notion of legal injuries, do we lessen the pain and stigma of other subjects? One difficulty, she notes, is that vulnerability depends on a cultural and political process of recognition, and some animals are more recognizably human-like than others. Making injury visible, therefore, means appealing to an essential sameness. Certainly, this recognition continues to undergird the human, leaving people with disabilities and others (including indigenous peoples whose humanity has long been seen as a question of their transition away from animality) relatively more vulnerable to community interests. Implicitly, this recreates some normative vestige of the autonomous subject, as Rasmussen points out, and leaves others whom the community must immunize itself against vulnerable to biopolitical state projects that continue to injure so that others may feel secure. This is apparent in the ways that Michael Vick is himself decried as an animal due to his injurious behavior toward the vulnerable dogs in his care. If the boundary between animal and human is not fixed, then one's protective "humanness" is something that one can lose, as Colin Dayan (2011) has brilliantly explored in her study of the "civil death" of slaves, prisoners, and animals. For this reason, Rasmussen argues that states should not be counted on to eliminate injury by emphasizing vulnerable subjects. But if the vulnerable subject is tied to our suspect notions of humanity, where do we find an adequate moral theory in which to consider inappropriate injury?

One direction for future research may be to explore injury in regard to animals and even those "things" westerners commonly see as nonliving and thus nonsubjects. Settler colonial states frequently trample and injure the cultural sensibilities of indigenous peoples in efforts to gain political and legal control of land (Wolfe 2006, Byrd 2011), but the legal system does not always recognize these actions as injuries. The recent struggle over the Dakota Access Pipeline that crossed Standing Rock land in North Dakota, and the ongoing challenge to the erection of one of the world's largest telescopes on sacred Mauna Wakea on the Island of Hawai'i are both examples of this. In both instances, indigenous peoples have asserted themselves as "protectors" to respond to injuries to water and mountain, as well as sovereignty, in creative ways. But in some (mainly indigenous) cultures, colonial injury is not only an injury to valued ways of life (Povinelli 2016). Some native Hawaiians, for example, have emphasized a metamorphic ontology in which some plants, animals, and even land forms are ancestors temporally living alongside people today (Goldberg-Hiller and Silva 2011, 2015). Thus, the injury to Mauna Wakea, just as the injuries to native plants by industrial agriculture, or the endangerment of kindred animals, has been articulated as an injurious loss of conviviality, not anchored, for example, in an idea of universal vulnerability. As the chapters of this book suggest, this idea that the individual and collective can no longer appreciate the populated world they helped make (and which ancestrally made them) may lead to more than a resurgent anticolonial politics. Perhaps, with speculative thought and empirical study, we might begin to explore the tortious idea that some have injured the planet, culminating in lethal climate change, in ways that are different than the legal system has conventionally thought about injury.

Another avenue to explore is that of the emotional economy, whereby pain is sometimes converted into injury. By calling this an economy, I suggest not only a study of individual affect, but also the ways in which emotions may be regulated in a more intangible and collective fashion. Mor addresses the significance of tragedy as a genre for understanding the pain of disability that many activists seek to transcend. Cataloguing and understanding the other genres that injury draws from, and particularly tracing the ways in which these genres are utilized within legal discourse and doctrine – the tropes they authorize and the narratives they privilege – might broaden our understanding of the imaginary constraints and opportunities in injury disputing.

The creation of injuries to conscience may be another fruitful direction for further thought about injury and culture not explored in these chapters. The frame for this type of injury can be seen in the American Supreme Court's ruling in *Burwell v. Hobby Lobby Stores* (2014) that corporate owners' religious freedom would be injured by requiring them to indirectly fund objectionable birth control for their employees.[1] Here, religious freedom is understood as a form of conscience that is vulnerable to the moral choices others make, requiring a new form of legal immunity. Similarly, other cases moving through US courts consider conscientious objection to public accommodations laws, specifically whether one must accept as clients same-sex couples wanting wedding flowers or cakes when proprietors hold personal scruples against same-sex marriage. Pharmacists who oppose abortion have also asked for the right to deny sales of some contraceptives due to conscientious objection. Certainly, recognizing injuries to conscience can be justified in terms of a liberal concern for privacy. In the cases described above, however, not only is conscience seen as socially and economically interconnected with others in nonliberal ways, but it tends to reverse the usual legal ideas of who can be harmed away from those "insular minorities," such as gays and lesbians, to employers or those with social responsibilities, who are now seen as most in need of immunity.

POWER AND INEQUALITY

This theme of inverted vulnerability conditioning the legal and political construction of harm echoes concerns raised by several authors here in other contexts and reveals the significance of power and inequality for our study of injury. Franks, for example, shows how injuries to the powerful are frequently exaggerated, ultimately discouraging empathy

---

[1] *Burwell v. Hobby Lobby Stores, Inc.*, 134 S. Ct. 2751, 2782 (2014).

and compassion for others who are less powerful. Thus, even when an injury seems imaginary and unverifiable, the claim of injury can mask other real or violent harms and immunize the powerful from scrutiny. Stand Your Ground laws are a good example. As Franks demonstrates, these laws not only draw from and reinforce patriarchal visions of the inviolate home-as-castle, but they also lead to more violent shootings. Similarly, claims of reputational harm to men in sexual assault cases can be judged more significant than those stemming from the rape itself. In Franks' examples, the injuries that count are those that are deemed excessive, at least from the perspective of the most powerful in the community, and incomparable to inconveniences that others in the community may face.

It would be interesting to study this sociological and political phenomenon more historically to think about how injury itself may lead to the constitution of new social hierarchies. We can see this process in the context of political struggles over rights, where some who represent dominant norms (heterosexuality, for instance, or "American" status) have identified rights for gays or for Indians as injuries and affronts to status requiring political mobilization (Goldberg-Hiller 2004, Dudas 2008). But these events have often been defensive and these norms were already dominant. Perhaps more studies of whiteness in the United States can aid this inquiry. David Roediger (1991) and others have shown how violence toward African Americans whitened the "black" Irish. Perhaps more inquiry into how this political use of injury altered the ability of the Irish and other subaltern groups such as Jews to voice their own injuries, and how this contributed historically to their growing recognition as white, might provide increased insight into what conditions make possible the legitimate articulation of injury.

Chen's chapter shows that the exaggeration of injury Franks locates in the American socio-legal landscape is also a motif in imperial contexts. The claim of victimhood by an imperial power creates the conditions for excluding and denigrating the alleged victimizer and subject of imperial control, thus easing qualms against excessive violence in times of war and conquest. Chen calls this the jurisprudence of injury and the morality of revenge, a particularly immunitary phrasing that shows the relationship between legal victimhood and the sanitizing language so common in many imperial struggles. Indeed, the discriminatory treatment of injury and rights, Chen explains, makes it perfectly reasonable to demand excessive retaliation and compensation for the damages one's own people suffer. Although such a discourse of injury can be challenged by those being dominated, mechanisms including the exclusion of others or control of historical memories make these counterclaims of injury harder to hear.

Franks' and Chen's arguments about injury inequality meet a contrary set of arguments in some chapters that focus on the ways in which injury claiming may produce a form of community that reinforces feelings of equality and perhaps broadens the experience of community belonging. Wada, for example, argues that there may be a new universalism established by the power of emotional feeling, which also provides a reason to support legal rules that will broaden the acceptable set of narratives in injury litigation. Fineman's emphasis on the vulnerable subject accomplishes something similar: if our legal and political institutions are able to acknowledge everyone's vulnerability, just as they can appreciate others' innate emotionality, it may lead to greater equality and a more inclusive understanding of community. And, at the same time, stronger counter-discourses to the exaggeration of injury might be found.

Barbas, too, argues that tort law might reinforce a democratic ethos. The growth of the idea of injury to one's image as injury to the self certainly involves an element of panoptic self-monitoring that is not essentially an expression of democratic power. For this reason, she points out, lawsuits over intimate forms of defamation only recirculate the harm they cite, and historically have been avoided despite the perception of injury. Nonetheless, some aspects of image injury seem democratic in that they thrive on the values of free expression while simultaneously conjuring the public right to consume images. It is the growth of the image-consuming public that ultimately claws back and limits what can be immunized from communal concern. While couched in the legal language of the public figure, these privacy rules are simultaneously a new mechanism limiting dispute formation around the idea of injury, while encouraging free expression.

In the interest of knowing more about the democratic regulation of images, it may be worthwhile to study those who have not historically been able to adequately manage their images within the law. This may include women, whose assumed vulnerability to sexual images is couched in protective patriarchal assumptions about their more fragile psyches. Race may also be a significant factor. What are the racial differences in the legal management of the self? Some evidence from incidents involving police violence against African Americans, such as the 2014 shootings of Michael Brown in Ferguson, Missouri, and Tamir Rice in Cleveland, Ohio, suggests that legal regulation may force young black males to manage their images differently than white youth. In line with empirical studies of unconscious racism (Lawrence 1987, Levinson and Smith 2012) young black men may be seen as particularly dangerous, drawing harsh or lethal treatment for actions that would be ignored for white youth. Is this partially a legacy of images that deny democratic presence or respectability, and, if so, what is its particular legal and social history? If, as Rasmussen has shown in her chapter, we only perceive legal injury in those beings who appear most human – beings that may include some animals and might disallow some humans such as prisoners – might we be able to map the kinds of percepticide that undergird the legal recognition of injuries?

In her chapter, Baxi shows the enduring injurious power of imagery in a postcolonial society. In India, colonial and racial imagery was made scientific, she argues, which set up the conditions for women's revictimization in rape prosecutions. The colonial image of the lying female subject, as she demonstrates, was incorporated into postcolonial medical textbooks that offered the basis for testing the veracity of rape, transforming diagnostic categories into experiential ones. The potentially lying sexual "habitué" was legally established until recently with penetrative tests that mimicked the sexual violence on trial. Baxi points out that this form of medico-legal humiliation contributes to men's lurid pleasure in the trial as these tests are disclosed, discussed, and used to elicit testimony not technically relevant to the crime. She also points out that even the once-dubious claim that children can be raped is dependent on the colonial image of the brown man who *would* and *could* rape a child, suggesting that the colonial tropes continue to haunt the current law. This haunting bridges historical time and jurisdictional spaces to make colonial violence real again for women injured a second time by the rape trial. Along with the immunitarian model, it also points to a rather unexplored area for further research: the uses of medical and other life sciences in the legal imagination of injury.

Koga's chapter likewise addresses a colonial temporality and spatial dislocality in injury discourse, one that she sees constituted in current agreements between China and Japan to defer reparation claims for Japanese imperialism. She finds between the layers of this transnational legal pluralism, ostensibly designed to silence injury, the spaces in which some victims can legally be heard. In an echo of the colonial dynamics once imposed, contemporary "frontiers" must be crossed, including statutes of limitations, sovereign immunity and the individual right to claim compensation. While these legal barriers recapitulate the Japanese post-war constitution's ongoing exclusion of imperial subjects, there are extralegal or quasi-legal *fugen*, supplementary statements written by judges in which the sufferings of Chinese victims are acknowledged despite the denial of their legal recognition. Koga's examples suggest the significance of the supplements to the law – ideas of equity in the West, or the citations of international legal decisions, perhaps – as legal venues worthy of more study. Perhaps in a world where liberal policies of immigration and asylum are once again being questioned, the extralegal behaviors of administrative officials who sometimes act to care for the injured and vulnerable despite contrary official policy might also yield new insights into the political dynamics of injury (cf., Honig 2009). Where the law remains closed to the acknowledgement of some injuries, or even the emotional expression of the associated pain, might we discover in other quasi-legal spaces valuable room for maneuver?

RECOGNITION OF INJURIES AND RESPONSIBILITY FOR HARM

Finally, I turn to the issues of injury recognition and responsibility for harm addressed by numerous authors in this book. Bloom and Galanter show how injury and medical enhancement change places in various contexts, and in divergent ways, suggesting that injury is fundamentally an interpretive event. Circumcision, foot binding or the "correction" of intersex characteristics were once seen as enhancements, whereas some are today clearly rejected or increasingly contested as injurious practices requiring oversight or intervention. During the same periods of time, what have been seen as injuries, such as tattoos or piercings, have increasingly been understood to be ethical choices about lifestyle, beauty and identification. The degree to which the membrane between harm and enhancement is shifted by social and political struggles, as well as by legal rules, may be a fruitful site for future research. Engel's chapter makes clear that some decisions are not necessarily conscious; lumping is not essentially a cost–benefit calculus, but may derive from cultural environments that suppress even the awareness of injury. In this way, his chapter points out, tort law may be rather marginal to our understanding, an outcome David Engel and Jaruwan Engel (2010) have shown to prevail in Thailand, as well.

If law remains at the margins, what other dynamics can we pursue to understand the transformation of disputes over injury? One direction might be to consider the ways in which some bodily practices reflect and resituate certain communal boundaries. Tattooing in the West, for example, has its origins in eighteenth- and nineteenth-century historical interactions with Polynesians, for whom prominent tattooing was common (the word "tattoo" is Polynesian in origin). Once ship captains (sometimes forcibly) brought home Polynesian "specimens," tattooing became a significant mark of the "primitive" and "savage," ideas that not only reinforced later colonial encounters, but were also reflected internally in forms of subaltern identity within European and American societies (Werner 2008). Interestingly, Polynesian motifs are a common aspect of contemporary tattoo art. How might we come to understand the ways in which broader historical encounters influence our notions of injury and the ideas of responsibility for the injuries that we hold?

The cultural interpretation of harm is undoubtedly confounded by temporal disjunctures, as numerous chapters have revealed, rendering law harmful as well as remedial. Colonial origins haunt postcolonial India in Baxi's critique of rape law, and Japanese colonialism in Koga's examination of Chinese reparations, muddling contemporary legal interpretations of events. Jain suggests that the complex wounds from mass production – specifically, the IVF industry that she examines – are entangled to such a degree that they exceed the ability of tort law to realistically recognize and address the harms of the "always-already injured." Unlike Baxi's findings, where science, burdened by colonial imageries of sexual violence, is able to secrete its own harm to women who have been raped by finding a niche in the courtroom, Jain argues that science and technology in the IVF industry "utterly evade any legal frame."

The refusal to collect medical data useful to regulating an industry that depends on the off-label use of potentially carcinogenic drugs when given to young egg donors means both that there is no possibility of informed consent to the risks involved, and that the relationships between practice and harm cannot be fully substantiated in court. The economic dynamics of the industry are likewise obscured by euphemism (such as the term "donor", which reduces the bargaining power of those who sell their eggs) and the patriarchal ideology of "family" that valorizes IVF procedures. Accounting for the suppression of clear economic or scientific notions of responsibility, Jain suggests that injury is rendered as a field somewhat impervious to a tort law bound to the identification of specific injuries that can be compensated. Instead, Jain claims, harm and health have become enmeshed so that "living now means living in a time of injury," such that specific injurious events can be challenging to identify.

Jain's model of a field of injury interrupts our notion of individualized and specific harm matched to legal remedy, but it does not explain or dwell on the origin of this field. Wenger explains that injury and remedy are not just complexly overdetermined as the field metaphor suggests, but fundamentally co-constitutive. In his example of the failed history of slavery reparations, law repels consideration of the reparations issue, ostensibly because of rules of sovereign immunity or the difficulty of conceiving generational responsibility, even though reparations for Japanese internment, the Holocaust and even tobacco smokers have all overcome similar formal barriers. The horrors of slavery are *sui generis*, and not amenable to reparation, Wenger argues, because the law has been built by elites who historically failed to see themselves in social positions suffered by slaves and others. Tort law reinforces hierarchies through the exaggeration of injuries, as Franks also notes, but also subtly through its rules privileging elite ways of life. We can see this privileging in rules for tort remedies, which consider lost wages without accounting for the gendered and racialized disparity in wages, and in tort tests positing "reasonableness" or "normal risk" that effectively disregard the unique experiences of more socially marginalized individuals or groups. Thus, tort law does not fail when it refuses to address slavery reparations; it actually fulfills its design as an intentionally inapt tool for holding masters accountable. Even in selective cases, where justice seems to be done by the law, Wenger argues that the spurious correlation of elite interest convergence is a better explanation.

Wenger and Jain join numerous other authors in this collection to argue that social justice will demand a critical rethinking of the complex relationship of law to injury. To the extent that these authors have shown injury and death for some to be for others a cultural and legal predicate of health and the good life, they implicitly point to a persisting immunitary dynamic. How do we begin to imagine a positive, healthy set of protections for ourselves that do not allow or require others to be neglected, harmed or killed? As compelling as this question may be for thinking about justice in the context of injury and the law, its answer remains elusive. This book has suggested numerous avenues for research that may refine this question. These pathways point to the significance of new understandings of the subject, different ways to think about social and political inequality, and emergent sociolegal models that transcend a hyper-individualized understanding of injury recognition and reparation that that may serve as catalysts for this inquiry.

References

Byrd, Jodi A. (2011). *Transit of Empire: Indigenous Critiques of Colonialism.* Minneapolis, MN: University of Minnesota Press.

Dayan, Colin. (2011). *The Law Is a White Dog: How Legal Rituals Make and Unmake Persons.* Princeton, NJ: Princeton University Press.

Dudas, Jeffrey R. (2008). *The Cultivation of Resentment: Treaty Rights and the New Right.* Stanford, CA: Stanford University Press.

Engel, David M., and Jaruwan, Engel. (2010). *Tort, Custom, and Karma: Globalization and Legal Consciousness in Thailand.* Stanford, CA: Stanford Law Books.

Esmeir, Samera. (2012). *Juridical Humanity: A Colonial History.* Stanford, CA: Stanford University Press.

Esposito, Roberto. (2008). *Bios: Biopolitics and Philosophy.* Minneapolis, MN: University of Minnesota Press.

(2011). *Immunitas: The Protection and Negation of Life.* Cambridge, UK: Polity Press.

(2015). *Persons and Things: From the Body's Point of View.* Cambridge; Malden, MA: Polity Press.

Goldberg-Hiller, Jonathan. (2004). *The Limits to Union: Same-Sex Marriage and the Politics of Civil Rights*, 1st Pbk. ed. Ann Arbor, MI: University of Michigan Press.

Goldberg-Hiller, Jonathan, and Noenoe K. Silva. (2011). "Sharks and Pigs: Animating Hawaiian Sovereignty Against the Anthropological Machine." *South Atlantic Quarterly* 110(2):429–46.

(2015). "The Botany of Emergence: Kanaka Ontology and Biocolonialism in Hawai'i." *Native American and Indigenous Studies* 2(2):1–26.

Harvey, David. (2007). *A Brief History of Neoliberalism*, new edn. New York: Oxford University Press.

Honig, Bonnie. (2009). *Emergency Politics: Paradox, Law, Democracy.* Reprint. Princeton, NJ: Princeton University Press.

Lawrence, Charles III. (1987). "The Id, the Ego, and Equal Protection: Reckoning with Unconscious Racism." *Stanford Law Review* 39:317.

Levinson, Justin D., and Robert J. Smith. (2012). *Implicit Racial Bias across the Law.* Cambridge; New York: Cambridge University Press.

Malabou, Catherine. (2008). *What Should We Do with Our Brain?*, 1st edn. New York: Fordham University Press.

(2012). *The New Wounded: From Neurosis to Brain Damage*. New York: Fordham University Press.

Nixon, Rob. (2011). *Slow Violence and the Environmentalism of the Poor*. Cambridge, MA: Harvard University Press.

Povinelli, Elizabeth A. (2011). *Economies of Abandonment: Social Belonging and Endurance in Late Liberalism*. Durham, NC: Duke University Press Books.

(2016). *Geontologies: A Requiem to Late Liberalism*. Durham, NC: Duke University Press.

Roediger, David R. (1991). *The Wages of Whiteness: Race and the Making of the American Working Class*. London: Verso.

Scarry, Elaine. (1985). *The Body in Pain: The Making and Unmaking of the World*. New York: Oxford University Press.

Werner, Annie. (2008). "Marking the White Body: Tattooing in the White Colonial Literary Imagination." Pp. 165–79 in *Transnational Whiteness Matters*, edited by Aileen Moreton-Robinson, Maryrose Casey, and Fiona Nicoll. Lanham, MD: Lexington Books.

Wolfe, Patrick. (2006). "Settler Colonialism and the Elimination of the Native." *Journal of Genocide Research* 8(4):387–409.

INDEX

Abe, Shinzo, Japanese Prime Minister, 308
adversarial system
   effects, 146
   oppressive nature, 152–3
Afghanistan, 309
agency, 12, 14
Agency for Super Donors, 159
Ahmedabad, Gujarat, District and Sessions Court, 267, 268
Aime, Wang, former comfort woman, 329–30
air bags, 126
Alexander, Marissa, denied Stand Your Ground immunity, 234
allegory, 138–9
   legal and everyday narratives, 138–9
   medical malpractice case
      legal discourse, effect, 144–5
      mother-child tie, 151
      parents of victim, grief, 151
      parents of victim, purpose, 145–6
Al-Qaeda, 309
Amendments, U.S. Constitution
   First, 215, 238–9, 239
   Ninth, 176
   Reconstruction, 263
American Board of Plastic Surgery, 194
American Society for Reproductive Medicine, 161
American Society of Plastic and Reconstructive Surgeons, 194
American Society of Plastic Surgeons, 194
American Tort Reform Association (ATRA), 129
Amnesty International, 96
animal rights
   shifting with respect to humans, 85–6
animal rights cases, 82–6
   Johnny Justice, Bad Newz Kennels, 85
   Tommy, chimpanzee, 83–5
Army Unit 731, Japanese, 319, 329
Association of Public-Safety Communications Officials (APCO), 129
automobiles, 125–7
autonomous subject
   critique, vulnerability, 81

autonomy, 63
Ayatollah Khomeini, 99

Beenaben, junior public prosecutor, Ahmedabad, Gujarat, 268
before the law, 319, 330
   parable, 320–1
Beijing, 323, 324, 328
Beijing University, 326
between the law, 319, 330–2, 341, 342, 343
Black Hole of Calcutta, 305
Black Manifesto, 251
Black, Rodney, white man, shot two black men on neighboring property, 237
Blackstone, William, 261
Boxer Uprising, 294
Brandeis, Louis, Justice, Supreme Court, 207
Brown, Corrine, Florida Congresswoman, 235
Brown, Henry, slave, separated from family, 249–50
Brown, Louise, first "test tube baby", 166
Brown, Michael, unarmed black man, shot by police, 237
Butler, Judith, vulnerability, 80–1

California Institute for Regenerative Medicine, 172
cancer, 156, 163, 164, 165, 166, 167, 168, 169, 170, 171, 172, 173, 174, 175, 179
capital punishment
   discretion, historical, 101–2
castle doctrine, 232–3
CEHAT. *See* Centre for Enquiry into Health and Allied Themes
Centre for Enquiry into Health and Allied Themes, 286, 289
chairs, cause of injury, 122–4
Chevers, Norman, British physician in India, observations on rape, 272
chilling effects, 239, 244
China, 294, 298, 299, 300, 301, 303, 304, 306, 307
Chinese Academy of Social Sciences, 328
Chinese Communist Party, 323
Citizens against Lawsuit Abuse (CALA), 129

369

INDEX

civil rights, 262
Civil War, United States, 251
claiming, 119, 130
  beneficial pain, impact of, 122
  cultural disapproval, impact of, 129–30
  invisible choices, impact of, 127
  naturalization of injury, impact, 123–4
  naturalization, impact of, 124–5
  self-blame, impact of, 128
Clinton, Bill, President, 160
Clinton, Hillary, 311
Clomid, 167, 173, 174
Colbert Report, The, 84
Cold War, 321, 329, 333, 343, 346
comfort women, 319, 329–30
Communications Decency Act, Section 230, 240
comparative fault, 127
consent, medicalization of, 275–6
Constitution, Japan
  Article 1, 339
  Article 17, 339
Constitution, Japanese, postwar, 320
Conyers, John, Congressman, United States, 254
corseting, 186
cost–benefit analysis
  air bags, 126
  rear-view cameras, 126–7
Council of Guardians, Iran, 98
Criminal Law (Amendment) Act 2013, India, 288

Daily News, London, criticism of Second Opium War, 303
Dakota Access Pipeline, 358
Davis, Jordan, unarmed black teenager, killed by Dunn, Michael, 236
Delhi High Court, 286
dependency, 58
Dershowitz, Alan, defense attorney, Mike Tyson rape case, 242
DES. See diethylstilbestrol
diethylstilbestrol, 170–1, 174
disabilities rights, 5
disability, 20, 355
  affirmative view, 33
    against tort doctrine, 34
    compensation, negative impact, 34
    problems with, 33–5
    progressive campaigns, contradictions, 35–6
    tort reform, reactionary risk, 34–5
  damages
    calculation, issues, 32
    pain and suffering, 32
    wrongful birth, 32
    wrongful life, 32
  dimensions of, 29
  dinstinguished from impairment, 36–7
  discrimination, 41
  legal studies, 27
  material equality, 45
  meaning of, 29
  personal experience, 37
  perspective, 28
  political equality, 45
  role for the state, 44–5
  social welfare policies, role, 44
  studies, 27
  tort approach, problems, 43–4
  tort law, functions
    compensation, 42–3
    deterrence, 40
    elimination, 40–1
    generally, 39–42
    prevention, 42
    prevention of disability, 40–1
  tort litigation, impact, 31
disability approach, 33
  implications for tort law, 33, 45
  pain, role of, 37–8
disability critique, 38
  role of the state, 44
  vulnerable subject, role of, 38–9
disability perspective, 27
  studies, critique of tort law, 28
  tort law, challenges, 32
  tort law, positive functions, 32
disability rights, 29
disablement, 44
disabling images, 36
dispute pyramid, 186, 354
dogfighting, 85
Dolly, cloned sheep, 160–1
Donor Angel, 160
Donor Source, The, 160
Dunn, Michael, killed Davis, Jordan, 236

Edwards, Robert, IVF scientist, 166
Elgin, Lord, 307
embodied vulnerability, 58
emotional economy, 359
environmental barriers, 36
ergonomics, 124
Esposito, Roberto, philospher, 351–3

Facebook, 202
false rape claims, 240, 241
FDA. See Food and Drug Administration
feminism, exclusion of minority voices, 261–2
Ferguson, Missouri, 237
Ferrell, Jonathan, unarmed black man, shot by Kerrick, Randall, 237

INDEX

Fineman, Martha, 38–9, 43
Florida, 233, 235, 236
Food and Drug Administration, 178
　regulation, 165
foot binding, 5, 186
foot binding, beneficial pain, 121
forbearance, 15, 112
forced labor, 319, 334, 335, 336, 337, 345
forgiveness, 15
(for)given time, 321, 329, 333
　described, 322
Forman, James, publisher, Black Manifesto, 251
forty acres and a mule, 251, 264
foundational violence, Japan, 341
Franciscus de Victoria, Spanish jurist, theologian, 296
Freedmen's Bureau, 251
Fujian, 298

Garvey, Marcus, leader, U.S. repatriation movement, 251
General Sherman's Field Order No. 15, 251, 264
Get Britain Standing, 124
good injury. *See* injury, good
Guangdong, 298
Guangzhou, 300, 303
Guoqiang, Li, Chinese survivor of Japanese forced labor camp, 322

Hammer, Marion, former President, National Rifle Association, 234
Hanaoka Uprising, 325
Hardy, Ed, tattoo artist, 190
Heydari, Hamid, Iranian murder victim, 96, 109, 110
Heydari, Mrs., mother of Heydari, Hamid, 96, 97, 106, 109, 110, 111, 112
Hirabhai, additional public prosecutor, Ahmedabad, Gujarat, 268
Hiroshima, 308, 309
Hobbes, Thomas, 351
Holocaust, 308
Hong Kong, 302
hormone replacement therapy, 163, 169–72, 174
　advertisement, 1960, 169
　product liability lawsuits, 169–71
hormone therapy. *See* in vitro fertilization, hormone therapy
House of Representatives, United States, 255
House Resolution 40, 254–5
HRT. *See* hormone replacement therapy
Human Rights Watch Report (2010), 287
Huss, Rachel, guardian, former Viktory Dogs, 85

image
　adversiting, role in developing, 217–18
　advertising in development, 209–10
　celebrity culture, 210, 218
　consciousness of, 1920s, 208–10
　culture, negative effects, 218–19
　injury to, 6
　legalization, 224
　legalization, effect of, 224–5
　mass media, culture, 210–11, 218
　society, 208
image, law of public
　expansion, post-war, 219–20
　freedom of speech, privacy right restricted, 221–3
　injury, sense of, 214
　libel
　　expansion, 1930s, 40s, 211–12
　　narrowing, 216
　publishers' rights, 214–16
　right to privacy, 211–12, 224
　　1950s and 1960s, U.S., 220–1
　　claims, petty nature, 212–14
　　public interest exception, 215–16
image-conscious self, 203, 224
　development
　　advertising, role of, 204
　　generally, 203–5
　　technology, role of, 204
　　urbanization, role of, 203–4
immunitary framework
　vulnerability, issues, 357
immunitary model, 353–4
　injury to conscience, 359
　subjectivity, 354–9
immunitary politics, 353
immunity, legal, 351–3
　paradoxical privilege, 352
imperial amnesia, law's, 320
imperial violence, Japan, 317–18, 319, 344
　lawsuits by Chinese victims. *See* postwar compensation lawsuits
in vitro fertilization, 156
　commercialization, profit motive, 162–3
　cost, 159
　egg donation
　　anonymity, 163
　　ethical issues, 162–3
　　health risks, 163–4, 166
　　hormone therapy, cancer risk, 164, 165
　　hormone therapy, drugs, 163–4
　egg donors
　　compensation, 161–2
　　lack of health tracking, 163, 166
　egg recruiters, marketing, 159–60
　family, expectation of, 179
　Food and Drug Administration, 165

371

INDEX

in vitro fertilization (*cont.*)
   Food and Drug Administration, regulation, 178
   government involvement, 176
   hormone therapy
      cancer risk, 168–9, 171–2
      drug mechanisms, 167–8
      procedure, 166–7
      research, 168, 172
   increased genetic disorders, children, 179
   industry, 158
   infertile women, treatment, 172–4
      cancer risk, increased, 174
      lack of follow-up, 175–6
      studies, 173–5
   insurance coverage, 178
   known-donors, 177–8
   marketing, 161, 178
   medical, capitalist nature, 157
   organ donation, ethical parallels, 177
   procedure, 158
   regulation
      political concerns, 176–7
incommensurability, medical malpractice
   competing narratives, 135–7
   lay compared with legal discourse, 138
   lay compared with medical discourse, 141
   within own narrative, 140–1
India, 307
inequality at law, 249
inequality, social, 4–5
inequality, socio-economic, 19–20
injury
   approaches to remedy, 117–18
      American, 118
   constitutional, resulting from inaction, 51–2
   cultural perception, shifting, 185–6
      enhancement, 186
      factors, 186
      plastic surgery. *See* plastic surgery
      tattoo practices. *See* tattooing
   dimensions of, 29–30
   experience of, 36, 354–5
   interconnected problems, 117
   naturalization of
      chairs, 122–4
      stairs, 124–5
   new identities, formation of, 356
   perception, cultural norms, practices, 2
   pervasive, 6
   power and inequality, role, future directions, 359–63
   recognition of harm, responsibility, 363–6
   resulting from state action, inaction, 50–1
   resulting from state neglect, 52–3

injury claims by state actors, 12–13, 15, 293–4
   colonialism, impact of, 294
   danger as basis for war, 310
   discourse, framing as more grievable, 303–4
   experience of shared precariousness, recognition of, 312
   modern era, 306–12
      China, 306–8
      injury discourse, 311
      Japan, 308–9
      Trump, Donald, 311
      United States, 309–10
   sensationalizing injury claims, 304–5
   victim politics, 294, 295
   victimhood. *See* international relations, victimhood
injury culture, 16–18
injury discourse
   failure to recognize victims, 306
injury hierarchy, 293
injury inequality, 3, 18, 231
   consequences, 244
   described, 231–2
   economic, 231
   elite perspective, consequences, 232
   freedom of speech, 232, 238–40, 243
      consequences, 240–1
   gender, 234, 235, 237, 239, 240, 243
      street harassment, 239–40
   injury construction, 18–19
   justifiable use of deadly force, 232–8, 244
   National Rifle Association, role in perpetuating, 235
   power relations, result of, 21
   prevention, burden of, 244
   racial, 235, 236–7, 237–8, 239
   relative injury judgments, 232
   self-defense reform, 237–8
   sexual assault, 232, 240–3,
      false rape claims, 240, 241
      Mike Tyson rape case, 242
      perpetrators, concern for, 243
      Roman Polanski, rape admission, 242
      Stanford Swimmer case, 241
      victim compared with perpetrator, 243
   sexual minorities, 239
injury narratives, 8
   causation, 8–10, 10, 12
   development, 12
   multiple, intermingled, 355
   responsibility, 9–10, 12, 21
injury, cultural construction, 4, 3–8
   beneficial pain, 119, 121–2, 131
   cultural environment, 120, 128–30, 132
   invisible choices, 120, 125–7, 131–2
   natural injuries, 119, 122–5, 131
   pain perception, 119, 120

INDEX

self-blame, 120, 127–8
supression of claiming, generally, 119–20
injury, experience of, 3–4
injury, good, 7, 185, 198
injury, meaning of, 1, 27
  disability perspective, effect, 27
  disability perspective, implications, 28
injury, social construction
  claiming behavior, impact, 131–2
  generally, 135
  incommensurability. See
      incommensurability, medical
      malpractice
  medical malpractice case. See medical
      malpractice case, Japan
  self-blame, 132
injury, socio-legal construction
  disability and injury, relationship, 27–8
injustice
  American tort system, failure, 132
  institutional, 62
Institute of Medicine, 172
interest convergence, 262
international relations, victimhood, 295–7
  as cause for just war, 295–6
  claims by dominant nations, 295
  colonial era, 297
  moral authority, inherent, 295
  revengeful violence, obligation, 296–7
Iranian criminal code, 8
  2013 revisions, 98
  constitutional period, 1906-79, 98
  post-revolutionary period, 98–101
  religious values, 97–8
Iranian criminal sanctioning
  crimtort system, 97, 101, 113
  dreams, role of, 110
  forbearance, 97, 104, 106
    affective space, 106, 107–8, 355
    historical comparisons, 101–2
    popular culture, 108–9
    process, 97, 107–8, 109, 111–12
  foregiveness
    dreams, role of, 110–11
  generally, 96–7
  reconciliation, 97, 104
  retribution, 104
  retribution, private right, 102
  shari'a, limits on state retribution, 103
  victim-centered approach, 97, 100, 96–7
Iranian murder case, 96, 106–7
  forbearance, 97
  forgiveness, 109–12
Iranian penal code
  1991 amendment, public injury murder, 100
  categories, criminal, 99–100
  delegation of rights, state and victims, 103–4
  distinctions among Muslim countries, 104–5
  homicide, treatment of, 100
  homicide, as private injury, 101
  Islamicization, 104–5
  religious ethics, role of, 104
  shari'a, integration of, 99
IVF. See in vitro fertilization

Japan, 308, 309, 323
Japan, imperial, 307
Japanese Civil Code, 318
Japanese Occupation of China (1937–45), 294
Jesus, 296
Jian, Zhang, Chinese lawyer, postwar
    compensation lawsuits, 325–6, 329, 330
Jianchuan Museum, 322, 324
John Olin Foundation, 129
Johnny Justice, dog, 82–3
Johnson, Andrew, President, United States, 251
Joint Communiqué, 1972, 321
just war, 295–6, 309
Justice Verma Committee, India, 288–9

Kadam, Dr., medical expert, Indian rape trial, 277
Kerrick, Randall, white man, shot unarmed black man, 237

Ladies' Home Journal, 205
Lady Hughes case, 301
LaPierre, Wayne, executive vice president, National Rifle Association, 235
Lau, Dr. Kamini, Additional Sessions Judge, India, 287–8
law and society, literature, 1
  tort law, study of, 1–2
Law of Islamic punishment, 98
law's imperial amnesia, 341
lawsuits, Chinese victims, 317
legal redress movement, 319, 321
legal subject as human, challenge
  case of Bad Newz Kennels, 77
  strategies, 76–8
legal subject as human, challenge to
  case of Tommy, chimpanzee, 76
legal subject, creation of, 12
legal subject, liberal, 13, 55, 86
  assumptions and exclusions, 56–7
  characteristics, 54–5, 56
  contrast with vulnerable subject, 59–60
  criticism, 78
  relation to state, 55–6
  social contract, impact on, 56

373

INDEX

lumping, 5, 22, 118, 120, 122, 123, 125, 126, 129, 130, 131, 132
  basis, cultural construction of injury, 119
  description, 118
Lupron, 168
Lyon, author, medico-legal text, 271

Makio, Tanaka, Japanese postwar compensation lawyer, 329
male circumcision, 5, 131, 187
male circumcision, beneficial pain, 121–2
Manhattan Institute, 129
Martin, Trayvon, killed by Zimmerman, George, 234–5, 236
Marx, Karl, 304
Masato, Japanese medical malpractice victim, 141, 142, 144, 147, 150, 151
Mau Mau Uprising, British apology (2013), 344
Mauna Wakea, 358
McBride, Renisha, unarmed black teenager, shot by Wafer, Theodore, 237
medical malpractice case, Japan, 6, 11, 135, 139–40
  allegory. See allegory, medical malpractice case
  competing narratives, 141, 146, 147–8
  conflicting perspectives, 143
  course of litigation, 142–3
  defense portrayal of plaintiffs, 146
  description of injuries, mother of victim, 147
  description of injuries, physician, 147
  dismissal, plaintiffs' lawyer, 148
  health care professional's narrative construction, 140–1
  incommensurability. See incommensurability
  injuries, 141–2
  legal discourse, strategy, 143–4
    defense lawyer, 149–50
    plaintiff's lawyer, 148–9
  narrative, parents of victim, 145, 152, 153
    description of grief, 150–1
    purpose of litigation, 145
  power of allegory, narrative, 152
  victim's, family's narrative construction, 140
medico-legal texts
  colonial origins, 271
  Modi, 2011 revision, 286–7
  Modi, two-finger test described, 273–4
  recent editions, 271
  shaping legal discourse, 271
  structuring trial testimony, 276–81, 284–5, 285
  Taylor, 278

technical rape, 281
trial role, 271
Mittal, Gita, Justice, India, 286
Modi, author, medico-legal text, 271, 274
Modi, author, medico-legal texts
  two-finger test, description, 273–4
Morita Noriko, Japanese lawyer working on behalf of comfort women, 325
Mukherjee, Siddhartha, oncologist, 171
Mumbai, 286

Nader, Ralph, 17, 156
Nagano Shigeto, Minister of Justice, Japan, denied Nanjing Massacre, 328
Nagasaki, 308, 309
Nanjing Massacre, 306, 308, 319, 328
Nanjing Massacre Museum, 328
Narita, Japan, 330
National Research Council, 172
National Rifle Association, 234, 235
New England Journal of Medicine, 174
New York Daily Tribune, criticism of Second Opium War, 303
New York Times Magazine, 84
New Zealand
  no-fault system, 45
NhRP. See Nonhuman Rights Project
Nobel Prize in Medicine, 2010, 166
Nonhuman Rights Project, 76
  goals, 84
  Tommy, chimpanzee, case of, 83
Noornissa, Indian rape victim, 276, 277, 278, 279, 280, 281
NRA. See National Rifle Association

Official Development Assistance, Japan to China, 321
Opium War, First, 294, 301–2
Opium War, Second, 294, 302, 303, 304, 307
  Western criticism of, 303, 304
organ donation, 177
Orlan, French artist, 195, 197
other-directed personality, 217
Outlook magazine, 206

Pacific Fertility Center, 161
pain, 15, 37, 354
  association with punishment, 127–8
  beneficial, 121–2
  claiming behavior, impact on, 120
  contextual nature, 185
  in disability, 37–8
pain and suffering, 32
Peace Constitution, 320, 339
  erasure of colonial, imperial subjects, 340
Peay, Muriel, woman cab driver, 202
penistration, 279, 281

374

People's Republic of China, 306
performance of misery, 31–2, 355
  damages, effect on, 31
  establishing liability, 31–2
personal image litigation, 202
  baseball player, unauthorized biography, 221
  bread vendor, newsreel footage, 213
  cab driver, Washington, D.C., 202
  defamation, 207
  early, libel and slander, 206
  exercise course, newsreel footage, 213–14
  Facebook Sponsored Stories, 202
  father's mail fraud arrest, 213
  gorilla physique, 211
  libel, 206
  process service, bathtub, 211
  starving glutton, 212
personal injury law, 15, 27, 39
personhood
  boundaries, making and unmaking, 77
Pfizer, 169
Philip II, King of Spain, 298
Pingdongshan Massacre, 319
plastic surgery, 5, 193–6, 196, 197
  cosmetic surgery, distinguished, 193–4, 194
  healing, as form of, 196
  history, injury repair, 193
  injury or enhancement, mediation, 193
  normalization, 198
  prevalence, increasing, 193
  regulation, deference to surgeons, 196
  regulation, relative lack, 193
  self-expression, as, 195
  surgeons
    mediating injury, enhancement, 193, 194–5
    role in determining injury, enhancement, 195–6
  surgeons, training, 194
Polanski, Roman, director, 242
political subject, 54
  constitutional era, 57
  evolution of, 54
  modern, 57–8
positioned subject, 137–8, 139
post-imperial legal space, 341, 343, 344
postwar compensation lawsuits, 318–19
  allowed by South Korea, 345
  between the law, 330–2
  China, acceptance of forced labor case, 321–2
  Chinese activists, 326–7
  Chinese lawyers, 325–6
  Chinese renunciation of reparations, 321
  Chinese suppression, 327
  class action not available, 332
  comfort women, plaintiff, 329–30
  Japanese lawyers, 327–9
    motivations, 327, 328–9
  legal frontiers, 333
    legal right to compensation, 336–8
    soverign immunity, 335–6
    statute of limitation, 333–5
  motivations to sue, 324
  plaintiff, forced labor, Li Guoquiang, 322–5
  privileging of formal economy over individuals, 321
  settlements, 346
Prempro, 169
primitive law, 102–3
public image, law of, 202, 203
  image-conscious self. *See* image-conscious self
  libel
    doctrine, expansion, 208
    litigation. *See* personal image litigation
  privacy, right to, 207–8
  public image, defined, 203
  reputation, protection of, 206–7
  right to privacy
    recognition of tort, 208
  torts, nature of, 202–3

Rajput, Mr.
  Indian prosecutor, 269–70
rape cases, India
  consent, medicalization of, 275–6
  courtroom vocabulary, 268–9, 279
    as male fantasies, 270–1
    distortion of testimony, 280–1
  distinguishing true from false virgins, 274–5
  historical, colonial era observations, children, 272
  medico-legal certificates, 267
  medico-legal language, 268, 280
  medico-legal texts. *See* medico-legal texts
  new examination protocols, 286
  Noornissa, rape victim, trial, 276–81
    testimony, medical expert, 277–8, 279–80, 282–3, 283–4
    testimony, Noornissa, 280
  partial penetration, 280
  public prosecutor, 268
  public prosecutor beliefs, Mr. Rajput, 269–70
  public prosecutor, Hirabhai, 268
  statutory, or technical, rape. *See* technical rape
  structuring of trial testimony, 276–81
  two-finger test. *See* two-finger test
rear-view cameras, 126–7

375

INDEX

reparations, United States, 249
  advocacy, 251–5
  Civil War era, 251
  Civil War, following century, 251
  cultural inertia against, 263–4
  denial, problems with, 256–7
  difficulty in obtaining
    law as master's tools, 262–3
  granting, problems with, 257–9
  In re African-American Slave Descendants Litigation, 10
  law as master's tools, 261–2
  lawsuits, 251–4
    Cato v. United States, 251–2
    In re African-American Slave Descendants Litigation, 251
    In re Slave Descendents Litigation, 252–3
    strategy, 253–4
  legal system
    ability to address, 256
    difficulties, 257
  legislative efforts, 254–5
  structural obstacles
    law as the master's tools, 264
  tort framework
    as barrier, 259
    failure by design, 261
    racial biases, effect of, 259–60
    value judgments, 260
  tort framework, difficulties, 257–8
resilience, 356–7
Restatement of Torts (1939), 211
retribution, 110, 112
revenge porn, 239
righteous suffering, performance of, 97
risk–benefit analysis, 125

Sarah Scaife Foundation, 129
Schiavo, Terri, 356
sedentary science, 123
Senate, United States, 255
September 11, 2001, terrorist attacks, 309
Shakeel, accused rapist of Noornissa, 279
Shanxi Province, 329
Sino-British Treaty of Nanjing (1842), 302
Sino-foreign relations, 293
  colonial powers, justification for war, 298–9
  failure to recognize Chinese injury, 302–3
  justification for war, internal contradictions, 299–300
  Opium Wars, 301–2
  resentment of Chinese, colonial era, 300–1
  unequal treaties, 294
  unwillingness to accede to demands, 297–8
slavery, United States, 249, 250–1
  Henry Brown, story of, 249–50

history, 249–50
legislative apologies, efforts, 255
reparations. See reparations, United States
torts and crimes, inclusive, 250
social contract, 54, 62
social disablement, 31
  causes, 31
social security, 44
society of victims, United States, 295
socio-legal research, 1
Sogand, wife of Heydari, Hamid, convicted murderer, 96, 97, 106, 109, 110, 111, 112
South Korea, 345, 346
Spanish Invincible Armada, 299
stairs, 124–5
Stand Your Ground laws, 233–4, 234, 235, 237
Standing Rock, land, North Dakota, 358
Stanford University, sexual assault case, 242
Starr Foundation, 129
state actors, injury claims. See injury claims by state actors
State Redress Act (1947), Japan, 339, 341, 345
statistics
  advertising spending, 1950s, 217–18
  claiming behavior, American, 118–19
  homicides following Stand Your Ground laws, 235
  in vitro fertilization, 159
  injuries, annual, American, 117
  injuries, cars backing up, 126
  mass media circulation, early 20th century, 210
  medical malpractice case, Japan, 139
  plastic surgery, 193
  tattooing, 187
statutory rape, India. See technical rape
subject, autonomous, 351
Summer Palace, Beijing, burning of, 307

tattooing, 5, 187–93, 196, 197
  as enhanceent, 187
  expressive component, 189–90, 190–1
  healing injuries, 191
  healing role, 192
  healing, historical role, 191–2
  normalization, 198
  prevalence, increase, 187–8
  professionalization, 190
  regulation, 187, 188–9, 192
Taylor, author, medico-legal text, 271, 272, 278
technical rape, 281–6
  child, constructed as provacative, seductive, 281–2
  consent, invalidity of, 281

INDEX

Thailand, 11
therapeutic jurisprudence, 285
Thoinot, author, medico-legal text, 275, 287, 290
Three Parent problem, 163
Tianjin, 324
Tianjin Martyr Cemetery, 324
Time magazine, 212
Tokyo Tribunal, 318
Tommy, chimpanzee, 76, 82
Tong Zeng, Chinese postwar compensation activist, 326–7
tort claiming
   social insurance, impact, 43
tort law, 27
   contrasted with other systems, 7–8
tort law, American, 118
   claiming behavior. *See* claiming
   codification, modernization, 102–3
   egalitarian alternatives, 44–5
   failure, 132
   individual nature, 30
   insufficiency of approach, 43–4
   lumping. *See* lumping
tort law, disability approach to, 33
tort law, functions
   prevention of injury, 42
tort law, need for reform, revolution, 45–6
tort law, purposes, 46
tort reform movement, 129–30, 155
Toshitaka, Hayashi, Japanese postwar compensation lawyer, 327, 328, 332–3
transnational law, 342, 344
transnational legal agency, 330, 331
transnational legal space, 330–1
Trump, Donald, President, United States, 311
Turner, Brock, Stanford University student, convicted of sexual assault, 242
Twitter, 240
two-finger test, 11, 271
   consent, 276
   critique of term, 289–90
   development of, 273
   Justice Verma Committee, abolition, 288–9
   medico-legal text, Modi, 273–4
   mimicry of penetration, 275–6
   mimicry of sexual violence, 267–8
   protest against, 286
   reintroduction, Delhi (2015), 289
   ruled constitutional violation, 287–8
   state sanctioned assault, 285
   to distinguish true from false virgins, 274–5
   transformation, rape to consent, 267
   truth-technology, 273
   validity in children, 274
Tyson, Mike, boxer, convicted of rape, 242–3

United States, 309
unjust enrichment, 258
unmaking of empire, 342
   difficulty, absence of law, 320
   difficulty, persistent imperial nature, 319–20
   in legal sphere, 346
   law and economy, intersection, 319
   role of law, 318
   within legal sphere, 331

Verma, Justice, India, 288
Vero cell line, 165
Vick, Michael, NFL quarterback, dog fight operator, 77, 85
Vick-tory dogs, 82
vulnerability, 12, 58, 60, 93, 356
   animal rights cases. *See* animal rights cases
   animals, help to realize, 357–8
   framework, focus to injury and causes, 77
   injury to place, nonliving objects, 358
   language, subjectivity, 79–80
   political, 80
   relation to stigma, 13–14
   relational, social nature, 80
   shared, community, 80–1
vulnerability analysis
   development of, 66
   embodied vulnerability, 58–9
   political implications, 71–2
   resilience, 63–4
      described, 63–4
      unequal distribution, effects, 64
   resources, 64–6
      institutions, role in managing, 65–6
      types, 64–5
   social contract, reimagining, 62
   state response to vulnerability, 68
   state-institution interactions, 66–7
vulnerability, shared
   subjectivity, grounding of, 78
vulnerable subject, 13, 38, 78
   advantages over autonomous, 81
   alternative to liberal, 53
   animal rights, applicability, advantages, 81–2
   animal rights, limits to approach, 87–92
   characteristics, contrasts with liberal, 59–60
   disability critique, role in, 38–9, 43
   individual and political agency, 79–80
   individual variation, impact of, 60–1
   institutional relationships, structuring, 62–3
   overlap, animal rights, 78–9
   state response
      individual, 69
      institutional, 68–9
   state, importance of, 70–1

INDEX

Wafer, Theodore, white man, shot unarmed black teenager, 237
Warren, Samuel, Justice, Supreme Court, 207
Whampoa, 301
Wise, Steven, founder, president, Nonhuman Rights Project, 83
World War, First, 193
World War, Second, 216, 307, 329, 341
wrongful birth, 32
wrongful life, 32
Wyeth, 169

Young, Ernlé, Director, Center for Biomedical Ethics, Stanford, 162

Zeng, Tong, Chinese postwar compensation activist, 326
Zhejiang, 298
Zhun, Geng, former leader of forced labor uprising, 325
Zimmerman, George, Stand Your Ground defendant, killed Martin, Trayvon, 234–5, 236

CAMBRIDGE STUDIES IN LAW AND SOCIETY

Books in the Series

Diseases of the Will
Mariana Valverde

The Politics of Truth and Reconciliation in South Africa: Legitimizing the Post-Apartheid State
Richard A. Wilson

Modernism and the Grounds of Law
Peter Fitzpatrick

Unemployment and Government: Genealogies of the Social
William Walters

Autonomy and Ethnicity: Negotiating Competing Claims in Multi-Ethnic States
Yash Ghai

Constituting Democracy: Law, Globalism and South Africa's Political Reconstruction
Heinz Klug

The Ritual of Rights in Japan: Law, Society, and Health Policy
Eric A. Feldman

The Invention of the Passport: Surveillance, Citizenship and the State
John Torpey

Governing Morals: A Social History of Moral Regulation
Alan Hunt

The Colonies of Law: Colonialism, Zionism and Law in Early Mandate Palestine
Ronen Shamir

Law and Nature
David Delaney

Social Citizenship and Workfare in the United States and Western Europe: The Paradox of Inclusion
Joel F. Handler

Law, Anthropology and the Constitution of the Social: Making Persons and Things
Edited by Alain Pottage and Martha Mundy

Judicial Review and Bureaucratic Impact: International and Interdisciplinary Perspectives
Edited by Marc Hertogh and Simon Halliday

Immigrants at the Margins: Law, Race, and Exclusion in Southern Europe
Kitty Calavita

Lawyers and Regulation: The Politics of the Administrative Process
Patrick Schmidt

Law and Globalization from Below: Toward a Cosmopolitan Legality
Edited by Boaventura de Sousa Santos and
Cesar A. Rodriguez-Garavito

Public Accountability: Designs, Dilemmas and Experiences
Edited by Michael W. Dowdle

Law, Violence and Sovereignty among West Bank Palestinians
Tobias Kelly

Legal Reform and Administrative Detention Powers in China
Sarah Biddulph

The Practice of Human Rights: Tracking Law Between the Global and the Local
Edited by Mark Goodale and Sally Engle Merry

Judges Beyond Politics in Democracy and Dictatorship: Lessons from Chile
Lisa Hilbink

Paths to International Justice: Social and Legal Perspectives
Edited by Marie-Bénédicte Dembour and Tobias Kelly

Law and Society in Vietnam: The Transition from Socialism in Comparative Perspective
Mark Sidel

Constitutionalizing Economic Globalization: Investment Rules and Democracy's Promise
David Schneiderman

The New World Trade Organization Knowledge Agreements: 2nd Edition
Christopher Arup

Justice and Reconciliation in Post-Apartheid South Africa
Edited by François du Bois and Antje du Bois-Pedain

Militarization and Violence against Women in Conflict Zones in the Middle East: A Palestinian Case-Study
Nadera Shalhoub-Kevorkian

Child Pornography and Sexual Grooming: Legal and Societal Responses
Suzanne Ost

Darfur and the Crime of Genocide
John Hagan and Wenona Rymond-Richmond

Fictions of Justice: The International Criminal Court and the Challenge of Legal Pluralism in Sub-Saharan Africa
Kamari Maxine Clarke

Conducting Law and Society Research: Reflections on Methods and Practices
Simon Halliday and Patrick Schmidt

Planted Flags: Trees, Land, and Law in Israel/Palestine
Irus Braverman

Culture under Cross-Examination: International Justice and the Special Court for Sierra Leone
Tim Kelsall

Cultures of Legality: Judicialization and Political Activism in Latin America
Javier Couso, Alexandra Huneeus, and Rachel Sieder

Courting Democracy in Bosnia and Herzegovina: The Hague Tribunal's Impact in a Postwar State
Lara J. Nettelfield

The Gacaca Courts and Post-Genocide Justice and Reconciliation in Rwanda: Justice without Lawyers
Phil Clark

Law, Society, and History: Themes in the Legal Sociology and Legal History of Lawrence M. Friedman
Robert W. Gordon and Morton J. Horwitz

After Abu Ghraib: Exploring Human Rights in America and the Middle East
Shadi Mokhtari

Adjudication in Religious Family Laws: Cultural Accommodation: Legal Pluralism, and Gender Equality in India
Gopika Solanki

Water On Tap: Rights and Regulation in the Transnational Governance of Urban Water Services
Bronwen Morgan

Elements of Moral Cognition: Rawls' Linguistic Analogy and the Cognitive Science of Moral and Legal Judgment
John Mikhail

A Sociology of Transnational Constitutions: Social Foundations of the Post-National Legal Structure
Chris Thornhill

Mitigation and Aggravation at Sentencing
Edited by Julian Roberts

Institutional Inequality and the Mobilization of the Family and Medical Leave Act: Rights on Leave
Catherine R. Albiston

Authoritarian Rule of Law: Legislation, Discourse and Legitimacy in Singapore
Jothie Rajah

Law and Development and the Global Discourses of Legal Transfers
Edited by John Gillespie and Pip Nicholson

Law against the State: Ethnographic Forays into Law's Transformations
Edited by Julia Eckert, Brian Donahoe, Christian Strümpell, and Zerrin Özlem Biner

Transnational Legal Process and State Change
Edited by Gregory C. Shaffer

Legal Mobilization under Authoritarianism: The Case of Post-Colonial Hong Kong
Edited by Waikeung Tam

Complementarity in the Line of Fire: The Catalysing Effect of the International Criminal Court in Uganda and Sudan
Sarah M. H. Nouwen

Political and Legal Transformations of an Indonesian Polity: The Nagari from Colonisation to Decentralisation
Franz von Benda-Beckmann and Keebet von Benda-Beckmann

Pakistan's Experience with Formal Law: An Alien Justice
Osama Siddique

Human Rights under State-Enforced Religious Family Laws in Israel, Egypt, and India
Yüksel Sezgin

Why Prison?
Edited by David Scott

Law's Fragile State: Colonial, Authoritarian, and Humanitarian Legacies in Sudan
Mark Fathi Massoud

Rights for Others: The Slow Home-Coming of Human Rights in the Netherlands
Barbara Oomen

European States and their Muslim Citizens: The Impact of Institutions on Perceptions and Boundaries
Edited by John R. Bowen, Christophe Bertossi, Jan Willem Duyvendak and Mona Lena Krook

Environmental Litigation in China
Rachel E. Stern

Indigeneity and Legal Pluralism in India: Claims, Histories, Meanings,
Pooja Parmar *Paper Tiger: Law, Bureaucracy and the Developmental State in Himalayan India*
Nayanika Mathur

Religion, Law and Society
Russell Sandberg

The Experiences of Face Veil Wearers in Europe and the Law
Edited by Eva Brems

The Contentious History of the International Bill of Human Rights
Christopher N. J. Roberts

Transnational Legal Orders
Edited by Terence C. Halliday and Gregory Shaffer

Lost in China?: Law, Culture and Society in Post-1997 Hong Kong
Carol A. G. Jones

Security Theology, Surveillance and the Politics of Fear
Nadera Shalhoub-Kevorkian

Opposing the Rule of Law: How Myanmar's Courts Make Law and Order
Nick Cheesman

The Ironies of Colonial Governance: Law, Custom and Justice in Colonial India
James Jaffe

The Clinic and the Court: Law, Medicine and Anthropology
Edited by Tobias Kelly, Ian Harper, and Akshay Khanna

A World of Indicators: The Making of Government Knowledge Through Quantification
Edited by Richard Rottenburg, Sally E. Merry, Sung-Joon Park, and Johanna Mugler

Contesting Immigration Policy in Court: Legal Activism and its Radiating Effects in the United States and France
Leila Kawar

The Quiet Power of Indicators: Measuring Governance, Corruption, and Rule of Law
Edited by Sally Engle Merry, Kevin Davis, and Benedict Kingsbury

Investing in Authoritarian Rule: Punishment and Patronage in Rwanda's Gacaca Courts for Genocide Crimes
Anuradha Chakravarty

Contractual Knowledge: One Hundred Years of Legal Experimentation in Global Markets
Edited by Grégoire Mallard and Jérôme Sgard

Iraq and the Crimes of Aggressive War: The Legal Cynicism of Criminal Militarism
John Hagan, Joshua Kaiser, and Anna Hanson

Culture in the Domains of Law
Edited by René Provost

China and Islam: The Prophet, the Party, and Law
Matthew S. Erie

Diversity in Practice: Race, Gender, and Class in Legal and Professional Careers
Edited by Spencer Headworth and Robert Nelson

A Sociology of Transnational Constitutions: Social Foundations of the Post-National Legal Structure
Chris Thornhill

Shifting Legal Visions: Judicial Change and Human Rights Trials in Latin America
Ezequiel A. González Ocantos

The Demographic Transformations of Citizenship
Heli Askola

Criminal Defense in China: The Politics of Lawyers at Work
Sida Liu and Terence C. Halliday

Contesting Economic and Social Rights in Ireland: Constitution, State and Society, 1848–2016
Thomas Murray

Buried in the Heart: Women, Complex Victimhood and the War in Northern Uganda
Erin Baines

Palaces of Hope: The Anthropology of Global Organizations
Edited by Ronald Niezen and Maria Sapignoli

The Politics of Bureaucratic Corruption in Post-Transitional Eastern Europe
Marina Zaloznaya

Revisiting the Law and Governance of Trafficking, Forced Labor and Modern Slavery
Prabha Kotiswaran

Incitement on Trial: Prosecuting International Speech Crimes
Richard Ashby Wilson

Criminalizing Children: A History of Welfare and the State in Australia
David McCallum

Global Lawmakers: International Organizations in the Crafting of World Markets
Susan Block-Lieb and Terence C. Halliday

Duties to Care: Dementia, Relationality and Law
Rosie Harding

Hunting Justice: Development, Law, and Activism in the Kalahari
Maria Sapignoli

Injury and Injustice: The Cultural Politics of Harm and Redress
Edited by Anne Bloom, David M. Engel, and Michael McCann

Ruling Before the Law: The Politics of Legal Regimes in China and Indonesia
William Hurst

The Powers of Law: A Comparative Analysis of Sociopolitical Legal Studies
Mauricio García-Villegas

A Sociology of Justice in Russia
Edited by Marina Kurkchiyan and Agnieszka Kubal